Music and Psychology

C. 31 May 1948 C.

The Hans Keller Archive
General Editor: Christopher Wintle

Music and Psychology
From Vienna to London, 1939-52

Hans Keller

edited by
Christopher Wintle
with
Alison Garnham

drawings by
Milein Cosman

published with the support of the
Jewish Music Institute
SOAS, University of London

Plumbago Books

2003

Publisher and address

Plumbago Books
P. O. Box 27832
London SE24 9YG

plumbago@btinternet.com
www.plumbago.co.uk

Keller, Hans, 1919-85

Hans Keller *Music and Psychology. From Vienna to London, 1939-52*
The Hans Keller Archive, General Editor: Christopher Wintle, drawings by Milein Cosman (1921 -),
edited by Christopher Wintle (1945 -) with Alison Garnham (1964 -)

Includes drawings and index

Published by kind permission of the Syndics of Cambridge University Library

Supported financially by the Jewish Music Institute SOAS (Millennium Award Scheme funded by the
National Lottery) University of London (www.jmi.org.uk)

Set in Calisto MT

Logo by Mary Fedden RA, OBE, © Plumbago Books and Arts, 2001

First published 2003

A CIP catalogue record for this title is available from the British Library

ISBN 0-9540123-1-3

Printed in Great Britain by CPI Bookcraft, Midsomer Norton, Bath, BA3 4BS

The Hans Keller Archive

Also available: *The Jerusalem Diary. Music, Society and Politics, 1977 and 1979*, drawings by Milein
Cosman, edited by Christopher Wintle and Fiona Williams, London, The Hans Keller Trust *in
association with* Plumbago Books, 2001, 234 pp. + 36pp. drawings. ISBN: 0-9540123-0-5

Contents

Frontispiece: Hans Keller in 1948 (drawing, Milein Cosman)   ii

Editor's Preface   xi

Acknowledgments   xix

A Note on the Text   xx

I From Vienna to London, 1939-42

Hans Keller Playing the Violin in the 1940s (drawing, Milein Cosman)   2

An Émigré in England   3

    1 England
    2 Amusements
    3 Lyons Corner House, Pissoir
       Notes Critical, All Too Critical (*On Nietzsche*)
       Miscellaneous Writings in German (*Report*)

Mental Shorthand   12

    1 In Brief
    2 Shielding you with Brevity (*Schonend, weil in Kürze*) (*Aphorisms*)
       Notes Selected Early Aphorisms
    3 Apropos of Leisure and Pleasure (*Aphorisms*)
    4 Mental Shorthand (*Aphorisms*)

Politics, Philosophy and Society   21

    1 Scientific Socialism – ad absurdum (*On Stalin and Marxism*)
    2 National Socialism and 'Being German'
    3 A Community of the Future (*On Zionism, Response*)
    4 Summary Report on the Revisionist Faction Within Your Youth Club,
       with a Proposal for a More Effective Scheme of Activities
       Notes Capital Punishment

Sex and Character, Yours and Mine   32

    1   You on Sex
    2   Man to Woman
    3   To Start you Sleeping
    4   Man, Woman and Midway Between

II *Psychology, 1942-47*

(1) Psychology and Sociology: Responses to Margaret Phillips (1942-47)

Dr. Oskar Adler, Leader of the Adler String Quartet (drawing, Milein Cosman)   40

Small-group Psychology   41

    1   Group Functioning of a String Quartet
         Notes Internment Camp (Isle of Man)
         Some Critical Remarks upon a System of Classification Used for
         Discovering the Conditions under which Groups Function (*Extracts*)
    2   The Childish Leader Senior Girls School
    3   St. Anne's Youth Club
         Notes *The Psychology of Social Unity (Report)*
    4   Psychoanalytic (Freudian) Group Theory and Its Critics
         Small Social Groups in England (Phillips) (*Contents*)

Language of Psychology   60

    On the Substitution of Freudian Terms by Popular Ones

From Community to Association   64

    1   British Tank Crew: Report and Commentary
    2   The Psychological Significance of Some Sociological
         Conceptions of the Group

Individual Psychology and Its Relation to Group Psychology   74

    Individual Psychology and Group Psychology
    Notes Hitler and History

(2) Psychological Observations (1945-47)

Prostitutes Wear Marriage-rings: Group Self-contempt   83

    1   Married-seeming Prostitutes

2 Prostitutes Wear Marriage-rings
   Notes Prostitutes: Private Census
3 Interviewing Prostitutes: First Interview
   Notes Correspondence with John Rickman
   Group Self-love

Psychological Essays   96

1 Self-knowledge
2 Sexual Hesitancies
3 The Need for Pets
4 Religion: the Psychoanalytic Standpoint
5 War, Peace and Psychology
6 Peace and Pessimism
   Notes Belsen: a Psychological Comment
   Psychological Writings (*Report*)
   The Psychiatric Psychosis

On Maturity (from The Psychologist)   108

1 On Maturity (*first set*)
2 What IS Maturity?
3 On Maturity (*second set*)
4 Maturity
5 On Maturity (*third set*)
   Notes Psychology and Ethics

Psychology and Gender   112

Male Psychology
Notes Human's Lib

III   Music and Psychology, 1946-52 (and after)

Peter Pears as Peter Grimes (drawing, Milein Cosman*)*   120

The Psychology of Opera   121

1 Three Psychoanalytic Notes on *Peter Grimes*
   Notes Open Letter to the Authors of *Peter Grimes*
   Peter Pears's *Peter Grimes* (*Letter*)
   Letter to Peter Pears
   A Sixteen-months-old Boy and His Mother Substitutes
2 First Opera Performances in England (including *The Rape of Lucretia*)
3 Off and On *The Little Sweep*
   Notes Keller's Writings on Benjamin Britten, 1946-52 (*Report*)

The Psychology of Film Music   157

    1 The Psychology of Film Music (Benjamin and Auric)
    2 Georges Auric at Film Music's Best

Creative Character: Its Psychology   164

    Benjamin Britten conducting at the BBC Maida Vale Studios c. 1946
    (drawing, Milein Cosman*)*

    1 Britten and Mozart
    2 Mozart and Boccherini
       Notes Towards the Psychology of Agatha Christie's Genius

The Psychology of Performers   186

    Kyla Greenbaum and the Psychology of the Modern Artist
    Notes Furtwängler, Menuhin and Szigeti;
    Not Famous Enough (Britten, Huberman, Kell, Pears and Whyte)

The Psychology of Composers and Listeners   197

    Musical Self-contempt in Britain

Psychology and Aesthetics   210

    1 Apropos of Beauty and Reflection
    2 "Bloody Little Fool": Sid's Kiss and the Problem of Taste in Opera

The Psychology of Genius (Two Essays from 1956)   221

    1 Towards the Psychology of Stravinsky's Genius
       Notes *Philosophy of New Music* (Adorno) (*Review*)
    2 Schumann after Freud
       Notes Biography's Truths: *Freud: The Man and the Cause* (Clark) (*Review*)

The Psychology of Music and Its Effects: Two Fragments   229

    1 Manifestations of the Primary Process in Musical Composition
    2 Notes on a Case of Dementia Praecox (Bleuler's Schizophrenia) and
       Attempts at a Musico-psychological Treatment

Aphorisms on Music   235

    1 Food for Music-love and -thought
    2 Short and Bitter
       Notes Later Aphorisms on Music

The Psychology of Everyday Musical Life   238

    1   Announce Opera Casts!
    2   Your Child and Music
    3   The BBC's Victory over Schoenberg
        Notes Musical Criticism (including Film Music Criticism)
        and Other Writings (*Report*)

Appendix: Two Stories and a Play

Hans Keller Writing in the Late 1940s (drawing, Milein Cosman*)*   248

Two Stories and a Play   249

    Freedom from Freedom (*Story*)
    Don Juan Again (*Story*)
    Notes Stories, Poems and Other Genres (*Report*)
    Antiwhatism: a One-Act Experiment Including
        Some Moral or Other (*Play*)

*

Index   284

Overleaf Keller's notes from the psychoanalytic literature taken around 1940. The manuscript forms part of the Hans Keller Archive in the Cambridge University Library. A general account of the Archive appears in the Editor's Preface below.

Jones Essays in Applied Psa. 23.

262/63 When we remember how extensively these repressed coprophilic tendencies contribute, in their sublimated forms, to every variety of artistic activity — to painting, sculpture, & architecture ~ θ i ℋ, ε, ℅ ε poetry on the other

287 That infantile interest for the sound accompanying the passage of flatus ♂ may be transferred in later life to the subject of music was first pointed out by Ferenczi Zentralbl. I 385¹)

fisteln — fisten to pass flatus)

Hermes God of music, wind, speech, money

———————————

Zentralbl. f. Psa I 1911 Ferenczi. über obszöne Worte.

Das infantile Interesse für die Darmgas- Entleerung
(die)
vergleitenden Töne war nicht ohne Einfluss auf seine
Berufswahl. ξ ↳ ℳ.

Editor's Preface

One day the children's children of the psychologists and
psychoanalysts will have deciphered the language of music.
(Arnold Schoenberg, *Style and Idea*, London, Faber, 1975, p. 511)

Introduction

Music and Psychology is really three books in one. First and foremost, it tries to show how
informed Freudian psychology came into British musical criticism in the post-war era through
the work of one remarkable figure, Hans Keller (1919-85). His 'overriding concern' with
psychology went on to become the distinctive feature, not just of his own writing, but of the
musical culture in general for the next three or four decades. Second, it tells how, as an
educated 19-year-old Jewish musician, Keller fled his native Vienna in the wake of the
Kristallnacht to join relatives in London (he was 'imprisoned, robbed, starved, and beaten up
by the Gestapo'), and how he recreated his Austro-German cultural interests in Britain during
his early years (from the end of 1938 until about 1952). To this end, he forged in his second
language a remarkably lucid, aphoristic prose style while pursuing an active professional life as
string-player, critic, psychologically orientated social worker and much else besides. And third,
it provides the first comprehensive listing of documents dating from 1939-52 held in the Hans
Keller Archive by Cambridge University Library. Many of these are published here for the first
time and are placed alongside reprints of the key published essays of the period. The books
inevitably interact, so that the social, political, philosophical, and cultural views provide a
backdrop for the musical and psychological ones. (Indeed, Keller himself adopted this pattern
for his *1975 – 1984 minus 9* (London, Dobson, 1977).) The whole thus reveals the foundations
of Keller's lifework and allows us to see how his early thought evolved stage by stage: it thus
represents a new kind of exercise, in the archaeology of music criticism.

The importance of the interaction, moreover, needs to be stressed. For although Keller
famously acknowledged that music moves according to laws inexpressible in words, he
nevertheless declined to separate art from life. For instance, in an entry of 13 June, 1979 for
his 'anti-autobiography', *The Jerusalem Diary* (London, Plumbago, 2001), he wrote, 'The first
drops of rain – and there is, ineluctably, the very same enjoyment of contrast that the sun
offers at home. The reason why unity and contrast are the essence of art is, surprise, that they
are elemental to life.' Thus, the studies of English culture, German philosophy, Stalin,
Zionism and sexuality with which the book opens, and the psychologically-orientated stories
and drawing-room play on British anti-Semitism with which it closes, all belong to the same
worldview. So too do the Freudian interpretations of reports on small social groups on the one
hand, and the implicit platonic categories he devised for music criticism on the other.

Music and Psychology roughly stops in 1952 when Keller was 33. The year saw the
culmination of the 'New Series' of the outspoken little journal *Music Survey* (1949-52) that he
edited with Donald Mitchell (it was reprinted in London by Faber in 1981); and it also saw the
publication of the provocatively partisan *Benjamin Britten: a Commentary on His Works from a
Group of Specialists* (London, Rockliff). From this time on, Keller's combative, anti-critical

style, his aggressive commitment to causes (in 'defence of great music'), his unique blend of interests described above, and his switch from playing to writing, were all firmly established. For most of the 1950s he lived the life of a freelance writer and reviewer, and then joined the BBC in 1959 for twenty golden but turbulent years. (The period is described by Alison Garnham in her authoritative *Hans Keller and the BBC: the Musical Conscience of Broadcasting, 1959-79,* London, Ashgate, 2003.) From 1979 until his death from motor-neurone disease in 1985, he returned to the life of a freelance writer and speaker, and coached string quartets at both the Guildhall and Yehudi Menuhin Schools of Music.

The character of the mature writings after, say, 1952 comes out particularly in his posthumous *Criticism* (London, Faber, 1987) and the selected *Essays on Music* (Cambridge UP, 1994). But to give a sense of how the psychological ideas planted in the early years came to fruition, several examples of his later writings have been included in the notes to this volume. A number of these come from obscure published sources or have never appeared in print before. These are 'Hitler and History', 'The Psychiatric Psychosis' (on Thomas Szasz), 'Human's Lib' (on women in the Reform Club), psychoanalytic comments on Furtwängler, Menuhin and Szigeti, two essays from 1956 on psychology and musical genius, and 'Biography's Truths' (on Freud) – all blend music, society, politics and philosophy with psychology. There is also a selection of later aphorisms to set beside the many youthful ones. That Keller's later (and more complex) thoughts are often elaborations of succinct early ones can be seen in this previously unpublished reflection on genius, music, psychology, Judaism, and suffering –

There has been an excessive, hedonistic reaction against the Judaic and Christian doctrine that suffering ennobles: the unthinking ego letting the id take over from the punitive superego. The situation is complex but clear. In the first place, you've got to have something to ennoble. In the second, it is demonstrable that Beethoven would have been the worse for not suffering, and Mendelssohn the worse for suffering. In the third, unless you are a genius like those two, you can't tell unless you've tried it all out. Genius just means not having to try: it's by far the biggest time-saver God ever invented – probably, as is the case with most good inventions, on the basis of personal experience.

– or in this piece of psychological advice (also unpublished):

Laughter, in our concealing civilization, remains a dependable indication of character, a short cut to undeclared, yet effective mental trends: people can help most reactions, but not laughing. There are stressedly mild individuals, sometimes even pacifists, but in any case respectably on the side of the underdog (without doing much about it except explode in a safe situation), who invariably and compulsively laugh when somebody they dare not openly oppose meets with a minor mishap – or a major one which they minimize. Don't be unkind to them, but beware.

On the other hand, two categories of writing from the early years are barely represented here: Keller's copious writing on cinema, and his reviews of concerts, operas, festivals, printed music, music books, records, and so forth. These fall outside the remit of 'music and psychology' are subjects for other collections.

Our 'three books' also reflect the time of the volume's publication (ours) and the three institutions supporting it. Music theory, analysis and criticism, especially in the Austro-German tradition, has for many years been a concern of the University of London, especially at Goldsmiths' College and King's College London. Keller himself taught on and off at

Goldsmiths' and contributed the opening essay to the journal *Music Analysis* founded at King's in 1982. *Music Analysis* in turn published a Hans Keller 'Memorial Symposium' in 1986: this included a comprehensive bibliography of his published work by Renée Atcherson. Both Colleges have supported the research for this volume, which began as far back as 1986, and many of their members have helped assemble it.

Second, in recent years the study of émigré writings, art, music, architecture and other activities has gathered apace, finding a recent focus in Daniel Snowman's *The Hitler Emigrés: The Cutural Impact on Britain of Refugees from Nazism* (London, Chatto, 2002). This kind of work has been encouraged by the financial sponsors of this book, the Jewish Music Institute, SOAS, University of London, which has set up an international forum on music and musicians banned and exiled by the Third Reich. Keller is in fact coming to assume pride of place among émigré musicians in many ways: he will be included in the revised *Dictionary of National Biography* (Oxford, 2004); a portrait by his wife, the artist Milein Cosman, has recently been taken into the permanent collection of the National Portrait Gallery; and his posthumously published *The Jerusalem Diary. Music, Society and Politics, 1977 and 1979* (London, Plumbago, 2001) won the book of the year prize for 2001 from the Royal Philharmonic Society. He was also the subject of an international symposium held in Vienna in April 2001, the proceedings of which are to be published in 2004 (edited by Gerold Gruber for Peter Lang AG, Frankfurt am Main). A Hans Keller Publications Board, chaired by Donald Mitchell, was formed in 2002, with the aim of encouraging publication from the Estate.

Third, after his death in 1985, Keller's papers were sorted into preliminary bundles at his home in Frognal Gardens, Hampstead by various people working under the guidance of Milein Cosman. In 1996, following an initiative from the Faculty of Music in Cambridge, at that time headed by Alexander Goehr, the University Library took over the main part of the estate. The Library then established an official 'Hans Keller Archive', and since then the papers have been further sorted and catalogued, a process that continues. At the time of acquisition, the Faculty of Music generously funded an archivist, Alison Garnham, and her work has provided a basis for this book. Although the catalogue of the Keller Archive is still incomplete, it is hoped that every item held in the Archive covering the years 1939-52 has been cited in the following pages, either in the notes following each essay, or in the reports placed strategically throughout the book. These reports deal with Keller's writings in German, the work with Margaret Phillips (*The Psychology of Social Unity*), the psychological writings, the writings on Britten, the music criticism (including film music criticism) and stories, poems and other genres.

Music and Psychology

Along with Arnold Schoenberg and many others in the twentieth century – composers, writers, artists, film-makers, business men, advertisers or whoever – Keller believed that psychology held the key to a new realm of understanding that would pit the logic of the unconscious against that of the conscious. He also believed that music held a special place in the new order of things:

> In rationalization irrational processes are modified so as to conform to rational laws, in musicalization rational laws are created so as to conform to irrational processes.

As he maintained repeatedly, he was interested not merely in describing 'the music', but in analysing 'the music behind the music'; and the branch of psychology that would most help him would be psychoanalysis. For, as he said at the start of his lecture to the British Psychological Society in 1950 (see Part III below),

> it is psychoanalysis in particular which is destined, in my considered conviction, to get the psychology of music out of its present embryonic state by shedding light on the psychology, not only of the composing process, but of the actual elements of musical structure and texture.

And one of the reasons that no one had done it before had to do with the psychologists themselves. As he wrote in *Apropos of Beauty and Reflection* (see Part III below):

> To take a special instance, the comparatively pitiable headway that psychoanalysis has so far made in its application to music does not prove that the results of psychoanalytic research cannot be used for explaining this form of art psychologically. The lack of psychoanalytic success in this direction seems rather to be due to the fact that most of the more original and capable psychoanalysts have so far been largely or wholly unmusical, the founder of this scientific branch, Freud, being himself on top of the list of musical ignoramuses.

In fact, Keller's interest was well established even by the early 1940s. In *Hans Keller and the BBC* (pp. 7-8), Alison Garnham writes how, in a letter to Mrs. G. Learner, Librarian of the British-USSR Association, of 24 March, 1981,

> Keller later recalled that his interest in psychology had dated back to his schooldays [in Vienna], remembering that, for part of his school matriculation examination, he had written an extended essay on '*The Brothers Karamazov*: A Contribution to Dostoyevsky's Depth Psychology'. He described the title as 'pretentious', adding that 'nowadays . . . I'm not interested in my contribution to Dostoyevsky's depth psychology, but in his to ours.'

Throughout the early years, he developed this interest by taking countless notes from the literature, first in German, then in English. The quest, being Freudian, inevitably linked music and sexuality. For instance, his attention was caught by this clinical remark of Otto Fenichel's:

> Under analysis, a number of such individuals finally admitted that music was not actually a matter of indifference to them, but that it was unpleasant; this feeling of unpleasantness proved to be connected with their repressed infantile sexuality. ('Outline of Clinical Psychoanalysis', *The Psychoanalytic Quarterly*, I, 1932)

Then, as far as the practitioners of music were concerned, he noted a comment of Havelock Ellis's (from the *Studies in the Psychology of Sex* (II, 1910, p. 295)) that

> as regards music, my cases reveal the aptitude which has been remarked among inverts . . . it is certain that various famous musicians . . . have been homosexuals. Calesia states (*Archivio di Psichiatria* 1900, p. 209) that 60% [of] inverts are musicians. Hirschfeld (*Die Homosexualität*) regards this estimate as excessive, but he himself elsewhere states that 98% of male inverts are greatly attracted to music, the women being decidedly less attracted (anal!).

From A. van der Chijs, moreover, in 'Über das Unisono in der Komposition' from *Imago*, XII, 1926, he learnt that unisons in musical texture may be indicators of a single love, in other words, homosexuality or 'pseudo-homosexuality'.

However, sexuality also embraced narcissism, and narcissism led to symbol formation and from there to the very foundations of music. So much is clear from a comment of Sigmund Pfeifer's transcribed from 'Problems of the Psychology of Music' (*Imago*, IX, 1923, pp. 452-62):

> Ferenczi has pointed out that the functional phenomena, in Silberer's sense, represent the part played by narcissism in the formation of symbols, and it is with just such functional phenomena that we are concerned in music.

In a Report of the Hungarian Psychoanalytic Society (22 October, 1921) from the *International Journal of Psychoanalysis*, Pfeifer noted that sources of pleasure in rhythm derived similarly from the

> binding of conscious attention through compulsive repetition, so that cathexis is withdrawn from repressing censorship and the way opened to wish-fulfilling, pleasure-producing tendencies

and that the

> economy of expenditure in ideas [makes such a] perception possible with the repetition of simple structures (cf. Freud's preliminary pleasure mechanism in 'Wit').

The report on Sigmund Pfeifer's 'Problems of the Psychology of Music' mentioned above also includes the suggestion that 'singing may be related to conversion hysteria developed on a fixation in the anal-sadistic phase'; and another piece by Pfeifer, a review of Robert Lachs's *Studien zur Entwicklungsgeschichte der ornamentale Melopöie* (*Imago* VII (1921), pp. 504-14) argues that ornament is a 'libido product' and a remnant from a paleolithic stage of music. There are other jottings, too, from the work of Willy Bardus (*Imago* V), Theodor Reik, Frieda Teller (*Musikgenuss und Phantasie*), J. S. van Testaar, A. Winterstern, 'Germain', Dr. Alexander Elster (*Musik und Erotik*) and Max Graf (whose book on the psychology of the composing process from Beethoven to Shostakovich Keller dismissed with uninhibited aggression in *Music Survey*, II, p. 193:

> It is the first book I am reviewing without having read it to the end, believing as I do that nobody who is capable of reading it to the end is competent to review it.)

Curiously, though, there were very few attempts at this stage to build a bridge between psychology and the 'actual elements of musical structure and texture' – something Keller saw anyway as the most challenging task for applied psychology. What remains of these efforts is a fragment on the 'Manifestations of the Primary Process' in music (see Part III below), together with a number of scraps of paper containing lists of the elements of music. These scraps refer to the theoretical work of Arnold Schoenberg and Hugo Riemann (on imitation) amongst others.

Yet, although he may have absorbed the general quality of their thought, Keller never really drew on most of these authors for his later 'theory of music'. (Something of this sort, though with different sources, was done by his friend, the psychiatrist Anthony Storr, in *Music and the Mind* (London, Harper Collins, 1992).) In any case, such a theory would need to have probed the link between music and aggression, inturned and out-turned, if it was to underpin Keller's observations on musical sado-masochism in Britten, Bartók and others. Indeed, what such a theory would have comprised is tantalizing: Keller noted (in German) the functions of music in relation to 'sleep, sex, death, eating, and religion'. When, however, he eventually announced his theory of (art) music with the notion that true innovation ('the foreground') takes place against the background of well-established procedures ('the sum total of our expectations'), he was in effect reasserting what Kant had already proposed in the *Critique of Judgment*, namely that artisans repeat what they know, but artists depart from it. On the other hand, the substance of Keller's arguments with respect to theory, analysis, criticism and repertoire remained for the most part Freudian, as is clear from his posthumous *Essays on Music* (1994).

The thought, however, was not entirely Freudian. For in 1942 Keller's work took the turn that gave it its distinctive character: he formed a professional bond with the sociologist Margaret Phillips. This lasted for about 5 years. (By the mid 1940s Keller had also come to know the eminent psychoanalyst J. C. Flugel: together Phillips and Flugel became his professional 'parents'.) At the time, Margaret Phillips was a fifty-year-old graduate ('my [twin] brother went to Oxford [but] I had to go to a provincial university'), a daughter of two 'highly intelligent' art teachers, unmarried ('panic-stricken but pursuing'), and author of *Education and the Emotions* (London, Allen and Unwin, 1939). As a person Donald Mitchell remembers her as 'very much the sociologist'; with typical candour she referred to her own appearance as 'non-descript'.

With her 'long experience as a member of staffs of schools and colleges, day and residential', she wrote, she had a strong sense of the 'extent to which personal happiness or misery depended upon the smooth workings of small groups'. In 1940, at the beginning of the war, she found herself in a coastal town as a member of an evacuated Teacher Training College. There, watching the unique social upheaval of mothers and children as they left one community for another, she decided to observe and record what she saw. Friends and students from the 'Universities, Training College, Adult Education Colleges and classes where some of us had taught or were teaching' also helped her. She drew up and circulated a questionnaire (reproduced at the opening of the 'Psychology' section below), defined a variety of small social units (again listed below), and collected personal group memoirs. In this she was aware of moving into territory that even Freud had not really probed, concerned as he was with the relation of the individual to the masses. After the war, she continued the work, focussing on both small groups in themselves and groups as part of larger organizations, and set the material 'in the culture pattern of this country'. She also related group models back to that of the family. She then interpreted the results according to categories evolved mainly by American group psychologists (among them 'Talcott Parsons, R. E. Bales and their Harvard colleagues'), and produced her book *Small Social Groups in England* (London, Methuen) in 1965. By this time she had become Principal of the Borthwick Training College, 83 New Kent Road, London S. E. 21, and could describe herself on the title page as OBE, MA, FBPsS.

In the acknowledgments, Phillips writes:

> The book in its early stages owed much to Mr. Hans Keller now of the BBC Music Department. My first draft was fully discussed with him, and I had hoped that the notes he then contributed might make a psychoanalytic commentary. His later professional preoccupations have however prevented this.

There is no doubt that the book would have been different if their bond had not, in effect, been ruptured by Keller's switch to music in the years following 1946 (she had hopes for the collaboration for many years after.) As the first part of the 'Psychology' section below shows,

Keller's responses to Phillips, which initially took the form of long letters, were of the utmost intensity, and gave Phillips interpretative tools that otherwise she could never have had. Their working method is described in detail in the introductions and notes to each of the items selected from the voluminous material. Of especial interest is the wartime report on a British Tank Crew. The commanding officer's text appears both here and in Phillips's book (albeit in slightly different versions). The present volume includes Keller's commentary and Phillips's additional remarks on the text as a 'first draft'; the notes reproduce the published response (of 1965) by Phillips alone. The response retains something of Keller's thought, though the overall effect is undeniably diluted.

The second part of the 'Psychology' section shows that around 1945 Keller embarked on social fieldwork of his own, especially on 'Married-seeming Prostitutes', and that he interpreted his findings against the background of Freud's ideas on sexuality. He coined aphorisms ('On Maturity') as he had done when he first arrived in England, and as before used the medium to refine his remarkable, newly acquired linguistic powers; and he wrote a number of psychological essays that extended what would be a lifelong fascination – albeit an outsider's – with English society. Through the encouragement of J. C. Flugel, he gave papers to the British Psychological Society, the first as a joint presentation with Phillips in 1945 (printed in the 'Psychology' section below), the second on his own in 1950 – this is also included in the 'Music and Psychology' section. The latter, on 'Musical Self-Contempt', openly transferred his concern with group self-contempt among Jews, prostitutes, and others to British composers and critics, and is a key transitional study. In 1946, he had finally published a scientific article written two years before on 'Male Psychology' in the *British Journal of Medical Psychology*: this was edited by John Rickman, a figure, like Keller, who aimed at a new mix of disciplines. It was this paper that firmly established Keller's style of the time, with its enumerated points, powerful teleological arguments, and utter lucidity and compression of thought.

It was from 1946 to about 1952, that Keller began to dissolve psychological concerns into musical ones. This can be seen in the first seven categories of the 'Music and Psychology' section below, which show the chronological evolution of this phase of Keller's thought. These writings also reveal what is implicit in most of his later criticism: namely, that he worked in platonic terms at the same time that he dealt with musical *actualité*. The newly edited psychoanalytic study of *Peter Grimes* (first published in 1995) owes for its family model to the joint paper for the British Psychological Society as well as to his own essay on 'Individual Psychology and Group Psychology': these in turn owe to the writings of J. C. Flugel and Sigmund Freud. The notes show how the short study of 'A Sixteen-months-old Boy and his Mother Substitutes' uses the same psychological sources as the opera study, and hence establishes another link between observational material and drama. The remaining categories probe the psychology of representatives of each part of music's golden triangle – composers, performers and listeners (not forgetting the categories of genius and creative character) – and add psychological advice to critics, administrators, teachers and broadcasters. There are also a number of musical aphorisms to set beside the earlier psychological ones.

Secure though these foundations may be, readers may yet wonder whether the blissful dawn of Keller's Freudian explorations – or, indeed, of the Jungian ones of contemporaries such as Michael Tippett or Robert Donington – yielded to the glorious day that so many had anticipated. For, it cannot be denied that, British musical criticism at the beginning of the new century is not in general orientated towards psychoanalysis. On the contrary, resistance is now widespread. There may be various reasons for this: as Keller often noted, the English are happier with the description of externals than the analysis of internals; there is ignorance among musicians (this is the first expository book of its kind); or, alternatively, the literary world may be bored with depth psychology in general. Even Keller eventually shifted his patch

Hans Keller

to 'the logic, the ethics and indeed the psychology of psychology'. There may be a further sense that whereas psychoanalysis serves therapeutic ends, music can achieve them more successfully without its help – as Keller observed, 'music gets a jolly sight deeper than psychoanalysis' (*1975*, p. 93). Yet, though some today are defiantly 'anti-Oedipus' (Christopher Bollas wrote recently, 'in modern cultures . . . attacks on psychoanalysis are thinly disguised attacks on unconscious life itself'), others (Matte Blanco) have continued to find renewed interest in the 'logic of the unconscious'. The debate, in other words, remains refreshingly open.

Especially in Britain, where psychology has contributed so much in the post-war years, this volume could well mark a new beginning. It certainly does not have to represent an archival footnote to a project that has long since come to a natural end.

Christopher Wintle
King's College London

Acknowledgments

Of the many who have helped with this book, pride of place must go to Alison Garnham, formerly of Goldsmiths' College London. She not only undertook the arduous task of cataloguing the papers in the Hans Keller Archive, but showed a keen and supportive interest in the project at all stages. The Syndics of the Cambridge University Library kindly granted permission to publish, and Richard Andrewes and his colleagues in the library helped in the day-to-day handling of materials. The Master and Fellows of Churchill College generously extended their hospitality during the research period in Cambridge on the recommendation of Hugh Wood, the Fellow in Music and former friend of Keller's. Joan Noble, Noa Lachmann and Geraldine Auerbach of the Jewish Music Institute, School of Oriental and African Studies, University of London, helpfully let me go my own way as they administered the project on behalf of the JMI Millennium Awards scheme funded by the National Lottery: they were a pleasure to work with. Irene Auerbach of King's College London with typical generosity gave up many evenings to provide the basic translations of the early writings in German. The editor then prepared these for publication. Julian Littlewood, also of King's College London, advised on technical matters with impeccable grace and set the music examples; the extracts from *The Little Sweep* and *Albert Herring* are reproduced by kind permission of Boosey and Hawkes Music Publishers Ltd. (London) and the Britten-Pears Estate, Aldeburgh. Bayan Northcott provided good and timely counsel. Donald Mitchell of the Hans Keller Publications Board, Peter Black of the Hunterian Museum and Art Gallery (University of Glasgow), Michael Fend (King's College London) and Amelie Roper (London Library) all offered materials or advice that, alas, has not all been used, but was still of help at the time. Sarah Wintle has been adept in trouble-shooting computer problems, and she, Alice and Emily Wintle are thanked for living patiently with this book for as long as the editor has. Finally, as always, there is the deepest gratitude to Milein Cosman, whose hospitality and unfailing support for the enterprise has stretched back many years. It is once again a great pleasure to be able to include drawings that she herself has chosen from the apparently bottomless well of her marvellous collection.

A Note on the Text

A book made up of essays written fifty years or more ago, some of which are in translation, some of which were published in journals with their own editorial styles, many of which appear in print for the first time, and all of which were the work of a young writer, makes a few editorial decisions imperative if there is to be any overall consistency. As with other posthumous publications of Keller's, the main concern has been to devise a new-old house style, whereby as much as possible of the original spelling, abbreviations and punctuation remains unaltered without yielding a text that seems remote in style to a modern readership. With the translations from the German, it seemed necessary to break up lengthy sentences and to condense ponderous expressions. With the English texts, even those that have previously appeared in print (such as the essay on 'Kyla Greenbaum') have benefited from extra paragraphing. Some unidiomatic word ordering has been adjusted (Keller's note to putative editors admits that his English might be imperfect); unnecessary neologisms have been replaced ('misogynism' by misogyny); and possessives have been given in full (e.g. Ernest Jones's). Italics have been removed where the phrase in question has entered everyday usage (in loco parentis, a priori) unless good reason was found for retaining them (as with the otherwise ambiguous *pace*). A very few concessions to modern practice involving changes of word have also been allowed (Keller used 'which' indiscriminately for clauses that in our modern view should begin with either 'that' or 'which').

The footnotes, or 'Notes', are essentially Keller's, and have amplified where possible to provide full bibliographical reference. Where Editorial notes have been added, or where ambiguity could arise, the additions have been indicated by square brackets, or by the denotation [Ed:].

I

From Vienna to London, 1939-42

An Émigré in England

Our knowledge of Hans Keller's early life in Britain comes from a number of manuscripts held in the Keller Archive in the Cambridge University Library: these are his earliest extant texts, and at the time of publication (2003) have yet to be fully catalogued. The writings establish the 20-year-old Keller's deep and discriminating knowledge of European culture. They also offer an insight into the charged feelings of a young émigré who had fled Vienna after being rounded up and tortured by the Nazis during the Kristallnacht *pogrom of the Jews on 9/10 November, 1938. The themes he addresses remained with him all his life: an awareness of being an outsider (or 'psychological observer') in whatever community he belonged; a commitment to Freudian psychology; an alignment with the great tradition of German philosophers and thinkers from Kant and Schopenhauer to his own day; the politics of Britain, Europe and the Middle East; the position of the Jews; radio and the media; sexuality; and the strengths and weaknesses of British society and culture. Very few of the writings are about music, notwithstanding the reference to Wagner in the context of the Nazis. Nor are many of them dated, though both their substance and the fact that several are written in German, suggests that Keller's literary career began at the latest when he arrived in Britain on 20 December, 1938.*

1 England

Far from wanting to come up with popular and mindless generalizations, I nevertheless believe in the existence of an 'English character', a belief that makes me want to draw attention to a number of emotional features typical of a large part of the population.

There is a well-known anecdote of the pupil who asked the rabbi whether humans live from the outside inwards or from the inside outwards, to which the rabbi responded with a thoughtful "you could say: yes." Ever since I've lived in England the ideas behind that question have gained new significance: for the Englishman, as opposed, for example, to the uninfected German, lives from the outside inwards. In Spengler's terms he is similar in this context to the man of civilization: his energy goes outwards, not inwards (as would be the case with a man of culture). He develops concrete thought to an extraordinary degree; isn't it remarkable that philosophy, this most abstract of all sciences, experienced the highest development of its *concrete* branch, inductive logic, with John Stuart Mill, an Englishman? In this country people think concretely with extraordinary consistency. Even religion here becomes a matter of *things*, it is placed on a real, plastic level, and apart from Hume no Englishman ever seems to have been bothered by doubts that threaten his understanding. This tendency of thought *seems* to extend the scientific horizon to the same degree as it apparently limits that horizon from the perspective of the theory of cognition. This tendency to out-turned energy can be observed right down to the smallest detail: nowhere else will you see such thorough study of daily newspapers as is cultivated in this country.

This matter-of-fact, vivid way of thinking is matched by a tendency to categorize without major complications, to layer, to simplify the tangled problems of life. Here is religion, there is life; here are the ideals, there is reality. Whereas Goethe (in *Tasso*) resignedly withdrew from the world of appearances into one of dream-images, Shelley finds nothing objectionable in a double life, [conducted on the one hand] in the real environment and [on the other] in the ideal, fictional dreamland of poetry. Nor does he shed a single tear over the lack of relevance of his imaginary world to the world about him. In this he understands classical aesthetics much more deeply than did any German classicist who, with mounting despair, confronted the diffusion of the opposing areas of thought and feeling. This naïve attitude towards the deepest problems of life must remain unintelligible to the 'sentimental', intellectual German. Shelley was an atheist. As a German (if you permit me this fantastic assumption) he would have been a decadent metaphysician. Yet as an Englishman he was capable of very neatly separating the irrational world in which he spoke and felt as a poet from the surrounding society, *into which* he thought in a materialistic way, and for this reason he deemed it permissible to call himself 'atheistic'.

This leaning towards a schematism rooted in concrete thought (which in the area of philosophy – with Wolf, for example – appears exceedingly strange) is the criterion of an original naivety that surprises the foreigner mightily. At first you think you are faced with a nation of fools; soon you realize your mistake, only to fall victim to the opposite error: to make a habit of finding naivety only in the idiot and the sage, but never in the intellectual or moral [make-up of the] man-in-the-street; then you seek the genius in every Englishman, only to come to the final conclusion that almost every member of this race bears naïve traits independent of his or her intellectual or moral capacities. Schiller used to read detective novels in his uncreative moments; Shelley liked going to the pond to sail tiny boats in just the way that we do to amuse our children.

The dislike of every complication in the problems of life (or of knowing about the complications) leads [on the one hand] to the neglect, or at least the simplification, of philosophical questions, but on the other hand to an intensification of detailed studies of the human being as well. The highest development of this process we find in Shakespeare, whose character studies outstrip many a psychoanalytical dissertation.

Those of us who have lived in Germany have always thought that Germans have a special access to certain complexes of thought, which, if they haven't invented, they've nevertheless discovered. However, it turns out that, certain ethical problems, whose treatment through Kant on the philosophical side and Schiller on both the philosophical and poetic sides we have all felt to be specifically and uniquely German, have been addressed just as deeply by Wordsworth and Coleridge from an artistic point of view. In this we are repeatedly surprised by a healthily naïve manner of thinking. The intellectual German, no matter how unproductive he may be, is complicated; the Englishman, no matter how creative he is, remains naïve and simple, without being primitive. How typical it is in this context that Dostoyevsky, the complicated fanatic of naivety, loved the English so dearly (but hated the French); maybe he found among the English the figures he had dreamt up, Prince Myshkin or Aljoshca Karamazov, at least to some extent.

The fading of [any] wellspring of judgment leads the Englishman to an unconditional and reactionary clinging to these romantic explosions and revolutions. Individual revolution you find only as a reaction against the dark sides of limited development: against conservatism that is suffering from hardened arteries, against fossilised tradition, against convention, and against conventional piety. Surely the over-developed consciousness of class and status, together with their fossilised conventions, are unwelcome developments. However, the innate worth of a Lord is as crucial and significant as is the acquired worth of a Gauleiter: today, with regard to these stratified relations we are prepared to make concessions. Even if the 'thank you' and the 'sorry' that you hear constantly from the mouth of an Englishman can be considered at least in part a convention, I find it much more attractive if one agrees to say 'thank you' as often as possible rather than to kick each other. If modern Germany continues along its present path, then it might well be that it is the kick that becomes the convention. We will judge this kick as [severely] as we appreciate the 'thank you' of the Englishman. A fossilised 'sorry' remains greatly more attractive than a living kick.

As a reaction against the social ossification mentioned above, certain individuals among English intellectuals stand out: the matter-of-fact (how could he be otherwise?) philosopher [William] Godwin, Wilde, and above all Byron who so completely falls out of my English framework and whose romantic cynicism, similar to that of Disraeli's, reminds us far more of Heine's than that of any other English poet. Shelley, who also revolted against English society, and like Byron fled it, did so on the basis of naïve (though also intellectually distinguished) opinions, which [would have] had to lead back to the conserving and fossilised society in some vicious circle, were it possible to put these judgments to the test; they appear to be categorical and static, incapable of development or withstanding changes brought about by time and circumstance.

That *inconsistency* which on the side of genius has brought the Germans so much good and on the side of the devil has brought them so much bad, is, as I have said, totally alien to the English. This manifests itself again in a manner that is at once pleasant and unpleasant especially in the English educational system. Here [the English] hold fast to good and bad practices with steadfast stubbornness; one-sided work, training the memory in great detail, which in an earlier age of a limited educational system might have had its point, is cultivated to this day and paid for dearly by the neglect of general topics offering an overview of life. Here the Englishman works *inductively*: from paying attention to detail he may go on to comprehend the whole, whereas the German is used to starting from the general insight and working *deductively* towards the detail. This latter way of teaching, however, rarely lacks a dangerous encouragement to superficiality.

A naïve race creates no music. Music, the most romantic, metaphysical, 'sentimental' of all the arts reaches its highest watermark in Germany. There one yearns and bursts through barriers (upwards, as in [Goethe's] *Faust*, downwards as in [Rosenberg's] *Myth of the 20th Century*); it is such a constitution that breathes life into music. Here in England they [merely] achieve a limit. There is hardly an important composer here; I personally think Purcell is still the relatively outstanding one. But alongside the lack of musical fertility there is a fundamental and harmonious love of music, of which Handel, Haydn, Mozart, Beethoven, and Mendelssohn happily took note. This harmonious love, which today is strangely focused on Bach in particular, has nothing in common with the searing Bach fanaticism of the musical German. If the German nevertheless seems to understand Bach more deeply, then the reason for this must lie in the fact that, the unhappy lover who yearns passionately for the beloved, but can never reach her, feels for her perhaps more deeply than does her happy husband. Thus the musical Englishman is happily married to Bach – so happily that Bach almost becomes a habit for him. German listening to music always bears a creative, active character, whereas English listening to music is entirely passive.

Thus the Englishman unconsciously represents a classical ideal, one for which Germans have always yearned in vain, without realizing how unclassical even the yearning is. In England physical training of the body is accorded outstanding importance, in this country sport enjoys an edified culture that has nothing with the enforced physical training of the hordes found in the Germany of today. Apollonian feelings and activities dominate this island, which is free from the deformation of dionysiac orgies: [the subjective idealist and nationalist] Fichte would have been impossible here; his grandchildren, the National Socialists, even more so; an enthusiastic, tolerant patriotism takes the place of an ecstatic, keenly destructive nationalism.

Everywhere we look in English intellectual life we find clear, intelligent, original minds and observant eyes. Lawrence's polemic against Freud left me dumbfounded. It is a polemic fought with weapons of the mind that have nothing in common with Freud's and which until then had been totally alien to me. Reading Lawrence's work left me rather confused. These two men would never be able to understand each other; to try to decide which of the two was right would be an infantile exercise: nothing would ever come of it.

In Germany the lower criminal murders, the higher and nastier one demonstrates intellectually the use of the non-use of morals and calls himself Nietzsche. Here, in England, such formally perfect disfiguration of human abilities is unknown, here you are simply either decent or not decent, but usually decent.

The tendency towards schematics and layering of which I spoke at the opening is not a drive towards ranking, but to a classification of things put beside each other. The different areas of life are juxtaposed equally but harmoniously: a skilful footballer is as 'clever' as a wise philosopher.

The Englishman hates the turbulence of a Faust just as he hates the seduction of a Gretchen (though occasionally he pays lip service to moral codes and the awareness of moral codes). The straightforward, open, intelligent attitude of this people might yet show it can have positive effect, even in the near future.

Source

German language typescript of 4 pages dating from c. 1939/40, reproduced here in translation. There is also an incomplete manuscript, *'Ein Emigrant sucht England'*, again of 4 pages, comprising the same material. In an observation in German included among the aphorisms of the time, Keller makes the same point about the English proclivity to think from the 'outside in', and adds, 'I, of course, feel a bit isolated here. I am daft and torn apart.' Another essay comprising two pages of typescript, 'Aus dem Englischen Musikleben' ('From English Musical Life'), was rejected by *Luzerner Tagblatt* in a letter of 11 October, 1946.

2 *Amusements*

'In our place', in the apparently so upright, but at least in the so consciously upright London, a truly sensual vision dominates the appearance of the streets in numerous parts of the town in the evenings: the so-called 'amusements' [arcade]. It would hardly be possible to describe these places or their details to anyone living in Paris; we refer to those well-known gaming shops in which, if not money, at least similar equally useful and valueless everyday articles can be won: cigarettes, chocolate, watches, etc.

It is worth visiting such a frivolous place once in a while. For apart from the hardly-ever-winnable articles that are there to be won, something else is on offer, [namely] watching the various kinds of players and gaming machines.

As far as the latter are concerned, we can define two fundamentally different groups. They represent two 'contradictory' principles of life; maybe they have been instituted deliberately: for every outlook should be catered for. One group unites within itself variations of the following procedure: after you have inserted a coin in a machine, a ball starts to roll, which, left to its own devices, careers for a bit around a field studded with little lamps. Each lamp that is touched by the ball 'counts'; a certain number of touched lamps is a condition for winning (usually: would be a condition for winning). All of this happens without any involvement of the player, who normally has to wait and see whether the ball will either lose for him or very nearly win.

The imaginative player believes that in this type of machine he sees the derisive faces of Mach and Freud; he hears their resigned voices: "Very well then, go and try your luck!" However, this trying for luck is rewarded by success only in the rarest of instances.

Disgusted by these deterministic machines from hell, the player may now turn to the other group [of machines]. The way these are constructed allows the player to exercise his own skill by trying to guide the ball into its intended hole. With joy he who now believes he has been promoted from object to subject sets to work. "Try your luck!" he hears coming from all the machines: a whole series of renowned gentlemen, from Kant through Fichte to Hegel, call out to him encouragingly. But oh dear! Even if with the deterministic game machines fate vary rarely allowed the player to be successful, here every attempt by the player himself turns out to be totally hopeless. It *always* results in 'very nearly'; never does the ball reach its goal. Annoyed, the player stands in front of his machine, Kant and is brothers in crime have fallen silent; but from the other corner of the room he hears Mach's triumphant howl: "Your free will is a fiction, your indeterministic world view a chimera!"

Truly, these London amusements are a condensed structural history of philosophy: an image of a drama, the exposition of which has ended today, but one that still needs a satisfactory solution.

The player will be annoyed: Fate has had little positive influence, and he none at all, on the path of the ball. How, then, could he win?

Indeed, how *could* you win there? Causality turns out to be fallible, subjectivity absent. We have to await the great synthesis: the gaming bazaar of 2039 may be able to exhibit a machine that demands the cooperation of the subject and another infallible causality. Maybe the development of philosophy will supply the necessary material for this new image.

Now to the players themselves, nearly always members of the male sex as the weaker gender would earn itself black marks if it succumbed to this temptation (I refer at least to the morally self-conscious London: on this occasion let us cross out the 'at least').

Here too we are capable of differentiating groups. First, there is that group of players who aren't players at all: they enter [the arcade] giving themselves an air of grandeur, typically crowding round the indeterministic machines (so that the whole business may attract interest), there to lose a few coins without their nervous system being affected in any way, only then to walk off again, partly with a superior air, partly with a disgusted air, and partly both, even smiling.

Most of the significant visitors are true players. Everybody knows, mainly from personal experience, the emotional constitution of that kind of person. The losses of a true player grow in proportion to his belief in winning. Members of this group work hard at the deterministic machines; this also makes sense: to play seriously means to be passive, to surrender [one's self].

And finally there is a small group of strange characters that attract attention: if you look more closely, they turn out to be pathological, over-compensating members of the petit-bourgeoisie. Too cowardly to lead a really naughty life, and too small to lead a really large life, they proudly search out such a little den of iniquity, smiling as if they stood for weighty frivolity, in order to be pleased with looking at themselves immersed in mire with the lowest possible intellectuality for quarter of an hour. "You don't play with sacred things" (for even iniquity, the devil is holy) is what you want to call out to them. You will forgive the author his trenchant criticism of this type of person if he closes with the admission that, as a representative of this last group, he himself frequently pays visits to the London 'amusements'.

Source

German language typescript of two pages dating from 1939, reproduced here in translation.

3 Lyons Corner House, Pissoir

'Corner Houses' were a chain of patisseries-cum-tea-rooms run by 'Lyons' that played a popular part in the life of mid-twentieth-century London. They included branches in Coventry Street and at the Trafalgar Square end of the Strand.

They stand there in quiet reverence neatly lined up: notice their bodies. By entering a pissoir you learn what the Temple of the Body is like. Here the God of the Body receives his sacrifices, here prayers take place. For prayer means at once giving and taking: and it is the sense of relief that is taken in spiritual prayer as well as in this corporeal one.

In this temple you realize the absurdity of asceticism. Asceticism means: encouraging the dominion of the spirit over the body, so that an attempt is made to turn the body, which is initially stronger, into the servant of the mind by ignoring its demands. Sometimes the attempt does not succeed. The place of sexual intercourse is taken by ascetic masturbation. Sometimes it does succeed. Fakirs sit on a bed of nails with a knowing smile. Nevertheless: no ascetic has ever undertaken not to urinate for two weeks. Each one of us has to make our way into that temple several times a day. There are points of the body that are so resistant that they cannot be coerced.

Nor can the body be seduced there. You can turn the erotic drive towards seduction, and that is why you are right to call yourself human. But in the temple described above you go further, and therefore you are right not to call yourself God. That is a drive you have not yet seduced.

[Indeed,] you are not yet God by a long chalk: for you are still more animal than god. Look: your friend says to you: "Hurry up, the *Matthew Passion* is about to begin!" You reply: " I can't come yet, I've got to pee first." Your friend accepts this as a valid argument. On the day that the words, "I can't pee yet, I've got to go first to the *Matthew Passion*", turn into a convincing argument, you will be more god than animal.

But that day is a long way off. For now lavatories are better attended than churches. To this we must add that, churches are by no means as important for the spirit as are lavatories for the body.

The lavatory is the true House of God. Here the body serves the body. The church, however, is the false House of God. That's where the spirit flees from the spirit under the illusion of entering into it. There the spirit gets quite beside itself. In the god-human the spirit will find itself from within. And the churches will presumably experience an upgrading: as there will be no further use for them, they will be used as lavatories.

They stand there in quiet reverence neatly lined up: notice their bodies. Not just in a Pissoir. Everywhere. In the army, at the theatre, and in front of the mirror. But only very few possess a mirror of the soul. And even they cannot bear the image in the mirror. But in that at least they show some taste.

We call death an end. Yet maybe it is a beginning: a beginning of the rule of the spirit. *One* symptom might indeed be apparent: after death, there shall be no more peeing.

NOTES

Source

German language typescript of 2 pages dated February 1940, reproduced here in translation. The reference to the *St. Matthew Passion* reflects the English taste for J. S. Bach noted in 'England' (see above).

Critical, All Too Critical
From My Observations on Nietzsche

Grey German beards sit and ascertain with mournfully wrinkled foreheads the source of corrupt, and in particular Jewish journalism, and triumphantly locate it in Heine. But why look into the racial distance when the problem can be found among the people of one's own times? Who is the self-representative Heine by comparison with the debased genius of style, the priest of the Devil in the cloak of misused dialectic, the scholastic of resignation in the face of a unified worldview, the most consummate, dangerous journalist, Nietzsche, who out of self-disgust thunders with them, the German beards, against the patchwork stylist Heine? Nor do you have to seek out the finest specimen of Jewish journalism amongst the Jews; after all we have Goebbels and his whole mendacious hypocrisy at our disposal.

Nietzsche cries out proudly that, if you read his work you couldn't derive any educated satisfaction from it. Oh, how wrong he is, how he deceives himself! Citations are indeed missing, for his thinking, with all its apparent originality, is bound by and rooted in education. Associations with his admittedly deep and dynamic knowledge supply him with a basis of independent thought; often he merely thinks in educational concepts that he subjectivizes with as much inspiration as wilfulness. But original thinking, of the sort we find, for example, in Kant and Schopenhauer, we do not see in Nietzsche. It is his pathological joy in polemics that should stop us in our tracks. To indulge in polemics means: to be stimulated by contrasts. Nietzsche's thought needs stimulus, he loves Wagner warmly for his greatness, which supplies him with a worthy opponent, a longed-for spur to thought. Nietzsche fights Wagner not for the sake of the matter in hand but for the sake of the fight. How different on the other hand is our kind of polemic that is conducted creatively, and not just for its own sake. Schiller's 'On Grace and Dignity' (Über Anmut und Würde), really a polemic against Kant's philosophy, ends up as an aggrandisement and extension of that philosophy. If we want to [find ourselves in agreement] with Hegel, who in this area was for once capable of constructive thought, then the various antitheses [that form part] of Schiller's polemical intentions with regard to their object, Kantian ethics, unite in that very dignified synthesis which characterizes Schiller's complete enterprise. Here the contradiction proves productive, but there, with Nietzsche, it becomes an intellectual work of art, not philosophy. I can safely climb up the ladder supplied by Kant and Schiller, but I always fall between the rungs of the Nietzschean one – in the end to find myself, exhausted, in Wagner's lap. Nonetheless, I bow down before the maximum development of his debased intellectual abilities.

If [the Viennese café-poet] Peter Altenberg [1859-1919] fires off contradictory sentences, then nobody with any common sense holds that against him. The charm of his ecstatic subjectivity makes up for the occasionally unstable quality of his judgment. However, with [a] philosopher things are different, he lays claim to objectivity, he wants to *judge truly*. The inconsistency which every thinker is permitted, nay, which stands as his criterion, in a philosopher not only comes into existence organically, that is, as part of his development, but makes it his duty to flag up any recantation or change of opinion. Nietzsche [in fact] does supply us with such a hint in *The Gay Science*, [albeit] in a somewhat presumptious and unnatural manner; but if you approach the Fata Morgana of his philosophy as a whole, which he himself describes as a closed entity, then the lovely spectacle fades away until finally it disappears entirely. A certain Plato taught me that the clarification of a concept has to precede its discussion. So how should I take it when Nietzsche on the one hand praises Schopenhauer for morality, but on the other hand treats Ethos, wherever else you look for it in him, without much respect; when on the one hand he demands 'simplicity and naturalness' as the highest goal of culture, but on the other hand damns naturalness and originality along with their effects for all eternity? Such things cannot serve me as philosophy, to shed light on truth. Rather, pseudo-artistic arguments flash forward arbitrarily for the sake of a coarse effect, often for the sake of an unworthy paradox. Let those flashes of light strike where they will: for me the dimmer, more permanent, and thus on the whole more luminous candlelight of Mr. Kant lights up more things, and deeper ones!

Friedrich Nietzsche dares to write the following sentence: "Who could ever believe in the truth of the feelings of a Heine! He reproduces with an ironic tendency . . ." How can a great thinker project such primitive analogies drawn from his own intellectual make-up onto other people? For this sentence fits Nietzsche beautifully, as he feels *only* the ironic – Heine on the other hand treats ironically what he has felt.

Source

Translation of a manuscript of 4 pages in German dating from c. 1939. It bears the title *'Kritisches und Allzukritisches. Aus meinen Betrachtungenüber Nietzsche'* ('Critical, All Too Critical. From My Observations on Nietzsche') and has been lightly edited here. The title is clearly a parody of Nietzsche's *Human, All Too Human* (1878-80), and the essay amplifies Keller's views on the writer, whose pithy, aphoristic mode of thought might, ironically, have been one of his influences. 'England' (above) includes a vilification of this 'higher criminal'.

Miscellaneous Writings in German: a Report

A larger German-language manuscript of 8 pages in the Keller Archive, beginning 'Heinrich Heine:', is a collection of fantasy reactions by heroes and villains, ancient and modern, to the invention of radio. The reactions capture a culture in turmoil and reflect as much on the Austria and Germany Keller left behind as on the England he was joining. They parody the styles of their 'authors' and are invariably witty, learned, and apt. The authors are (in order of appearance in the ms.): Heine, Wagner, Walter von der Vogelweide; Nietzsche; Lao Tse; Knut Hamsun; Biblical Old and New Testaments; Hitler; The Hon. Neville Chamberlain, Eden, and Lord Halifax; G. B. Shaw; Dostoyevsky; Bruckner; a German Impressionist; a German Expressionist; a German Naturalist; Goebbels; Altenberg; Karl Kraus; Hegel; Schopenhauer; Goethe; Schiller; Plato; and Kant. It is of course appropriate that Keller, who later spent twenty years in the BBC (from 1959), should turn his attention so early to its prime instrument of propaganda. Here, in translation, are some of the reactions:

Richard Wagner:
>"Since TV has been added to it, the radio appears as a not inconsiderable additional medium for the execution of the thought of the *Gesamtkunstwerk*."

Nietzsche:
>"My God, how we will have to allow ourselves in future to be attacked incessantly by the far-too-many people who pretend they've got morals or that they are idealists!"

George Bernard Shaw:
>[Q:]   "Mr. Shaw, what do you think of the radio?"
>G. B. S.:   "That all depends upon what the radio company thinks of me!"

Fyodor Mikhailovich Dostoyevsky:
>"Please keep me away from this product of superficial Western invention. I haven't yet finished with God and human beings, especially with Russian human beings . . ."

Karl Kraus:
>*Subscriber:*   "What do you say about the loudspeaker?"
>*Viennese:*   "It does speak a bit loud."
>*Subscriber:*   "Yes, I always have to shout at mine, speak louder!"
>*(Curtain)*

Plato:

> | *Socrates*: | O my dear Phaedrus, whence do you come and whither do you go? |
> | *Phaedrus*: | From a radio-talk, O Socrates, and [now] I feel I must go for a walk outside the town. Why, O Mighty One, do you never speak on the radio? |
> | *Socrates*: | That manner of speaking, dear friend, is inappropriate for a man to whom the gods have not granted the wisdom of such radio speakers as Lysias, son of Kephalos, to name but one; because, for my sins, I am incapable of teaching if I am not being taught by my pupil at the same time in some fertile exchange. That Wisdom, by which one might talk with a silent and, more than that, an invisible friend, has been denied to me by Zeus. |
> | *Phaedrus:* | Truly, you have spoken well, O Socrates; I hasten to pass on your words to the Artistic Director of the radio company, Dr. Blumenkohl. |

Lao Tse:

> "But the radio is a bad thing, for whoever deals in music is preoccupied, and preoccupation leads away from truth, and truth lives in calmness that liberates inner contemplation."

The New Testament:

> But the radio is of Evil, for it supplies to him who does not pay attention that for which he who does pay attention has to seek out . . .

Adolf Hitler:

> "I emphasize with unconditional and unconditioning emphasis that, as an unknown soldier from the World War, I would rather sacrifice my own life than admit that the radio is not one of the most potent weapons in the struggle for the national honour of our great people. Great Germany, *Sieg Heil!*"

Anton Bruckner:

> "Jesus! If only my Eighth could be performed on the radio! But I could well understand it if that was stooping too low for the gentlemen of the radio company."

The Honourable Neville Chamberlain:

> *Debate in the House of Commons*
>
> *Eden:* Is the Prime Minister yet in a position to give an unambiguous statement on the problem of the radio?
>
> *Chamberlain:* Her Majesty's Government considers it its duty to state that it is dedicating its particular attention to this problem though o'er hasty decision would do more damage than the use [of radio] round the world, which has already been thrown into confusion by baseless rumours. On the other hand, there is much that can already be said on this subject, namely that I have agreed with the Foreign Minister to make a decision next week in the hope of bringing the problem to a speedy resolution.
>
> *(Enthusiastic applause from part of the Conservative benches. On the next day, Lord Halifax issued a similar statement in the House of Lords that met with enthusiastic and unanimous support.)*

In the Archive there is also: (a) an untitled single sheet of typescript beginning '*Oder: der Primitiv ist selbstbewusst*'. This comprises two sketchy paragraphs, the first asserting the self-possessed, conceited nature of both the primitive person and the genius in contrast to the nature of the pathological self-doubter; the second compares the wise person and the stupid one. If Dostoyevsky calls intelligent people 'Idiots', then he does so for good reason. Keller is unable to find the deep source of this parallel as he is 'an average person' – unlike Socrates who, for all his denials, knew a thing or two; (b) an untitled typescript of two pages beginning 'Und nur noch "etwas" . . .' Starting in the course of a second section, this fragment continues through to third and fourth sections. The subject is the 'intoxicating relationship' of 'something' to 'nothing', the latter being the 'pure something because it lacks representation'. It is possibly a summary or transcription of a philosophical text, as neither the style nor the substance is recognisably Keller's; (c) a typescript of two pages, '"Vom Noch-Nicht" zum "Nicht mehr"', a ponderous fragment addressing the concept of the 'average', its statistical emptiness, and its relation to human beings; (d) a fragment, '*Aus der Liederbuch für höhere Söhne. A Parody and Improvement on Prussian Humour*'.

Mental Shorthand

1 In Brief

In the Keller Archive there are 5 typed sheets of thoughts and aphorisms in German, and several more sets in English. Together they show the range of Keller's thought and, as with Nietzsche's later writings, form the crucible of his style. In their appearance and concerns, the five pages suggest a date of c. 1939. Two of these pages belong together and bear the title 'In Kürze'. They are reproduced here in translation:

Tact. A tactful person overlooks the strengths of another in a tolerant way. Overlooking another's weaknesses: that is just good moral upbringing. But sensing a superior fellow human being, one does not allow that person to feel one's own non-existent strengths: *that* is indeed tact.

Recently I was chatting to my four-year-old niece. In the course of telling me something, she began to hesitate: "I know what it is, but I can't express it." What a healthy attitude that places imagination ahead of linguistic formulation! I was obliged to think of Hegel who, were he honest, should have said often: "I can express it, but I don't know what it is."

I get annoyed at people who are convinced of their own genius simply because the Reich's propaganda minister has declared that they are degenerate. Dr. Goebbels isn't quite that infallible in his misjudgements.

Programme music. Programme music is a creation of notes tied to static facts, thoughts, or feelings. I consider static in this context to mean the complete pre-existence of the state of affairs at the time of musical composition. Thus a love song is not a creation of programme music as it arises directly from the dynamic feeling of love; however, a song about love may indeed be described as programme music.

Logic is the teaching of the laws of correct thought. What a nuisance that these rules have to be created by *thinking*! Who will prove to me that the rules according to which the rules of correct thinking were formulated are correct?

Ethics. I. There are people who do good in the hope that Fate will provide some material recompense in this world. Then there are those who hope for a reward from God: an equally unsavoury business. There are others still who are content with the unworldly reward of respect for their great deeds from those around them. There are also those who are secretly good. Not that you should believe that these people do good for the sake of the good: they too profit by the fact that their environment knows nothing of their goodness. And finally there must once have been a Christ who did good purely out of inclination. But that man must have been the only one in this category.

II. You can hold out the left cheek because you are too weak not to hold it out. You can hold it out in spite of being strong enough not to hold it out. And you can hold it out *although* you are too weak not to hold it out. Yes indeed, society or other unhealthy circumstances may put you in the situation of having to grovel: but you can *nevertheless* be humble.

Idealism.

I. I was imprisoned with criminals and idealists during a German pogrom [the Vienna *Kristallnacht* of 1938]. The idealists killed the Jews dead. The criminals (a burglar and two pickpockets) gave them something to eat.

II. Strictly speaking, an idealist would have to be immoral a priori – as far as he is an idealist of the good. For he would do good because he wanted to do good, because he would have to want to do good. The innately good person [on the other hand] loves to do good, he tends to goodness and he knows nothing of his good deeds; he has not performed them intentionally, thus he isn't an idealist either, though the nature of his moral activity is similar to that of a dog who eats because he likes to eat. If [however] the dog said, "now I am going to eat, otherwise, God forbid, I might have hunger in my belly and be unable to look after my young any more; but I'm not [in fact] at all hungry," then he would be an idealist, for he would then have motivated his actions in a rational way.

Now you could say that it is still possible for somebody to *tend* to do good and to motivate that drive in a rational way and then to proceed to act accordingly. That person could then be a moral idealist. But an inner voice tells me that where there is motivation something is rotten. Motivation means fighting oneself, in the mildest of cases finding excuses in the face of one's own badness.

It is a good thing in a discussion to speak as little as you can, and above all as briefly as you can. Thus you rob your partner in discussion of the opportunity to prepare his own torrent of words while you yourself are speaking. If you follow this recipe, it might even happen once in a while that your partner in discussion – lacking anything better to do – will actually listen to you.

Beyond this a discussion is only then of creative value if the participants are of a like mind. In other cases it becomes a tedious collection of concurrent monologues.

There are Jews caught in a delusion of super-objectivity formed out of unjustified inferiority complexes, the urge for pointed sayings and a blasé delusion of self-deprecation which cannot be taken seriously: they go so far as to propagate National Socialism as a great idea. They have devised a whole philosophy out of such teaching, one that holds the 10 commandments in contempt. I have personal experience of how National Socialists, who are as decent as they are stupid and spirited, have accepted this philosophy with enthusiasm. We can well do without such blessed activities of our 'fellow people'.

I do not understand your admiration for the person who is busy and works really hard. One person flees into the opium den, the other into work. Only the latter will seriously try to convince us that he has achieved something. We are quite happy to let him think as he likes: for in truth he is just talking to himself.

Certainly it is harder to build up than to tear down. But many critics think that tearing down is easier than it is. Even if you are tearing down you can also build up: Lessing, Polgar.

2 Shielding you with Brevity
(Schonend, weil in Kürze)

These aphorisms were published on 25 October, 1941 in Zeitspiegel, *an émigré German-language publication based in London. They are reproduced here in translation with the originals appended.*

Inertia arises by recognizing the disastrous results of one's diligence. Laziness is reluctance to create anything; inertia is reluctance to destroy anything.

Conscience pricks, law threatens.

A pessimist is one who has dug a hole for others and is surprised that he hasn't fallen into it himself. An optimist is one who has dug a hole for others and is surprised that he has fallen into it himself. Pessimism and optimism have one thing in common: their predictions are always wrong.

Sometimes it can prove useful to run into open doors; in this way everyone knows that they are open.

It is not easy to be tolerant in the face of intolerance.

The equable person imagines he is long-suffering. But only the patient person can be long-suffering, and only the impatient person can understand patience.

God protect us from someone with a persecution-complex who is being persecuted.

The phantasist sees things as they are not and never can be. The poet sees things as they are not and always could be. The former dreams the non-existent into events; the latter reads the non-existent out of events. Both despise appearance, yet only the poet knows the reality of that which has not appeared.

Virtuosity: the weaker the capacity for expression, the stronger the addiction to variety in the means of expression.

He who is poor in spirit approves of things in fiction that in life would fill him with disgust.

Without Mozart we would never have known what an opera is, without Wagner we would never have known what a Mozart opera is.

We may only put ourselves below another, or put another above ourselves. Those who put themselves above another are inferior to the one they put below.

Take heart: there are more repentant sinners than fallen saints.

Even the pedant will lose his pen*. But always where he wants to find it. [* *lit.* penholder]

Today's commonplace is the day-before-yesterday's joke. Some even recognized it as a commonplace the day-before-yesterday.

Theatre or cinema: things which can be understood in everyday dealing between people without having to be said are said on stage **for the sake of the listener** and are therefore not understood. The lack of realism in the action does not come from the unreality of the events, but rather from the reality of the listener, who, as it were, is allowed to participate in the action.

German Originals

Die Trägheit entsteht aus der Erkenntnis der unheilvollen Ergebnisse des eigenen Fleisses. Faulheit ist Unlust, etwas zu gestalten, Trägheit ist Unlust, etwas zu verderben.

Das Gewissen mahnt, das Gesetz droht.

Pessimist ist der, der anderen eine Grube grub und sich wundert, dass er nicht selbst hineingefallen ist. Optimist ist der, der anderen eine Grube grub und sich wundert, dass er selbst hineingefallen ist. Pessimismus und Optimismus haben dies gemeinsam: immer das Verkehrte vorauszusehen.

Zuweilen erweist es sich als nützlich, offene Türen einzurennen: damit auch alle merken, dass sie offenstehen.

Es ist nicht leicht, der Intoleranz gegenüber tolerant zu sein.

Der Gleichmütige bildet sich ein, langmütig zu sein. Langmütig aber ist nur der Geduldige, und geduldig nur der, der die Ungeduld kennt.

Gott behüte uns vor einem Verfolgungswahnsinnigen, der verfolgt wird.

Der Phantast sieht die Dinge, wie sie nicht sind und niemals sein könnten. Der Dichter sieht die Dinge, wie sie nicht sind und immer sein könnten. Nicht-Vorhandenes träumt jener in die Ereignisse; Nicht-Vorhandenes liest dieser aus der Ereignissen. Beide verachten den Schein, doch nur der Dichter weiss von der Wirklichkeit des Nicht Erschienenen.

Virtuosentum: Je geringer die Ausdrucksfähigkeit, desto stärker die Sucht nach Mannigfaltigkeit der Ausdrucksmittel.

Der Kleinliche im Geist findet im Roman verehrungswürdig, was er im Leben verabscheungswürdig fände.

Ohne Mozart hätte man niemals gewusst, was eine Oper ist, ohne Wagner hätte man niemals gewusst, was eine Mozartoper ist.

Nur sich selbst darf man unterordnen, nur einen Anderen überordnen. Der sich selbst überordnet, ist dem Untergeordneten unterlegen.

Nur Mut: es gibt mehr reuige Sünder als gefallene Heilige.

Auch der Pedant verliert seinen Federhalter. Aber immer dort, wo er ihn aufzufinden wünscht.

Der Gemeinplatz von heute ist der Witz von vorgestern. Manche erkannten ihn schon vorgestern als Gemeinplatz.

Theater oder Lichtspieltheater: Dinge, die im lebendigen Verkehr zwischen Menschen verstanden werden, ohne gesprochen werden zu müssen, werden auf der Bühne **dem Zuhörer zuliebe** – gesprochen und daher nicht verstanden. Das Unwahrscheinliche der Handlung kommt nicht von der Unwirklichkeit der Vorgänge, sondern von der Wirklichkeit des Zuhörers, dem gleichsam Teilnahme an der Handlung gestattet wird.

NOTES

Source

Zeitspiegel, 43, 25 October, 1941, p. 10.

The published column concludes with one further item: 'Österreichischer Flüsterwitz: Hitler, Himmler, Göring und Goebbels fliegen nach Wien. Plötzlich stürzt das Flugzeug ab. Wer wird gerettet? ??? Österreich.' ('Whispered Austrian joke: Hitler, Himmler, Göring and Goebbels are flying to Vienna. Suddenly their plane crashes. Who gets the benefit? ??? Austria.') In Keller's copy, this item is heavily crossed out.

Zeitspiegel was a London-based German-language publication of the Austrian community with a strong émigré orientation. On the same page as Keller's aphorisms appeared various notices – for talks about the war, for plays, revues and dances, as well as for jazz and classical concerts (e.g. Edith Vogler playing Bach, Schumann and Schubert). The events were held at a number of venues around the capital, including the Austrian Centres in Paddington (126 and 132 Westbourne Terrace, W.2.) and Swiss Cottage (69 Eton Avenue, N.W.3).

Keller's contribution was one of his earlier publications in England (the earliest came in 1939), and the aphorisms may have been assembled after his release from the internment camp on the Isle of Man in the autumn of 1940 (see the 'Psychology' section for details). They help show a culture at the very point of transition, for some recur in slightly altered form in the English-language aphorisms (see in this Part below).

*

As mentioned above, the Keller Archive holds three further typed pages of unpublished and untitled German-language aphorisms from about this time. The following is a selection (in translation):

Selected Early Aphorisms

Love comes from God, hate from Man, envy from the Devil. Richard Wagner had all three in him.

If Hitler is mere apparition, what on earth is the thing-in-itself Hitler?

He who dishonours Moses is unworthy of Christ* – and, listen Israel! – vice versa.
    [* *Wer den Moses nicht ehrt, ist den Christus nicht wert*]

Being well read is the result of ignorance of the great goals in life; education is the result of knowing them.

Nothing ventured, nothing gained. Correct. But he who does venture will hardly gain. For the only one to gain is he who expects no gain and therefore never finds himself in the situation of not venturing.

With a single stroke, the contended émigré was robbed of his protective routine of daily habits that defined the nature, value and purpose of life. Bereft of this apparently protecting rampart, he is forced either to go under for lack of any real aim in life or, rather, to live a meaningful life.

Any suicide, before he commits the act, should be confronted with an unexpected and unintended, unplanned, surprising threat to life. He will be surprised at his will to live. (This insight I gained empirically in a German holding camp.)

You can spot a fool by the fact that he thinks you're stupid if you can't answer one of his questions. In such unanswerable questions I have managed to discern a principle that becomes apparent in the following example. The questioner points to a green easy chair and asks *why it is red*. A basically similar question belongs to the time when the world began.

Dialectical success creates the same feeling of bliss as a well-taken goal in football. Nor is it worth any more than that.

Freud's treatise on 'Civilization and its Discontents' seems to me like setting up a shop that sells skates in the Sahara. We should bow down with deep respect before Freud's knowledge of neurosis therapy: in Vienna the establishment of a first-rate skate shop is to be welcomed and makes sense. But in the Sahara?

That apart from the transcendental 'up above' there is also an irrational 'down below' can be seen in the Germany of today. Yet I must say, I'm not in agreement with Thomas Mann's compromise of a rational middle.

In order to experience an emotional event fully, you must have the feeling even before it happens of having already experienced it. It is in this sense too that Akibas's comment, "There is nothing new under the sun", has to be understood.

A wrong turning in language: The determinist thinks himself not able to determine.*
    [*HK's English]

3 *Apropos of Leisure and Pleasure*
(*Aphorisms*)

This and the next set of aphorisms were written in English, and appear never to have been published. They were typed out neatly and date from about 1941.

Not anybody who can enjoy leisure is mature, but anybody who can't, isn't.

The surprises we love most dearly in a show are those that don't surprise us, but would surprise us if we weren't so clever.

There are plays that must be played better than they are.

The superficial listener is happy that the performance whiles away his time. The penetrating listener is unhappy that time whiles away his performance.

Every creative genius is succeeded, not only by his heirs, but also by legacy hunters.

Lack of imagination may be the reason why we don't like a good show; an exuberant imagination may be the reason why we like a bad one.

Paradoxical as it may seem, there should be something leisurely about our leisure time activities.

After an evening out with the other sex, A remarked to B that two sexes were quite enough.

"I don't believe in entertainment. It isn't really necessary." "That's just why I believe in it."

An artist needn't know what he has to say as long as he says it.

There are people who cannot enjoy themselves without worrying about having, for the moment, nothing to worry about.

A joke in a significant play must be one that you don't get if you think it is one.

True entertainment offers a holiday, not only from being moral, but also from being immoral.

When we envy a celebrity we mustn't forget that he envies us our envy.

Art is a convincing compromise between denial and interpretation of reality. Trash is a compromise between denial and acceptance of reality, convincing for people you don't like.

Youth lives on fore-pleasure, age on after-pleasure. There needn't have been any actual pleasure in between.

I don't want to be unkind, but history seems to show that it is often better to entertain people than to entertain ideas.

Go out with one who always cares and never minds.

It is a curse of our civilization that we tend to debase leisure by regarding it as a duty.

What at first seems to be a commonplace entertainment may still turn out to be an entertaining commonplace.

The main difficulty for the serious artist is to be frank without being a bore.

So often the platform turns playing into placarding.

To composers, playwrights, performers, actors, audiences: there is only one convincing way out of many a phrase, and that's the way into the next.

Boring ourselves we try to entertain one another: boring one another we try to entertain ourselves. Nor is there anything wrong in this essentially human rhythm.

Whether or not music be the food of love, love is the food of music.

4 Mental Shorthand
(Aphorisms)

Aphorisms are not valuable on account of their substance, but on account of their function. They transmit little truth, but they provoke the desire for it.

Many women offer more than they eventually would like to give, many men ask for less than they eventually would like to demand.

There are three spheres of life where pity is much more immoral than indifference: Love, Art, Science.

Insofar as there are nothing but exceptions to the rule, 'No rule without exception', this rule is valid.

The trouble is that whenever our feelings of contempt would seem fully justified they aren't present. The best nourishment for contempt is an uneasy – but not too uneasy – conscience.

He who hates the woman he loves behaves much less unpleasantly than he who does not hate her, but does hate his love, and loves his hate.

The newborn cries while the bystanders smile: the dying smiles while the bystanders cry.

Only he could be considered completely mature for whom time does not pass either too quickly or too slowly.

It is difficult to be tolerant towards the intolerant.

Importance attached to others results in knowledge about them. Importance attached to oneself results in ignorance about oneself.

Mother to child in a café: "Eat up nicely or you will never be a big girl!" It is significant that we shower the greatest amount of lies upon those of whom we expect, unconditionally, the largest degree of truthfulness. In fact, we treat our beloved children even less respectfully than our grown up enemies, though the former pay us an (undeserved) compliment – in desiring to be big.

It is a commonplace fact that a bad fellow may be capable of a good deed. We must not judge the moral standard of an individual by what he is able to do, but rather by what he is able not to do.

In certain conditions of intense excitement, inanimate objects almost seem to live. Extreme apathy causes living beings almost to seem dead.

We have to make a sacrifice for having success. We are sacrificed by misfortune.

Tardiness frequently arises from the recognition of the unfortunate results of one's own diligence. Laziness is unwillingness to create, tardiness often unwillingness to spoil.

The fool is simple without being profound, the mediocre is profound without being simple.

Everyone's life is an escape. It all depends on the spot we escape to.

If wish is father of the thought, fear is often its mother.

A child pretends to make something because it cannot really make it; the childish adult flirts – pretends to make love – for exactly the same reason: because he cannot really make love.

He for whom honour and prestige are identical is without the former.

We cannot concentrate without being distracted from something or other. Distraction may be a sign of concentration, or of the lack of it.

Conviction enters upon the mind when doubt is so strong that it has to be silenced, and weak enough to submit to this procedure.

Don't despair: there are more repentant sinners than fallen saints.

We are degraded to dogs by those ladies around Piccadilly: we smell them before we see them.

One should persuade men to use make-up and gorgeous clothes. Then they would discard perhaps some of their unbearable mental make-up.

Charles Laughton lives just as much when he is acting as Hitler acts when living.

There is nothing more terrible than a persecuted persecution maniac.

Anyone who is really honest is so about his sex life. You think that in this case there are very few sincere people? Quite so. Except among prostitutes, of course.

The reasonable is distinguishable from the practicable in that the former was an illusion yesterday, whereas the latter will be one tomorrow. Today they both possess reality-value.

The result of the attempt by which men endeavour to regain what they have lost is called 'progress'.

NOTES

Attached to the typescript 'Scientifischer Sozialismus – ad absurdum' printed below are two 'sketches' (in effect aphorisms), one of which does not appear elsewhere:

> Kant says: 'The moral law inside me tells me, there is a God.' Ivan Kramasoff says: 'The immoral law inside me tells me, there is no God.'

Politics, Philosophy and Society

1 Scientific Socialism – ad absurdum
(On Stalin and Marxism)

This forthright polemic challenges Stalin's justification of the Russian attack on Finland in 1939-40 by reference to Marx, Engels and Lenin, and ends with an early, but characteristic defence of individualism. It shows that, however much Keller may have thought of himself as a-political (and it would have been impossible to categorize him politically as, say, belonging simply to the centre-right or speaking with the voice of liberal conscience), he nevertheless responded sharply and sensitively to world events.

It is more than a cheap enterprise to want to show the current manoeuvre of the USSR as having its roots in a Marxist view of the world. However, if in what follows that very thought is elaborated, at least as a suggestion and as far as context allows, then there must be some fairly good reason for it.

The concept of the absolute, or the unconditional, is totally alien to the worldview advanced by Marx under the label of dialectic materialism or 'scientific socialism'. As Engels deduced from Hegel's *Philosophy of History* (which Marx had turned upside down), 'everything that exists, is worth perishing' (Friedrich Engels, 'Ludwig Feuerbach and the End of Classical German Philosophy'). The lie of today is the truth of tomorrow: that is what Marxist dialectics teach. The prophet Isaiah foresaw the path of dialectical materialism when he wrote, 'Woe unto them who make light out of darkness and darkness out of light, who call the bad good and the good bad, and make the sweet from the sour and the sour from the sweet.' (Isaiah 5: 20)

Aristotle's (or Parmenides's) law of identity, which only has real value as a concept if it transcends the times, does not, according to the socialist viewpoint, find any manifestation other than that rooted in time [and place], and is thus truly eliminated. For practically, that is to say applied to certain ideas or understood as applied to reality, the axiom of identity is meaningful only in the sense that, with regard to strictly abstract concepts – for example, 'good' and 'evil' – these concepts are not only the same as themselves but will *remain* so. This point of view, however, will not meet with understanding in places where the view is held that life starts with apparitions and not with the self [*Ich*]; the latter may only be a reflection of appearances and especially of their economic forms. By means of the idea thus gained of the relativity of all moral ideas, the most uninhibited opportunist gains free rein because he is in a position to elevate his crime to the expression of historical law or (to use a dialectical technical term) the negation of negation, the truth of tomorrow: he can thus defend himself against theory. However, the fulfilment of Kant's categorical imperative, which he calls 'an expression of bourgeois class morality at a certain stage of historical development' and for which he claims eternal validity, might have cost fewer Finnish and Russian lives.

It has always been obvious that, a worldview mustn't make valid demands on life if it contains the mere fundamentals of dialectics without also embodying some ideals. However, there are no ideals without ideas, which in their turn have to be absolute and not relative, even though their forms and manifestations may vary. Today's world comes to grief through *resignation in the face of idealism* and through the partial acceptance of pseudo-idealism that privileges consciousness of any one drive to the 'ideal' (and thus allows wilfulness and not the will to reign).

There are, so to speak, two great paths for mankind, an outward one and an inward one. The former originates in polytheism and with an increased understanding of the causal relations in Nature grows in strength towards pantheism; it then turns into atheism and materialism through the deliberate neglect of the critique of understanding and of the exploration of the evolution of individuality. The constant companion on this path of development seems to be awareness of predestination. We find this in Sophocles's and Spinoza's determinism, as well as finally in materialistic determinism (in his dissertation on the natural history of religion, David Hume drew attention to the deep relation between polytheism and atheism with the words, "these apparently religious people (he is speaking of the polytheists) are really superstitious *atheists* of a kind and do not recognize any being that would match our concept of Deity"). Now materialism as long as it remains mechanical is a mere ideology and as unreal as any abstract philosophy. But as soon as it becomes dialectical its fundamentals are so poorly constituted and have such a wide conceptual circumference that with its help you can proceed to an apparently gapless interpretation of the history of the world, to a materialistic view of history. This makes it possible for Josef Stalin – in whom, notwithstanding his scientific socialist education, we must deny any moral qualities, or [anything] in the age of the chemistry of the soul we simply have to shy away from calling 'conscience' (which is very much not the case with his teachers Marx, Engels and Lenin) – to make himself, through an immoral action, the fulfiller of an oh-so-dialectical history.

That things could achieve this strong materialistic impulse was, of course, probably caused to some degree by the further misfortune that great genius-like nature/realists like Darwin and Zola were capable of delivering to many a muddled mind. The obedient trained materialist of today is no longer capable of perceiving an essential difference between cause and effect on the one hand, and principle and consequence on the other. He is an objective realist (or does he merely think he is?) and swears by the experience, the environment, as being the *foundation*, not the trigger, for life: [that is to say, he swears] by the a posteriori of the spirit.

The second path of development, which hardly ever makes itself known today through actions, but which nevertheless continues to be cultivated, takes as its starting point the immediate recognition of individuality and its power, namely love. In a rational form we find this path manifested in the idealistic philosophies of all ages and nations, in its irrational version it appears in the great monotheistic religions. Those worldviews emanating from this line find the basis of life in the spirit, find their reason for being (*causa sui*) in the I (*Ich*), from inside themselves, and not from the outside. They search in the individual not just for a general speciality, a characteristic, a species as in the animal kingdom, but rather for a *unique* being, a personality that is essentially different from any other personality. To them has been opened up insight into the absolute, a priori values that stand above the times, insight into moral standards; they do not see in the Will some mere playing around with consciousness.

To this place, to the reflective (*besinnlichen*) [and] not to the meditative (*beschaulichen*) life, that's where many a human being of today should return.

Source

Translation from German of a typescript of 5 pages cast in article form: '*Scientifischer Sozialismus – ad absurdum*'. This includes a covering letter addressed 32 Herne Hill S.E.24, England and dated 16.II.40 to the *Jewish Review*, Jerusalem, inviting publication. (There is no evidence that the piece was accepted.)

2 National Socialism and 'Being German'

The most burning and topical question that preoccupies much of the thinking world today concerns the existence or degree of homogeneity in the outlook adopted by National Socialism and the ordinary German. The German opposition may well have the right to express a word or two on this problem, which is of such huge as well as practical importance. But if we are to speak about 'being German', of the ordinary German, and thus of the typical people, then we have to proceed with all the more caution, as we often find even with serious contemporary authors the sinister tendency to draw deductions from imperfectly induced factors – that is, to generalize beyond what is justified, for example by introducing into otherwise serious discussion the concept of race without a glimmer of knowledge about its raison d'être.

The nature of National Socialism, this theory of inexhaustible changeability, can be summed up in one sentence that will serve to clarify our problem: <u>National Socialism is pseudo-'being German'</u>. The falsification and the lie – those are the constant factors in a movement the defining characteristic of which is inconsistency: the pseudo-dynamics. For the Nazis are no interpreters, nor are their epigones, of what may be called German decency, their idea is not even plagiarism, not even reflected 'being German'. No, the fermenting factor of their work is the *pretext*. They say that the good end justifies the worst means, but their deeds show that in the best cases the bad end desecrates even the good means. As wrong as the former is, so is the latter right. One need only think of the Strength-through-Joy Organization, to which in essence there should be no basic objection: and one thinks further of the misuse of that institution with the aid of the seductive propaganda machine, the main tool in the service of falsification.

There was a time in Germany when people engaged in debate over the Path to the Good: here people called for justice, there for charity, here for humanity and socialism, there for Christianity, here for Goethe, there for Dostoyevsky; the noble battle between the rational and irrational pathfinders was fruitful because there was a common goal. What do we find today? A pseudo-synthesis. Behind the pretext of serving the good, Alfred Rosenberg[1] indulges in forbidden metaphysics, in mystical prattle, and Adolf Hitler in invalid materialism.

Thus there is nothing left for us, the German opposition inside and outside Germany, but to set the true 'being-German' [against] that pseudo-evolutionism, that is to say the *in*volutionary movement which, with the aid of deceit, wraps up everything that has ever been developed. If there are many who say that Nietzsche's philosophy already bore the kernel of the national socialistic outlook, then we have to say that, Nietzsche honestly preached an aesthetic amorality, whereas the Nazis, under the cloak of morals, have not undertaken a single moral action, and have misrepresented even *their* Nietzsche (as well as their Wagner) with an artless art. Whatever the German had to offer by way of heroism and ecstatic enthusiasm, National Socialism falsified into tyranny and bestial fanaticism. Kleist and Fichte: they sang and fought for their fatherland, the Nazis bawl and murder. What is there that cannot be used for the purpose of deception? Today we must live through the dishonouring and falsification of Fichte's 'Speeches to the German Nation'; we don't just see the denial but also – and this is the most dangerous – the prostitution of truth, of morality, of beauty: of all that which a good German knows how to appreciate and is capable of creating. Is Hitler himself not the personification of the pseudo-genius?

Every true philosophy may be called the project of an esoteric biology. Under Hitler philosophy has sunk to pure pseudo-biology. What does National Socialism, which critically banishes critics, know [of the premise] that the criticized has to be lived through first, that only that deserves the name of dialectics? Where are the blooms of German criticism such as Lessing or Winkelmann, what does Nazism know of the great critics of pure reason? Who today can afford the luxury of submitting pure rationalism to criticism when one may not criticize pure irrationalism?

The Nazi movement calls itself a revolutionary movement. The irruption of a reversal that threatens life, however, is nothing but pseudo-revolution. It is an uproar with an object [that is conducted] under the pretext of a subject that in truth never existed, it is an uproar against rebellion, against the true German revolution which in spite of everything will not allow itself to be kept down.

Finally will you permit me the aphoristic risk of describing the propaganda minister Dr. Goebbels, the pupil of Gundolff, as an unconscious pseudo-German Jew?

The fight against human values is a common experience. But never until now has it been accompanied by such diabolical hypocrisy. For a short period the hypocritical criminal is a step ahead of the honest judge, because the latter hesitates so long before he makes judgement against the former, and before, [supported] by enough evidence, he no longer sees any danger of a miscarriage of justice. Hitler was protected by his own hypocrisy and conscientious fear of his opponents from an early ruin, something that should already have come to him as a 'confessed criminal'. But today no hypocrisy will help him; it is just a good thing that he goes on pretending that he cares only for the German people: for from this point of view his claim that he is the voice and *the* man of the German people hardly gains in credence. If Kant says that religion is accepting all duty as divine order, then it is the understanding of all duty per se that differentiates the German from those who in the old pseudo-manner still dare to utter the name of God.

Source

Translation of typescript in German of 5 pages, with Keller's name and address added in manuscript, dating from c. 1939. Keller refers to himself as part of 'German' opposition even though he was born in Austria. This is technically correct. When Hitler annexed Austria on 14 March, 1938, all Austrians became de facto German citizens.

1   [Ed:] Alfred Rosenberg, whose name, thinly disguised, may have been appropriated (ironically) for Keller's play *Antiwhatism* (see Appendix below), was editor of the *Völkischer Beobachter* and author of an undistinguished discussion of race and culture, *Mythos der 20. Jahrhunderts*, a book that Keller viewed with disdain (see 'England'). He later became a senior Nazi.

*

A further, incomplete typescript in German in the Archive conveys Keller's immediate reaction against a short article 'by a German correspondent' in *The Spectator* of 14 April, 1939, p. 637. This finds in Hitler and Mohammed the most convincing of all comparisons (though the author would prefer it if Hitler and Chaplin, both 50 at about the same time, were to swap roles, the tragic for the comic.) Unlike Mohammed, a part-divine founder of religion (argues Keller), Hitler, the diabolical destroyer of religions, has behind him the Antichrist model of Friedrich Nietzsche, as well as the work of Alfred Rosenberg described above.

3 A Community of the Future
(On Zionism, a Response to Dr. Mayer Ebner)

The State, however, is [an entity] inconsistent
with the Jewish principle and foreign to the law of Moses
(Georg Wilhelm Friedrich Hegel: *Vorlesung über die
Philosophie der Geschichte*, Part 1, Section 3, Chapter 3)

What Dr. Mayer Ebner expounds [on the Jewish question] is logically beyond reproof. But if you try to understand the premises and part-results of his reflections as a whole, then you arrive at a fresh starting point that lends the discussion of the entire problem a hitherto unsuspected new dimension.

I

Dr. Ebner says: 'We [Jews] are more than a religious community and less than a nation.' The criterion of nationhood is common land and common language. Even if you look at Palestine, the Jewish community possesses neither. On top of that, it never possessed it, but only seemed to, as Hegel correctly points out in the chapter cited above: ' . . . that a real bond of Statehood did not exist . . .' etc. We Jews are not only 'less than a nation', but also and at the same time more than a nation, as will be shown in what follows. What has held us together since time immemorial, and the shared characteristic that allows each one of us to be called a 'Jew', is something essentially intellectual and finds its part-expression in our religion. Many will consider a constant life as persecuted minority as the reason for this non-national, immaterial formation of the community; many, however, will consider that what we have in common is the source of persecution. If we look at the matter in more detail, however, we see that it is neither common heritage nor persecution that can be seen as cause or effect, one upon the other. Rather both should be understood as correlatives, which, rather like day and night, have a common cause. If alongside the mutual regular relationship there is any *influence* of one manifestation upon the other, then this takes the form of a catalyst but not of origin.

II

Dr. Ebner thinks: 'The fact (of the hatred of Jews) as such is an unarguable premise.' That is put in almost too mild a way. In every non-Jew lies at least the possibility of an anti-Semitic attitude; in Kantian terms, the view that 'The Jews are our misfortune!' is in a way a synthetic a priori judgment, that is to say, an enlarged judgment independent of the experience that triggers it off ('it doesn't matter, the Jew will be burnt anyway'), or to put it aphoristically: the non-Jew views the world in space, time, and anti-Semitism. Anti-Semitism is thus an elementary manifestation and only needs the Jews for it to materialize. In view of the current relation of Jews to non-Jews, there is an astounding parallel between the fate of the Jewish people and that of Jesus Christ to which I have already drawn attention in my article on the subject in the *New Diary* (Paris, 7, January 1939, p. 31). For wherever a human being is ahead of his time, the apparently irrational hatred of his contemporaries is directed at him. If we can only manage just for once to distance [ourselves] from the fact of 'contemporaneity', then it becomes evident to us that, for example, Christ, as a result of his stage of development, belonged to a time that lies in the distant future. This is the case to a lesser extent with all geniuses, so that 'not being recognised by one's contemporaries' has become their characteristic from the outset (and evidence for the excuses of the untalented). If we want to take this parallel between a Jewish Jesus Christ and the entire Jewish community further, then we will come up with some impressive results:

III

Dr. Mayer Ebner's suggestion for a basic solution, indeed, doubtless the outstanding planning of Zionism per se, is a projection of the state of development of the times in which Jews live today onto their own [present] stage of development, which will match the level of a world for which we can't hope for a long while yet. The essentially intellectual form of today's Jewish community is that trans-national form of community that in some distant future will take over from the material form of a *people* and a nation. Something of this sort has already been divined by the great thinkers who turned against their own peoples, because they wanted to deny their own *national* link to [them], because as far as they could see, [the notion of nationhood] was backward. I would merely call to mind, Schiller, Goethe, Schopenhauer, Heine, Nietzsche, Grillparzer, Shelley, Byron, Otto Weininger. As long as there are nations and peoples Jews will be persecuted and scattered, and it will never be possible to make a nation of them because they have already reached the stage of development at which the concept of nation is an empty one. Only with persuasion will they all be coerced into searching for a common home, something they wouldn't even think of doing if it weren't for the pressure of persecution. It is their task [rather] to act as the persecuted exemplar, as a signpost to the future, the developmental form of which they already embody and for which they suffer: [in such a future] it will only be possible to have a trans-national intellectual community, [to deal with] which the means of force will no longer be adequate. Already today the Jew shows how [such] force should then be met: in a sensible way, by means of a tolerant superiority (in this I am thinking of the typical Jewish 'that's the way it's supposed to be' ('*soll sein so*') which is the expression of a quietly thoughtful attitude in the face of naked aggression, an attitude, which in a German holding camp I could admire in my Jewish fellow prisoners): [that is to say,] in a moral manner but adopting a brave humility, the outstanding examples of which are the passion of Christ, and the Jewish people.

NOTES

Source

Typescript in German of 5 pages, reproduced here in translation, for which there is also a draft in manuscript, '*Eine Gemeinschaft der Zukunft*'. This characteristic response to an unspecified (and untraced) statement by Dr. Mayer Ebner appears to date from early 1940. Keller's attitudes (which never seem to have changed) also stand behind his play *Antiwhatism* (included in the Appendix). They may also have informed his address to the World Jewish Music Congress in Jerusalem in August 1978 when he created uproar by suggesting that Smetana's music was good in spite of, and not because of, its nationalism.

In addition to the letter printed in *Das neue Tagebuch*, Paris, 7/2, 7 January 1939, p. 31 mentioned above (probably Keller's first publication, apart from a childhood story, 'Inge's Cloud Journey'), the Archive holds a further letter (in German) to the same journal, dated 10 January 1939, comprising 4 pages of typescript. This defines 3 layers of meaning for the debased term *Weltanschauung* ('worldview'): (i) among the self-satisfied, pro-Nazi intellectual underclass (who cling to work ethic); (ii) among the intellectual upper class underpinning the blow Hitler gave the German Reich through philosophy (Hitler justified his own position through philosophers, poets and writers); and (iii) among the enthusiastic intellectual middle class, who use the word constantly and tirelessly in its full meaninglessness. As a reaction to all this, the working Jewish émigrés in exile continue to work, the super-intellectuals among them still concern themselves with philosophy ('the situation of the oppressed becomes the crucible for cleansing'), and their middle-class, previously close to psychic suicide, is saved by putting meaningless terms in the bin.

4 Summary Report on the Revisionist Faction Within Your Youth Group, with a Proposal for a More Effective Scheme of Activities

For the Brit Trumpeldor, London, in memory of the many enjoyable hours the author was allowed to spend with a number of Betarim in Vienna, with genuinely heartfelt good wishes.   *Hans Keller*

Keller's address to the 'Brit Trumpeldor' dates from April 1940 and again establishes his passionate involvement with Jewish issues, sexuality, capital punishment, and (informally) small-group psychology in the period immediately following his arrival in Britain. He did not in fact deliver the address personally as he was prone at the time to sudden attacks of stammering, something he explains in a letter included with the typescript in the Archive. In any case, as he also remarked, he wanted to be free to monitor the reactions of the listeners anonymously.

The Brit Trumpeldor was an organisation (or covenant, expressing an agreement between God and his people) named after Josef Trumpeldor, an almost mythic Zionist killed at a very early age; the Betarim were young right wing-militants, some of whom Keller knew in Vienna and London; the Zionists were supporters of the Zionist Congress that paved the way to the State of Israel, and heirs to the vision of an assimilated Austrian Jew, Theodor Herzl, 1860-1904 (as expressed in The Jewish State, *Vienna, 1896); whereas the revisionists (or revisionist-Zionists) were a militant right-wing group committed to violence – 'pre-1948 Jewish terrorists', as Keller later described them – whose leader was Vladimir Jabotinsky – 'my boyhood's pet aversion' (Hans Keller,* The Jerusalem Diary, *London, Plumbago, 2001, p. 59).*

I Introduction

Right from the beginning I think it's essential to introduce myself briefly to my listeners. Though I'm conscious of being a young Jew, I can't describe myself as either a Zionist or a revisionist. I'm not the former, because I see Jewry as a purely spiritual, trans-national community, which should point towards an immaterial, communal stage in the development of Mankind, and which for the time being has to put up with its suffering. Hegel had already grasped this point when, in his lecture on the philosophy of history [I: 3/3], he said emphatically: 'The State, however, is [an entity] inconsistent with the Jewish principle and foreign to the law of Moses.' I can't be described as the latter – as a revisionist – for another reason: it is my most deep-seated belief that no individual may be party to the sacrifice of even a single human being, whether or not it were for the laudable aim (laudable in his own eyes, that is) of saving 10 other lives thereby. Under no circumstance can I see the decision over life and death as one for a human being to take.[1]

These are fundamental attitudes about which we can argue as little as we can about the reality of Space or Time. Meanwhile, as God hasn't denied me a tolerant attitude to other viewpoints out in the world, thanks to which I never consider any belief of mine to be universally applicable, I've always been able to maintain an intimate contact with Zionist circles and especially with revisionist ones, and I've often enjoyed many friendly disputes with young revisionists over the problems of Jewry and the young. Indeed, if I'm not guilty of misplaced vanity, I've often [found that I could] make a real contribution to solving a [whole] variety of youth-related problems by putting forward a number of modest suggestions.

In view of my deep interest in Jewish questions and the problems of the young, I was truly delighted to seize the opportunity yesterday (20 April, 1940) when a friend invited me to pay a visit to the local revisionist youth group. Out of respect for his invitation I cast myself, as always on such occasions, in the role of silent observer; now I feel compelled to make public the impressions I've formed from a combination of [my reaction to two] short reports and other experiences of club life, and add to them a proposal [of my own].

II Exposition

A: The Two Reports

These [reports] have made an admirable impression on me for their seriousness and manly idealism. There was criticism of a general shallowness, negligence, and, as one speaker put it, "lack of discipline" among club members, [concern] that the seriousness of the situation was not sufficiently taken into account, etc.

The criticism can't be faulted. However, the few suggestions for improvements, and [the manner of] their announcement, were deficient because they didn't get to the heart of the matter. On the basis of my numerous observations of youth groups, all of which suffer from the same complaint as the one made yesterday – even though the aims of the respective societies don't lack energy – the nub of the matter strikes me as follows:

B: Sober conclusions from the facts that can stand up to any argument except one accompanied by cynical or racy smirks.

1   The role that sexuality plays in the entire emotional life of human beings is overwhelming. Today this is scientifically and philosophically incontestable – we need only refer to what the Jews Sigmund Freud and Otto Weininger have revealed.[2] The sexual instinct is fundamental and capable of pushing all other inclinations and duties into the background, even among the conscientious.

2   The average age of the members of the revisionist club I had the pleasure of visiting yesterday is, I reckon, somewhere between 17 and 20 years. This is the age at which sexuality is relatively more pronounced even than later; it is the stage of puberty and post-puberty, the time of sexual crisis, imbalance, irritability, and of the natural over-valuation of the sexual instinct.

3   As a trigger for sexual arousal, which need not produce physical so much as – certainly – psychological effects, the mere presence of the other sex is enough, offering as it does the opportunity for various kinds of association.

4   From a sexual viewpoint dance has a dual significance. First, it offers the opportunity for arousal as it presupposes mutual contact; second, as the Leipzig zoologist Gustav Jäger has demonstrated, rhythmic movements release sexual pleasure because the weak arousal they cause makes the protein disintegrate, which in turn liberates emotional substances in the modification of sexual pleasure. From this it is clear that, because of the total dissolution of concentration caused by sexual arousal, however weak it may be, a political talk during a break in the dancing will have something of the same effect as a lecture on Kantian philosophy in a lunatic asylum. As a former passionate socializer and dancer myself, I know this to be the case only too well.

5   We Jews are usually endowed with a rather strong sexual drive, and suffer more than others from detumescence, or, relatively, from [a greater] impulse to contract [out of shyness].[3]

6   As the sexual problem is latently an underlying problem of all Mankind, manifestly an underlying problem of youth, and an especially acute problem of Jewish youth, the latter must not ignore it. Only the realist (as opposed to the materialist) earns the right to call himself an idealist.

7   There is a danger that your Zionist club will be used for nothing other than 'canoodling', whether it be actual or imagined, or indeed only dreamed-of (but still leading to loss of concentration). According to what I observed yesterday there is at least the possibility that part of your membership, albeit a small one, uses the club as a mere pretext for the pursuit of its private sexual aims, perhaps without fully realising it. I don't blame the members in the least for this: after all, they'll have to lie to themselves, citing impersonal motives, for which one shouldn't blame them given their critical age. However, none of this is in the interest of the club, which, as yesterday's speaker said, is no mere social club, nor, as I said, merely a club for sublimated sexual action, reaction, abreaction and arousal.

8   Men and Women are fundamentally different, and so too are young men and women. Only the virago is an Amazon, and only the manly woman is a rationalist. From this it follows that a political education, particularly one [conducted] under military auspices as in your case, can be the same for young men and women only in the smallest measure.

9   A strong sexual constitution, such as we Jews usually possess, is no symptom for deficiency in other respects; on the contrary it usually even coincides with great capacities in other ways.

10   *Mere*-sexuality is of little worth, *a*-sexuality even less so. The synthesis is, *enhanced*-sexuality. However, in your gatherings most of [what should be] *enhanced*-sexual [activity] is *merely*-sexual. Thus the fault lies in your gatherings, not in the majority of your members.

From what has been laid before you there emerges as a logical consequence:

III Proposal

1   Everything to do with the idealistic side of the club *mustn't take place at the same time* as its 'social' side.

2   In practical terms this means that the benefits of monastic 'asceticism' should be linked with the benefits of behaviour that is not too inhibited: dance evenings and serious evenings should be organized, but both *separately*.

3   As far as social and political training is concerned, most of it would best be done in single-sex groups. This precludes distraction, and beyond that each gender will receive instruction appropriate to it alone. However, according to the nature of the topic, much can be worked at together. The previous speaker would be mightily surprised to watch that 'attitude', which last night he criticized fairly, totally vanish were this to happen; otherwise things will always end in warnings and retribution.

4   From such a scheme it would become immediately apparent who was seriously interested, for if, for example, 30 members were present for social evenings, but only 1 of them for serious ones, then the best thing would be to close the club anyway.

5   It is beyond question that evenings of pure socialising, of conversation, of exchange of opinions, etc. should remain *sexually mixed*, an arrangement that in this case might bring nothing but positive and fruitful benefits. My proposal should not – God forbid – create the impression that I was unctuously advocating the life of a eunuch.

6   All this must happen only if the community declares its agreement.

7   Therefore a vote should be held on this issue.

8   The voting should be held in secret, so that anyone could oppose the motion without feeling intimidated. Everybody against should have the opportunity to explain their opposition anonymously, without being put under pressure.

9   To be honest, gentlemen: the presence of an attractive woman is enough to make us ignore the Devil in Eastern European politics and the fate of the Jews in Copenhagen, and for some length of time too. And why not? Everything has its time and place: kissing, and saying "Nebbich" ["How unfortunate I am"], as well as drawing the consequences from this saying of "Nebbich". But none of you will succeed in doing both things *at once*. Bodily exercise of a non-military kind can also take place in mixed company, as physical concentration is always easier.

10 Only by these means will you turn Jewish boys into young Jewish men, and only in this way will you have a practical opportunity of choosing from the members. You'll never find out anything just by 'looking at individual cases in the greatest detail'.

11 The only proof of the validity of my suggestion lies in the eating: *by experiment*.

12 Presumably the majority of members fall into the category of [having an] *enhanced-*sexuality. These people, so to speak, enjoy an excess of energy that isn't currently absorbed by their club-life. Let them dance; but when you have something serious to tell them, don't do it between foxtrots, or rather when the other sex is all-too-close.

13 If something of this kind is set up, then a more controlled conduct will emerge even on the purely social and dance evenings, as the laxity that has been criticized [hitherto] is nothing other than unconscious over-compensation for the apparent restraint hitherto attached to the dance evenings.

14 As I'm not used to the technical procedures, it may be that one or other of the points I've listed so far isn't practicable. Therefore I must emphasize that these are merely the foundations of a solution. Nor would successful polemics against inessentials weaken the basic framework.

15 This basic skeleton is an attempt to find a balance between the powerful sexual complex and the suppressed intellectual one. This can achieved in theory only, a point I can easily demonstrate through an obvious example. In nature we hardly ever think the temperature is right: at best it is 'a bit too hot' or 'a bit too cold'; the perfect balance is an extreme case that exists in the mind, one that we can apply successfully only to something inanimate and unchanging. The closest approximation to such a conceptual balance is therefore the most we can hope for.

16 Finally, there is one more thing I should mention: as I don't have much free time I am writing this little tract by night after a visit to the London Betar. Thus it was only in the tube that I really had the opportunity to turn over in my head the data [I had gathered] and [to make] deductions from it. On the basis of this I must beg humble forgiveness from my listeners for any faults in the presentation and for any other lacunae. Nevertheless, I do believe I've been able to say the most important things, the ones closest to my heart.

IV Conclusion

Far be it for me to want to use what I've put forward here as a pretext for playing the Great Man, [or] to wish to be thought of as adopting a lofty position, or [even] to appear to assume the dubious role of a moralizing preacher. I am – if I may express myself more colloquially – more the snotty-nosed brat, the Lemach and the Nebbochant, than are nine-tenths of my esteemed listeners. There is nothing in what I've been saying that I've learnt just from the observations and reports of my contemporaries; rather, I'm drawing on my own experiences every bit as much, as I've already said. We intellectual Jews are masters of self-criticism: everything I've put before you derives from this source too, and is its outcome.

I've no intention whatsoever of wheeling out the worn-out platitude that, where there is a way, there too will be the means; if my proposal can be shown to be impractical, then I'll have to resign myself to the fact, at least up to a point.

I've permitted myself this one licence: to identify things by their names and not just by their effects. In this respect I have proceeded in a somewhat radical fashion, guided by a thought as simple as it is beautiful, taken from a work that only Mr. Julius Streicher could make popular in various circles, namely a thought from the Talmud (which I quote in English translation) –

Truth is heavy, therefore few care to carry it.

NOTES

Source

Translation of a typescript in German dating from Sunday 21 April, 1940 (the day after Keller's first visit to the club when he heard two papers at 10.00 p.m.), bearing the ponderous title (recast in the translation):

SYNOPTISCHE REDE ÜBER EINE ALLGEMEINE MÖGLICHKEIT EINER EFFEKTIVEREN GESTALTUNG DER AKTIVITÄTEN DER REVISIONISTISCHEN PARTEI INNERHALB IHRER JUGENDGRUPPE.

Dem Brit Trumpeldor London im Andenken an viele genussreiche Stunden, die der Verfasser mit zahlreichen Betarim in Wien hat verleben dürfen, mit recht herzlichen Wünschen unterbreitet *von Hans Keller.*

1   [Ed:] Keller's opposition to capital punishment was life-long, and he campaigned tirelessly for its abolition in Britain. A later paragraph from the early 1970s puts the case in a nutshell (see below).

2   [Ed:] See the Hans Keller/John Rickman correspondence in the 'Psychology' section of this book for a discussion of Keller's reaction to Sigmund Freud's remarks on Otto Weininger.

3   [Ed:] Keller may be referring to the phenomenon of male sexual shyness. See his essay on 'Sexual Hesitancies' in the 'Psychology' section of this book.

Capital Punishment   Abolitionists, are you asleep, just because all is well at home? The world's worst, a country's worst, an organization's worst, invariably happens just because all is well within your own narrow four walls. First, the unanswerable case – in the unlikely event that any reader of this [book] needs it. It isn't a question of the sanctity of human life at all – or any such concept which many might regard as vague. Elementary justice will do – justice being human, and hence inevitably fallible; from which it follows that there cannot, in justice, be any irreparable punishment. Secondly, to go no further than Western Europe, the current facts. There are five countries left in which this medieval element of criminal law still obtains – Belgium, France, Greece, Luxembourg, and Spain. Vis-à-vis Belgium and Luxembourg, reformative excitement would be a little academic: Belgium hasn't had an execution for over half a century, Luxembourg for a quarter of a century. Greece (three executions in the past year) and Spain are likely to remain unaffected by your excitement and mine. But France? One had thought that the last execution took place in March 1969, one month before De Gaulle rejected a plea to commute their death sentences. The French conscience, like ours, is resigned – but the other week, Roger Boutems and Claude Buffet were guillotined after Pompidou sometimes more sensitive to pricks from outside than to its own internal conflicts and convulsions, which it has learnt to live with.

Sex and Character, Yours and Mine

Sexuality was a dominant topic in Keller's writings in the 1940s, as is evident from the 'Summary Report' (above), his essay 'Sexual Hesitancies' and the fieldwork on 'Prostitutes' who 'Wear Marriage-rings' (see 'Psychology' below). As with Sigmund Freud and Otto Weininger before him, the subject was not just a matter of burning personal concern, but a gateway to individual and group psychology. Here are four more unpublished texts on the topic (in the original English) from the Archive. These date from around 1941.

1 You on Sex

Are you sure that, when discussing sex problems . . .

. . . you aren't flying out against the horrible fact that people like to enjoy themselves and – what's even worse – one another?

. . . you are informed about the subject matter? Your own sex life, plus a number of obscure hearsays, are not a sufficient source of information.

. . . you are able to tolerate tastes and inclinations different from your own if only they harm nobody?

. . . you are capable of not envying people for pleasures you may have no opportunity, or no power to enjoy?

. . . you can tolerate intolerance?

. . . you are determined to treat things you're feeling awkward about just as openly as somebody who wants to annoy you would treat them?

. . . you won't hurt people seriously with your opinion on so delicate a subject?

. . . you don't twaddle about these problems simply on account of the sexual stimulation with which such talking may provide you?

. . . the importance you attach to the subject is at least half as great as the importance you attach to what you are saying about it?

. . . the others will not misunderstand you?

. . . you aren't really propagating Jimmy's views because Jimmy has had such a lot of sexual experience and because Jimmy is so clever and because Jimmy's views on sex are so sober and clean (and because, after – or is it above? – all, you love Jimmy)?

. . . the others are as serious about the topic as I hope you are?

. . . you know that appearing modest and being filthy, and appearing shameless and being decent, are two not very unusual combinations?

. . . you are able to realize things prior to intensely liking or detesting them?

. . . you don't tend to cover conclusions to be drawn from your own sex life and that of others with the palliating mantle of refined hypocrisy?

. . . your intellectual attitude towards the other sex is not influenced by an overdose of either sexual enmity or sexual attraction?

. . . you do not merely want to say something, but that you have something to say?

If you are sure, think again whether you are. If you aren't sure, shut up.

2 *Man to Woman*

How often man feels ashamed of his gratitude to you. He ought to be ashamed of himself.

Whenever you are in a situation where you are considered inferior by society, but superior by psychology, activities that aren't your business become your duty.

I'll never forgive you your making us flirt with you. I'll never cease thanking you for making us make love to you.

It has been alleged that between man and woman there exists an unbridgeable gulf. I only see a river. Never mind whether that's bridgeable as long as you can swim.

When we say that this woman isn't so nice a person as she seems to be at a time when we are in love with her, we forget that she isn't so distasteful as she seems to be at a time when we are in love with somebody else.

You may have to treat your husband as a child; always treat your growing son as an adult.

What a pity that there aren't some competent neutral neuters to decide on the question of sex differences. You and we, however impartial we may try to be, will always be influenced by deep-lying prejudices. But then wouldn't there be the danger that the neutrals would concentrate on our respective shortcomings rather than on our respective assets?

Our greatest fault lies in regarding your superior qualities as weaknesses.

The other day Alison Settle wrote in the *Observer* that home was the centre but not the boundary of your life. I hope we'll help you to feel quite at home outside the home. And I hope you won't forget to make us feel at home at home.

I wish we used our mental make-up as openly as you paint your faces.

You don't get on our nerves by having the last word, but rather by having it in the right place – now and then.

Why on earth do you feel pleased when somebody is in love with you for whom you don't care a bit? We, in the corresponding situation, feel extremely ill at ease.

The misogynist is really a man-hater. He hates his feelings of affection towards women, feelings that are distinctly masculine.

For ages you have inspired us to do things. Now you yourself have started doing things – as yet with little inspirational assistance on our part.

Every woman knows how to give pleasure; every mature woman knows how to bestow happiness. (Pleasure experienced as happiness is gratification resulting in satisfaction.)

You often show us how right it is not to mind who's right.

If a member of either sex mentions quality X as being the point in which a worthless woman differs from a worthless man, you can be sure that X is their common characteristic.

We don't mind self-display in women, we merely object to the display of something different from the self.

3   To Start You Sleeping

[HK:] Blinded by the fierce rays of their self-esteem, some writers tend to forget that one of the profoundest functions of literature is to get the reader to sleep. Whether we writers like it or not, reading is doubtless the most widely used soporific.

In the following, I've been trying to take heed of this fact. Knowing from my experience that the soporiferous value of many a piece of otherwise quite acceptable reading matter is dangerously decreased by the circumstance that somehow or other, although already sleepy, you've got to continue reading, I have endeavoured to free the reader from the threat of this compulsion. Thus, while the length of the preceding and the present sentence ought to serve as initial doses of my sleeping drug, the following items will be sufficiently short, self-contained, and, I trust, boring, to enable the reader to drop off at any point with a perfectly easy mind, and just to DREAM IT OUT:

Many are the women who make a man's manners their mannerisms.

The only certain way out of a love affair is yet rarely safe, for it usually is the way right into the next.

A man who would never be moved to tears belongs to a peculiar type of creature, to be found among both men and women – namely, a Woman trying to be a Man.

Man's love is enduring as long as it is not yet reciprocated. Woman's love is enduring when it is no longer reciprocated.

There are women who call the impression they want to make on others 'self-expression'. Yes, the reader's uneasy feeling, beneath his agreement, is right: not only women.

Man's hate for Woman bears witness to the curious forms love may take.

Not being worth his while she readily thinks that she isn't worth hers.

Most unhappy relationships would consist of a man who needs a mother being tied to a woman who needs a father, if there were not so many consisting of a man who needs to father tied to a woman who needs to mother.

Trying to prevent oneself from falling in love results in falling in love with the wrong one.

Critics of women, beware of pointing to the lack of things you fail to notice!

Overshadowed, though not outweighed, by differences, the similarities between the sexes go unrecognised.

The first date is seldom an appointment without fear on either side.

Let's not make up our mind about her making up her face without considering our making up our mind.

Whilst he whispered: "Never could I love anyone more than I love you," and whilst she thought he lied, he knew he spoke the bitter, bitter truth.*

Man is on the lookout for the woman who always cares and never minds.

Part of Don Juan's tragedy was not that he had no pleasure in morality, it was that he had none in immorality.*

Reflecting on men and women, one comes to the conclusion that two sexes are quite enough.

> (*With acknowledgement to *Kite* [these sentences appeared in the journal as part of the short story 'Don Juan Again', December 1945, p. 16, printed in the Appendix below])

4 Man, Woman, and Midway Between

Man is on the lookout for the woman who always cares and never minds.

Both the dreamer and the poet see things as they aren't. But only the poet sees them as they could be.

Part of Don Juan's tragedy was not that he had no pleasure in morality, it was that he had none in immorality.*

Even the pedant loses his pen. But only in the very place where he desires to find it.

Whether or not music be the food for love, love is the food for music.

If the worst comes to the worst, our moralizing demoralizes us far enough to make us worry others about our having nothing to worry about.

In human partnership there is not always love where there is no hate, but there's always hate where there is no love.

Death-phantasies are the liveliest.

"You're to blame: you left her." "I'm not to blame: I left her behind."

Art is a convincing compromise between denial and acceptance of reality.

An awkward difficulty in the way of democratic matrimonial life arises when a controversial issue is put to the vote.

We shall never convert criminals by convicting them if we don't heed their convictions.

First he was raptured because she seemed to have stolen his heart; later he was raptured to realize that she had only borrowed it.

Is it a joke or is it humorous? That depends on whether we laugh at it once, or often smile at it.

"Give" and "take" in love are most effective when they are identical.

A woman with a past has more sex appeal than a man without a future.

What many a man wanting a wife is searching for is freedom from freedom.

There are women who manage to follow you by walking in front of you.

Most people who try to laugh in their sleeve haven't a sleeve to laugh in.

When I'm down, my wife is always ready to refresh me with a few words (spoken, of course, by me).

A subtle surprise is one that doesn't surprise the reader, but would surprise him if he weren't so clever.

A woman's most dangerous rival is a new edition of herself.

In love, one hesitates when noticing that one is going to mean what one is going to say.

Don't despise self-love. Even love starts at home.

Intellectual development: as the child grows into the man and learns to be ashamed, he acquires comparisons to cover up his fallacies.

Between the sexes, it is often fatal to learn from experience. Though there are only two sexes, there are, in the broadest sense of the term, numberless sexualities.

Though the relation between their ages was upside down, they never quarrelled: she was old enough and he was young enough to know better.

We lie in order to provoke lies in others that we accept as truths.

Hating her love of you is yet more comfortable than hating your love of her.

Monogamous promiscuity: just as many real women may stand for one imagined woman, one real woman may stand for an imagined harem.

Tolerance is but the realisation that nobody is to blame for one's deficiencies.

Looking at mankind, said the cynic (or was it the realist – I don't remember), one inclines towards the view that there are more premature births than premature deaths.

"If Ann were free to talk about sex she wouldn't talk about anything else." "Really? Susan would start talking about something else."

The teacher's development proceeds from being his pupils' pupil to being his own.

Freud discovered that when we lose something there often is unconscious intention behind our mishap. Was there something of the sort involved when I lost her love?

Those who live in the past think they cut themselves free if they look at the present with future eyes.

The point about romantic love (don't know whether there is one in it) is that its expectations are their own fulfilment.

So often regret is an excuse, successful not even with oneself, for not removing its cause.

As long as men and women are the judges, the right thing about men and women cannot be said.

While artistic wisdom knows of every course that life may take, it does not know the meaning of "of course".

A durable lover must be more than a skilful lovee.

There is no failure without a preceding illusion of success.

As long as we try to make a virtue out of sex we show that we still regard it as a crime.

The good critic does not lose hope that others will do what he would but can't. The bad critic does not lose hope that they won't.

To cut a short story short: because she was his first woman it seemed to her as though he were her first man. As a matter of fact she remained his first, and he her last.

The only thing one can do about many a thing is it.

The writer's main aim (and difficulty) is to be frank without being a bore.

However much one may consider the prostitute inferior, she has chosen her profession in order to feel superior.

If we can't change her, we can still change the point of view whence we are looking at her.

"Such is life" is one of the platitudes that always have a deep meaning.

She carried the world's Misery and Guilt on her husband's shoulders.

A woman may forgive a man for not realizing his ambitions, but she'll hardly forgive him for not realizing hers.

Others' actions and one's own thoughts are what one tends to regard as evil.

What does he want a mother for if he must start fathering her[?]

The sexes will always need each other, if only for the purpose of self-love by proxy.

A significant joke is a joke that you don't get if you think it is one.

People who wish they could commit temporary suicide should consider that they go to sleep every night.

There's always something fishy about our truths, which makes us communicate them to others.

She says she's making friends whenever she desires to make rivals.

The child who cannot tolerate postponement of satisfactions is yet more realistic than the man who is wont to postpone them indefinitely.

Thought on the golden wedding: 50 years ago I believed that I had lost every battle except the last; today it seems that I have lost every one except the first.

Reflecting on men and women, one comes to the conclusion that two sexes are quite enough.

NOTES

Keller continued to write aphorisms and brief texts for the rest of his life, jotting them down – and occasionally typing them out – on any scrap of paper that came to hand: in addition to the aphorisms printed elsewhere in this volume, a selection appears in 'Hans Keller (1919-1985). A Memorial Symposium', *Music Analysis*, 5/2-3, 1986, pp. 368-70.

II

Psychology, 1942-47

(1) Psychology and Sociology:
Responses to Margaret Phillips (1942-47)

Small-group Psychology

1 Group Functioning of a String Quartet

Keller's first formal involvement with small-group psychology came with this response to a questionnaire he received in July 1942. This was drawn up in 1940 by the sociologist Margaret Phillips and passed to him by 'Miss G. Marle' in the Lake District, where he was touring with a string quartet. (For a discussion of Phillips, see the Editor's Preface above.) His response took the form of a 26-page letter and demonstrated the 'psychological trend' of his thought. It is a document of great intensity and includes a preliminary critique of the questionnaire itself. He writes: 'The two particular groups I am choosing for this purpose are (a) the population of an internment camp [on the Isle of Man] in which I resided for several months, and (b) a string quartet of which I have been a member for several years.' Section (b) is set out here, and a separate summary of section (a) in the notes (section (a) itself is too diffuse to publish). Keller's quartet had formed in Vienna and reconvened in England, though its membership fluctuated (in Austria Franz Schmidt had played 'cello); at this point it would have included Dr. Oskar Adler (leader), Hans Keller (second violin), Sybil Maturin (viola), and Keller's mother ('cello).

*The following paragraphs respond to the headings drawn up in Phillips's questionnaire (the relevant sections are set out below); as Keller chose not to answer every one of Phillips's points, their numbering is discontinuous. Keller's response appears to be rooted in Freud's seminal essay, 'Group Psychology and the Individual' ('*Massenpsychologie und ich-analyse*', 1917): this defined groups in terms of aim, leadership, and membership. The themes of display, courtship and Eonism (found in the remarks on the Internment Camp) were addressed by J. C. Flugel in the* Psychology of Clothes *(London, Hogarth Press, 1930). Both the questionnaire and the text have been lightly edited.*

The exercise brings together the two cultural approaches Keller describes in 'England' (above): by drawing up categories for observation, Margaret Phillips works in the English way, from the 'outside in'; by probing the internal dynamics of the group, Keller works in the Continental way, from the 'inside out'. It appears that Keller met Phillips only in the following year, in August 1943, and that this was his first encounter with her work.

Questionnaire *(Margaret Phillips)*

OBJECT OF THE INVESTIGATION

To discover the conditions under which groups function (or fail to function) effectively and harmoniously both internally and in relation to the outside world.

METHOD PROPOSED

The study of particular groups over a period of time either by members of the group or by observers in close contact with it. Where possible it is suggested that a diary be kept and notes written up whenever developments occur. It is likely that a study of the same group by two or more members (observers) independently would yield good results. I shall be grateful for any help in enlisting the co-operation of other [observers] likely to be interested – especially in making any independent study of the same group. Points that might be noted include the following:

I   *To what extent does the group achieve or fail to achieve:*

    1   *Internal unity and co-operation*
    2   *Effective collaboration with other groups*
    3   *Harmony with the outside world*

II   *How is this to be accounted for? The following factors are suggested for consideration:*

    1   *Leadership*
    2   *Common aim or purpose*
    3   *Common activities and enterprises undertaken*
    4   *Common religious or political convictions, philosophy or scale of values*
    5   *Common pattern of living*
    6   *Common training, ritual, ceremonial*
    7   *Common social or educational background*
    8   *Common interests outside the group*
    9   *Degree of group-consciousness achieved by the members – e.g. as to the group's aims and methods, its history, tradition or record of achievement*
    10   *A written constitution*
    11   *The form of government, e.g. autocratic or democratic*
    12   *Financial responsibility*
    13   *The size of the group*
    14   *Groups within the group*
    15   *Rivalry or competition with other groups*
    16   *External opposition: a common enemy*
    17   *Common internal grievances*
    18   *Differences of age, sex, class, temperament, race or nationality among members*
    19   *Personal ties or differences between individuals*
    20   *Does change in personnel of group affect unity?*

III   *Does the degree or nature of unity change as time goes on? [If so,] why?*

IV   *What needs of the individual does the group satisfy? Are the benefits he receives or the services he renders more important in attaching him to the group?*

V   *How do the attitudes to the group of the leader, the official [and] the ordinary member differ?*

VI   *How does the level of living and thinking within the group compare with that achieved by the individual?*

N.B.   It is not necessary to answer these questions as they stand. They are only intended to indicate the scope and the direction of the inquiry. All information will be regarded as confidential and so used as to give no clue to the identity of either the writer or the group. Any suggestions for the improvement of this outline will be welcomed.

Response *(Hans Keller)*

II.I   Leadership of the group, and its role in achieving internal unity

Leadership in the string quartet has been responsible for much of the internal unity, and for some disintegrational processes.

(1)   From the purely musical point of view, a string quartet without a leader who possesses a great amount of authority and initiative is unthinkable. The fact that usually members of such a group are fully aware of this condition contributes a great deal towards the suppression of jealousy, envy, and rivalry, and to the widest possible unfolding of the submissive tendencies, whatever their psychic origin. In our case this could be observed very clearly (i) because the 1st violin's authority and initiative was so great that it did not offer any weak points where he could have been attacked, and (ii) because the other members of the quartet showed, for the most part, a degree of musical and artistic education which would have made it difficult for them to rob the leader of his influence, even had he possessed less. His position as leader was over-determined, so to speak.

(2)   Nevertheless, as I have indicated before, his authority did give rise to manifestations of rivalry and envy, and thus for a short period, disintegrative processes were observable. It follows from (1)/(ii) that this could happen only if at least one of the other members was not capable of exhibiting the necessary degree of artistic education. This was the case with a female viola player who was a member of our quartet (necessarily) for a short time. Not only did her behaviour and her attitude towards the leader and towards the rest of the quartet exhibit signs of envy (in regard to the position of the first violinist), but she also rebelled obviously against the endo-psychic loss of individuality and power which came about through the strong influence which the leader exerted even on her – a fact to which she herself seemed frequently to have been alive. In other words: just as those members who fulfilled condition (1)/(ii) suppressed their 'revolting' tendencies and gave free reign to [discernible] submissive tendencies, the viola player in question was painfully aware of the fact that her submissive tendencies exhibited a considerable activity against her will. She consequently attempted to protect her endangered individuality by both concealed and open revolt, this attempt being also correlated to, and intensified by, her envy, her wish to be a leader herself. It might be interesting to note in addition that she displaced part of her manifestations of these anti-leader tendencies upon the other two members of the quartet, and this she did in a twofold manner: on the one hand, she rebelled against the other members, identifying them with the leader (this process being facilitated by the great amount of loyalty which the other members displayed to the leader); on the other hand, she often tried to treat the other members as her own protégés who were misused by the leader and who consequently needed her protection and her leadership. Thus she acquired in her estimation the position of at least a sub-leader who, moreover, owing to her (spasmodically imagined) superiority over the leader, could be considered, in other respects, the real leader of the quartet.

The main cause of the displacement can be sought in her partial submissive acceptance of the leader's influence, whilst the twofold form of the displacement (rebelling and leading) is, as regards its determinative factors, too obvious to need a further explanation. Shortly after she had retired from our quartet she formed a chamber music ensemble in which she was the actual leader, the subordinated members all belonging to the male sex. (In our quartet she had been the only female.)

Let me add that I do not, for a moment, believe that the decisive factor which I mentioned sub (1), i.e. the degree of artistic education, is one which can be accepted, without further analysis, as a psychologically workable variable, without regard to its dependence both upon the kind of development of the psychic organisation of which it is a manifestation, and upon the external circumstances which may condition either its free display or its involution. However, a discussion of this detail would lead us too far afield from the realm of interpretative observation, and would perhaps force upon you conclusions, the hypotheses underlying them you may not feel willing to accept.

II.2   The Common Aim of the Group

There are some interesting details to be mentioned with regard to one specified practical common aim, namely public performance. A string quartet is, by its artistic nature, an ensemble in which most of the members are impelled to restrain to a great extent those tendencies to display their personal artistic powers and their technical skill in which, on other occasions, say at soloistic performances, they are used, indeed, mostly entitled, to indulge. I do not speak of the quartet's first violinist in this connection, because the player who has to perform the leading part is, even from a purely artistic musical standpoint, least compelled to this suppression.

Many writers would regard any tendency to display as of an exhibitionistic nature. Whether we accept such a view or not, we have to bear in mind, in this specific case, that a performing musician always is to some extent acting as if he were courting his audience. Remember that we must regard exhibitionism 'as fundamentally a symbolic act based on a perversion of courtship,' that the perversion on which it is based is not qualitatively to be distinguished from those displaying tendencies which are in normal cases, subordinated to the sexual organisation, and that every form of courtship, *ex definitione*, implies an element of display. In an isolated, intensified, exaggerated form such display would have to be regarded as bearing perhaps all of the essential characteristics of exhibitionism proper, though in a much more limited, and much less obvious degree, and, of course, in a much more sublimated form and accordingly on a different psychic level. Remembering all that, we cannot escape the conclusion that where we have to deal with an act of courtship (whether on the sexual level or not) in which the tendencies to display are pretty strong, or even appear to predominate, we have to suppose that at the root of these tendencies there should be found urges of a narcissistic nature. As regards their qualitative traits, they would be at least related to the basis of what, under exceptional conditions of constitution and development, we would consider to be manifestations of a clearly exhibitionist nature.

Now to continue. It was very easily to be observed in our quartet (as in others) that some of the players showed, according to different occasions, three different 'playing attitudes', as it were. The different occasions are (i) playing for the enjoyment of the players themselves, (ii) rehearsing for a public performance, and (iii) the public performance itself. The attitude of the players in question in the case of (i) was one of more or less successful, in any case of fully intended, suppression of the tendencies to display. During (ii) there still could be detected the strong artistic intention to suppress the tendencies: however, the approaching event of the public performance already showed its influence upon the player: whilst executing passages of a relatively soloistic kind, the tendency to display began to break through in a way not fully justifiable by his own artistic standard, i.e. his artistic conscience. At (iii) finally, the suppressive intentions and their efficacy were weakened remarkably, and at the same time the tendencies to display appeared with all the potential energy behind it. Purely accompanying figures were played frequently as though they were cadenzas, and most of the original intentions were flooded by the now much stronger, and at least developmentally much more primitive, tendencies to display, so that for the time of the performance, and also as regards the player's retrospections, his own artistic standard and conscience, and the judgments influenced by it underwent partly a paralysis, and partly a regressional modification. He would have been surprised, had he been able to hear a gramophone record of the performance.

After having observed this process in others, I investigated as critically as possible the changes of my own playing attitude and observed very similar results in myself.

Thus the common aim [of performance] which has now been discussed had a detrimental effect upon the achievement of internal (artistic) unity and co-operation and, from the standpoint of a strictly musical-artistic scale of values, the way from (i) to (iii) is one of deterioration and involution, just as it can be termed, dynamically, as one of evolution.

II.4   The common religious or political convictions, philosophy or scale of values of the group

Affinity of individual philosophies and scales of values is, in my experience, almost a necessary condition for a successful functioning of artistic co-operation, not only in that it binds the members together through congeniality outside the specific artistic activities, but also because very frequently it constitutes a correlativum to common attitudes towards artistic values and modes of artistic interpretation and reproduction. I have come to this conclusion not only by observing the development of the string quartet of which I am a member (the personnel of which varied at some time), but also after inspection and interpretation of numerous other groups of an identical or related nature. [Re. II.7] [A common] social background hardly comes into play in this connection. [Re. II.9] The more the artistically influenced group-consciousness was developed, the more successful were the suppressive tendencies, and therefore the more was achieved in respect of unity.

II.18   Differences of age, sex, class, temperament, race or nationality among members of the group

The greatest amount of unity seems to be achieved in a string quartet the members of which are all of one sex. This descriptive conclusion has been arrived at by me as well as by the leader of our quartet in consequence of long-time experience both with the quartets in which he and I played, and (indirectly) with those the development of which we had the opportunity to observe. Where the personnel of the quartet, with regard to sex, is mixed – and here we arrive at a detail where I am able to state something about the age factor – it would appear that a high degree of unity can be achieved on condition that the female members (at least) are not too young. But as these conclusions have been arrived at in consequence of inductions on a predominantly symptomatic level, I think I should warn you to accept them with caution, notwithstanding the fact that I believe in their validity. But let us also consider the sexual factor itself more properly: from my experience it appears that whenever some form of sexual tension (in the narrower meaning of the term) exists between two members of the quartet, there is much more probability that if other strong counter-forces are not present, this fact will make against unity. On the other hand, where there exists between two members an actual sexual relationship, as for instance when a married couple plays in a quartet, this condition does not make against unity; indeed, it often seems to contribute towards internal co-operation, provided that the conditions of the sexual relationship itself are favourable, and that other counter-acting forces, as for instance a secret longing of a third member, are absent.

But this is only a seeming contradiction, for the following reasons: (i) the unity and high degree of co-operation achieved through the one-sex-condition has, inter alia, its source in the (then more probably prevailing) affinity of artistic outlook of the different members; [on the other hand] the unity achieved through the existence and the influence of a frictionless sexual relationship owes much of its existence to the emotional equilibrium both between the partners themselves, and among the rest of the quartet, where it comes about through the very strong suggestive influence (in this case based upon processes of identification and projection) which a happy relationship [in these] favourable conditions always exerts. Now there is no doubt that affinity or identity of artists' outlook which is based upon the direction the development of instinctual energy takes ([among] members of the same sex) is of greater significance for artistic unity and co-operation than an emotional equilibrium, the latter moreover frequently accompanying the former. If (ii) we finally take into account the fact that counter-forces, such as jealousy, will more easily make their appearance under the conditions that prevail in the sexual-relationship case, we will give up the thought that such a relationship might contribute to unity. For the thought contradicts the statement that the maximum amount of unity will probably be found in a quartet consisting of members of one and the same sex.

But again I have to warn you: the fact that one proposition does not damage the validity of another is in itself no proof that the other proposition is undamageable: the basis I gave to the aforementioned symptomatic induction is probably valid, but I may have left out other determinants which might wipe out the actual effectiveness of the known ones.

As far as my observation goes, I cannot make any statement about the factor of class difference; differences of nationality did not play any role at all.

II.19   Personal ties or differences between individuals in the group

During one period my mother was one of the members of the quartet; the amount of internal unity during this period equalled that during others.

II.20   Change in personnel [and its effect upon] group unity

Artistic unity is endangered temporarily through changes [in personnel], because it is only possible through a long process of co-operation to achieve that high standard of internal unity which is required in the present case for artistic purposes: this fact holds good even under very favourable conditions. On the other hand, if the change only involves persons who at some previous period have already co-operated with the quartet or its leader (as was the case with my mother), the fact of the change itself has no serious influence upon unity.

V   The difference in attitude to the group of the leader

Outside the playing itself, there cannot be noticed any difference between the attitude of the leader to the group, and between that of other members; at least not inasmuch as such a difference would be conditioned by the two facts of 'being-a-leader' and 'being-an-ordinary-member'. Within the playing activities, the leader assumes an almost entirely dominating role, whilst the other members' attitude towards the rest of the group is one of equal associateship. The leader succeeds not only in expressing his necessary instructions in a modest way (the characteristic of 'domination' applying more to the frictionless way in which the instructions are obeyed), but also in making his will and influence effective through the medium of his playing itself. The latter process is the most sublime and impressive way of successful and unopposed domination I know. It would be interesting to know how far identification plays a role in this process; but this would be no easy task.

VI   The level of living and thinking within the group compared with that achieved by the individual

In consequence of the exalting effect of the group activity, the level of thinking within the group is generally, at least as concerns the majority of members, a higher one than, or at least equal to, the level achieved by an imaginary individual typifying the average individual level of the existing group. But this is a precarious question.

Source

Undated single-spaced typescript letter of 26 pages written in July 1942. It begins 'Dear Madam', and is written from 'Glebe House, The Promenade, Bowness-on-Windermere, Westmoreland'.

Keller closes by saying that he understands from 'Miss [Gertrud] Marle' that, in return for his letter, Margaret Phillips would be prepared to respond to a questionnaire of his own relating to his current project on the endo- and extra-psychic roots of 'modesty and shame' (a topic also addressed in 'Modesty' from J. C. Flugel's *The Psychology of Clothes*, London, Hogarth, 1930, pp. 53-67). The project would address, *inter alia*, 'the appearance of shame-modesty processes in mythology, religion, poetry, art and perhaps even in music (Brahms's later works).' Both questionnaire (4 pages of typescript with manuscript additions) and response (6 pages, also mixed typescript and manuscript) are held in the Archive.

Keller asks 28 questions grouped under 5 categories. These 'keep within the sexual realm', notwithstanding 'one or two excursions into non-sexual spheres', and deal with: (I) experiences in childhood, (II) problems with physical developments in adolescence, (III) the excitation of desire in others through make-up and perfume (together with the fear of excitation), (IV) embarrassment (blushing, feelings of shame, nudity before others), and (V) attitudes to female modesty. Keller realizes that some of the questions might be unanswerable or intrusive (e.g. (II), Q. 3: 'Have sexual activities of any kind, whether phantasmal, masturbational, coitional or otherwise, resulted in a feeling of shame and guilt during the period of your adolescence? Why?'); but he does also ask, (VI) 'Can you indicate, with regard to the questions you *do* answer, the approximate degree of internal difficulties which you had to overcome before answering them, and can you give an introspectional analysis of these difficulties?'

Phillips's reply is impressively candid and by and large comprehensive. For example, in response to (IV), Q. 1, 'Do you blush easily? When? Why?' she writes: 'I think I am most embarrassed nowadays when our Principal, who has a genius for saying the wrong things at staff meetings, does it again. The symptom I notice most is one I used to notice in my father – the rhythmic movement of one foot, the knees being crossed. Oh, and I am acutely embarrassed by tender passages on films – can't bear them. That may be why I practically never go to a film.' Then, in reply to (IV) Q. 8, 'Imagine: if circumstances forced you to be, for a short period, naked in the presence of somebody who would especially stimulate your bodily sense of shame, and you were put before the alternative either to remain perfectly quiet during this period, or to move about continually, which of the two would you prefer? Give reasons,' she exclaims 'What a question! However did you think it up? I have no idea. I should try to emulate Lady Godiva, if possible.' But in her afterward, partly in response to (VI), she admits that she now has 'a feeling of stepping back in my own persona after playing a very silly part.' What does Keller want all this information for? Hadn't the questions all been answered by the 'humourless' Havelock Ellis (and 'what a mess "he and his wife" had made of their marriage')? The questionnaire struck her as 'so trivial and unreal' because sex couldn't be isolated 'from a total state of mind'. Female modesty, anyway, was a virtue only 'in a man-made world'; sex in England and the West generally was a 'cultural artefact'; and what she had 'against the whole dam business is that it turns our minds inwards on ourselves, whereas romantic love turns them outwards.' More still, 'my generation was brought up, not on sex, but on women's suffrage, social reform, settlements and slumming, which partly explains perhaps my feeling about the emptiness of the enquiry.'

Internment Camp [Isle of Man]

Following Hitler's offensive in northwest Europe in the spring of 1940, an offensive that threatened Britain (especially after Dunkirk), Keller, along with many other émigrés, was interned on the Isle of Man in May of that year. In the autumn of the same year he was released at the recommendation of Ralph Vaughan Williams, who chaired the Board that heard individual cases (see: Daniel Snowman, The Hitler Émigrés, *London, Chatto and Windus, 2002, pp. 105-15). The following is a summary of Keller's experiences, cast again in categories familiar from Phillips's questionnaire.*

Size, Stability and Change of Personnel   1000-2000. Newcomers after the time of my arrival relatively few (compared with releases which continually proceeded on a varying scale). The latter kind of changes (releases) had considerable impact on harmony and conflict. The aim of the group was, of course, its dissolution, release. Every individual release excited (1) envy (agreeably suppressed) (2) hopes (on the part of those who had applied for release on the same grounds as the respective 'releasee'). The almost universal 'release obsession' involved a degree of emotional interest in releases that sometimes even defied attempts at complete rationalisation. On the impact of the general release idea, as distinct from occasions of individual releases, see below.

Age   The separation of the age factor from other interrelated conditions is in this case impossible for the conscientious observer.

Sex   [There was] a growing longing for the presence of the other sex, [with the] resulting instability making for conflict. [On the other hand,] the fact of common grievance made for harmony. [There was an] over-accentuation of individual's past experiences, [with] older members narrating to younger ones their sexual past: some degree of unity [was] achieved through the existence of such bonds that rested on a common phantasy life. The increase of sublimation in other individuals [was] also the consequence of frustration; [there was an] intensification of homosexual tendencies; [and] Eonistic tendencies (transvestism) manifested themselves in theatrical performances (there was no observational indication as to the increase of these tendencies).

Social Status   A strong cohesion between members of the same class [was matched by] animosity between different class members: [but the] conflicts [were] always individual.

Cultural Background, Outlook, Interests   If they were common to a number of individuals, these served as a cohesive element, especially where common activities arising out of them gave rise to the formation of sub-groups (football, music, philosophising). On the other hand, within the cohesive frame and in most individual cases subordinate to it there also arose such feelings of jealousy as are commonly to be observed amongst congenials. The majority [were] Jews [exerting] a cohesive influence reinforced through Nazi opposition. Different outlooks within this frame caused minor conflicts.

Structure   Officer in charge of camp – camp leader (refugee) – houseleaders. The officer [was] father for some, the camp leader (called the camp father in a previous camp) [was] father for many, the house leader (house father) [was also] father for many; the connective element was jealousy and on the other hand rivalry. Family feeling [was especially strong among the] Jews! The attitudes of house-leaders [were]: (1) dominating (a small section of them), (2) moderate, modest (with a far-reaching suppression of dominating tendencies). (2) almost always makes for unity in at least some degree, (1) makes for opposition, but also for unity regarding submissive individuals.

Relation of Individual Members to Each Other and to the Group   To each other: [This] can best be described by pointing to the difference between the present relations and those in a town of equal size. The mentioned unifying elements manifested themselves in the fact that negative attitudes were never as outspoken as they would have been in a normal town; they were also rarer. On the other hand, the regressive factors [allowed] the positive as well as the negative attitudes to proceed on a more primitive level. On the positive side, this was shown (1) by the element of dependence, either on a father, a brother or a son, entering the picture with great intensity, friendships being much more of a necessity and much less of a luxury than under normal conditions; (2) by the easily detectable ambivalence which many of the 'positive' attitudes showed. The ambivalence would have been weaker and more concealed under normal conditions. This second point overlaps with the primitive aspect of the negative attitudes. Though more powerful hostilities would remain latent and sometimes were even overcome where they would have broken out under different circumstances, minor antagonisms, whether within the frame of ambivalence or more isolated, received over-accentuation. The correctness of these observations is proved by the fact that many friendships, seemingly so intimate and firmly founded, as well as many negative relationships consisting in petty hostilities, ceased as soon as the partners were released. Note that I have only stressed the differences between this society and a normal one. Analogies, such as the formation of permanent friendships, need no special comment.

To the group: Majority: "Function as well as you can as long as you have to exist; cease to exist as soon as possible." Minority: "I don't care how you function or whether you function at all. This is hell, anyway, I don't mind which special kind of hell I'm in. I want my freedom." (I exaggerate, or rather I'm diving below the outer surface. Social inhibitions mitigated this attitude, which was also opposed, on deeper levels, by the need for personal relations. However, if the attitude was sufficiently strong, the individual tended to satisfy this need without coming into serious conflict with his 'don't care' [attitude], i.e. he stuck to as few objects as possible, avoiding an extension of his friendly feelings to the group. The strong uniting factor of common Jewry and common fate prevented manifestations of hostility against group life, indifference being the general characteristic of the attitude of these individuals.) Small minority: "I don't want to be released, I prefer this life to the life outside." They were accordingly social. The reasons they gave for their preference were mainly economical. Behind the infantile tendencies [stood the attitude] "Let someone care for me . . . here I'm protected."

Source

Typescript of 3 pages from about 1942. Keller's document breaks off with the start of a new section, *Groups within Groups*. This was to fall under two headings: (i) subgroups based on common aims, and (ii) sub-groups consisting of dwellers of different rooms and houses. He remarked that the 'formation of these groups [were] predominantly beneficial for general unity'.

Phillips also includes a report on internment camps in her *Small Social Groups in England*, again covering the period May-October 1940. This does not include Keller's material, although she acknowledges use of his term, 'group narcissism'. She also draws on his 'group self-contempt'.

[From:] Some Critical Remarks upon a System of Classification Used for Discovering theConditions under which Groups Function

Keller's response to Phillips included a long, formal critique of the questionnaire itself. Keller takes note of her hope that it conveys 'the scope and direction' of her project, which is 'to discover the conditions under which groups function (or fail to function) effectively and harmoniously both internally and in relation to the outer world', but argues that the scope is, or should be, wider still. She needs to cut through the 'network of intra- and inter-individual psychic causes' at a 'deeper level' (a) by reconsidering her methodology and (b) by extending her inquiry. Under (a) he writes:

To give a definition of 'group', [it] is necessary [to have a] mental representation of at least two groups; after I have found the common characteristics of these two, I am in possession of a *tertium compariationis* for a provisional definition, of a *fundamentum divisionis* for a classification. The more these two groups will typify extremes, the more probable it will be that common characteristics which we abstract from them will be valid for any given group. Two of the main lines along which I have to travel in my search for the extremes appear to me to be signified (1) by the number of group members; and (2) by the degree of organization achieved by the group. As it appears that a small group can more easily attain a high degree of organization than a large one, I try to picture (i) the smallest possible group with the highest possible degree of organization, and (ii) a large group with the highest possible degree of organization. Under (i) there comes to my mind inevitably a happily married couple, whereas under (ii) the conception of a theatre audience seems to me to be useful.

Under (b) he divides the inquiry into 'phylogenetical and ontogenetical aspects' which 'conveniently, if artificially' further divide into 'a theoretical and . . . a more practical part'. The phylogenetic part would involve

. . . a comparative investigation into the group life both of higher mammals and of more primitive races on the one hand, and into manifestations of group life on a level of more progressed civilization on the other . . .

whereas in the ontogenetic part 'the sexual factor should not be underestimated' and the views on sexuality of Sigmund Freud and J. C. Flugel (Men and their Motives, London, 1934) should be considered. (Keller pays homage to Flugel's 'extraordinary intellectual powers' that 'astound even those who are amongst his adversaries'; he also refers to Gustav Jäger (Die Entdeckung der Seele, Leipzig, 1880, I) and Havelock Ellis.) Here the inquiry could profitably look at children's groups, adolescents' and pre-adolescents' groups (such as scouts). This investigation would then lead to an analysis of interrelations between environmental and psychosexual factors within the group:

With regard to the environmental factors, marriage would obtrude itself on us as being particularly interesting in its different ways of [influencing] group life (I am speaking of extra-familial group life, of course) . . . Of special importance would be an inquiry into the questions (i) how far marriage, in being itself an equivalent, sometimes even more than that, for group life, effects a weakening of social tendencies; and how far on the other hand (ii) marriage tends to contribute to the intensification of social tendencies, e.g. through the (however small) outlet (a legitimate outlet) group life offers to the polyandrous and polygynous tendencies of the matrimonial partners.

After suggesting that, where applicable, 'there might be valid reason to investigate the relative consequences of different extents of periods of time spent together by the group members upon the group life at different ontogenetical stages . . . and accordingly into the importance of the relative length of intervals between the periods of group activity', Keller advocates as a starting point for the study of group life (without going into details) . . . the theoretical and practical study of family life with special regard to the development of a child's relation to his parents, brothers and sisters.

2   The Childish Leader

One naturally wonders why the childish leader should be 'constantly recurring' in our material. The answer may be, because there is a connection between leadership and childishness. More exactly, it can be suggested that a widely prevalent form of immaturity manifests itself in a wish to be leader.

This 'adult' form of the desire to play at being parent [is] due to an undue dominance of the super-ego, as distinct from the ego. We have previously seen that such dominance is indicative of an undeveloped personality.

In the present case, the ego, unable to bridge the gulf between itself and the super-ego by behaving to the latter's demands, tries to overcome the tension created by this gulf by identifying itself with the super-ego (the parent) and thus to boss an outside 'child' instead of being bossed by the super-ego.

This identification with the super-ego does not succeed very far for the very reason for which it has been set going, i.e. because of the great distance between ego and super-ego. Further, great gulfs between super-ego and ego, symptomatic as they are of immaturity, are likely to go hand in hand with dependence on external parent figures.

Thus the attempt to be a parent figure is accompanied by an increased need for a parent figure: 'the parent needs the group members not only as his "children" . . . but also in some sense as [his] "parents".'

The associations that have been discovered between the idea of one's parents and that of one's children may also operate in the case of parent figures and child figures and may thus promote, and be promoted by, this double need to find 'children' and 'parents' in the same object. In one sentence, the double need can be said to be based on a weak ego that cannot do without the primitive claims of an inner parental agency, and the support of an external one.

Source

Typescript from the early to mid 1940s. The essay forms the first of the four parts of Section VII of the joint book planned with Margaret Phillips (this is described in the Notes below): the other parts are devoted to 'Group Self-love' (see below), 'Group Self-contempt' and 'Hate in other Directions'. These last two are themes Keller addressed on various occasions (notably in 'Prostitutes Wear Marriage-rings', reproduced below). The references to 'our material' are to work included in the joint book under sections V and VI and elsewhere in VII. Phillips herself edited the essay and her main corrections have been incorporated here. The comments, however, did not make their way into Phillips's *Small Social Groups in England* (1965).

3   Senior Girls School

This is just one of many case studies that were to be part of Keller's joint book with Margaret Phillips (see the Notes *below) and takes the form of a commentary by Keller on Phillips's findings. The exercise reflects their particular interest in the 'Psychology and Ethics of School Staff Groups', and the nature of leadership, gender, frustration and aggression. Phillips did not in fact use the material for her* Small Social Groups in England *(1965).*

1   Lack of maternal qualities in the headmistress; presence of some masculine qualities

I have remarked [in my introduction] that these women's groups tend to consist of a high number of masculine women. Where masculinity shows it will of course be accompanied by a corresponding lack of maternal qualities, because the masculine line of development implies consequences of the castration-complex other than those involved in the development of the (actual or substitutive) maternal attitude. There is, however, a further point to be considered in the present instance of (as we must more generally call it) lack of leadership. The masculine side of leadership is also absent to some extent. It is true that, as Phillips observes, some masculine qualities seem to be there, but these are certainly not of what appears to be the essence of masculine leadership, viz., qualities which stimulate the super-egos of the group-members and thus serve to bring about identifications amongst them. We might therefore say that the Head Mistress presents an instance of pseudo-masculinity, or, more exactly, pseudo-masculinity in some respects. On the surface level we might be led to remark, "Of course, after all she is a female." Yet a moment's reflection must show us that the fact that some masculine qualities are present in an unusual degree whilst others are absent is in need of explanation. ('Masculine' is here to be taken as denoting qualities which are predominantly found in men.)

The explanation is not difficult on the basis of psychoanalytic theory; it can I think be given in one sentence. Whilst a female will be capable, in consequence of her penis-envy having developed in the direction of the identification with the male, successfully to imitate maleness in many respects, such [imitation] will hardly extend over much of her super-ego sphere, because the absence of castration-anxiety must have had its effects in her case as in the case of the feminine female.

It therefore appears that the present Head Mistress would have been in need of being led in order at least to have a chance of being a successful leader herself.

Whilst there is not the least doubt as to the importance of the factor of (lack of) leadership which monotonously pervades the whole lot of our material, we must I think be especially careful not to overlook other factors in view of the apparent preponderance of this one. 'Lack of leadership' is the answer to the question, "What is wrong with the group?" We can, however, put another question that only partially covers the sphere of the afore-mentioned one: "What is wrong with the group members?" This question naturally emerges when one considers the continuous flow of aggressiveness that distinguishes this group. More precisely, the question would run, "Given the present lack of leadership, is a considerable decrease in aggressiveness, caused through change of other circumstances, imaginable?"

Accepting for the moment a neo-psychoanalytic theory (which either to agree to, or to reject I have not yet found any opportunity) according to which, 'frustration, and only frustration, is the cause of aggressiveness',[1] there could indeed be very much done to reduce aggressiveness. But the reduction in frustration in which such a cure would consist would of course have to happen mainly in childhood. Yet it seems in the present instance that school life imposes an extraordinary amount of frustration on the individuals, one that could be profitably reduced (whether the above-mentioned theory is true or not).

2 Hostility to new members

This is particularly striking in the present instance. The similarity with children's groups is obvious. How far this factor is a regressive one is a precarious question when one does not know much about the personalities outside group life. But in view of the very primitive level of group-relations altogether, one that is very probably not that of the individuals' other processes, a regressive element can be presumed. This seems the more probable if one considers the large amount of strain falling upon group members; strain of any kind, in threatening the usual channels for adjusting oneself to circumstances and of adjusting the latter to oneself, tends to work for regression. The regressive element at present under consideration, i.e. that which manifests itself in a strong degree, unusual for adults, of hostility against the 'foreigner', has a parallel in the nation's life of not long ago which the reader may remember: under the strain of the threatening Nazi invasion [in the spring and summer of 1940] one proceeded to choose as a beatable enemy (scapegoat) a new section whose anti-Nazi feelings were as ardent as those of any other group or individual on the globe. German and Austrian refugees were interned on security grounds. To many of the latter as well as to many of their British friends this came as a shocking surprise; to those with some psychological insight it came as a matter of course.[2]

It seems that a high level of self-sacrifice and service to the group can only be bought at the expense of processes (liable to come to the fore in a psychic emergency) that according to generally assumed standards of valuation are not rational either.

This is not to say, however, that the latter processes cannot appear without the former. In the case of the nation's attitude to the threatening invasion, we have seen such behaviour as doubtless saved civilisation. In the case of the present group, whilst the irrational and immoral elements are undoubtedly present, there is not much to be seen of practicing, let alone saving, civilisation. In the latter case, we have a very weakly developed association, in the former we have an extremely strongly developed one. Amongst the main reasons for the successful formation of this strong association was the concentration of aggressiveness on an object outside the group in conformity with our group ideal. That our aggressiveness largely conformed to our (previous) standards of conscience was, incidentally, a reason why we succeeded in regressing relatively little.

The unity in hostility, though less consistent, less super-ego-syntonic, and weaker, is of course also to be observed in the present group. As Phillips correctly remarks, sub-groups reunite through common hostility against outsiders. These outsiders may be within the larger group, as [with] the just discussed newcomers, or the headmistress, or they may be altogether outside the group, as [with] the staffs of the [Senior] Boys or the Junior Schools. I would like to add that unity solely consisting in hostility (not merely unity caused through hostility) is the only kind of appreciable unity we encounter in this group.

NOTES

Source

Typescript of 5 pages dating from the early to mid 1940s.

1   A theory of which a prominent representative is [Roger] Money-Kyrle (*Aspasia, The Future of Amorality*). See also, [John Dollard et al.,] *Frustration and Aggression*.
2   [Ed:] Keller was among those interned for several months in 1940 on the Isle of Man: see 'Internment Camp' above.

4   St. Anne's Youth Club

Keller urged Margaret Phillips to publish her 'free and easy' document to which he here responds. As a work of 'considerable length' and a 'source of pleasurable enrichment of knowledge', he said, ' it ought to teach both the psychologist and the educationalist a thing or two.' The reflections on leadership continue the theme of the three previous essays; those on sexuality in a youth club that of the 'Summary Report' from Part I of this book. Keller's reference to the work on young people by the psychoanalyst Willi Hoffer (whom he knew personally) shows another source for his study of group life.

In the following, which is again case study material for their joint project (though also eventually unused), detailed references to the document have been omitted and the text has been lightly edited.

The most striking point about this club is its successful development – this with human material which, from a common point of view, is the most 'difficult' imaginable. We must not, however, let our judgment be disturbed by common prejudices, but must critically ask ourselves whether these club members do not after all exhibit characteristics which would tend to contribute to the club's successful development, characteristics at the same time the lack of which in less 'difficult' youths would at least prove partly harmful to group unity as well as to individual satisfactions. Looking naively at the state of affairs, we are presented at once with an affirmative answer. For a primitive horde is more likely to consist of many people with common tastes than a group of highly developed, and therefore differentiated, individuals. We only have to remind ourselves that differentiated group members have to regress, not without endo-psychic conflict, to a more primitive level (the 'greatest common measure') so that their main interests become those of the group as a whole, in order to realise that in this respect a group has an easier life when it consists of members whose (primitive) 'greatest common measure' does not necessitate regression. One finds it hard to convince oneself that the actual difficulties inherent in such a 'difficult' group outweigh this great advantage.

We shall consider below the satisfaction of these common interests. Before that, let us throw a glance on what we already know to be an important question, i.e. that of leadership. One could sum up by saying that, whilst empirically (at least as far as our material goes) we are here presented with female leadership at its best, it could be, theoretically, perhaps even better.

To substantiate these abstract notions. Striking about the leader is her tolerance and her enjoyment of her job. These two interconnected factors probably rest on a great capacity for empathy (identification) and on maternal tendencies. Negatively, the lack of endo-psychic conflict seems to be of importance. We cannot say, with an easy scientific conscience, far more about her personality, since she is wont to keep herself in the background, not only in group life, but also in describing it. This fact itself, however, induces us to form a further conjecture. The passivity of her leader attitude as well as her non-egotism is surely conducive to the formation of the community-atmosphere and of simple associative elements (as are included in the conception of 'common decency' of which something can be found in any ego-ideal). To be sure, she actively pursues her passive policy (if 'policy' be allowed to denote such spontaneous tendencies). Though she is a good example of an efficient leader being led by the capacities of those she leads, one would surmise that she would easily be an even better instance of this sort if her intuitive psychological understanding were assisted by psychological knowledge.

So as easily to understand some of the satisfaction of common interests that the group life offers we might profitably inspect [your] 'brains trust' questions that, one can suppose, will relate to topics of interest. Of the 25 questions, 8 relate to sport. As can be seen from the report itself, sport is indeed a mighty attraction. The same observation can incidentally be made by the reader of Willi Hoffer's study of youth-group life (in S. Bernfeld, *Vom Gemeinschaftsleben der Jugend*). The advantages that such activities offer centre on the possibilities for relatively primitive instinct gratification under the cover of some elementary moralisation, such as the super-ego (ego-ideal) conceptions of 'keeping fit' and of 'team spirit'. On the instinct side, auto-erotic, narcissistic, and exhibitionistic tendencies are satisfied; further, shifting nearer to the manifestations of the death instinct, we would certainly find considerable masochistic satisfactions (on which Hoffer lays particular stress in regard to the group under his observation); as an indication of this, the boys' response to Mayo's discipline may be cited. [This is] again on the side of aggressiveness, for 'unity in hostility', even where it does not appeal to the ego-ideal, makes one feel more justified than when one is aggressive alone.

An interesting point would be the satisfaction of heterosexual and homosexual impulses. Unfortunately the author does not provide us with information regarding the sex life of the group; were it not for occasional references to sexual matters, the unprejudiced (or, as I would prefer to say, the prejudiced) reader would think that direct impulses did not concern this group. We are left with descriptions of sublimated forms of homo- and hetero-sexuality, i.e. of manifestations of homo-social and hetero-social impulses.

If we want further knowledge on satisfactions inherent in the club situation, we must discover the psychological significance of some of the author's observations on the club's progress. The 'alternative to home' is a substitute for Oedipus-bonds and -aggressions. The break away from the family, natural at that age, is eased by the provisions of a family substitute. There being a female leader, the Oedipus situation is more complete for the boys, with whom, accordingly, she 'gets on better'. Incidentally, it is probable that her own loves direct themselves more easily on to boys, which on the surface level is self-evident, whilst on the more primitive level the Oedipus complex and the castration complex, by dint of which there exist psychic links between the idea of penis (male), child (substitute), father-and-son, would seem to be the driving forces behind such a seemingly simple and obvious attitude. It would have been interesting to know to what extent the leader was a conscious sex object.

The 'change' referred to in the document links up with our 'break-away', whilst 'warmth' signifies a substitute for the home, or, for many, rather a substitute for a home image, in that they find in the substitute what they did not perhaps to that extent find in the original. The 'alternative to the pictures' is perhaps a more essential one than the author is aware of, for the dramatic activities provide scope for such energies as would otherwise drive the individual to a more passive enjoyment of phantasy life. These activities are of importance for imitative (identificatory) tendencies that cannot easily be worked off in reality. In another way phantasy-satisfaction (in the pictures) is substituted in the club life: in providing, in reality, scope for various instinct gratifications (partly already enumerated), they make less realistic satisfaction partially unnecessary.

The 'alternative to the street' is again an alternative in breaking-away from the family, i.e. a social breaking-away instead of a more anti-social one. Club bonds also substitute public-house bonds, and the desire for alcohol decreases with the intensity of frustration. So as really to weaken the latter there must be an outlet for anti-social, anti-authoritarian attitudes. For apart from Phillips's by-now well-known 'need to be needed', there is also, I would suggest, the more directly narcissistic 'need not to be needed'. Outlet for aggression, especially aggression against a parent figure, will easily weaken this need inasmuch as it is based on resentment. Here the no-wise bossy mother-figure is again of importance, for she not only tolerates (for instance) the verbal discharge of aggression against her, not only enjoys and to some extent understands revolt, but is also 'actively passive' in her experimental 'club half-hours' which she understands to function towards the lowering of frustration. Yet it would seem that the absence of something to fight against is one of the few more obvious obstacles in the way of successful group life; an external hate-object would perhaps make successes of the not-too-socially inclined individuals.

Perhaps the most important lesson we have to draw from this document is how much internal unity can be achieved without an external hate-object.

Finally, a word is needed on the contribution the observer makes to our knowledge about homo-social and heterosexual tendencies. Frequent references to frictions on mixed nights make it clear that in this group life homo-social tendencies are stronger, or encounter weaker resistances, than hetero-social ones. This accords with the assumption that during adolescence manifest homosexuality is relatively intense. From an educational point of view, the introduction both of single-sex and of mixed nights would seem to prove a valuable measure. Not only is scope thereby given both to homo-social and to hetero-social inclinations (and aversions), but sex antagonism which probably always tends to make its appearance under collective circumstances, is to some extent countered by mixing, i.e. by the other sex losing some of its strangeness, whilst at the same time resentment against mixing should not assume undue proportion since there are frequent opportunities for separation.

The weakening of sex antagonism would seem to be one of the more important tasks for educational psychology and sociology, though the deepest causes of hostile attitudes towards the other sex probably lie in both the male and the female castration complex [whose special] surface treatment as applied in the club under consideration must have a strong counter-acting influence (where it does not encounter definitely neurotic resistances): for it is assisted by the forces of attraction between the sexes which, after all, also seem to exist. The crucial question, 'Co-education or unisexual education?' a question which moralists (whether of the moral or the anti-moral brand) have always been quick to answer, but to which psychologists, and particularly psychoanalysts, have not often dared to give any straightforward reply at all, does perhaps ask for the compromise reply, 'Both.'

To be sure, the forces of attraction between the sexes do not at present easily assert themselves in a diffused and aim-inhibited manner. Our endeavour to have the matter both ways, i.e. our demands for monogamous heterosexual and promiscuous hetero-social attitudes, seem to have ended in something of a composite failure. On the one hand we meet, under the cover of the monogamous ideal, considerable sexual promiscuity, whilst on the other, under the cover of politeness, we hit upon sex-hostility. It would therefore seem as though the specialisation of love towards which both our childhood-circumstances (plus education) and our ego-ideals drive us, is not strong enough to satisfy our group ideal where the latter demands it, i.e. in the sphere of little aim-inhibited genital and pre-genital impulses, whereas it is too strong where our group ideal would have only little of it, i.e. in the sphere of widely aim-inhibited loves.

But let us not pursue the matter further lest we be tempted definitely to enter the sphere of evaluations.

Source

Typescript from the early to mid 1940s.

The Psychology of Social Unity: *a Report*

The handful of examples reproduced above and below represents the tip of the iceberg of the Keller-Phillips material held in the Archive, all of which was directed towards a joint book, *The Psychology of Social Unity*. There are 4 distinct outlines for this project, and although the book never materialised, Phillips eventually published *Small Social Groups in England* (London, Methuen, 1965) under her own name, with a generous acknowledgment to 'Mr. Hans Keller' (reproduced in the Editor's Preface above). The table of contents of the book is listed at the end of this report. A full study of this material and its evolution from the draft of the 1940s to the book of the 1960s would have to be undertaken by a historian of sociology but is unnecessary here.

In addition to the responses and essays included in this book under the heading 'Psychology and Sociology', Alison Garnham lists the following items, some complete, some fragmentary, most (if not all) dating from between 1942 to 1947 (only some dates are given), and many annotated by one or both authors (the exact authorship is not always clear):

The Project

1   'Psychology and Ethics of School Staff Groups', a joint report of some 98 pages of typescript, annotated by both authors, and intended as a single article though some of its material was earmarked for the book.
2   'Chapter II. Freudian Theory of the Group', 5 pages of typescript.
3   'Psychoanalytic (Freudian) Group Theory and Its Critics', 3 pages of typescript (reproduced below).
4   'Object-cathexes in Group-relations', in 4 versions (typescript/manuscript/carbon with some annotations): (a) 'Object-relations in Group-relations', 4 pages; (b) 'Object-cathexes in Group-relations' (carbon of (a)); (c) 'Object-cathexes in Group-relations' (draft, 3 pages); (d) 'The Cathexis-group', 6 pages, (incomplete). Cf. 'Individual Psychology and Group Psychology', 14 pages (reproduced below).
5   '[Chapter] III. From Community to Association', 21 pages (cf. the section of this name below).
6   '[Chapter] VI. Evolution of the Family Pattern; Youth Groups', 21 pages.

7   '[Chapter] VII. Uniting and Disruptive Factors in the Group', 37 pages.

8   'To [Chapter] VII:' HK's commentary on MP's Chapter VII, in 2 versions: (a) 19 pages, typed on the reverse of drafts of 'Certain Elements in the Psychology of Leadership', and (b) 10-page incomplete carbon, annotated with a covering letter by Margaret Phillips.

9   Untitled carbon of 30 pages, beginning 'Certain Elements in the Psychology of Leadership . . .' typed on the reverse of earlier drafts and the beginning of a questionnaire on 'The Nuremberg Trial: a Psychological Study of Reactions'.

10   'Chapter IX. Village Groups; Women's Groups', 39 pages (by Phillips).

11   '[Chapter] IX. From Intra-familial to Extra-familial Group Life', a 5-page commentary by Keller on (10) above, typed on the reverse of drafts for 'The Need for Pets' (reproduced below).

12   'Chapter XI. Groups Working Together', 31 pages (by Phillips, with several references to Keller).

13   '[Chapter] XI. Groups Working Together (2)', 29 pages (by Phillips, again with references to Keller), collected with a further item by an unknown author working as feature/leader writer on *The Sun*, 'Group-associations in a London Daily Newspaper', 6 pages of typescript.

Case Studies for the Project (in addition to 'Internment Camp', 'St Anne's Youth Club' and 'Senior Girls School' reproduced above):

1   'Advanced Course Group 1944', 6 pages together with draft of 5 pages (some sections dated 29/30 January, 1945).

2   'BPS Social Psychology. 1 June, 1945', notes on a meeting of the British Psychological Society, 4-page manuscript by Margaret Phillips.

3   'Life in [an] ATS billet', 2 pages, the first typed on the back of a letter of 17 July, 1945 from the Lancashire Federation of Women's Institutes to 'Mr. Argent'.

4   'Co-educational Institution for Working-class Students', 4 pages.

5   'Oram Hostel', 4 pages.

6   'Study of a Jewish Synagogue', 3 pages.

7   'WEA Committee, Mill Hill and Edgware Branch', 3 pages.

8   'Women's Training College and Staff', 8 pages, with 'Staff of Women's College', 1 page, and a page of notes.

9   'Society of Friends', 5 pages.

10   [On HK's Football Team in Vienna], 4 pages, beginning: 'the following remarks relate to a group which ceased to exist about 8 years ago.'

11   'Women's Co-operative Guild', 6 pages (incomplete) with 2 pages of notes.

12   'R. A. F. Training School', 3 pages.

13   'Miss Everness' Bridge Party', 1 page, with notes on 'Advanced Course Group' (cf. 1 above).

14   'A Girls' Circle', 4 pages with 2 pages of notes.

15   'Factory Group. (Surgical Equipment)', 3 pages with 2 pages of notes.

16   'Remarks on 3 Nurses' Groups', 4 pages, with notes, some on the reverse of a letter fragment dated 18 February, 1945.

17   'Nursery Staff', 4 pages, with 'A[nna] Freud Nursery Staff', 1 page.

18   [Study of flats], 3 pages, with 'Private Note to Margaret', 1 page.

19   'Edwards. Study of a Group of 5 Students at a Training College', 3 pages.

20   'Hillcroft College', 4 pages.

21   'Church College', 1 page.

Fragment (3) from the *Project* list above provides a definitive statement on psychoanalysis by Keller in the form of a draft introduction to a larger chapter. It was probably written at the end of 1944:

Psychoanalytic (Freudian) Group Theory and Its Critics

In order to learn to know ourselves, we first have to become strangers to ourselves.
([Theodor] Reik, *Surprise and the Psa'aist*)

'A mother and her daughter aged about 15 were talking in the bus, and the mother mentioned psychoanalysis. "What's that?" asked the daughter. "It was invented by a German called Frood," was the reply. It is used in schools, and the teachers find it very interesting, but it is very bad for the children.' (Reported in *The Lancet*, 28 October, 1944.)

It seems something of a minor nightmare to present psychoanalytic group theory to a mixed circle of readers, made up of (a) those who could have given the above explanation, (b) those who smile at Frood and his alleged nationality, but find the rest of the statement appropriate, (c) those who smile at the whole of it, but would not smile at a statement formulated in a more highbrow manner yet testifying to even less a degree of knowledge of the subject, (d) to those children who find psychoanalysis very bad for themselves, (e) to the teachers who find it very interesting . . .

Psychoanalysis concerns itself largely with things with which we do not want to concern ourselves. It is therefore only natural that we do not want to concern ourselves with psychoanalysis. The question is whether we should stay natural and reject what we otherwise might come to regard as a piece of reality properly understood.

Lies and illusions are more auspiciously promulgated than truths. Admittedly truths are also accepted at times. But, in most cases, not before they have been exhaustively misunderstood. Psychoanalysis would seem a nice, if particularly sad, example of this. Yet acceptance, even misunderstanding acceptance, of this science, still grows slowly and painfully. If ever psychoanalytic theory should prove a lot of nonsense, it will range in the history of the human intellect as one of the few outstanding examples of lots of nonsense not being spontaneously and universally accepted. It is for this reason, if for no other one, that this discipline, which 'still retains something of the reputation of the bad boy of science' (Flugel), deserves the interest even of those biased in another direction than the present writer.

There is no great danger that the latter will seduce anybody to embrace psychoanalysis. He is of the take-it-or-leave-it rather than the there-there-come-come-it-isn't-so-bad-after-all type. To those who find people arrogant this will seem arrogant. To him it appears to be a recommendable, nowise superior attitude. For should not a writer refuse to take his readers as a crowd of idiots wholly incapable of grasping things which are not exceedingly simple so as to suit their intellects and strikingly tasty so as to suit their emotions? But if he refuses to adopt this attitude found in members of nursery- and asylum-staffs, he has to confine himself to the objective presentation of what seems to him valuable knowledge. He may make allowance for their not being experts in the sphere in which he works. He may, for this purpose, find himself compelled to simplify a little and to sacrifice exhaustiveness – just as they would if they expounded him their special knowledge. But he must not make allowance for their supposed incapacity: he must not soothingly say: "Alright, call him Frood, if you find it difficult to remember and painful to pronounce 'Freud'. It's quite a nice name, after all, isn't it?"

Small Social Groups in England *(Phillips): Contents*

Margaret Phillips defines the starting point of her book *Small Social Groups in England*, London, Methuen, 1965, (312 pp. + indices) thus (p. 13):

> The size of a small group is necessarily vague but there seems to be a general disposition at present among social psychologists to regard as 'small' a group all of whose members are known, at least by sight, to everyone of them, and this limit suited my intentions very well.

The groups are explored in two ways reflecting the book's division into two parts, 'Small Group Development and Structure' and 'Environment, Organization and Groups'. Part I deals, as far as it realistically can, with small groups 'with as little reference as possible to the organization of which they are part or the wider society in which they are set'. Its subheadings are predominantly theoretical, using 'platonic' categories some of which Keller would have recognised (Disruptive Forces in the Group, The Mother-Leader, The Father-Leader, etc.). Part II, by contrast, uses groups that are part of organizations: 'I also consider the effect of the wider environment and am confirmed in my guess that as "no man is an island", neither can a small group be.' Here the categories define different communities and associations (The Village, Defence Groups, Three Christian Communities, Teaching Staffs, etc.). Appended is a glossary, in which some terms are sociological (association – 'the group in its "working together" phase', community – 'the group in its "living together" phase', formal and informal structures etc.) and others are psychoanalytic (ambivalence, narcissism, regression, group self-contempt and self-regard, etc.). The latter terms are Keller's legacy. The contents are as follows:

PART I   SMALL GROUP DEVELOPMENT AND STRUCTURE

1   Object and Method of Study
2   Outline of Group Development: Room X – Internment Camp Group
3   Disruptive Forces in the Group: Young Adult Group – E. N. S. A. Group
4   The Physical Setting of the Group: Life in a Bell-tent – Meeting of a Learned Society – A Residential Conference
5   Two Phases of Group Life: Radical Policy Committee – Evacuation Centre
6   The Family Pattern in Small Groups (the Mother Centre): Training College Council – Women's Services Club – Girls' School Staff – Crossways Cottage – A Cinema Operating Group – A Literature Group
7   The Family Pattern in the Small Group (the Father-leader): Scientific Journal Club – Bridge Team – Farming Group – A Threshing Team

PART II   ENVIRONMENT, ORGANIZATION AND GROUPS

8   The Village: VE Day Celebrations – Coronation Celebrations – Village Discussion Group
9   Women's Institutes: Survey of Wartime Institutes – Birth of an Institute – An Institute at Home to Visitors – An Institute in Training – An Institute Moving Outwards – A Democratic Institute – Village, Institute and Federation
10   Defence Groups: A Fire-fighting Unit – A British Tank Crew – Recruit Psychology – A Wireless Section – A Signals Training Corps – A Wireless Training School – RAF Accounts Section – RAF Squadron and Its Leader – Training Course for Discussion Group Leaders
11   Three Christian Communities: A Community of Nuns – A Protestant Community – The Society of Friends
12   Nurses and Hospital Pattern: Hospital Life 1930-45 – A Nurse's Training in the 1940s – A Nurse of Today
13   Teaching Staffs: An Independent Boarding School Staff – A Direct Grant School Staff – A Leaderless Staff – A Secondary School Head – The Staff of a Primary School
14   Conclusion
15   A Sociologist's Footnote by Brian Wilson

Glossary, Bibliography, Index of Records used, General Index

The final chapter, a 'Sociologist's Footnote', is by Bryan Wilson, a 'Reader in Sociology in the University of Oxford'. After contrasting Phillips's concerns first with micro- rather than macro-sociology (the European model) and then with the way Americans rely on groups to create a conformity within a society that lacks traditional stratification, Wilson points out that in Britain, where individuals enjoyed 'a fixed conception of a stable social order', a sense of group-identity was not fundamental. 'Groups,' he writes, 'arise in societies marked by high rates of social mobility.' The group in wartime Britain was thus a new phenomenon. As W. J. H. Sprott, author of *Human Groups*, noted, traditionally, humans could be just as healthy if they were non-joiners. The downside of groups is that they do indeed encourage conformity, and thus permit manipulation. Wilson also points to a further professional resistance to small group studies. These are thought to concentrate on 'affective functions' rather than the 'structured relationships of interacting roles' typical of trade unions, or political parties. Nevertheless, he continues, structured institutions may depend for their success upon informal small groups within their walls. Such groups, indeed, may readmit necessary individuality even though they may also foster opposition. It is the capturing of the 'real life' quality of such groups that Wilson claims to admire in Phillips's work.

It was, of course, the sense of small groups turning aggression inwards as a response to an indestructible larger organization that stood at the heart of Keller's notion of group self-contempt, a sense generated, perhaps, through his experiences in Nazi-occupied Vienna. It also prompted his 'real-life' fieldwork with prostitutes, as will be seen later in this section.

Language of Psychology

[On the] Substitution of Freudian Terms by Popular Ones

This argument forms the core of a letter from Hans Keller to Margaret Phillips of 9 November, 1944, and is a response to her query as to whether Freudian terms could be substituted by popular ones. The letter has been adjusted in one or two small ways for the sake of readability. It falls into two parts: I General Comment, II Super-ego and Conscience. Keller follows Freud closely throughout, especially in his discussion of the super-ego. In, for instance, the New Introductory Lectures on Psychoanalysis *(1933), Lecture 31, Freud writes: 'As you see [from my diagram], the super-ego merges into the id; indeed, as heir to the Oedipus complex it has intimate relations with the id; it is more remote than the ego from the perceptual system [the conscious].' Again, towards the end of Lecture 32 Freud draws a distinction between super-ego and conscience. In a discussion of the 'unconscious need for punishment' he remarks: 'It behaves like a piece of conscience, like a prolongation of our conscience into the super-ego . . . if only the words went together better, we should . . . [call] it an "unconscious sense of guilt".'*

I GENERAL COMMENT

I am not in favour of [the substitution of Freudian terms by popular ones]. Freudian terms were created out of a necessity, not out of pleasure at finding some incomprehensible words. This necessity largely arose out of the conception of the unconscious, which is no popular conception yet, however popular the word and its misconceptions may be. This conception, together with the recognition of the resistances and repression that it implies, as well as with the realisation of the significance of the Oedipus complex and sensuality, is one that represents a very bitter truth to the ego. For a long time to come, the latter will, more or less deliberately, grasp at any opportunity to return, under the cover of alleged progress, to pre-psychoanalytical outlooks. Two fine examples of such reactionary processes are, of course, the teachings of Adler and Jung. Now the proposed substitution would offer a unique occasion for such reactionary activities, as indeed it has already done. The occasion would be unique because the very substitution (unless popular terms are endowed with new meanings, which in most cases is simply impossible to achieve) would logically represent a reaction in the direction of pre-Freudian thinking. New things can hardly be expressed in old words. And if these newly found things are, on top of their novelty, extremely unpleasant and therefore at first largely incomprehensible, the chance that they will be properly understood vanishes, I should think, not only far-reachingly, but completely. According to the accepted meaning of the old words, the substitution would objectively represent a major reaction. Whatever there would remain of the Freudian sense would be drowned in the subjective attitude towards the result of the substitution, so that the reaction would become complete. I shall, in the second paragraph on this subject, show some of the catastrophic objective consequences that such substitution would entail, by means of an analysis of the substitution of 'conscience' for 'super-ego'.

There are two ways in which concessions could be and have been made ([I am thinking of] J. C. Flugel, Anna Freud and Edward Glover.) Of the first I am rather suspicious, the second seems more acceptable to me:

(a) Although the substitution of Freudian terms by descriptions of what they mean, often shortened and incomplete, is far more advisable than the above substitution, it wouldn't seem to be a straight course and is definitely dangerous. May I quote Freud:

> . . . but I did not want to do it because I feel inclined to avoid making concessions to weakness. You never know where you are going to land once you have entered upon this course; you first give way with regards to words and then, gradually, you also yield with regards to the matter itself . . . and finally, he who is able to wait need not make any concessions.

(b) The second way is to introduce the technical terms sparingly, but to furnish them with descriptions of what they mean, as simple as possible yet as complete as possible. In most cases it is best first to bring [forward] the description and afterwards to introduce the term. This seems to be the ideal course if one wants to make concessions. Whenever the (shortened and simplified) description does not really give a correct picture, the reader (especially the sufficiently educated reader) can (be advised to) consult more technical works if he wants to arrive at a thorough knowledge of the conception in question; one has offered him the catchword with the help of which he may proceed if he wants to.

II   SUPER-EGO AND CONSCIENCE

'Conscience' is a surface conception, 'super-ego' isn't. Indeed there aren't many psychical processes that are more conscious than, say, the pangs of conscience (under certain circumstances), whereas there aren't many psychical processes that are less penetrable by the conscious mind than the greater part of the processes within the super-ego. Is it in need of an explanation when I say that to identify an upper bit of the super-ego with the whole of it (this diving deep into the id) is a procedure which is bound to massacre the dynamical and topological relations so laboriously uncovered by psychoanalysis?

In order to arrive at an understanding of the super-ego one has to consider its history and its origin. The shortest description of the latter is that the ego creates the super-ego out of the id. This may sound pretty mysterious; I shall explain it presently. At this stage I want to point out that as the super-ego is created out of the id, it is likely to be less near to consciousness than the ego – which in fact is the actual state of affairs.

As we know, the super-ego's existence starts with the more or less complete decline of the Oedipus complex. The determination of this fall is manifold. On the one hand there is the hereditary (phylogenetic) factor: the new phase of psychic development which sets in with the fall of the Oedipus complex is no doubt strongly predetermined. On the other hand, accidental factors play an important part too, just as they play an important part regarding death, though the fact of death, and often even much of its particular form, is organically predetermined. According to Freud the main accidental factor is the castration threat (with the male) in consequence of which the child's ego turns away from the Oedipus complex. Other factors are the effects of education and of the general threat of the loss of being loved.

Now what exactly happens during this 'turning away from the Oedipus complex'? The first thing is that the object cathexes characteristic of the Oedipus complex are being withdrawn and substituted through identifications. The parent authority is introjected into the ego where it forms the nucleus of the superego. The latter perpetuates the incest prohibition and thus ensures the ego against a return of the libidinous object cathexes. What happens with the tendencies that have caused the latter's existence, i.e. with the libidinous impulses belonging to the Oedipus complex? They are partly desexualised and sublimated (a process which is characteristic of a transformation of an object-cathexis into an identification), another part is being 'aim-inhibited' and thus transformed into tender impulses. With this whole process the latency period sets in.

The turning away from the Oedipus complex constitutes a repression, but (a) not merely a repression, and (b) a repression that exhibits an important difference from most of the later repressions:

> (a) Under ideal circumstances the complex is not merely repressed, but eventually destroyed with the help of the above transforming mechanisms. The less ideally the whole process works, the more the complex remains in existence, the more it has merely been repressed, i.e. the more it forms an unconscious element of the person's psyche, an element located in the id.

> (b) The mentioned difference between the present repression and later repressions lies in the nature of the repressive agency. In the present case the repressive agency is the ego. Later repressions mostly occur under the participation of the super-ego, which, during the present processes, is only *in statu nascendi*.

I hope it is clearer now why I said that the ego creates the super-ego out of the id. Impulses of the latter that went to form the Oedipus complex are used for the formation of the super-ego. Thus the super-ego tends to communicate with the id, the more so when the overpowering of the Oedipus complex was not successfully accomplished. Conflicts between the ego and its former object-cathexes can continue in the form of conflicts between ego and super-ego. The fact that a large part of the super-ego is unconscious strikes us as a matter of course. Not only does its connection with the Oedipus complex, which itself belongs of course to the unconscious, engender this topological characteristic, but the ego may also tend (as is especially the case with hysterics) to offer energetical resistance to the painful perceptions which threaten from the side of the super-ego's criticism. The nature of this resistance will be the same as that of the resistances against intolerable object-cathexes, namely repression. Through the ego's 'fault', therefore, guilt feelings that are part of the super-ego are debarred from becoming conscious. This form of repression is of the greatest interest. It is again a repression that is activated through the ego (see (b) above). But in the present case there is a still more striking difference as compared with other repressions. Whereas in other cases the ego represses under the command of the super-ego, in this case it REPRESSES THE SUPER-EGO!

I said that the present notes should represent an analysis of the evil consequences of the substitution of 'super-ego' [by] conscience, but I have not mentioned 'conscience' up to now. This was done intentionally, for my remarks clearly imply this analysis: insert 'conscience' wherever I write super-ego and you will see what happens to the conception. The most drastic example of the fact that such a substitution will not work is probably the following:

> The increase in power of the unconscious part of the super-ego is a deadly threat to the personality out of whom it *can* make a criminal. The possibility of connecting a hardly bearable unconscious feeling of guilt with something REAL offers the prospect of relief. This prospect, together with the claims that the need for punishment puts forth, is

strong enough in certain circumstances (ego still fairly aggressive, weak reaction-formations, conscious super-ego undeveloped and under sway of its unconscious roots, and other factors) to urge an individual (especially a youth) towards crime. Guilt feelings are in this case not the consequence, but the motive of the crime. What about saying that a person with a strong conscience may tend to become a criminal? That his strong conscience may drive him into crime? Of course you *could* do it and say that conscience doesn't really mean conscience. But on the next occasion, when the fact that conscience doesn't really mean conscience is not so obvious, the reader will willingly discard his knowledge that conscience doesn't really mean his conscience and will return to the natural opinion that conscience means conscience.

So it does. It is an important part of the super-ego, which, however, has other important parts whose similarity with 'conscience' is overshadowed by their surprising diversity.

NOTES

Source

Typescript dating from the early 1940s

Another, 1-page fragment from the Archive, 'A Terminological Suggestion', also reflects Keller's concern with the language of psychology. Keller's preoccupation with jargon emerged later in life at the start of his 'Schoenberg: The Future of Symphonic Thought', *Perspectives of New Music*, 13/1, 1974, pp. 3-20, where he addressed the apparent obscurantism of 'Princeton analysis'.

From Community to Association

In the mid 1940s Keller and Margaret Phillips worked on a variety of 'small group' case studies, including this report from an (unnamed) Officer commanding a British (Sherman) tank crew in the Second World War. Their reactions took two forms: (i) direct comments upon the report, and (ii) a joint paper to the Social Psychology Section of the British Psychological Society on 29 September 1945, 'The Psychological Significance of Some Sociological Conceptions of the Group'. The report, in a rather tidier version, was included in Phillips's Small Social Groups in England *(London, Methuen, 1965, pp. 177-81) and Phillips's published response is included in the notes below. The paper placed the findings within a differential study of 'association' (a group 'working together') and 'community' (a group 'living together') and related both to the model of the 'family'. It fell into four parts, with alternating contributions from Phillips and Keller. Both forms of reaction are reproduced here, although only Keller's parts of the joint paper are included (Phillips's are not available).*

1 British Tank Crew: Report and Commentary

Commanding Officer's Report

The group was made up of five men, none of whom were regular soldiers:

(a) *Harold Goode, driver of the tank, and a Lance Corporal.* He was always the troop leader's driver and was the best driver in the troop. When I was not with the crew, Harold automatically took over command. Although he lost his stripe later at his own request (when asked to command a Buffalo) he was the obvious leader of my crew in all small decisions. An excellent cook, he prepared our meals either himself, or else by supervising others. He was very conscientious. His main interests were (i) his son and wife (to whom he wrote every other day in all conditions), (ii) football, and (iii) driving and maintaining his tank, in which he took great pride.

(b) *Charlie Ingham, co-driver of the tank and hull gunner, and a trooper.* Ingham was a very conscientious worker and thoroughly reliable, but he longed with all his heart to be out of the Army. He wrote every day to his wife a long letter, written painstakingly in copybook hand in a slightly stilted style, always talking in the gloomiest of tones. "Once again I take up my pen, my dearest wife, in this long and weary war . . ." But despite this, he went through extremely trying experiences with good cheer, and was always as bright as any of the others.

(c) *Kenneth Coombes, the turret gunner, and a trooper.* Single, and without a mother. His interests were (i) to do any job accurately and carefully, and (ii) painting (decorating). I find it difficult to say what was so good about Ken. He was very, very conscientious. His kit was always in perfect condition and he always had a crease in his trousers. Often, when I've looked and felt like a tramp, I've been amazed at his cleanliness and neatness. He was very quick at picking up targets, and his guns were always in first-class order. Never have I seen him ruffled or worried, even in tricky positions. He was very quiet and seldom voiced his opinion. But he was recognised as one of the squadron's most reliable men, the backbone of the crew.

(d) *George Ikin, wireless operator, and also a trooper.* Single and an only child. Main interest: reading. George was the best informed of the crew – at school till perhaps 16 years old. He could be relied on to get a message down in writing accurately if I missed it myself. He followed the battle intelligently so that often I would tell him to give me a report of what had been happening if I had been away on a reconnaissance. Small, like Kenneth, he normally went about with him. He was always very cheerful and cracked quite good cynical jokes.

(e) *Myself, a lieutenant.* You must remember that I am discussing a group of which I am myself a part; also that I am an officer and bound to see things in a different light from the men.

*

The only time I was with the group was when we were in action, or on the move, or operational in any other way. At other times the officers returned to their mess life. When we were together, however, we were very much together, in the extremely cramped conditions of a Sherman. We went through almost every kind of extreme cold and discomfort together, and fought several battles together. In between we drank tea made hastily by the roadside and shovelled down 'M & V' (meat and vegetables) heated up in the tin on the tank cooker. At nights, when operational, Goode and Ingham slept in their seats in the front of the tank, Coombes and Ikin slept on the turret floor, curled up in an impossible position, and I slept out on the engine deck at the back. We ate, slept, fought, thought, washed, drank and swore together. Yet I was the only educated man among them and I was in command of the crew and of the three other crews in my troop.

It seemed to work very well. It was quite possible to maintain perfect discipline and perfect harmony. The crew all worked together automatically. Three of them came from Yorkshire and all from the North. They were all conscientious and reliable men, the absolute strength of our battalion's fighting men. I got to know them, and they got to know me, as well as this was possible for men of different ranks. They used to give me their letters every day to censor and often there was something one [of them] wanted me to advise him about. Nearly always I had to find out myself first of all from somebody else! Men like this are very loyal if they think anything of their own officer and they will always come to him rather than an outsider, even if the latter is better informed. (I spent a busy three days learning all about mortgages and building societies the other day!)

To ensure smooth working in the conditions in which a tank crew finds itself, its life must be in accordance with a system. Thus, Harold Goode was in charge of the crew when I was away. He arranged the meals, what we were to eat and when we ate it, and saw to it that the rations were properly distributed. If any of us got titbits sent from home we put them into the tank ration box and Harold dished them out.

Similarly, all the personal kit, ammunition, bedding, etc., was kept in its correct place, so as to make the most use of the space. With a crew as conscientious as mine, it was not only unnecessary, but unwise for me to suggest that such and such a thing needed doing – and it was done. This is usually the case with a Troop Leader's crew, as he always has the best crew.

Whenever we stopped to bivouac for the night each of us had his own job. Nearly always I had to visit the Squadron Leader to get the latest tactical picture and the orders for the move during the night or in the morning. While I was away the crew would be busy getting the 'bivy' up and the tank cooker on the go, and the beds laid out ready for the night.

When I returned I would pass on the information to my other tank commanders, and then Harold Goode would announce that supper, or the washing water was ready – according to the time and the arrangements he had made. We would have to dig slit trenches before we could get started on a meal if shelling was expected.

The men were always keen to hear the tactical picture and after the 'O Group' I always gave my crew a summary of the position, with my map, and in the same way my tank commanders passed it on to their crews.

In action we did our job mechanically. There was usually a fair lot of talk on the wireless and nobody but myself used to say much on the inter-communication system of the tank. Now and again somebody would have a witty remark to make over the I. C. – usually a crack at one of the officers' wireless messages.

In Shermans I had a Troop Sergeant, and two Corporals, each commanding a tank of their own with a crew of their own. During operational periods the men lived on their own tanks in the way I have described above. If, however, we stopped in a town for two or three days, whenever possible I got hold of a house or barn for the troop and everybody lived there together. Always, however, they lived in their crews. For instance, if, luckily, we got a complete house instead of a barn, each crew would have its own room. But all our activities were as a troop. Sometimes we had discussions, or technical quizzes, or more often, sports and games against other troops. There were four troops in the Squadron on Shermans, five on Buffaloes.

Dissension within the troop was very rare, though on one occasion not long after I joined the troop one man came and asked me to transfer him. It appeared that the rest of the crew had always been together, whereas this man was a newcomer. In the end the crew remained together amicably for the next six months. The newcomer turned out [to be] one of the leading lights of the troop. He is now a Lance Corporal, and will probably be a Sergeant within the year.

An interesting point is the tremendous keenness of the men to stay in their own crews. When we transferred from Shermans to Buffaloes to train for the Rhine crossing, it meant a troop made up of six crews of four, as opposed to four crews of five. This meant four newcomers to the troop and a general upheaval [that] caused me a great deal of brain racking. At the end of the Buffalo period the men returned to their old crews, or as near as I could get it.

Troop spirit was strong, in the same way that crew spirit was strong. I have seen several instances of men being transferred from one troop to another for technical reasons, which has caused so much friction and dissatisfaction on their part that they have eventually won their way back to their own troop. The same applies on the level of Squadron and Regiment. In my own case, for instance, it was a real blow when I was to leave my Squadron. I miss them very much and will do so for a long time.

The more we have been through together, the more we have come to respect one another, and to regard our little world as the universe, and to view everything through glasses coloured by it.

Hans Keller:

The observer's bias seems to be fairly strong in the present case.

It has already been said [in our other work on the Forces] that we find Army groups among the most united as well as among the most disunited groups. Whilst the peaceful Army group has to bear the frustrations involved in Army life without being able to release aggression outside the group, the group in action has singular opportunities to discharge masses of aggression in an outward direction.

But cannot life in action involve greater frustrations than peaceful Army life? Here we have to distinguish between like and common frustrations. In peaceful Army life, we have a great number of *like*, and a small number of common frustrations. Army life in action offers plentiful *common* frustrations, and under their influence as well as under other deep-reaching common experiences (such as the release of primitive aggression) what have been until then *like* frustrations are at least partly experienced as common frustrations. While the binding effect of *like* frustrations can be negligible, their disruptive effect can be considerable, just as the uniting effect of common frustrations can be.

Considering the study in more detail, our attention is first caught by the pride in and love of the tank. We note that this pride [which] goes somehow parallel to the pride in and love of an object, while being in itself a form of group love, considerably enhances group love as we know it. But as a rule, it is a living object – the leader – who is the common love-object ('object of identification'). Perhaps in the case of an inanimate leader the group's identification with 'him' (or is a tank a woman? The possibility of the tank as womb – and therefore mother-substitute – obtrudes itself) attaches itself more predominantly to the ego (as distinct from the super-ego) than in the case of the animate leader (the latter's – observer's – role is the usual one).

*

[*With regard to the group members*:] In the case of Goode and Ingham [(a) and (b)] we realise the possibility of extra-group heterosexual relations (indirect in the present case) reinforcing the individual's homo-social intra-group ties. [Both men wrote to their wives regularly.]

[As far as the egregiously reliable Coombes is concerned,] the question arises here, what, psychologically, is the 'backbone' of a group? We suggest that the 'backbone' has leadership (super ego) function minus those functions that depend on official leader status, and that he [Coombes], the backbone, is himself led by – projects his super-ego onto – the official leader. In the present case the 'backbone' would be leader No. 3, if we include the tank amongst the leaders. [Leader No.1, of course, is the officer in charge.]

There seems to be a special advantage, both for the group and for him, in [his] position of 'backbone' within the group. The fact that he is 'one of us', i.e. does not enjoy a privileged position, must make the excitement of displaced father-hatred towards him difficult.

Leader No. 4 (the order is that of appearance in the present comments) is Harold Goode. Superficially he functions in part in a motherly way; it is imaginable that the associative link, 'cook, food-distributor' has an effect on group members. Maybe this motherly touch enhanced the efficacy of his more fatherly leadership. If that was so, the Soviet slogan, 'Every cook must learn to govern', ought perhaps to be complemented by, 'Every governor must learn to cook.'

The non-secretiveness of the 'parent' – the Lieutenant – [shown by his always giving his crew 'a summary of the position', just as the tank commanders did to him] seemed to have [had] a favourable effect on group unity. Perhaps such a rational attitude is especially needed under army conditions, because there the occasions for regression and negative transference can be manifold. A little bit of that transference is released [in this case by 'somebody' now and again having 'a crack at one of the officers' wireless messages'] towards higher, more distant, less loved parents, but in a sublimated way (via wit). [As to the] hostility to the newcomer to the troop, [this] is not, to be sure, the only factor in the dissension: one of the most obvious, one of the least original, yet one of the most important results of our investigation is the recognition of the regularity with which it occurs.

[As to the tank crew regarding 'their little world as the universe', this is] an impressive description of group narcissism.

Margaret Phillips:

In this apparently united group we note as so often before the meticulously worked-out pattern of living serving at any rate in part as a leader-substitute. We note, as in the R. A. F., the good parent who is near to his children and shares the experience with them; we note the scope given for individual skill and responsibility – the children are growing up. Though as has been said the members of the groups would cheerfully leave the army for civilian life, they will not leave this army group for any other.

NOTES

Source

Typescript of Margaret Phillips's, with annotations by both writers, dating from the mid 1940s. It was to form part of Chapter X of their joint project, 'Groups Working Together', a chapter dealing with groups in the Armed Forces. Other notes of Phillips's in the typescript refer to the Home Guard and the Civil Defence Services. ('Since these groups are largely formed on a neighbourhood basis, such feeling as already exists for the neighbourhood is easily transferred to the group.')

In her *Small Social Groups in England* (1965), Margaret Phillips commented on the report on the British Tank Crew in a way that subsumed Keller's 'father' and 'mother' functions at the same time that it added new perceptions of her own. Her comments are unexpectedly brief:

> We note here that the group structure follows from the structure of the tank. The resulting family pattern, with the tank itself as home and protection, the 'father' as instrumental leader and group maintainer and the 'mother' as cook and housekeeper, provides both instrumental and expressive satisfactions. Hence the members' strong feelings for the group, and their resistance to disruption.
>
> The group-maintenance work (of which more later), which is here performed by the officer, may be in part the result of his own temperament. But it also suggests the implementing of Montgomery's policy of full information for every man as to the general situation and the part he has to play in it.

'Father' and 'mother' functions, which Phillips, guided in all likelihood by Keller, derived from J. C. Flugel's *The Psychoanalytic Study of the Family* (London, Hogarth, 1921), were accorded two separate chapters in *Small Social Groups in England*, 'The Mother Centre' (Chapter 6) and 'The Father-leader' (Chapter 7). Another chapter dealt with 'Disruptive Forces in the Group' (Chapter 3). Elsewhere in the book Phillips acknowledges the influence of Kate Friedlander's *The Psychoanalytical Approach to Juvenile Delinquency*, London, Kegan Paul, [n.d.].

2 *The Psychological Significance of Some Sociological Conceptions of the Group*

The following are the two contributions Keller made to the joint paper with Margaret Phillips of 1945 for the British Psychological Society. The first followed a presentation by Phillips, 'Introduction: Method. "Association" and "Community". These are related to the family', and was timed at '14 minutes'.

(a) The Family Pattern in Relation to 'Association' and 'Community'

We now proceed to a short review of how the family pattern relates to the association on the one hand and to the community on the other. Regarding the association, psychoanalytic research has of course furnished us with a fairly complete picture of present processes and their past sources that go to form the group.

Concerning the present processes, the group leader has proved to be a very important, indeed – as we might be inclined to add in view of recent experiences – sometimes a painfully important person. For it is he on whom group members tend to project their super-egos, and it is he who, consequently, causes group members to identify themselves with one another.

If we ask why this should be so, our reply leads us to the past processes in the individual's family life which justify us in speaking of a family pattern in the present connection. The group leader is felt to be a parent-substitute and is as such a suitable object for super-ego projection. For it was the real parent who, in childhood, powerfully contributed to the formation of the super-ego. You may remember Freud's statement that the super-ego is heir to the Oedipus Complex. That means that the infant, after he has been forced to give up his incestuous aims towards the parents, builds up within his own ego permanent parental institutions charged with energy withdrawn from the actual parents. In other words, the parents are 'swallowed' in a mental sense, in a similar way as, at a previous stage, parental substance – the mother's milk – had also been swallowed in a physical sense.

For various reasons that have by now been fairly clearly established, the internal moral institution that is thus created is to a great extent more primitive in its internal behaviour than was the attitude of the actual parent. If thus its relation to the parent is not one of striking similarity, both from the point of view of the outside observer and of the individual's own conscious system, it retains, nevertheless, in the more primitive layers of the mind, a strong parental significance. Consequently, persons who, in later life, are regarded by the individual as being in loco parentis, have a great chance of establishing immediate contact with the individual's super-ego. The group leader, on account of various associative links, and not least because he himself is liable to feel and act in a parental manner, is easily regarded as a parent figure.

Now in consequence of an interaction of social and more purely psychological circumstances, the role of the father is often a very predominant one in what happens to, and in, the super-ego. Amongst the many factors which are responsible for this – and I do not for a moment think of neglecting sociological ones – I would like today merely to stress one point which is clear from surface inspection: the fact, that is, that strict morality, at least in our society, emanates from the father rather than the mother, the latter frequently occupying the position of a forgiver and mediator. Since the super-ego necessarily has an immensely strict aspect due to the child's inturning of his inhibited sadism, the probability is great that this strictness, and the cognate notion of authority, will be more particularly linked with the father than with the mother image.

In terms of group life, the father leader plays a more dominant role than the mother leader in all those situations where the stern aspects of group members' super-egos are brought into play. It is clear that it is the association, rather than the community, that incessantly claims the super-ego's attention.

However, the difference between the paternal and the maternal aspects of the super-ego cannot be drawn neatly; strictly speaking, it cannot be drawn at all. Although one can recognise different super-ego systems, some pertaining to the mother-type, others to the father-type, there is a great deal of overlapping between their functions. I think we should try and keep this in mind when Phillips will later on tell us about father and mother roles in groups we have studied.

To summarize for the moment, psychoanalytic group research has established the following points:

1   The role of the parent (mostly father), of the parent substitute (leader), and of group members' super-ego;

2   Identification between group members on account of common super-ego projection onto the leader.

We see quite clearly that this interpretation covers everything of importance that happens within an association.

Turning now to the community aspect of group life in its relation to the family pattern, we find that although classical psychoanalytic group theory covers a wide field, here also there are yet some points that merit closer inspection than has been devoted to them so far.

Though there is a great deal of identification between members going on in the community, this seems to be less due to super-ego stimulation than in the case of the association. What there yet remains of group members' super-ego projection seems to point to such systems of the super-ego as are of the mother- rather than of the father-type. Indeed community life seems partly to hark back in the individual's life to a pre-moralistic, pre-purposive stage, a stage therefore in which the mother's role, as compared with that of the father, has been more in the foreground than it was at the close of the Oedipus situation.

Consequently, the leader does not play so predominant a part in the community as he does in the association. His, or rather her, function, as far as it is present, is rather of a protective, tender, loving, comforting nature rather than of an authoritative, purposive, striving one.

Moreover, whereas the father-leader is primarily an object for super-ego projection, the mother-leader in the community seems to be to a considerable extent a love-object. This again reminds us of a stage in the individual's history prior to the dissolution of the Oedipus complex.

Further, just as the individual's attitude to the association leader is reflected in his attitude to the group, in that both attitudes are essentially identificatory in character, so the community member's object-love, more exactly his aim-inhibited object-cathexis in regard to the leader, is reflected in his object-relation with group members. Yet I have come to the conclusion that there is more identification in a community than there is object-love in an association.

Finally, the community lays great stress on the satisfaction of physical needs and thus again points to an early stage in the individual's development. Indeed, in view of the conclusive results that have been obtained regarding the existence of the desire to return to the womb, it does not seem too phantastic to point out that the yearning for, and delight in, a community which protects the individual from the hardships of the outside world and which brings a great deal of immediate satisfaction (as distinct from the more deferred satisfactions of the association) might well be shown to be based on the yearning for pre-natal cosiness.

Let me conclude this section of the paper by returning from our intra-uterine existence to an example taken from the immediate present, an example that shows – though I hope you will not take me too seriously with regard to it – the joint appearance of the community and the associational in a group that is – by its appearance, an association.

We – I mean us here – as far as we are anything in the way of a group, seem to be a pretty pure association. We have assembled for a distinct purpose, and we might disperse as soon as this purpose is accomplished. The leader of our group seems to be, not so much a person, as the conception of social psychology. At any rate, it is social psychology on to whom, or which (I really don't know which is the more appropriate in this special case), we do a bit of super-ego projection, and through whom we identify ourselves with one another to a moderate extent. So far so good. But if you have a look at this notice [*The lecturer shows notice of the meeting*] you will find that the only thing which is underlined there is a reference to tea which, fortunately, we shall enjoy afterwards. Indeed, in our correspondence with the Hon. Sec. on the subject of the present paper, the question of tea occupied quite a prominent position.

Thus physical needs and personal contacts gain recognition even in what might otherwise be regarded as an assembly of rather dry highbrows.

I did not, however, bring this example in order to show that we are, after all, nice people, but in order to indicate, in a semi-serious manner, that the community element will obtrude itself, even in comparatively pure associations. We shall, in the further course of this paper, indicate that a neglect of mother-regarding tendencies may be of serious consequences to the development of associative group life – however fortunate the inhibition of the development of some associations may be.

The second of Keller's contributions followed the second of Margaret Phillips's presentations, 'Mother-figure and Father-figure in the Group', and was timed at '16 minutes'.

(b) From Community to Association

We are now in a position to view the psychological significance, not merely of the communal aspect of group life on the one hand and of its associational aspect on the other, but of the relation of these two aspects to one another.

This relation, specially if one tries to abstract accidental factors that tend to obscure it, frequently seems to take the form of a transition from community to association, whilst the converse process, that from association to community, seems to take place under strain or frustration.

Viewing these facts against what we know to be the psychological characteristics of community and association respectively, one is forced to assume that the transition from community to association parallels individual development, roughly speaking, from childhood to maturity.

Though the suggestion that the group can repeat to some extent the history of the individual may come as something of a surprise, it does not psychologically seem difficult to comprehend. In the case of the individual as well as that of the group, there grow out of the satisfaction of primitive needs, or more exactly out of primitive needs, the possibilities of more evolved needs which have the primitive ones at their root.

For the purpose of showing some of the details of this parallel I shall avail myself of results at which Phillips has arrived without being influenced by the present piece of theory.

First, she says, associations will gain from their communal aspects being also developed. In the same way, that is, as the development of the child's intellectual, social, and aesthetic interests will gain from smooth instinctual development.

Second, Phillips suggests that the community lives in the present, the association in the future. We know, of course, that in the case of the individual, growing-up proceeds from more immediate satisfactions to deferred satisfactions.

Third, our collaborator concludes, the community, whilst being the basis of the association, is in itself best built on the satisfaction of elementary physical and psychic needs. Equally, that is to say, as in the case of the individual, psychic life starts on the basis of the satisfaction of physical needs, and the first stages of psychic development are, to transfer Phillips's words to this context, 'best built on the satisfaction of elementary physical and psychic needs.'

Fourth, we have heard that the building of the community is typically the work of women. The building of the individual's start in life is, we know, out of necessity the work of women.

Indeed, as previously indicated, the unborn child's relationship to his mother is, as far as exclusion of associative elements goes, the most perfect community imaginable.

Fifth, Phillips shows that the community, when compared with the association, is formless and unconscious. The parallel in individual development is obvious.

Now it can be safely assumed that all of us present are agreed upon the well-established fact that the differences between so-called individual and social, or group, psychology is more apparent than real. Consequently, if we examine our parallel minutely, we are not so much dealing with the repetition by the group of individual development, as with the repetition or reproduction by group members of primary group experiences – family experiences – on their part. This formulation, which is psychologically the more accurate, sounds also less pretentious than our first contention, in that it is directly based on a principle with which we are nowadays sufficiently familiar: the principle, that is to say, of individual repetition, however modified, of infantile patterns.

After having submitted to you the main trend of this argument, I have to confess that I have presented it in a little too sunny a light. Further considerations with which I shall not today exhaust your patience show that the whole matter is not quite so simple and neat as it might seem from what I have said. It appears upon reflection that an important qualification has to be kept in mind when one talks about such repetitions as I have described. May I just remark on the essential point of this qualification. What, to be quite exact, is actually repeated in later group life are modified characteristics of different successive stages of individual, and especially childhood development. This, I should think, is the most general and perhaps the most concise form into which one can so far press the inferences drawn from the study of the transition from community to association.

We now turn our attention to the all-important question of group members' hostility in regard to both the community and the associational aspect of the group and to our transitions between these two aspects. In order to vindicate the great variety of possible forms of group sadism I shall give you two extreme examples from the accounts of group life we have studied.

The first is a tank crew in action. This crew is under the leadership of an officer who, according to circumstances obtaining, has very much direct contact with the group, as much contact, we are inclined to say, as only a sergeant has under other circumstances. There is an extremely high degree of unity and cohesion. We know of course that one of the reasons for this is that the group can express a very large amount of common hostility, and that this hostility is super-ego-syntonic as well as ego-syntonic (Phillips usually murders me when I use those terms).[1] One can further observe that the group progresses and regresses from community to association and vice versa, according to whether there is rest or action. We are indeed confronted with a parallel to the periodical fluctuations between waking life and the regressive phenomenon of sleep. The tank, a close and protective room – or should we say collective protective clothing – has a favourable influence on community life.

When the group is in action and behaves like an association, the officer in charge of it has the function of a conductor, if I may say so, of the hostility orchestra. He clearly seems to have a father-significance.

When the group recedes into a community, mother-functions seem to spring up within it, including the late father. There is no hostility within the group. This is in part due to the fact that so much hostility has been spent on the associational level, and in part due to the transitions from community to association and back to community occurring frequently.

May I in passing draw your attention to a small contribution we are able to make to the question of variable leadership function, in view of such transitions as I have just now described.

Freud, in 1921, said that officer and sergeant were father figures. Brill, in 1945, states that as far as he could discover from his study of traumatic neuroses, the captain stands for the father, but the sergeant for the older brother. We note that the older brother stands in the middle between father and child, mother and child, father and mother. As the mother he is the mediator. Now we on our part find that the shorter is the psychic distance between officer and men, the more chance has the officer to be regarded, in part, as a mother. May I remind you in this connection that the German for 'sergeant' is 'Feldwebel', a 'small field-woman'. You will also remember the song, 'Kiss me good night, sergeant major'.

Moreover, apart from individual variations due to difference in super-ego structure, father-, mother-, and brother-significances seem to vary according to the phase of the group life, according to the degree of communal or associational life the group happens to be in. Yet I do not doubt that there are, apart from these processes, comparatively stable super-ego projections that are not much affected by transitions between community and association.

We haven't got much time left, but fortunately my second example can be described in one sentence. A bridge group meets in order to fight on the associational level, however, primitive, in the form of bridge playing, and on the communal level in the form of offending and attacking each other. Here we have on both levels hostility *within* the group, in fact hostility is the only thing, almost, that happens within it.[2]

The whole group life is a fascinating proof of the fact that group cohesion is not, as is generally supposed, the same as unity. There is no unity at all in this group, but there is plenty of cohesion. We see that under the appropriate circumstances hostility, sadomasochism, within the group can have a binding effect. I might add that true to the Freudian group conception, the lack of unity in this present group is clearly due to lack of leadership.

Viewing these two examples we realise that it is quite impossible to follow a naïve inclination to present general rules as to what happens to hostility on the way from community to association or the other way round. Yet it seems to me that provided we deal with long-range progressions or regressions of group life we might eventually succeed in formulating a number of qualified conclusions of a fairly general nature.

Meanwhile, we might as well revert, recede, regress to the communal aspects of our own present group life.

NOTES

Source

Typescript dating from 29 September, 1945.

1 [Syntonic: attuned with other aspects of the individual's personality – here, with the super-ego or ego.]
2 [The meeting is described in Keller's typescript notes on 'Miss Everness's Bridge Party'.]

Individual Psychology and Its Relation to Group Psychology

This essay is crucial for an understanding of Keller's transition from 'Psychology' to 'Music and Psychology': for it develops the Freudian idea adumbrated in the previous essay that individual psychology has its roots in group psychology and that the basic model is that of the 'family'. If, as it seems, the ideas were developed early in 1946, the essay would immediately precede the Three Psychoanalytic Notes on 'Peter Grimes'*, which shares its concerns.*

Individual Psychology and Group Psychology

> Wir dürfen aber wohl den Einwand erheben, es falle uns schwer, dem Moment der Zahl eine so grosse Bedeutung einzuraümen, dass es ihm allein möglich sein sollte, im menschlichen Seelenleben einen neuen und sonst nicht betätigten Trieb zu wecken.
> (Sigmund Freud, *Massenpsychologie und Ich-Analyse*)[1]

Psychologically, man is never alone. Throughout his life, including his pre-natal existence, he is directly or indirectly influenced by other people; directly when they are present, indirectly when they are absent. Life in the normal sense, as distinct from pre-natal existence, is nevertheless a period of relative solitude. For never again after his birth is the individual so absolutely one with another person as he is before the event. Psychoanalytic investigations have shown that this is no mere armchair speculation, but an important, extensively applicable psychological fact. We never quite outlive the catastrophe that our birth presented to us. The Talmudic saying, 'Blessed are those who never were born' betrays something of that unconscious attitude which gives rise to what is technically known as the intra-uterine phantasy, or womb-phantasy, i.e. the unconscious and somewhat reactionary desire for the status quo, the unconscious slogan 'Back into the mother's body!'. As far as its content goes, this slogan is only natural and reasonable. Its flaw, as with so many other slogans, is the unlikelihood of its being executed.

Where we cannot have what we want, we have to avail ourselves of an Ersatz product. At every stage of our life we try and make do with whatever assumes, in the unconscious, the significance of a womb-substitute: first the mother, seen this time from the outside, then the family, the home, and then a group to which we attach home-feelings.

The first (and most cohesive) group of which we are a member is a little far off in time. Moreover the details of its functioning, if we knew about them, would prove rather boring in that they all would point in one direction: satisfaction. As the following documents will show, this is not always the case with later groups. If we therefore want to select a group in the functioning of which can be found the prototype of *all* later group feelings, negative as well as positive, we had better stick to the family.

It is the latter, then, with which group psychology proper starts. And since our psychic contact with members of our family is present from birth onwards, there is not, strictly speaking, such a thing as individual psychology – unless, of course, what is meant thereby is the study of the individual as a member of a group. This, fortunately, is self-evident. There are some psychoanalytical discoveries that are not yet accepted as such. For instance, the fact already alluded to that a grown-up's reactions in what we are used to call a group are not essentially different from his early family reactions. This fact, intimately connected with the conception that there is nothing but 'group-psychology', furnishes the key to the psychoanalytic theory of group life.

The Family

> It is the displacement of the emotional attitudes originally adopted towards members of the family (and in particular the parents) on to other persons, groups or objects, that more perhaps than all else, makes the family life a subject of such great importance to the sociologist.
> (J. C. Flugel, *The Psychoanalytic Study of the Family*)

Virtually all of us grow up in some sort of family where we are bossed. Many of us also grow into some sort of family in which we become the bosses. Both these families are of importance to our extra-familial group-relations. However, the child being the father of the man, the family in which we spend our childhood is of immeasurably greater significance for our later group-life than that in which we are fathers of children. Indeed the latter family brings back attitudes that were formed in the former.

The Child's Family

That our parents are the source of so many of our group metaphors has been so well known that it failed sufficiently to arouse our interest before we were introduced to psychoanalysis. A few examples: Mother Church, Alma Mater (University), Motherland, Reverend Mother, Matron; 'Vaterland', 'Landesvater', King (Sanskrit root gan-beget, ganaka-father), Padre, Holy Father, Little Father (Czar of Russia). An interesting example of father and mother being combined is 'la patrie'. In one of the following documents we shall encounter 'house-fathers' and 'camp-fathers'.[2] All these examples have a common characteristic: the parent-name is always an honorary rather than a derogatory title. But, as psychoanalytic investigations prove, our parents were not only objects of our love, but also, largely on our unconscious level, of our hate, i.e. our attitude towards them was 'ambivalent'. It being definitely uncomfortable to love and hate one and the same person at the same time, we tend to split this ambivalence as opportunities offer themselves. When we transfer our parent-regarding tendencies onto objects (largely groups and group leaders) in the world at large, we frequently manage to divide the objects, more or less exactly, between 'good parents' and 'bad parents'. The good parents who become the object of love-impulses are liable to be adorned with parent-names, whereas the bad parents, whose parent-significance is unconscious because hate against the parents is not easily tolerated in the conscious mind, do not on the surface betray their parent-significance so easily. Thus it has been pointed out that whereas the King (see above) who is given a position above the hates of the population is considered the father of the country, the Prime Minister, on to whom much of the hostility originally flowing against the father is directed, is not so obviously regarded as a parent-figure.

Previous writers, however, have not drawn attention to a very interesting point in this connection. The title 'Father of the House' is bestowed for the longest unbroken service, not as might be expected by an outsider necessarily on the Prime Minister. Again, the honorary parent title is fixed to a good parent, one who recommends himself through his untiring services to the children (the association of whom with the original father proceeds along the age-link).

It might of course be argued that our ascribing so great a significance to these parent metaphors is nothing but analogy and need not be indicative of an actual transfer of attitudes. Indeed, there are psychologists as well as anthropologists who, whilst using the family and other units for the purpose of comparison, would not go so far as to propound a causal connection between the elements of the analogy. (In quite a number of cases even the attentive reader is left in the dark as to whether the writer is merely comparing or ascribing a cause.) Now psychoanalytic investigations leave no doubt as to the nature of the psychic connection between real fathers and metaphoric ones, and the psychoanalytically versed is in a position to recognise in the attitudes towards the latter a more or less modified repetition of the earlier attitude towards the former. Yet, even apart from the psychoanalytic considerations, it is clear that behind the universal tendency towards the formation and acceptance of such metaphors there must be motives at work that point to intimate psychological connection. These motives can only rest on the realisation (conscious or not) that the metaphorical parents have to some extent the significance of the real parents; alternatively they may wish they did.

It is true that this parent-significance need not be directly related to parent-regarding or parental attitudes. Rather it can be based on the realisation that the metaphorical parent-function is essentially similar to the real parent-function, its most essential aspect being procreation. Metaphors of an impersonal and highly abstract nature furnish such instances as, 'The wish is father to the thought.' Yet even here one might guess that at the root of the thought lies another thought, 'The father's wish is my (the child's) thought.' However, where there is a person involved, there often lie provable, deep parent-regarding or parental feelings behind whatever there may be of an essential logical similarity. Thus, the afore-mentioned 'The child is father to the man', besides satisfying intellectual claims through the common factor of (pro)creation, is no doubt also determined by the man's identification of his father with his son, a process which psychoanalytic investigations have brought to light.

The associative links between an original and a later [substitute] parent are (1) mental or physical characteristics, including age, (2) present and past circumstances [and] (3) family relationship, as when the amount of excitation, or 'affect' (psychic tension), originally evoked by parental stimuli and thus attached to the idea of parents is partially displaced on to a brother or sister, so that the ideas of the latter become invested with some of the affect ([i.e.]become 'cathected').

In the course of normal development such displacements proceed in ever-wider circles, passing from attachment to family-figures to 'cathexes' of persons who are not so closely associated with the parents. Should, however, the link between the original object (parent) and the later one remain very close in adult years, we are confronted with incomplete development due to 'insufficient displacement' (Flugel).

Close investigations, proceeding directly and through the analysis of the adult's mental life, have proved beyond doubt that the nature of this original attachment to the parents is a sexual one. The discovery of infantile sexuality is indeed one of the greatest achievements of psychoanalytic science, though one which has been met with enormous resistances, the latter being identical with those which the individual sets up against what he represses, or, in other words, against a large part of his own infantile mental life (repression is clearly an unconscious process, as you cannot consciously make something unconscious). At the same time the validity of this discovery is one by which psychoanalytic theory stands or falls.

For later group life, as indeed for all other aspects of the individual adult's mental life, a certain group of infantile psychic processes in which the child's sexuality is far-reachingly involved is of the utmost importance. These interconnected processes are comprised under the name 'Oedipus complex' and centre without exception round the wish (in the case of a boy) that the father be dead and the mother [be] in the boy's sole possession. This thesis again encounters the most absurd, though psychologically easily comprehensible, resistances, and is again one of the foundation stones of depth-psychological theory. (Nor is it quite clear what, from the standpoint of the adult's conscious emotional life, the excitement is about, for one gathers that if a man kills his rival this has something to do with honour – yet when a child merely wants to kill his father (identifying 'to-be-away' with 'being-dead') this is supposed to be so dreadful that one cannot believe it.)

The boy's attitude of rivalry towards the father (as that of a girl towards the mother)[3] is however opposed by other tendencies. According to the bisexuality of infants, he frequently develops the so-called 'negative Oedipus complex', i.e. a tender attitude towards the father together with a jealous and hostile attitude towards the mother. But even prior to this homosexual object-cathexis, the boy has already entered a more primitive, indeed, the most original, form of tie with another person, i.e. identification (in the present case with the father). The difference between an identification and an object-cathexis is most simply explained by the statement that, in the case of identification one is 'what one wants to be', whereas in object-cathexis, one is 'what one wants to have' (Freud). (It is clear at the time of the Oedipus complex this identification, which from the beginning is an ambivalent process, sounds a markedly hostile note. For the father is not only the ideal the child wants to be, but also in the position in which he wants to be.)

We see now more clearly in what way the child's attitude towards each parent is ambivalent. The negative part of this ambivalence is largely inhibited, both through the opposite tendencies in the mind and through external circumstances. Moreover, the positive part is also partly inhibited, inasmuch as it would manifest itself in the desired sexual activities. Consequently the Oedipus complex is repressed and eventually to a greater or lesser extent extinguished.

Such partial extinction is only possible if the repression preceding it is accompanied by a transformation of the repressed impulses. These transformations, in short, proceed as follows. The object-cathexes, partially abandoned, are partly displaced or even 'sublimated' (i.e. unconsciously and gradually displaced onto spheres more in accordance with the ethical and aesthetic standards of the child's environment, whereby the impulses change both their 'aim' and their 'object'). Another part is 'aim-inhibited', i.e. modified into tender attitudes that do not urge towards grossly sexual goals.

However, these processes are but the accompaniment to the substitution of object-cathexes [previously] relating to the parents through identifications. This substitution is of the greatest importance for a particular system in the mind, one that has been given the exceedingly Latin name 'super-ego'.[4] The particular nature of identification most significantly involved in the substitute-ties with the parents is that of 'introjection', a process by dint of which happenings in the outside world are reacted to as though they originated in the individual himself.[5] The introjection of parent-authority results in the acceptance, indeed incorporation, of parental demands, both imagined and real, so that these are now felt to be part of the self. The 'sternness' of the parents is taken over by the agency to which the introjected ideas become attached, i.e. by the above-mentioned super-ego. The latter thus constitutes the moral system of the mind. In the adult, this system is largely unconscious; only a relatively small part of it is what we are used to regard as our 'conscience'. In order to understand why moral processes are kept unconscious (repressed) it is necessary to outline the nature of the super-ego.

The critical reader will have noticed amongst the gaps in our description there is a glaring one. What, he is entitled to ask, has happened to the negative part of the attitude towards the parents? Is this hostility also sublimated and displaced, and what is its role in these new identificational ties?

The answer is that there are parallel displacements and sublimations of the more aggressive tendencies[6] and that the identification described above which succeeds the object-cathexes also involves a drastic transformation of the pugnacious tendencies connected with the Oedipus complex.[7]

This transformation is at first sight perhaps a little surprising: it consists in the child's aggressiveness being directed against the self, in-turned or, as the psychoanalyst has it, 'introverted'. It seems indeed to be in part a general characteristic of instinct that it undergoes, under certain conditions, either an out-turning or an in-turning. Outside psychoanalytical investigations, this is perhaps most easily observed when one studies the manifestations of the sex instinct, including all such indirect (sublimated or aim-inhibited) tendencies as are comprised under the popular term 'love'. One then finds that an individual whose love life in the wider sense is severely inhibited tends to have an increasing regard for himself, whereas conversely a person who falls in love is liable temporarily utterly to disregard his own person. That means that self-love is convertible into object-love, and vice versa. With regard to aggressiveness the surface-observer is not so easily in a position to note such transformations, yet when we think of the pious person who reacts to aggressive desires by atoning for them we get an idea of the more superficial aspects of this process of introversion.

Now when we say that the child introverts his aggressiveness this means that he attaches a great part of his hostile impulses against the parents to the parent-institution which he has set up in his own mind, i.e. to the super-ego. The super-ego's strictness towards the ego[8] consequently involves (a) the parent's strictness, and (b) the child's aggressiveness. It must not be thought, however, that these two factors are in the child's mind independent of one another at any time in his development. We have spoken above of the 'imagined or real sternness' of the parents; it behoves us now to make a little more clear in what way the child is 'imagining' that the parents are stern.

For this purpose we have to acquaint ourselves with a most primitive mechanism, one that has come to be recognized even outside psychoanalytical circles, probably because there is relatively little difficulty in inferring some of its working from everyday observation. It is the process of 'projection', which represents the first defence mechanism against unpleasurable excitations coming from the mind. It involves the unconscious ascribing to the outer world of processes that originate in the self, but are not recognised as doing so. By dint of this defensive process the child rids himself of his own powerful aggressiveness against his parents which he is unable to satisfy directly by attributing it to them.

Though all of us make use of this mechanism to some extent, it is in the adult a sign of abnormality where it so strongly prevails that it seriously interferes with our reality-sense. That such adult children (or in other words, insane persons) can do a lot of harm if their trouble is not recognised in time can unfortunately be seen very clearly at the present time. Hitler spent his life largely in projecting his desires for world-domination, extermination of other races, etc., onto the Jews who no doubt were a bad parent in his eyes. He then proceeded to react with defensive aggression against his own impulses, which he had partly attached to this outward agent.

NOTES

Source

Typescript marked '26th Feb' and almost certainly written in 1946 (Hitler is referred to in the past tense) if not later. Margaret Phillips herself edited the text and some of her adjustments have been incorporated here; the essay has been lightly re-edited for publication.

1   [Sigmund Freud, *Group Psychology and the Analysis of the Ego* (1921), trans. and ed. by James Strachey (1922), London, Hogarth Press and the Institute of Psychoanalysis, 1967, p. 2: 'But we may perhaps venture to object that it seems difficult to attribute to the factor of number [i.e. of people comprising a group] a significance so great as to make it capable by itself of arousing in our mental life a new instinct that is otherwise not brought into play.' Freud continues: 'Our expectation is therefore directed towards two other possibilities: that the social instinct may not be a primitive one and insusceptible of dissection, and that it may be possible to discover the beginnings of its development in a narrower circle, such as that of the family.']

2   [Cf. Keller's observations on the 'Internment Camp' (Isle of Man) earlier in this 'Psychology' section.]

3   But for the girl, as for the boy, the first love-object is the mother.

4   Linguistically sensitive souls tend to direct their resistances against psychoanalysis on to this name, which, I am told, is not a nice one. The only apology I am able to make is that the original name is 'Über-Ich', a term to which such protests could not apply. [However,] you can hardly expect the translators to introduce the word 'Over-I' or 'Over-me', since to do so would [add to] the entertainment of the reader.

5   Introjection is perhaps identification par excellence, since it is most closely related to the origin of all shades of identifications, i.e. the child's 'introjection' of the mother's milk and body (the latter of course only in phantasy). We have already mentioned that identification is the earliest tie, and we can add now that it naturally originates in the earliest phase of psychic development, namely [in Freud's] 'oral' phase, when the child's sexuality is mainly directed to the mouth-zone.

6   It is an empirical fact that love and hate never appear in their supposed pure form but are always found in some combination and that love-tendencies always have an aggressive element.

7   It is hardly necessary to state that the gradual, lengthy development of interconnected processes is, for the sake of a terse exposition, cut up and compressed into the present scheme.

8   The 'ego' in psychoanalytic language means integrated organisation of psychic processes (which dominates motility, i.e. the channels for the discharge of excitations into the external world). It is *not*, as frequently supposed, identical with 'conscious', for there are ego-processes (the resistances mentioned above) that are unconscious.

Keller's essay opens with a quotation from Freud's 'Crowd Psychology and the Individual' and ends with psychoanalytic remarks on Hitler. It thus parallels a (slightly later) essay by Theodor Adorno, 'Freudian Theory and the Pattern of Fascist Propaganda', written in collaboration with Max Horkheimer. Adorno observes: 'While Freud did not concern himself with the social changes [in an era 'which for socio-economic reasons witnesses the decline of the individual and his subsequent weakness'], it may be said that he developed within the monadological confines of the individual the traces of its profound crisis and willingness to yield unquestioningly to powerful outside, collective agencies.' (Theodor Adorno, *The Culture Industry*, London, Routledge, 1991, p. 134)

Keller's earliest remarks on 'National Socialism and "Being German"' are included in Part I of this book. He returned to the topic of Hitler repeatedly in life, never more trenchantly than in the following review, where he combined his now psychologically-based observations with a characteristic rejection of 'history'. ('History' is a topic already addressed from a political standpoint in 'Scientific Socialism – ad absurdum', see Part I of this book). The piece appeared in the *London Review of Books*, 5-18 February, 1981, p. 14.

The books under review were:

Norman Stone, *Hitler*, London, Hodder, 1980
James and Patience Barnes, *Hitler's 'Mein Kampf' in Britain and America: A Publishing History 1930-39*,
        Cambridge [UP], 1980
Peter Paret, *The Berlin Secession: Modernism and Its Enemies in Imperial Germany*,
        Harvard UP, 1980
William Vaughan, *German Romantic Painting*, Yale UP, 1980

Hitler and History

My title is intended to be quadruply functional: the four books raise four interpenetrating problems – and not one problem per book either. That Hitler himself remains an incurable problem is proved by our civilisation's continued, compulsive preoccupation with his personality – which a George Steiner even undertook to reinvent: his *The Portage to San Cristobal of A. H.* has been reviewed in these pages, nor are Norman Stone, James J. Barnes and Patience P. Barnes always less fanciful. And if Hitler's personality remains an unanswered question, so, too, does the history of National Socialism – which a book like Robert Harbison's recent *Deliberate Regression: The Disastrous History of Romantic Individualism in Thought and Art from Jean-Jacques Rousseau to 20th-century Fascism* (1980) interpets as dreamfully as Steiner recreates Hitler. The reason why I quote Harbison's enormous subtitle in full is that it is symptomatic of one of our age's grand delusions – of the belief that Hitler has a specific history in German Romanticism. It is a delusion which Peter Paret and especially William Vaughan are quite ready to take for reality, while Norman Stone's own dreams about 'the positive qualities of Hitler, his real achievements' (thus Professor J. H. Plumb's Introduction) aid and abet it: if Hitler was some sort of genius, he is part of the history of German nationalistic genius. The whitewashing of Hitler goes together with the soiling of his past.

Last but first, there is what for me is the most insoluble problem of all – history itself. I have never understood it as a discipline, simply because I consider the minimal incidence of error too high for intellectual comfort. So far as I am aware, I have only one predecessor (Karl Popper's case against historical destiny is a different proposition: disproved, in my view, by any prognostic philosophy of history that proves itself – above all, Spengler's *Decline of the West*). But it must be admitted that the reasons for Schopenhauer's hostility to history differed from mine: it was *post hoc ergo propter hoc* that he considered history's ineluctable fallacy. We see his point – about which, however, there can always be argument. Wrong facts, on the other hand, are demonstrably unavoidable: neither the power of Norman Stone's intellect nor his conscientious research is in question.

For any given purpose, the historian needs more facts than he has at his disposal or is able to ascertain, verify, confirm. There are, of course, levels of factual illusion – nor is a historian of Norman Stone's recognised calibre able to escape the most elementary level: he tells us that 'Sir Neville Chamberlain, the 69-year-old British Prime Minister, flew to meet Hitler at Munich.' The face of the secretary to whom I am dictating this piece remains unmoved while she is taking down this quotation – but then, in 1938, she was minus 15, whereas I was plus 19. What would her face have looked like if I had dictated something about Dame Margaret Thatcher? Her face now clinches my point: we under-react to untruths about the past and over-react against truths about the present.

The Barneses could never have written their meticulous 'Publishing History' if they hadn't been downright obsessional about factual accuracy. Yet they tell us that Hitler got his German citizenship in February 1932, 'just in time to run for the presidency of the Weimar Republic.' Again my secretary's face remains unmoved – less forgivably so: 'the Presidency?' It was the Weimar Republic's president, Field-Marshal Hindenburg, who appointed Hitler to the chancellorship, and it was the chancellorship for which Hitler had run. Hindenburg died in 1934, and as Stone reminds us, 'Hitler, without opposition, proclaimed himself president and subsequently also head of the armed forces, which had to swear an oath of personal loyalty to him.' Thus a tiny mistake inevitably creates, or makes possible, prolonged historical confusion.

But while Stone's is, inevitably, the more important book – a competent biography of Hitler is of greater relevance to what life and death are about than a competent [history] of *Mein Kampf* – there are, in fact, one or two places where the Barneses score over him, where their facts beat his desire to be unprecedentedly, unconventionally factual. With a serious historian's weighty flippancy, he observes, for once deceived by Hitler's own lies, that *Mein Kampf* 'cannot be taken as a blueprint for anything save Hitler's royalties'. This verdict would have made me suspect a lesser scholar of never really having read the Führer's testament of illiteracy and, yes, magnetic stupidity – until the Barneses would have reminded me that there are two ways of looking at *Mein Kampf*. 'In retrospect it usually made sense; in prospect it deceived as often as it revealed.' An eminently reasonable differential diagnosis. For the sake of his historical aphorism, a leading historian has, paradoxically, refused to look at the past in retrospect.

And although his clear account (as distinct from his evaluation) of Hitler's life is, to my knowledge, absolutely free of factual error, surrounding mistakes are legion – which is not a criticism, because I must insist they are bound to be. The Gestapo and the SS, for example, are described as 'much the same thing'. You might as well thus describe grass and greenness: all Gestapo was SS, but there was plenty of SS (including a school mate of mine) that wasn't anywhere near the Gestapo. Then there is a careful list of concentration camps in general and women's camps in particular – excluding the one where my grandmother was killed in her nineties.

Again, if the Nazi bureaucrats had 'worked with efficiency', I wouldn't be alive: I was released from pre-extermination prison although a Gestapo warrant for my arrest had been issued while I was still inside. Two of those bureaucrats, moreover, subsequently failed to identify me and to have me arrested, while a third placed the contents of my Gestapo file at my (or rather a half-Jewish cousin's, his former girl-friend's) disposal in exchange for an appropriate bribe. 'In the early years of Nazism, anti-semitism contributed to Hitler's popularity.' Contributed? I didn't know a single Nazi, budding or full-grown, who had the slightest interest in anything else. In short, history is for readers who weren't there when it happened.

Unfortunately for three of our historians, I was a victim of the *Kristallnacht* pogrom (about six weeks before my escape to England), if 'victim' is the word for one of the tiny proportion of eventual survivors. All the Barneses seem to know about the event is that 'Jewish synagogues' (what other synagogues are there?) and Jewish private property were destroyed, while 'some of the Jews could only walk the streets and pass their time in restaurants': this is an eye-witness account of a day when we were beaten, tortured, and articulately prepared for an early demise which, for some, was to prove almost immediate.

So one turns to Stone in the hope of reality, a bit of it. He does at least mention '90 murders' (I don't accept either the figure or the possibility of ascertaining or assessing the correct number, doubtless a multiplex multiple), duly reports the burning down of synagogues and 'several' Jewish houses, and contends that '35,000 Jews were taken to concentration camps for forced emigration.' In Vienna alone, according to the Nazis' own statistical survey, 1,950 Jewish dwellings were destroyed or ransacked, nor is the figure of 35,000 arrests remotely credible: again in Vienna alone, 70,000 Jews were arrested as early as March 1938, when the majority of the city's 200,000 Jews (including myself) escaped arrest, while in November, I hardly knew anybody who hadn't been arrested.

But the climax of Stone's misinformation is our alleged 'forced emigration' – the precisest possible opposite of the truth: emigration was a Jewish dream, usually unattainable; what was forced upon us at that stage was imprisonment and the concentration camp – whence, for the vast majority, there was only one possible eventual emigration, to the gas chambers. And if Mr. Stone thinks that 'the British in particular [had] a distinguished record from [1938] on' so far as 'generous' admittance of Jews from Nazi territory was concerned, I am ready to give him a list of personal friends and acquaintances, all gassed, who would be alive today if the British had admitted them, in or after 1938, to this country or Palestine. My own British visa I owed, exclusively, to my English brother-in-law [Roy Franey] and his financial guarantee: without him, the gas chamber would have been an absolute certainty.

The central Nazi slogan was not 'One People, One *Country*, One Leader' but, all-importantly, 'One Empire' (*ein Reich*): there is no chapter without such none too minor mistakes – which, however, do not mar Norman Stone's biographical achievement. In fact, when I say that he goes wrong in the evaluation of Hitler's life, I am concerned with and about the man's *public* life, for the picture of Hitler's character, of the uninteresting person that was Hitler, is immaculate: 'He lived for power, and his image of a man of power dictated his way of life. The private Hitler was a boring and banal figure . . .'

So was the public Hitler for anybody who had retained his sanity – and it is this crucial fact that we are not yet sane enough to realise. In my long-considered submission, he was a stupid, semi-literate paranoiac, a text-book illustration of both persecution mania and megalomania, and it was the German war generals who, 'appalled', 'thought that Hitler was mad' who have evinced the most realistic insight so far – naturally so, under the pressure of reality. 'In his own way, he was an intellectual.' So is every psychotic idiot who thinks he is. On 7 December 1930, he 'made a brilliant, emotional address' which, as an 11-year-old, I questioned my father and uncle about: was this not a raving half-wit? Had I missed anything? No, they said – for at that stage, receptive insanity was confined to party members, whereas, by now, it even affects critical historians.

As for Hitler's historical role, any such madman would have done; and 'his real achievements' are Stone's fantasy, though by no means his alone. It is deeply depressing to find that the historian's occupational obsession with objectivity drives a man of stature into downright silliness – for his 'major reappraisal of Adolf Hitler' teaches us, in the words of the publisher's publicity sheet, that 'he did not destroy German democracy – on the contrary, in January 1933 Hitler provided the first majority-based government Germany had in three years.' What undiluted nonsense! Fortunately Stone's own account disproves it: the Nazis never got more than 37.6 per cent of the vote in [any] election worth its name.

Now it might be thought that at least a historical monograph like Peter Paret's could be absolved from history's original sin, the inevitability of wrong facts; if the denotation of the subject is sufficiently narrow, its connotation might be proportionally free of fancy. Maybe, maybe not; I personally have not come across a guiltless specimen. So far as Paret's own fascinating 'detailed history' of the Berlin 'secession' from academicism is concerned, the irony is that it is too narrow a denotation (in the strictly logical sense, meaning the 'aggregate of objects that may be included under' the word 'secession') that produces the gravest factual error, which is one of indefensible omission.

That is to say, while Paret does not forget the secessions of Dresden, Karlsruhe, Stuttgart, and Weimar, while two Swiss artists, Arnold Böcklin and Ferdinand Hodler, are naturally included in the 'aggregate of objects', since they were 'regarded as essentially German', the equally German Viennese secession is utterly neglected, though such names as Gustav Klimt, Josef Hoffman, and Kolo Moser leave one in no doubt about the historic, rather than the merely historical, role it played in the history of German Modernism, not to speak of its enemies. But of violently wrong elementary facts, at least, the study seems entirely free, simply because it isn't the history of anything big, wide, long. *German Romantic Painting* is in all conscience – with the result that all levels of factual error are, of necessity, represented in this impressive chronicle, not only of the Romantics' art, but also of their aesthetics and worldviews.

2 Psychological Observations (1945-47)

Prostitutes Wear Marriage-rings:
Group Self-contempt

Keller's enquiry into why prostitutes wear marriage-rings was conducted under his own auspices around 1945, though it is clear that he discussed his findings with Margaret Phillips, John Rickman, Willi Hoffer and others too. His underlying concern was with 'group self-contempt', a topic he also probed in connection with Jews (see the Appendix for his play, Antiwhatism*) and which Margaret Phillips herself had pointed out in connection with teachers. The concern with sexuality and its interpretation on Freudian lines continues a theme already explored in the first part of this book.*

1 Married-seeming Prostitutes

I Statement of Probable State of Affairs   II Interpretation with Regard to the Psychology of Prostitute's Customers [Appended: III   A Note on Prostitution and the Dissociation of Male Sensual and Tender Sexual Tendencies]

I

According to a private census which the present writer made in different parts of London with a view to discovering the ratio of prostitutes wearing a marriage-ring and those wearing none, this proportion would appear to be something like 7:3 in favour of the first-named. As far as he is aware, there is no reliable up-to-date [set of] statistics or estimate about the proportion of actually married prostitutes. It is therefore difficult to decide how great, if present at all, is the number of such prostitutes as wear a marriage-ring without being married. However, although the percentage of married prostitutes has probably risen considerably during war time (in a relatively recent conversation the present writer had with a prostitute the latter thought that 50% of all the members of her profession known to her were married (including widows), a high percentage of whose husbands were serving overseas – an estimate whose first part might seem exaggerated), we can hardly convince ourselves that all the marriage-rings we encounter on the hands of prostitutes are indicative of a past or present state of marriage. It is probable that there are a number of prostitutes who wear a marriage-ring without real justification.

The following analytical note represents an attempt to justify the contention that this endeavour to seem married may be a reasonable undertaking from the prostitute's professional point of view, in that the marriage-ring may be a point of attraction to certain customers. If we thus may assume that the respective prostitute is alive to the fact that she can add to her attraction by this means, the *married* prostitute's wearing a ring could be regarded as [a] sign both of her being married *and* of her wishing to seem married. It does not, at any rate, seem to damage her attractiveness, for in that case she would take it off, unless unusually powerful motives deterred her from that realistic course.

II

Various psychological factors, apart from the professional motive, may underlie the above-mentioned marriage exhibition. Being married is a respectable state, a state that in the minds of most people is not associated with prostitution. There is no doubt that there are prostitutes who more or less consciously desire respectability, and would therefore tend to show off a sign of their [longed-for] fair social standing, even when such [a] sign was at the same time indicative of actual matrimony. (On interviewing another prostitute, the present writer was confronted with a peculiar psychological picture: she showed a marked general lack of inclination morally to evaluate – with one exception: she exhibited an exaggerated moral contempt for prostitutes. Thus she could never forgive the Duke of Windsor for marrying what she called a 'society prostitute'. (Note the contraposition of marriage and prostitution. She herself was unhappily married.)) A deeper penetration into such and other psychological motives would seem, however, to be a dangerous undertaking, for there is too little psychologically usable observational material against which to appraise various hypotheses. Let us therefore stick to the task we have set ourselves, one that will proceed on the firm ground of verified conclusions.

In the first place we have to get a clear picture of the type of man whose *vita sexualis* centres around intercourse with prostitutes. As he cannot be said to love his sexual objects in the sense in which the bridegroom loves the bride, we can note as the most obvious characteristic of his psychosexual organisation a strong dissociation of the sentiments of tenderness and sexuality as properly understood. This antagonism between the sensual and the tender impulses rests on an unconscious infantile incestuous fixation, in consequence of which the individual chooses such sexual objects as do not remind him of his unconscious sexual object, i.e. such persons as do not rouse his worship and excite his tenderness. The sexual object is degraded, whereas the over-estimation that is normally related to the sexual object is being reserved for the unconscious object and its representatives. However, there are also impulses that do not accord with this attitude. A common trait in the psychic life of male adolescents is their tendency to associate the mother with the prostitute, to make, as it were, a prostitute out of the mother. The motives underlying this tendency prove to be attempts at bridging the gulf between tenderness and sexuality.

[Addendum:]

III

[Men, therefore, who frequent prostitutes] have not solved the Oedipus situation: their direct sexuality is kept under repression whenever a woman whom they deem valuable (i.e. whom they associate with their mother) presents itself. The original cause of this repression is the father, the successful rival. In order to be able to satisfy their direct sexual needs, those men are forced to avail themselves of women who are not associated with the mother-imago: women whom they [hold in] contempt.

It is well known that [such] men who have not overcome the Oedipus situation tend to repeat it, i.e. to have affairs with married women, so that they have again a rival whom they can fight, this time more successfully.

NOTES

Source

The quality of the handwriting in the manuscripts for both parts, I/II and III, suggest a date around 1945 when the majority of the interviews with prostitutes were carried out.

The marginalia cite: Sigmund Freud [*Beiträge Zur Psychologie des*] *Liebeslebens* [1910, *Gesammelte Werke*, 8, London, Imago, 1943], pp. 73, 82-3 [trans. by James Strachey as 'A Special Type of Choice of Love Object Made by Men', *Standard Edition*, 11, pp. 163-75; also in, *Pelican Freud Library*, 7, London, Pelican, 1977, pp. 227-42], and Ernest Jones [*Papers on Psychoanalysis*, second edition, London, Baillière, Tindall and Cox, 1918] p. 555.

Among the Keller papers is a separate sheet, possibly written in a more mature hand, referring to other sources: *A Handbook of Social Psychology*, edited by Carl Minchinson [n.d.], p.35; Catherine Cox Miles, *Sex in Social Psychology* [n.d.], p. 772 ('Two human tendencies are especially expressed in the persistence of prostitution: the desire for convenient and immediate sex indulgence without social responsibility and the urge for variety. Both are apparently stronger in men than in women.'), and S. Putnam, 'The Psychology of Prostitution' in, S. D. Schmalhausen and V. F. Calverton, *Woman's Coming of Age*, New York, Liveright, pp. 310-72. Another note cites J. C. Flugel's *Psychoanalytic Study of the Family* [London, Hogarth, 1921], p. 107: 'one possible motive [for prostitution] is the desire to have to do with married men and to harm their wives'; the same reference addressed 'men's hypothetical desire for "married" prostitutes' and the idea of the 'mother as prostitute' (p. 110). The same sheet refers to Glover, and to the 'Papers [1918] of Ernest Jones' (p. 558) on wickedness ('naughty'), prohibition, etc.

Another stimulus came from Ives Hendrick's *Facts and Theories of Psychoanalysis*, 1934, from which Keller singled out three passages:

> p.110   Similarly, in women, prostitute-like behaviour, repetitive tendencies to quarrel violently with men they have attracted, and obviously masculine drives of a sort which leaves them thwarted in their hopes of being loved by men are shown in analysis to be problems of the phallic period. Many cases of frigidity and of abnormal social inhibition are due to a strong unconscious sadism which survives in the unconscious from this stage of libido development.
>
> p.130 ff.   The most severe case I have seen of psycho-neurotic symptoms and character reactions determined by unconscious aural sadism was a woman of good family . . . no capacity for tender feelings . . . had for a time chosen to be a prostitute in order 'to see how filthy human beings could be' . . . Occupancy of two apartments. One on a good neighbourhood, cared for immaculately, [she] never received callers there. Other in undesirable neighbourhood: she enjoyed its extreme disorderliness and general disreputability . . . [the] two apartments represented unconscious phantasies of her own body. (1) vagina (capacity for voluptuous sensation there unthinkable) pure, (2) anus, vile, [able to] defile all men . . . denied herself and partners all normal genital gratification, used vagina as unconscious representative of anus.
>
> p. 132   (condensation of phantasies:) [she] will be punished for any vaginal or tender feeling towards a man, even in phantasy.

Keller's report refers to his 'private census' on the topic of prostitutes' anti-prostitutionalism. Another manuscript, with abbreviated entries rather than polished prose, shows how the census was conducted:

2 Prostitutes Wear Marriage-rings
Interviews with Prostitutes, Summer 1945

I 5 [shillings]. Hyde Park. Strongly moralizing.

Great stress on prostitution as side line. ("I have no life.") Only in this (Hyde) Park. Outside I'm just as any other girl. Don't practice intercourse. Just play about, relieve their feelings and let them play with me. I'm fair (stern). They want their money's worth. No intercourse (1) because I'm married and have 4 children, I reserve that for my husband, (2) I don't want to bring the children a disease home. Great stress on strict business. No pleasure for her, pleasure with her husband. No friends among prostitutes, they are treacherous. After saying that she was going home by bus, she was seen half-an-hour later talking with 2 prostitutes, not giving [any] sign of recognition to me. Great stress on entirely for money and family, if she has money she doesn't do it. No pleasure from handling and being handled. How so the latter? Strictly business . . . but you must get excited when somebody plays with you[?] Perhaps he doesn't find the right spot. Perhaps I hide it. You can't hide it, can you[?] Well I shut my feelings off . . . feelings for husband. [*In the margin*: 'geographical morality']

II Tottenham Court Road. Did not ask for payment for these few questions (the only one as yet).

Practising afternoons. In many ways an exception:

(1) Hardly any trace of nemesistic displacement.
(2) No suspicion.
(3) Is enthusiastic about the profession: (a) "likes the thrill of it", "always meeting new people". West End is a magnet, only happy when in the streets in the West End, and (b) Money: no saving, high standard of living, no taxes, just now earned £2 in 5 minutes.

No pleasure in promiscuous intercourse, "strict business proposition" (same choice of words as Hyde Park side-line-mutual-masturbator). Why not? Because you have to hurry along and think of the next one who might be on the streets while you aren't there. But most of the girls have one boy friend with whom they have pleasure. After being questioned and [showing] hesitation she says it is the same with her. Asked about the wearing of wedding-rings, she suggests that all of them have been married (though they may be separated, widows, husbands away). So is she, and has a 12-year-old daughter. She has been 9 years on the streets. (Proud statement.) Asked further why they wear the rings she says, probably as "a symbol of respectability". Asked about the prevention of venereal disease, she adduces:

(1) that after 9 years you are no fool and see if a man is alright
(2) "the usual things, douches" etc.
(3) a doctor friend by whom she is examined weekly

Prostitutes: Private Census

Keller's papers also include a generous handful of snatches of interviews with other prostitutes. These are not as evolved as the texts printed here, and show a range of response from the friendly to the suspicious and the downright contemptuous. For example, on 5 September, 1945, Keller interviewed a number of prostitutes, his replies being 'noted down immediately after each case'. He approached one girl aged between 20 and 30 years plying her trade in the Piccadilly Circus/Shaftesbury Avenue/Leicester Square district: "Why do you all wear marriage-rings?" (Friendly:) "Most of them have been married at one time or another." "That's no reason to wear them." "It is no reason not to wear them, it makes no difference to anyone, you see." Keller then interviewed another, this time aged between 30 and 40. He asked the same opening question; she was again friendly, but avoided his eyes. "Well, for once the majority are married." "Any other reasons?" "If you go to a flat you can go there when you say you're married. That's one reason." The last words prompted him 'to continue to ask for [a] further reason'. "No girl likes to be called an old maid . . . why, are you writing a book?" When he reached his sixth prostitute, who was aged between 25 and 30, he found her less obliging. To the same opening question, she replied, "That's their own business. Why be so nosy?" She withdrew and Keller asked himself, "Why be so rude?" On 6 September, another girl replied to the question defensively, showing her hands: "I don't know. I have no ring. I don't know." Keller pondered the significance of what some had not said though others had. Next day, at Victoria Station, a prostitute cried out at him, "What do you mean, most of us wear marriage-rings?" She showed him her wedding ring and engagement ring: "I have no wedding-ring. That's no wedding-ring." "Isn't it? I thought it was." "No it isn't!" She hurled abuse after him. Ten days later, on 17 September, he interviewed a French prostitute (the interview is, or appears to be, numbered 207(!)): "I never saw a wedding-ring. Sorry." Keller noted that 'she had a wedding- and an engagement-ring.'

The interviews still continued a month later. On 20 October he noted: 'One prostitute in Shaftesbury Avenue agreed in a friendly manner to have an interview next week (½ hour, 10 [shillings]. My proposition). Unfortunately, I forgot that I have no time at the appointed time. (Her *free day* (Sunday) which she has every week.) Another one, near Piccadilly, flatly, though not rudely, declined any interview-suggestion.'

3 Interviewing Prostitutes: First Interview

Whereas on the whole the psychologist gets paid for the knowledge he receives, he has to pay if he wants to acquire psychological knowledge about prostitutes living in their usual surroundings, for he will find that a prostitute charges between 2/6d and £6 for one hour's interview, the prices varying in direct proportion to the fees she charges, or is used to getting, from her customers, i.e. varying also according to the part of the city which is her professional sphere (one may roughly say, the further away from the West End, the cheaper).

It is therefore something of a sacrifice for anyone to whom these amounts of money mean a lot to embark on interviewing prostitutes (the present writer is, for the time being, interviewing prostitutes who charge no more than 5s.) If he does it nevertheless without even knowing whether he will get his accounts published, he must have strong reasons for this:

1   Modern psychological (psychoanalytical) investigations have revealed that apart from the (important) economical factors there are psychological factors of great significance to the problem of prostitution. (Men who have a certain psychological development behind them tend to choose prostitutes, more or less exclusively, as sexual objects, more or less independently of what other opportunities may offer themselves.) Whereas the psychology of men who are drawn towards prostitutes is fairly clear by now, the psychology of girls who are drawn towards prostitution and the psychology of prostitutes themselves has not yet been clarified to the same extent (in spite of some remarkable contributions to the solution of this problem, either by individuals, or by collective bodies (such as the League of Nations)).

2   The attitude of most people towards 'prostitutes' is far from natural. Utter condemnation and senseless glorification are both found extremely frequently amongst individuals who have so little knowledge about the subject that they actually believe they have some. Deeply as such attitudes are rooted in more primitive recesses of the mind, they receive considerable support from the individuals' ignorance.

It is often only a matter of how often one's head is knocked against facts whether or not one finally realises them. It is to be hoped that efforts like the present one will help to break down that somewhat hypocritical barrier which our society has erected between prostitutes and the rest of us. This process is to be regarded as a necessary one if we want to be in a position to form that humane and at the same time realistic attitude which is a prerequisite of knowledge of human beings, and therefore of solutions of human problems.

The prostitute I want to discuss in this first article is a married part-time suburban worker of 45. When I say that she is a part-time worker I refer to her prostitutional activities that she carries out in another suburb than the one where she lives, at such times as are convenient to her to conceal this occupation from her husband. The latter, who is a drunkard, secures [for] her her subsistence; she spends the money she gets for her prostitutional services [on] drinks. (I am not, of course, in a position to test the truth of her statements, but mild cross-examination and the fact that [the] pseudological inclinations use[d] betray themselves come to my assistance.) She has no children. She has no room where she could go with her customers, but uses bombsites instead.

During the extensive and fruitful interview (she manifested appreciable intelligence) three points about her emerged, which, I think, are of some interest:

1   She exhibited a striking degree of what the psychoanalyst would call manifest narcissism and exhibitionism, i.e. a tendency to admire her self and to provoke the admiration of her self in me. During the interview this tendency primarily related to the intellectual sphere (in the child this tendency first relates to the body and is later 'displaced' onto other spheres), i.e. she endeavoured to show off her knowledge and her intelligence (stimulated to some extent, no doubt, through the interviewer being of the intellectual type). Remarks like "I'm not so stupid, eh? Ha, ha," or "You're surprised that I know such a lot, aren't you?", in reminding me of the child's "Look how clever I am," suggested to me a rather infantile stage of part of her mental make-up. These remarks were frequently repeated throughout the interview.

2   In part I was really 'surprised that she knew such a lot'. It was her knowledge of sex psychology that was remarkable. She delivered something of a lecture on male sexuality, which, if only formulated a little differently, would hardly have been different from a psychologist's lecture. In [particular] it became clear that she had a very fine understanding of the dissociation of the sexual instinct, as well as of the partially tragic consequences to which such a split, if marked, may lead. One could say that on the descriptive level (i.e. apart from the developmental aspect of the question) her lecture was exhaustive.

3   What was perhaps the most striking point about her was the almost complete absence of an evaluating attitude towards anything (with one significant exception which I shall adduce below). She did not praise, nor did she condemn, anything or anybody (I omit her self-admiration in this connection). One had the impression that the question whether anything was 'good' or 'bad' hardly interested her.

The mentioned exception (apart from self-praise) was as interesting as was the rule. It consisted of her utter contempt of prostitutes. As I have had the opportunity to observe that other prostitutes exhibited the same attitude, and since I have found that this 'contempt of one's own group' tends to manifest itself wherever a group is persecuted, or at least neglected, by another one which occupies an authoritative position (cf., *inter alia*, female misogyny and Jewish anti-Semitism), I want to enlarge on certain psychic mechanisms that seem to me to contribute to this phenomenon, one, it will be admitted, of great sociological impact.

For that purpose I have to grow a trifle technical. The reader will kindly reinforce his patience by realising that the reason why I do not omit a fairly specialized discussion is that I refuse to take him, as so many 'specialists' do, as an idiot.

There are various things which may happen to human aggressiveness if it cannot, through external or more purely endo-psychic circumstances, express itself in its original way. It depends on the nature of these circumstances what actually happens in a given case. Out of these many ways in which an individual may deal (mostly unconsciously, in the Freudian sense) with his aggressiveness, let us consider two:

1   The aggressive impulse may be 'displaced' from the original object to another, mentally associated one, as happens on a more conscious level when we angrily tear a letter instead of punching its sender on the nose.

2   The exchange of a secondary object for the original one takes a special form when the former is not an external object, but the self. The impulse is in-turned (introverted) in such a case, as when the child, unable to discharge his aggressiveness against his parents (not merely because he is powerless, but also because he loves them), makes their would-be-rejected demands his own, being aggressive towards himself (conscientious) whenever there arises [some] danger that they may not be fulfilled.

To return now to the prostitute's contempt for prostitution, the fact that she is a member of a group which to some extent is persecuted by authority implies (a) that her aggressiveness is stimulated through the hostile attitude of authority, [and] (b) that she cannot discharge it against the proper object (authority) both because she is powerless and also because she has, in the course of time, partly accepted this authority which, if ever so slightly, intruded her conscience as a parent substitute. Now I suggest the way she deals with her increased and at the same time inhibited aggressiveness largely consists in a combination of the above described mechanisms. From the fact that she formed an aggressive attitude towards prostitutes we are bound to conclude that she *introverts* her aggressiveness inasmuch as she takes them as herself, identifies herself with ('introjects') them; and that she *displaces* it as far as her feeling of self does *not* extend over them. Thereby she kills two birds with one stone. On the one hand she is in a position to condemn herself (we remember that her conscience is to some extent dependent on authority), on the other hand she is able to avoid the painful consequences of self-condemnation by making the introversion a mild one, i.e. [by] mixing it with a displacement on to other persons. The latter involves also in the present case what in depth psychology is called 'projection', i.e. the ascribing of impulses which are not recognised to originate in the self to others: her own unconscious guilt feelings manifest themselves in her considering other prostitutes (to use the expression) as 'dirty'.

The analysis of processes that seem to me to be involved in that peculiar attitude of group self-contempt has by no means been exhausted in the foregoing. What may have been exhausted are the editor's indulgence and the reader's patience.

NOTES

Source

Manuscript dating from c. 1945 (by when the fieldwork was probably complete) or 1946/47 (see letters below).

Keller returned several times to the theme of 'Group Self-contempt', notably in his paper to the Social Psychology Section of the British Psychological Society, 4 November, 1950, on 'Musical Self-contempt in Britain', and in his related essay, 'Resistances to Britten: Their Psychology', *Music Survey*, 2/4, Spring 1950, pp. 227-36 (reprinted in his *Essays on Music*, edited by Christopher Wintle, Cambridge UP, 1994, pp. 10-17).

A further manuscript, possibly from as late as 1947, shows how the investigation of prostitutes' self-contempt was to take its place alongside investigations of Jewish self-contempt and female misogyny in the project with Margaret Phillips, though apparently in a different (or earlier) form to that included elsewhere in this section. There are 4 large hand-written sheets numbered pp. 9-12 and heavily annotated. The themes are in general sufficiently familiar not to need repetition. However, the following extracts add to Keller's observations on money and prostitutes' rates:

Few prostitutes hide their open contempt for their profession, and many also manifest it in a subtle way, i.e. by wearing – whether married or not – a marriage-ring so as to look married. The wearing of a marriage-ring is, of course, over-determined, among other things, indirectly, by the customers' Oedipus complex (cf. Freud), but this is not the place to go into the other determinants. In order to prevent their open contempt being exaggerated in order to please him, the present writer usually introduced the topic with a remark like: "I wish I could make as easy money as that." (It must be added here that most prostitutes seem to have a considerable fund of their conscious and preconscious layers of their super-ego – which seems intensely sadistic in its topographical aspect – pervaded by business considerations: the over-riding and often powerful duty to which pleasures are sacrificed is to make money.) Among the reactions he elicited was the following: Prostitute (shocked): "Do you call that *easy*?" (She enlarges upon the low opinion she has of her profession.) Investigator: "Well, if you don't like it, there are other ways of making money." Prostitute (mothering the investigator's stupidity): "But not *so easy* money, not *so easy*."

Although they have no Trade Union, prostitutes have what one of them called 'trade union rates'. For instance, with prostitutes stationed in the West End, 30s. [£1 and 10 shillings] is the minimum rate for 'short time', general intercourse indoors. A prostitute stationed near Victoria, where the minimum is £1, who asks 30s. for 'short time' and £5 for 'all night', and who does not work every night, estimates her weekly earnings (not her profit) at £40. 'All night' prices in the West End are sometimes higher than £10. Among a prostitute's professional expenses, apart from rent and maid (who, however, often receives payment directly from the customer) are the expenses involved in 'being pinched' (loss of money and working hours), if she is not able to establish rapport with the policeman in question.

Correspondence with John Rickman

That Keller hoped to publish his findings on prostitutes in the British Journal of Medical Psychology *– where he had published 'Male Psychology' in 1946 – is apparent from an exchange of letters in the spring of 1947 with the psychologist John Rickman, the journal's innovative editor. The exchange began on 3 April with a request from Keller, writing from 30 Herne Hill, S.E. 24, for permission to republish his earlier article (he described this as 'something of an open letter to all women psychologists'). Rickman, writing from a London address and 'doctoring' Keller, granted permission on 5 April (the article duly appeared in 1947 in* World Psychology*):*

Dear Dr. Keller,

Brit. Jnl. Med. Psych. art. 'Male Psychology'

As far as this journal is concerned you can publish this paper again in any form you like; it is usual of course to state where it was first published but I don't like the 'with kind permission of the Editor' stuff – just say first published in abbreviated form in *Brit. J. Med. Psych.* 1944 [*sic*] XX, iv, 384-388.

I haven't heard of a periodical called 'World Psychology', it sounds rather grand, so grand that it would be well to look into its credentials. Nor have I heard of the British Institute of Psychologists.

With kind regards,
Yours sincerely,
John Rickman

Herne Hill: have you taken over Havelock Ellis' house; he was No. 30, wasn't he?

Keller replied on 9 April (the Archive holds two versions of this response, of which this is the longer):

Dear Dr. Rickman

Many thanks for yours. I recently had a look (tho' not a very thorough one) at WORLD PSYCHOLOGY; it seems to be all right. The grand title, I gather, is to indicate its international character and function. President of the federation is Prof. Marc Lanval of Brussels. The journal intends to publish 'authentic articles on all aspects of Psychological Science (medical, industrial, religious, educational, experimental)'.

No, I don't think Havelock Ellis was No. 30.

I wonder whether you, or rather the *Brit. J. Med. Psych.*, would be interested in any of the papers I am planning to write. Here is suggestion number one:

Thesis: in groups whose members are, or regard themselves as being, in some way persecuted by members of other groups that occupy an authoritative position there tends to develop an attitude that can be called 'group self-contempt'.

Examples: Jewish anti-Semitism, female misogyny, prostitutes' anti-prostitutionalism. In addition Margaret Phillips (*The Education of the Emotions*), with whom I am working on group research, has drawn my attention to the prevalence of this attitude in teaching groups. Finally, [A. M.] Meerlo's article 'Psychopathic Reactions in Liberated Countries' (*Lancet*, 7.4.45) seems to furnish further confirmation of my assumption.

Prostitutes' anti-prostitutionalism does not seem to be well known, if it is known at all. I should therefore like to quote a particularly neat instance: a prostitute (of low rank within her group) told me that she had always loved the former Prince of Wales, but that she could not forgive him his marrying what she called a "society prostitute". (In a conversation on the subject [Willi] Hoffer suggested that I shouldn't quote this example in a paper, for reasons of taste. I wonder. Isn't it possible to say that in a strictly scientific paper such considerations of (unrealistic) tact do not apply?)

Description of phenomenon: a group is aggressively treated by another group in authoritative position. Because it is aggressively treated its own aggression is aroused; because the persecuting group is in authoritative position, the persecuted group's aroused aggression (to which displaced ucs [unconscious] parent-hatred powerfully contributes) cannot be discharged towards the original object (the persecuting group), nor can it easily be displaced outside the group. The persecuted group's aggression, that is to say, is at once aroused and suppressed.

The persecuting group, in loco parentis, establishes communication with the persecuted group's superegos via introjection and projection. This will be still more the case if the persecuted group's members have grown up in or near the social setting in which the particular instance of group self-contempt develops (Jews, prostitutes, women, teachers, but not populations under the Nazi yoke). Communication facilitates inturning of aggression on the part of [the] persecuted group's members (modified repetition of childhood situation). But what happens is not a simple introversion. Aggression takes a middle course between introversion and displacement (on to another external object, i.e. one's group as apart from oneself), oscillating to and from between these two objects, the self and the external substitute object, according to circumstances. Inasmuch as the group is introjected into the persecuted group-member's ego, aggression against the group means aggression against his own ego. Inasmuch as the group has not been introjected, there is the usual process of displacement and projection. Not to speak of the necessary conflict within the super-ego.

It is important to realize that group self-contempt may be great fun for the individual who harbours it; he may indeed come to depend on it. For he is able to satisfy, at the same time, his need for punishment and his extra-punitive tendencies. If his character, and a particular situation, asks for a great deal of extra-punitiveness plus a little bit of intro-punitiveness, he'll behave like another prostitute whose utter contempt for prostitution was strongly associated with the feeling that prostitution was really something that did not belong to her. If more intro-punitiveness is needed in the mixture, he'll behave like the orthodox Jew who believes that Jewish irreligiosity is the cause of anti-Semitism and at the same time takes the greatest part of this very guilt upon himself, or like the misogynistic woman who thinks that women are rotten and that she, therefore, is rotten.

Probably group self-contempt is favoured by the castration complex, especially by the female or quasi-female (Jewish) one. You may remember Freud's remarks on Otto Weininger's combined anti-Semitism and misogyny. (Can't locate the reference.)*

Summary: a group persecuted by society is the latter's scapegoat. The fact that it is a group (not an individual) contributes to the scapegoat's scapegoat being only partly himself.

Moral: group self-contempt must manifest itself, to a varying extent, in intra-group aggressiveness. Now if the individual depends on his group self-contempt, *intra-group aggressiveness can make for group cohesion.* Consequently that holy axiom of social psychology, i.e. that intra-group cohesion [rather than unity] is proportionate to extra-group hostility, is, as it stands, wrong. Unity is one thing, cohesion another.

Terminology: 'Group self-contempt' is descriptive, but I don't like it very much, because a group has no self and because I am sick of metaphorical group psychology. 'Nemesistic displacement' would be a more exact, tho' somewhat severely technical term. (In adopting the term nemesism as designating in-turned aggression, I follow the suggestions of Rosenzweig and Flugel). For nemesism and displacement are the two essential elements in the process I've been describing. Strictly speaking nemesism is of course itself a special kind of displacement and the term 'nemesistic displacement' could therefore be taken to represent a tautology. Since however 'displacement' is practically only used in regard to external objects, and since moreover the very fact that one speaks of nemesistic displacement ought to make it clear at once that [in] another case brought into combination with the latter, there shouldn't be any confusion.**

With kind regards,
Yours sincerely,
[Hans Keller]

---

* [The reference comes in a footnote to Freud's 'Analysis of a Phobia in a Five-year-old Boy', *Jahrbuch für psychoanlytische und psychopathologische Forschungen*, Band I, 1909; reprinted in *Sammlung kleiner Scriften*, ii, 1913; translated by Alix and James Strachey in, Freud, *Collected Papers*, III, London, Hogarth Press, 1925, p. 179. Freud writes: '. . . the castration complex is the deepest unconscious root of anti-Semitism; for even in the nursery little boys hear that a Jew has something cut off his penis – a piece of his penis, they think – and this gives them a right to despise Jews. And there is no stronger unconscious root for the sense of superiority over women. Weininger (the young philosopher who, highly gifted but sexually deranged, committed suicide after producing his remarkable book, *Geschlecht und Charakter* [1903]), in a chapter that has attracted much attention, treated Jews and women with equal hostility and overwhelmed them with insults. Being a neurotic, Weininger was completely under the sway of his infantile complexes; and from that standpoint what is common to Jews and women is their relation to the castration complex.']

** [Keller's letter covers much the same ground as the third and fourth parts of his contribution to Chapter VII of the projected book with Margaret Phillips, 'Group Self-contempt', and 'Hate in Other Directions' (typescript, pp. 8-18), though more concisely and lucidly. (The first part is reproduced earlier in this section, under the heading

'The Childish Leader'.) The third part begins with a brief allusion to their work on Auxiliary Fire Brigades: 'By midsummer 1940, [the] absence of raids, sharpening public criticism of [the] Fire Service's cost and firemen's inactivity gradually built up acute shamefacedness amongst members of [the] group, having [an] inevitable effect on cohesion and comradeship etc.'. It also cites Rosenzweig as well as Flugel (*Men, Morals, and Society*, London, Duckworth, 1945, p.78) in adopting the term 'nemesism' to designate inturned aggression (as distinct from narcissism, which designates love directed towards [the] self). The fourth part is in effect a resume of the other three:

> It remains to point out that nemesistic displacement and its consequences must be distinguished from (1) simple intra-group aggressiveness not engendered by it, and (2) group members' nemesism (of which the group aim may be an indication). The boarding school groups seem to be dominated by a nemesistic philosophy as do the Quaker groups, and group members' behaviour also points to their being nemesistically inclined. If this assumption were correct, we would expect to find that the Polycrates complex [cf. J. C. Flugel] reigns powerfully among group members. In fact, the observer of the boarding school group devotes a paragraph to the rationalisation of this complex as it affects group members.
>
> Further, our assumption is indirectly supported by the fact that even angels must do something with their aggression (as far as earthly editions go, they largely introvert it). The external world does not get very much of it, for the groups are largely non-combatant. Intra-group, not intra-individual, aggressiveness, likewise, does not seem to be discharged lavishly, though the 'group-narcissistic' observer's denial of it must be received with caution. (The group's group narcissism will, of course, actually minimize intra-group aggressiveness, but this same narcissism will prompt the observer to minimize it still further in his observations.)]

John Rickman replied on 17 April:

Dear Dr. Keller,

Forgive the long delay in replying to your interesting letter of the 9th inst. addressed I take it partly to me and partly to the Editor of the *Brit. J. Med. Psych.* who you know are almost identical. The latter cannot enter into any discussion on unwritten papers – it is a general editorial policy not to do so; but the split personality I have referred to above enables me to reply with enthusiasm to your letter.

A paper on the relation between 'Intra-group Aggression and Group Cohesion' is badly needed in my opinion (may I reserve or copyright that title for a short paper of my own but without prejudice to every encouragement to you to produce your paper.

It is important I think to introduce something analogous to clinical experience, i.e. not generalities but material from observation of groups which can be described and delimited, so that readers may be able to participate in the observations intelligently.

There is another point. I rather fancy that papers almost exclusively devoted to anti-Semitism would not be readily absorbed by readers because there have been quite a lot of them and they are all much the same, or so they seem to the casual reader at any rate.

I shall look forward to seeing the paper.

Yours sincerely,
John Rickman

P. S. About Hoffer's objection to the publication of the prostitute's comment about Mrs. Simpson: why drag in Edw. VIII? The story is scientifically speaking just as good if you say 'a prince's fiancée who had been divorced' – surely Russia and Germany between them before the First World War could provide enough examples to save you a libel suit and save Edward Windsor embarrassment?

On 'page 9' of the 4-page fragment on 'money' and rates cited on pp. 89-90 above, Keller appears to have replaced 'Edward Windsor' with 'a male film star':

> A prostitute of long (and low) standing . . . after enlarging considerably upon her love, or rather her former love, for a male film star, said that she could never forgive him his marrying what she called a society prostitute. While the writer is ignorant of the exact connotation of the term 'society prostitute', its application to the film star's wife indicated that the prostitute's requirements in respect of chastity were somewhat severe.

No paper was eventually submitted to Rickman. But a further characteristic absent from the exchange with Rickman that might have been included was the 'opposite' of group self-contempt, namely group self-love. This was explored in the second part of Keller's contribution to Chapter VII of the joint project with Margaret Phillips (the third and fourth parts are discussed above, and the first, 'The Childish Leader', is printed earlier in this section). Here is the full text:

Group Self-love

[One of the consequences of the group-uniting factors described in] Freud's *Group Psychology and the Analysis of the Ego* [is] 'group self-consciousness'. This proves to be a convenient starting-point for one or two none-too-theoretic conclusions. The first question that arises is, who is conscious of what? A metaphorical reply, 'a group is conscious of (certain processes in) itself' does not lead us far: for a group has no consciousness and no self. But if it is the individuals who are conscious, and if only they have selves, why has the concept 'group self-consciousness', self-contradictory as it must seem then, been found useful – indeed why did it suggest itself?

The answer is that emotionally we do not care whether or not a group has a self; once, that is to say, we have identified ourselves deeply with the group (leader, purpose) we tend to invest it with our own self, to regard it as part of ourselves.

Consequently, group self-consciousness means *the individual's consciousness*, however dim, *of the group as self*. It is clear from [our material], as also on theoretic grounds, that in the formation of group consciousness [there] is essentially involved the displacement or extension of group members' narcissism ('love directed to the self', as [J. C. Flugel calls it]) on to the group. It will thus be profitable to collect phenomena of group self-consciousness that are reducible to self-love, self-admiration, etc. – it is doubtful whether there any other[s] – under the concept of *group narcissism*.

Now there are two kinds of narcissism, i.e. such as attaches to the real self and such as attaches to the ideal one (ego-ideal, part of super-ego). Correspondingly, there would seem to be two kinds of group narcissism. In accordance with Freud's group theory [and our own observations] the individual may regard and love the group (a) as part of his ego and (b) as part of his super-ego. The former process will be more predominant in his relations with co-members, the latter in his relation to the leader, leading ideas, purpose, tradition, etc.

When simple ego group narcissism develops there tends to occur what could be called an 'extension and externalisation, outside the group, of morality'. For inasmuch as the group is regarded as self, what would otherwise have the significance of altruistic attitudes towards co-members assume the significance of selfish attitudes. Consequently, altruistic tendencies will seek satisfaction outside the group.

However, there are many factors that oppose that externalisation of morality. For instance, when group narcissism relating to the super-ego is very powerful, and when at the same time group purposes on to which the super-ego is projected do not include morality to be practised towards the outside world, the externalisation of morality may be lacking. [In our material] it is true that the observer speaks of loving prostitutes and other people not immediately eligible for group membership, and also of the group being 'willing to give outside help and information when required according to practicability,' but practicability seems to be a rare phenomenon, for 'harmony with the outside world is achieved by having practically no contact with it,' and 'this could not otherwise be maintained as the whole atmosphere and tempo is irreconcilable with present-day conditions.' This isolation from the outside world seems to point to an excessive degree of group narcissism (even of the 'real self' kind) which in its turn might indicate an extraordinary degree of original individual narcissism on the part of group members, under which circumstances altruistic tendencies tend to be drowned. Thus, where simple (ego) group narcissism is excessive, an absence of externalised morality can be expected.

However, this absence is not total in the present case. One has to know about an individual's altruistic efficiency before one can foretell whether he will, when developing group narcissism, externalise morality. Another factor that works against the externalisation of morality seems to be that the groups have external groups within themselves. The children (who, in one of the groups, are twice the number of the rest of the group) are group objects rather than group members. Upon them, it seems, is lavished what would otherwise be farther externalised morality. There is little doubt, however, that love and care for the children are themselves narcissistically toned, though on a level that must give the individuals moral satisfaction: one is impressed by something of the possessive mother's attitude when one reads: 'Many children are incurable. They will never find a place in normal society, and for these it is intended that they shall always remain a part of the life [here].'

Generally, an individual will only externalise morality as a result of his developing group narcissism if he has morality to externalise: one cannot on the strength of group narcissism alone base any conjectures as to the probability of externalisation of morality – indeed, an excessive degree of group narcissism, indicative as this is of narcissistically inclined group members, would seem to foreshadow lack of externalised morality.

We shall see later that an increase in the size of the group may also go to weaken externalisation of morality, for identification and group narcissism will in that case not embrace each individual group member, but rather the abstract idea of the group, so that altruistic tendencies can still be satisfied within the group, co-members retaining to a varying extent the significance of non-selves.

But given exceptional circumstances, morality can be strongly externalised: [this] can happen quite intensely even in very large groups such as the state. For instance, in wartime, consequent on intensified identification and group narcissism amongst state members, such of them as display altruistic tastes tend to develop plans concerning the betterment of the world. This process is of course promoted by reparation tendencies due to guilt aroused by warfare and projection of guilt ("It is not we who need to be bettered, it is X"). However, but for externalised morality as engendered by group narcissism, reparational impulses would be more confined within the state boundaries. Projection of guilt can of course take place within the state as well; there is plenty of scope for compatriots to reconstruct each other, as distinct from themselves.

On the other hand, the state at war shows how (as we have already indicated) an excessive degree of 'ego' group narcissism plus, in this case, an equally intense amount of 'super-ego' group narcissism – in other words: nationalism, chauvinism, jingoism, patriotism (note the 'super-egotistic' word, *pater* (Latin) = father) – can spell lack of externalised morality (except for mere guilt projection).

Psychological Essays

Keller's psychological interest was not limited to the theory and fieldwork described so far, but also ranged more generally over politics, society, culture and sexuality. The following essays return to and extend the topics addressed in the first part of this book, but now do so from a more focussed point of view. The style of the first essay expands aphorism, with each paragraph 'unpacking' a paradoxical proposition.

1 Self-knowledge

Self-knowledge is at the root of an undistorted understanding and appreciation of the outer world.

That this proposition has become a commonplace does not necessarily mean that its significance is fully grasped. It would indeed appear that many a commonplace owes its very existence to the concealed desire to overlook and neglect its importance – for who cares much about a commonplace?

However, even where it seems as if the importance of self-knowledge were appreciated, close inspection often shows that what is appreciated – though it be concerned with the self – is not exactly knowledge. In other words, there is no kind of deceit that hides so easily behind the appearance of knowledge as does self-deceit.

That this is so is due to the fact that one tends to 'think' ('feel' would be plainer) both too much and too little of oneself. That is to say that self-knowledge is commonly distorted by a spontaneous over- and under-estimation of one's own personality.

There would thus seem to be necessary a twofold preparation for the attainment of self-knowledge, viz. to admit to oneself (1) that one isn't so important as one hopes to be and (2) that one isn't so unimportant as one fears to be.

Source

Typescript dated 21 November, 1945. The essay was intended for *The Psychologist*, which had published the first collection of maxims 'On Maturity' in July that year (see below). However, it did not appear until 1995 (posthumously) as part of the volume *Three Psychoanalytic Notes on Peter Grimes*, edited by Christopher Wintle, London, Institute of Advanced Musical Studies (King's College London), 1995, p. 35.

2 Sexual Hesitancies

The advice "Pull-yourself-together-don't-worry-don't-be-ridiculous," once so much in vogue amongst the medical profession, has in the course of time lost a great deal of its popularity amongst psychological advisers (amongst the advised it never had so very much to lose).

Nevertheless there are certain mental troubles where at least such part of this advice as can be comprised under the words "Why worry?" is obviously sound and in accordance with what body of knowledge medical psychology [can] dispose of at present.

Indeed readers of this magazine [*The Psychologist*] may remember that in certain cases they were advised in a similar direction on these pages. Nor is it a matter of chance that in special instances where the "why-worry" advice is suitable it is also eagerly welcomed.

What is perhaps the instance par excellence of mental discomfort that is largely or wholly resolved by such simple recommendation is *the anxiety arising on occasion of temporary impotence during the attempted commencement of sexual relations.*

This impotence (if taken popularly the word is too severe and our title suits the state much better) together with a greater or smaller degree of anxiety is an extremely frequent phenomenon, as its temporariness. According to my observations (which, it must be noted, do not relate to neurotics) there are surprisingly few men who altogether escape the physical part of the experience, though its duration varies widely, i.e. from hours to weeks.

The mental part of the experience, the anxiety feeling, can be prevented by our advice being given beforehand, or it can be eliminated by such advice being given during the state of hesitancy. One has of course to add proper information as to why the worry is justified.

This information consists in the simple statement that what the individual tends to worry about, i.e. that he is actually and permanently impotent, abnormal, unsuitable for marriage and whatnot, has no foundation in fact. It needs a distinct neurotic element to make a man continue worrying to any serious extent after he has been told there is nothing unusual about these hesitancies.

The latter can be regarded as but both a special and a common (though commonly unknown) version of stage fright, and in a way a harmless version of stage fright at that: for there are not many artists whom this malady afflicts only temporarily.

We have to accept the frequent occurrence of this minor friction at the start of heterosexual relations as a little sacrifice for our cultural achievements. Those readers who have gathered some psychoanalytic knowledge will easily see that the Oedipus complex (which the 'Medical Psychologist' treated in two issues of this journal not long ago) is at the root of this 'normal symptom', involving as it does repression of sexuality and more especially some dissociation between the tender and the sensual elements of the sex instinct.

This latter observation brings us to the fact that the indicated hesitancies . . . are annoyingly painful if not encountered by enlightenment, [a fact that] is far too little known. Most people, believing themselves to be more or less of an unfortunate exception in this respect, are ashamed to let others know about their experiences.

A little more frankness on the part of each of us would indeed ease the burden of those of us who are doing research work in this as in other questions, and would thus contribute to general wellbeing. "You ought to be ashamed of yourself!" is a frequent, though frequently ineffective exhortation. "You ought not to be ashamed of yourself!" has not often been heard yet, although such an invitation has a profoundly moral function in cases like the present. As to its efficacy: this will increase, as ethical efficacy generally, with knowledge.

Source

Typescript (which appears to have a page missing, as indicated here in the penultimate paragraph) dated 12 August, 1945. The essay was intended for *The Psychologist*, and was written under *nom de plume* Keller used on several occasions around this time, 'Psychological Observer'. The pseudonym was apt: later in life, in a short, unpublished extension to *The Jerusalem Diary* (1977/79), he proposed keeping a London Diary, explaining (on 11 November, 1979) 'I shall look at our life, our society, our national characteristics as if I were a visitor to this country: as an ex-foreigner, I should be well suited for this task. Let's start with taxis . . .'

3   The Need for Pets

'We are experiencing a big demand for practically every breed of dog, provided it is young and healthy,' an official of the Dogs' Home at Battersea stated according to a newspaper report. While in pre-war days, at the time before the New Year licences fall due, there would be an influx of dogs into the home, 'the flow today is in the opposite direction.'

The interest of those of us who take heed of the results of scientific research is immediately aroused. The question arises of what the possible change in the attitude towards animals may be symptomatic, and how this change fits into the general socio-psychological picture of our time.

Common observation furnishes a starting point for our considerations. Pets, we all agree, are frequently children substitutes.

In fact they offer a number of advantages over children to certain of their owner's tendencies. The very word 'owner' indicates one advantage: one can be possessive towards one's pet without unpleasant consequences, without an uneasy conscience. Also, possessiveness encounters less immediate obstacles in the case of dogs than in that of children. Further, one has smaller responsibilities towards pets, and their education offers fewer problems. Their manifestations of love, coming as they do from non-humans, are exceedingly satisfying.

On a deeper level, we find that in possessive love is involved a considerable amount of ill-concealed self-love (and the need to be loved that springs from the latter), as well as tendencies towards mastery which in their turn spring from aggressive impulses. Indeed, the education of animals is more of the 'I'll teach you to . . .' sort than that of children.

The psychoanalytic body of knowledge offers further insight into the emotional significance of animals. We know of the great role animals can play in the mental life of children and of savages. This role, it has been shown, is determined by the suitability of animals to serve as parent substitutes. In the case of children's animal phobias it is the 'bad parent', the unconsciously hated parent, whom the feared animal signifies.

The question may arise at this point how an object can at the same time be a child and a parent substitute (supposing the animals retain some 'parental' significance in adult years). As a matter of fact there is evidence that one tends unconsciously to identify one's children with one's parents, a process of which the tendency to treat one's children as one would have liked to treat one's parents is a sign.

Each factor so far enumerated tends to show that the increased need for pets is a miniature indication of one or both of two phenomena which are at present observable amongst our society, viz., the manifestations of mental regression (return to a function of an early stage of development) involved in, and outliving, warlike attitudes and wartime circumstances; and the manifestations of reactions against such regression, reactions in the form of, *inter alia*, impulses towards reparation.

Let us specify these abstract considerations.

Firstly, love of an outward object that is strongly tinged by self-love is a primitive form of love. Moreover, the joint appearance of love and aggressiveness towards the same object (ambivalence), such as is often involved in one's relation towards pets, points to early stages in psychic development. The shunning of responsibility in regard to one's love relations points in the same direction. So generally does the increased emotional importance of dogs.

Secondly, as regards impulses towards reparation, the need to be loved by, and to love, an animal may well be based in part on the guilt reactions to the stimulation and satisfaction of hate impulses (war).

The animal is a convenient object for compromise satisfactions between regressive (e.g. aggressive) claims on the one hand and reactions to them on the other. Further, Man having proved, at least to such parts of our thinking as are strongly under the dominance of emotion, somewhat unworthy of our love, there is the temptation to leave him to his fate and to spend our love on objects that offer greatest reward, or at least less disappointment. But behind this and other seemingly realistic motives that may draw us, now more than at other times, towards animals, I suspect [there is] one of the reparational kind which I only bring forth with some hesitation. For such readers as are not acquainted with the results of psychoanalytic investigations may find my observation rather grotesque.

It has been indicated that in childhood an animal easily serves as a 'bad parent' substitute. Now when we remind ourselves that conscience, including its unconscious primitive part, is to some considerable extent a parent derivative, the thought forces itself upon us that in being nice to animals an individual might unconsciously try to atone for his 'sins' (war aggression) by asking the parent (animal), the forerunner of conscience, for forgiveness, by silencing conscience through loving a primitive substitute for conscience's (partly imaginary, partly real) originator.

Whether or not we accept this interpretation we must agree that the fact that the animal (dog) was once, in the child's imagination, a hating (and therefore feared) agency would make it exquisitely eligible as the primitive external conscience's representative for the dog lover. For the primitive unconscious conscience (i.e. part of what in psychoanalysis is called the super-ego) shows considerable hate towards the rest of the personality.

This whole process of reparation, though a reaction against aggressiveness, would of course in its turn be of a highly regressive nature.

A word, or rather a warning, finally, on regarding the ethical value, or otherwise, of the need for pets. Here as elsewhere in mental life, tendencies cannot be ethically evaluated (or, as some of us might think in view of the foregoing, devaluated) unless one examines, in each individual case, the total social and endo-psychic situation into which they are woven.

Source

This essay appears to have been written in immediate response to a report in the London evening paper, *The Star*, 21 December, 1945. There is no evidence that it was published at the time, though it appeared posthumously in *Three Psychoanalytic Notes on Peter Grimes*, London, 1995, pp. 37-9. The theme is closely related to Ernest Jones's 'reversal of generations phantasy' invoked during the third of the Notes on *Grimes* (see 'Music and Psychology' below).

4 Religion: the Psychoanalytic Standpoint

Again and again the question is asked, especially by those religious individuals whose endo-psychic resistances do not altogether forbid them to pay heed to psychoanalytic considerations, what are the exact claims that psychoanalysis would put forth regarding its often suggested invalidation of religious beliefs and doctrines?

A principal review of this question seems therefore called for, and if this review is short it might also be welcomed. Yet, however short, the psychoanalytic reply to this question cannot be what is unfortunately known as 'clear-cut'. Clear-cut answers, though they may be cut for the sake of clearness, are also often cut at the expense of validity.

Apart from the original Freudian contributions, what is perhaps the most comprehensive description of the significance of psychoanalytic discoveries for religious value is to be found in J. C. Flugel's *Men, Morals and Society*.[1] The author, a writer of the psychoanalytic school who is at the same time one of the few men of our time having a detailed knowledge of the most varied psychological theories, states at the outset of his treatment of our present problem that 'a distinction must be made between *understanding* and *disproof*' of religion by psychology, and especially by psychoanalysis. The latter cannot claim to have disproved religion, but it cannot reject the accusations, or the praise, as the case may be, that it has to some extent undermined the supposed validity of religious contentions.

Now whilst 'disproof' is a thoroughly exact conception, 'undermining' is not so *a priori*. I think the briefest and also most general way of indicating in what way psychoanalysis appears to have 'undermined' religion is to direct our attention to the fact that this psychological discipline has shown that what it considered to be a proof of religion, i.e. the existence of certain endo-psychic processes (religious experiences), is not dependent on the truth of religious claims in the cognitive sphere.

For psychoanalytic investigations have made it clear that these religious experiences will come into existence, broadly speaking, in consequence of the 'Oedipus complex' – 'the individual's affective attitude towards his family, and in its narrower sense his father and mother' – having been mastered, i.e. by reason of something which does not include the reality-value of religious truths.

Thus psychoanalysis has removed the often-suggested inevitability, indeed also the probability, of the connection between subjective religious experience and the assumed validity of the results of religious cognition.

For instance, the fact that the existence of God was experienced by an individual could be shown to be determined by the child's relation to his parents (Flugel descriptively calls God the Super-parent), determined by processes, that is to say, which did not, or, more exactly, need not, include the actual existence of God.

It is in this way that psychoanalysis turned, as R. B. Catell has pointed out,[2] the old ontological argument somewhat upside down, an argument according to which God's existence followed from the fact that we had an idea of Him. For depth psychology has shown that our idea of Him had to come about in any case, so that (the genesis of) this very idea rendered His existence insecure.

The reversal of the ontological argument is, it will be noted, not complete: in Flugel's words it is such only 'to some extent'.

A complete reversal would involve the disproof of God's existence through our idea of Him, and this has not been, indeed cannot be, accomplished.

NOTES

Source

There is no date to the manuscript of this essay, though its appearance and reference to a 'recent' publication of 1945, suggests that it was written in early December of that year. It was first published posthumously in Keller's *Three Psychoanalytic Notes on Peter Grimes*, London, 1995, pp. 35-7.

1   J. C. Flugel, *Men, Morals and Society*, London, Duckworth, 1945, p. 236.
2   R. B. Catell, Psychology and the Religious Quest, London, 1938.

5 War, Peace and Psychology

As I recently pointed out,[1] it would be [as] conducive to our knowledge as to the prevention of future Hitlers' successes if we arrived at a more thorough understanding both of the social aspects of individual paranoiac aggressiveness and of group paranoia by subjecting Hitler and [his] accomplices to psychological research. By relegating him to the sphere of the insane, this would also serve the purpose of preventing his becoming a martyr.

That war, as indeed any 'Kampf' [struggle], is to a considerable extent a psychological problem was long ago lucidly expounded by Freud, and in this country (among many others) by Ernest Jones and Edward Glover. Psychological investigations of the Nazis, and thus of Nazism, would of course only be an infinitesimal step in the direction of the solution (if any) of this problem. Yet it would be an important step, not only more directly on account of the enrichment of psychological knowledge needed in this respect, but also indirectly, in that the prominence of such inquiries would probably contribute to the popularisation of what one could call the 'psychological attitude' towards crime in general and war in particular. For it is the lack of this attitude that, *inter alia*, is a serious impediment to the abolition of individual and collective crime alike.

Our spontaneous attitudes to crime are largely determined by primitive unconscious reactions against our own unconscious drives. These attitudes can broadly be classified according to whether they are predominantly irrational tendencies (a) towards retaliation, or (b) towards forgiveness. Both are extremely human, i.e. not to be found among animals which do not get into the position to forgive an aggressive agency because they are incapable of brooding revenge against it.[2]

The 'psychological attitude' makes use more freely of another very human trait, namely the capacity intellectually to realise things happening in other people. Such understanding of mental processes is of course also lastly based on a very primitive mechanism, called 'identification' by psychoanalysts. By dint of it we are able to put ourselves into the position of other people ('empathy') and thus to react to their experiences as though they were ours, or, on a more developed level, simply to imagine or infer their reactions.

The proposition that to understand means to forgive is not altogether cogent. Understanding rather makes the questions both of forgiveness and retaliation at least temporarily unimportant. As far as psychological understanding is correlated with ethical mental processes, it implies prevention and cure.

Scope and depth of our understanding of the psyche are limited by the consequences of unconscious conflicts. A decrease in the latters' intensity engenders an increase in the efficacy of our psychological reality-sense. A radical reduction, or even extinction, of unconscious conflicts (of 'war in the mind', as a psychoanalytical observer aptly put it)[3] can however only be brought about by special methods (psychoanalysis).

Yet intellectual (cognitive) processes, gradual though their effect may be, can themselves play their part in strengthening undistorted psychological insight. If the afore-mentioned unconscious factors allow them to function fairly efficiently, the absence of specialised action to deal with unconscious 'war' need not deter them from achieving increasingly realistic results. Passionately pursued for the sake of realism, with sufficient contempt for our own affective prejudices as far as we get a glimpse of them, our tendencies towards understanding eventually show us at least where heaven lies.

As far as the present subject goes, heaven would seem to lie near the place where criminology gives way, wholly though not exclusively, to psychology and psychopathology (the latter only when scientific valuations have reached a fair degree of definiteness). Not exclusively – for must we not grant the sense of humour its claim to exercise, here as elsewhere, its refreshing function?

Scientific suggestions, particularly psychological ones such as hinted at in this article, often appear as anti-climax. However, an anti-climax to illusions serves a useful purpose.

Past ideas as to the prevention of war have proved illusory. Not that we should therefore neglect military, political, economic measures. But the effect of these will be the greater the more they are based on knowledge of human nature.

The stress on both the good and the evil in man has been somewhat overdone during the past few thousand years. But a new accent, that on what he looks like, with a corresponding partial suspension of spontaneous evaluation, is making itself felt. The causal succession: (1) 'What do we want the mind to look like?' – (2) 'What does it look like?' is superseded – very gradually to be sure – by: (1) 'What does it look like?' – (2) 'What can and should be done about it?'

The growth of this 'psychological attitude' is our hope, indeed much the only hope, for the future of an element in human existence the past of which has not perhaps been very impressive: for the future of happiness.

The way to scientific hell (the abode of condemned errors), and hence to a hell of a more general sort, such as can be found in its extreme forms within a German concentration camp or a gas chamber, is paved with emotional valuations.

NOTES

Source

Typescript dating from April 1945, addressed 32 Herne Hill, London S.E.24. For a more a fully evolved discussion of Hitler's paranoia, see Keller's review from 1981, 'Hitler and History', included in the notes to 'Individual Psychology and Group Psychology' earlier in this section.

1   [*Evening Standard*, 4 April, 1945. Keller had won a prize for the best suggestion as to what to do with Hitler if he was caught (the letter was published in the same paper the day before). After reporting that he had himself faced the Gestapo, Keller proposed a searching psychological study of the Führer before turning him over to whatever fate awaited him.]
2   Cf. R. Money-Kyrle, *Superstition and Society*, 1939, p. 105.
3   Charles Berg.

6   Peace and Pessimism

A condition for the establishment of permanent peace, if that is possible, is a ruthless and realistic pessimism on the part of peace workers. And peace workers, however indirect, we all shall have to be if we want to abolish war.

Pessimism, in this connection, does not mean resignation. It simply denotes an attitude of realisation that pessimism – the worst – is possible in matters of aggressiveness between human groups, and that the worst is probable if steps are not taken which up to the present have never been taken. This is the lesson that the past, and more especially the almost present past, teaches everyone who does not allow his judgment to blur the issue.

If to that pessimistic attitude is added a fair dose of what is technically known as meliorism, i.e. an attitude according to which progress in peacefulness is possible, the peace worker disposes of the best prerequisites for his job. As far as our present scientific knowledge goes, such meliorism is equally realistic.

Completely unrealistic, on the other hand, is that irrational optimism regarding the future of peace that so easily takes possession of our minds and will often present itself under the disguise of scientific reflections.

We might profitably inspect just one example of such logically unfounded, though seductively rationalized, optimism with regard to our past would-be achievements in the advancement of peace.

C. J. Colombos, a notable authority on problems of peace, stated in 1929: 'The progress that the world has made in the cause of peace in the last ten years surpasses every previous effort. For the first time in the world's history, there is a 'common conscience of mankind' intent upon avoiding war and realising that peace is necessary for the development of human progress and civilisation.

A comparatively young scientific discipline, namely that of psychology, and more particularly a still younger body of knowledge within that discipline, i.e. psychoanalysis, can at the present time already both confirm the soundness of our attitude of 'melioristic pessimism' and contribute suggestions as to the steps to be taken in accordance with this attitude.

To the psychologist the fact that humans, especially when under group influence, can easily revert to the state of inhumans is not in the least surprising. The exploration of our primitive and largely unconscious aggressive impulses and the mental (endo-psychic) conflicts to which they contribute has made it possible to comprehend such violent *external* conflicts as are involved in war far more thoroughly than was possible before; to one equipped with scientific psychological knowledge there is no longer anything inhuman in inhuman behaviour.

Whilst thus having arrived at a secure basis, however preparatory, for viewing an important bunch of factors that contribute to war, the psychologist sees himself compelled at the same time to suggest that unless *psychological* knowledge is applied to, and *psychological* measures are taken regarding the problems of war and peace, there is not much reason to suppose that in future human groups will behave more peacefully than they have in the past.

At present, exact psychological knowledge is confined to a circle, mainly of specialists, who are not actively concerned with politics. The new steps which psychology would propose would amongst other things consist in radical changes in this respect. Not only the politician, but everyone in a responsible position regarding public welfare, would have to be acquainted at least with the basic results of psychological research. Further, he would have to be able to consult a specialist body on all questions with which he cannot deal with adequately owing to lack of psychological knowledge. Moreover he himself would have to prove that his mental state is such, or has become such in consequence of a psycho-therapeutical process, that his actions are not unduly influenced by irrational mental reactions.

This is only a glimpse of the changes required for the abolition of war. As a matter of course, psychological research bodies, state-financed on a generous scale, would have to be continually active, enquiring further and further into the conditions and modes of aggressive manifestations, and paying special attention to the working of our primitive punitive tendencies, both those that aim at self-punishment and such as are directed towards the punishment of others. These scientific bodies would have to work in close collaboration with other scientific groups such as sociologists and anthropologists. Most intensive enquiries would have to be undertaken into child- and youth-behaviour, both individual and collective.

This brings us to another aspect of our prospective changes, i.e. that of education. Consequent on, and even in conjunction with these investigations, education, from infancy onwards, would have to undergo radical changes. Psychological as well as anthropological studies have shown beyond doubt that aggressiveness can most profitably be dealt with (and often is most absurdly dealt with) during early life.

These few and incomplete indications[2] may give the impression that our proposed steps involve something in the nature of a 'psychological dictatorship', and therefore threaten the individual's freedom. As a matter of fact the contrary is the case. Scientific ethics based on psychological knowledge must needs not only recognise the individual's need for freedom, but also appreciate its moral justification.

Does all this seem fantastic? So does war, in temporarily peaceful circumstances. If we fall back once more into that scientifically unfounded state of carefree optimism which is partly the result of our emotional reactions to our own aggressiveness, and which, through our impulses towards wish-fulfilment, presents us with illusions, not with realities, then a far less melioristic pessimism will be justified, however little pessimism will be actually present.

Why should we refuse to heed the results of one of the not too many scientific disciplines that have not contributed towards destruction?

NOTES

Source

Typescript evidently dating from some time in the weeks or months following the end of the war, with Keller's nom-de-plume 'Psychological Observer' claiming authorship.

1   See 'Peace', *Encyclopedia Brittanica*, fourteenth edition.
2   For a fairly exhaustive treatment of many of these questions, see Edward Glover, *War, Sadism, and Pacifism* [London, Allen and Unwin, 1935]. [Glover also wrote on 'War and Pacifism' in *Character and Personality*, 4, pp. 100-21.]

With this typescript is a hand-written opening of an essay prompted by a (then) recent book about a concentration camp. It is headed with an epithet from Freud on 'War and Death': ' . . . by which I mean that . . . we are led to regard human nature as 'better' than it actually is!' Keller writes:

Belsen: a Psychological Comment

When a friend, a psychologist who is not bound to the psychoanalytic outlook, sent me the July issue of *Horizon* and suggested to me that I should write a psychological comment on Alan Moorhead's *Glimpses of Germany: Belsen*, I realised that the time had come when extra-analytical psychologists, and thus perhaps also a section of the general educated public, felt the *need* (as distinct from [some] more passive attitude) for psychoanalytical treatment of 'Belsen' problems. For in asking for my opinion, this psychologist asked for considerations strongly influenced by the Freudian body of knowledge.

It was with this impression, coupled as it was with the recollection that *Horizon* has proved to be one of the few journals offering space to expositions of straightforwardly psychoanalytic considerations, that I set aside diverse scientific scruples and decided to put down the following observations.

One bunch of these scruples was concerned with the fact that I myself was subjected to beatings by the S. S. in 1938 in Vienna; I was 19 then and it might be suggested that through experiencing and witnessing such physical maltreatment the risk of a relatively high degree of irrational (if rationalized) reaction to 'Belsen' problems was great.

On the other hand, there is the fact that such experiences furnish valuable observational material and may thus be of assistance in forming a clear picture of what cannot yet be regarded as processes adequately understood.

Keller wrote his full (and poignant) account of 'Vienna 1938' as he had experienced and understood it in the *Listener*, 91/2348, 28 March, 1974, pp. 397-99. It was reprinted as the first chapter of his *1975 (1984 minus 9)*, London, Dobson, 1977. See also: 'Vienna: Myth and Reality', *London Review of Books*, 5-18 June 1980, pp. 8-9, and 'Hitler and History', *London Review of Books*, 5-18 February, 1981, p. 14 (reprinted above).

Psychological Writings: a Report

The Archive holds a few other psychological essays of this time. The conclusion to 'Women Who Wear Trousers' is cited in the notes to 'Male Psychology' (below). 'Observational Experiences' include 'Sex and Aggression: I. Immorality', an account of a tussle in Piccadilly; 'Public Privacy', reflections at Elephant and Castle tube station at 11.30 p.m.; and 'Peace Time Thrills – or Not', brief thoughts on a London bus.

Keller wrote extensively on psychology and psychiatry from the mid 1970s onwards in articles and reviews as well as in the third chapter, 'Psychoanalytic Congress 1975', of *1975, 1984 minus 9* (London, Dobson, 1977). See, 'Music and Psychopathology', *History of Medicine*, Vol. 3, No. 2, Summer 1971, pp. 3-7 (reprinted in Hans Keller, *Essays on Music*, edited by Christopher Wintle, Cambridge University Press, 1994, pp. 29-34); 'Composition and Psychopathology', *Listener*, 91/2355, 16 May 1974; and 'Towards the Psychopathology of Mental Health', *Spectator*, 239/7783, 10 September, 1977, pp. 12-13.

In the years 1977-81 especially, he championed Thomas Szasz, the controversial anti-psychiatric Professor of Psychiatry who was based at the [New York] State University Hospital of the Upstate Medical Centre, Syracuse. See: '*Karl Kraus and the Soul Doctors: a Pioneer Critic and his Criticism of Psychiatry and Psychoanalysis* by Thomas Szasz', *Spectator*, 238/7769, 28 May, 1977, p. 19; '*Schizophrenia: the Sacred Symbol of Psychiatry* by Thomas Szasz; *The Theology of Medicine: the Politico-philosophical Foundations of Medical Ethics* by Thomas Szasz', *Spectator*, 240/7809, 4 March, 1978, pp. 22-23; '*Sex: Facts, Frauds and Follies* by Thomas Szasz', *London Review of Books*, Vol. 3, No. 14, 6-19 August, 1981, p. 9.

*

The following (unlisted) essay, which, as far as is known, exists only in typescript, probably dates from the late 1970s. It is a good example of Keller the mature 'psychological observer':

The Psychiatric Psychosis

Readers unversed in psychiatric facts, as distinct from ever-popular psychiatric fancies in the guise of facts, may not know of that historic occasion in a loony-bin when a sociological visitor was shown round the place by a psychiatrist: he was intent upon learning what he could from the step-sister science. You might say, sociology is not a science – but then Thomas Szasz might say, psychiatry isn't either. Anyhow, the visitor came up against a sparsely clad gentleman with a deep educational outlook on his face who was not prepared to indulge in small talk, as distinct from humble giant talk, and all but scared the visitor out of the room with his radical views of the world in general and the soul in particular.

"Who are you?" the visitor asked eventually, when he could get a word in edgeways. "Jesus Christ," the gentleman answered winningly, ready to offer the other cheek as soon as convenient, should the first one now be endangered. But the visitor was marginally puzzled: "Who told you that you were Jesus Christ?" "God!" the gentleman retorted, now in a thunderous tone. From the other end of the room, equally thunderous, an awe-inspiring voice intervened: "No, I didn't!"

Well then, what made the occasion historic was that nothing happened inside the sociologist. Had he had the imagination and intelligence, he would have realised that he had been given a living illustration of the relation between sociologists and psychiatrists, variable as are the answers to the question who is or who isn't Jesus Christ, and who is or isn't God.

Kathleen Jones is professor of Social Administration at the University of York, and less than a year ago, the Royal College of psychiatrists invited her to deliver the fifty-first Maudsley lecture [entitled] 'Society Looks at the Psychiatrist'. She soon got cracking and, for the duration of the lecture, was prepared to forget all about disagreements between sociological Jesus and psychiatric God. Indeed, she demonstrated their common receptivity to dependable delusions (if that's not too much of a tautology). In due course, the evidence of her ill-concealed filiation from God was joyfully published in a recent issue of the *British Journal of Psychiatry*, and has thus become the text of the present essay. Kathleen Jones thinks she argues that psychiatry should care about sociology, but she cares so much about psychiatry that she would dearly love to have a foot in it, and no doubt has.

However, as we paddle *in medias res*, we have to define one relevant delusion – and I don't mean the common delusion of 'mental health' either, with which Prof. Jones does, of course, operate throughout, assuring us at the same time that 'we are all "disturbed personalities"', and that 'life consists in learning to deal with one's own problems and those of other people.' Speak for yourself; for me, life consists in discovering things, and as for other people's problems, I'd never dream of 'dealing' with them unless they invite me to, in which case, more often than not, I succeed in showing that when one stops creating problems, few survive. But then, both observant sociologists and observant psychiatrists are professional problem-creators, and you can't expect them to renounce both their material and their spiritual livelihood.

No, the delusion I want to throw into relief is a symptom of an as yet undiscovered psychosis: there's a collective psychosis – one up on what the old-fashioned Freud thought of as 'collective neurosis' – which the de-individualized part of the psychiatric world has fallen victim to, and which Prof. Jones is only too eager to share – in her attempt to insinuate herself with God. About persecution mania, to be sure, we all know – but why had its opposite to wait until, listening to many a psychiatric delirium (nowise *tremens*, alas), I discovered it?

It is the delusion of not being persecuted. The psychiatric world did not, of course, invent it. History is full of examples, the most tragic being the European Jews in the 'twenties and 'thirties, many of them: by the time they noticed they were being persecuted, and that their persecution had come to stay, it was too late to escape. Psychiatry's psychotic denial of Thomas Szasz's persecution of (legally or psycho-technically) compulsory psychiatry, of psychiatry-as-she-is-practiced, cannot decently be mentioned in the same breath; none the less, it's the same old human psyche breathing, shallowly. What's worse, while Hitler was a raving lunatic out to kill, Szasz is a raving rationalist (called irrational by Professor Jones because she mixes him up with [R. D.] Laing) out to redeem. Hitler only existed *en masse*; Szasz only exists alone – which makes the persecution more easily deniable. Now, if he were not a psychiatrist himself, if the persecution were not from within (like mine of music criticism, musicology, and education), the psychiatric psychotics could, at least, plead that they were merely facing amateurishness, proportionately ineffective. As a matter of fact, they do – thus delusionally denying that they are facing professionalism, proportionately effective.

Kathleen Jones toes the line. Her sociology comes in handy: she argues in terms of movements and schools, real or imaginary, not in terms of individual thought. Early on, she tells us that 'the psychiatrist has at his command the insights derived from the psychoanalytic tradition' (read: Freud's insight), and by the time she reaches Szasz, he has become a mere member of 'the "anti-psychiatry" school' (and is thrown in the same dustbin as Laing). In reality, Szasz agrees more with Freud than he does with Laing, and Laing agrees more with Freud than he does with Szasz; quite realistically, the two gentlemen are not on speaking terms. In short, while Laing thinks that it isn't the schizophrenic that's sick but his environment, Szasz thinks that nobody is sick unless thus diagnosed by un-metaphorical medicine, as opposed to psychiatry adopting the medical model.

Where, high-handedly, she does talk about Szasz specifically, Prof. Jones gets him wrong: he appears 'uninterested in the problem of what choice the patient has if he cannot afford to pay.' The so-called patient's choice is, in fact, about the only thing Szasz is interested in. He favours the means test; below a certain level of income, the psychiatrist's potential client 'gets a chit' that enables him to pay for any psychiatric services he requires (stress on 'he').

In question-begging response to Szasz's submission that if you've done something wrong you should be punished rather than treated, she airily remarks that 'the effects of such a view may well be harsher than those of the older liberal philosophy.' Szasz is not concerned with what's harsh or less harsh, but with what is rational and, hence, right. Assuming, for the duration of a paragraph, the mantle of psychiatric professionalism, she reminds the hallucinated amateur Szasz that 'the hard slog of clinical practice does not leave much time for fantasies about the conquest of society,' just as she approvingly quotes Tony Clare about 'the great mass of Britain's two thousand psychiatrists, junior and senior,' who 'go about their clinical activities without engaging in much public discussion of their attitudes concerning ideological issues outside their speciality.' But according to Szasz, there are moral issues outside their speciality that, however, they should govern – just as we would not allow a psychiatrist to rob his patient for an alleged therapeutic purpose (my comparison). Thus the hard slog of persecuting the patient is easily denied, the threat of Szasz's persecution of psychiatrists psychotically averted – by hallucinating things he never said, and ignoring things he has said.

Mental health operators, psychiatrists and sociologists, I mean you well: don't wait until it is too late. For the purpose of returning to reality, of shedding the psychiatric psychosis, nothing but a straightforward, professional discussion between you and Szasz will do – preferably in the *British Journal of Psychiatry*. Meanwhile, I myself visited a loony-bin, where I ran into a rather impressive lady, highly articulate, who told me all about the psychiatrist's duty to investigate his patient's social needs, and her own interdisciplinary involvements. "Who are you?" I asked her. "A sociologist with psychiatric rights and duties." "Who told you you were?" "Ha, a leading psychiatrist." From the corner of the room came a thunderous voice: "No, I didn't." "Who are *you*, then?" "A leading Kleinian." For them, of course, formative life finishes at minus 6 months or so.

On Maturity
(*from* The Psychologist)

Keller had previously used the aphorism to explore aspects of everyday life (see part I above), but now uses it psychologically to probe an abstract idea. The aphorism was in fact well suited to revealing how the manifest and the latent can stand in a paradoxical relationship. These reflections 'On Maturity' for the little magazine *The Psychologist* also inaugurate the first of many Keller 'columns'.

1   On Maturity (first set)

Intellectual maturity is reached when disbelief is superseded by doubt and conviction by opinion.

Emotional maturity is reached when self-love is as weak as one's love for one's neighbour is strong.

Sexual maturity is reached when one's sex-life is as important to another one as it is to oneself.

Ethical maturity is reached when moral satisfaction no longer varies according to the degree of effort underlying one's actions, but according to the extent of their positive effect.

Artistic maturity is reached when both need for and contempt for applause are superseded by the desire to be understood.

Maturity in reasoning is reached when the malicious joy one experiences at detecting another's fallacies is superseded by satisfaction at detecting one's own.

Conversational maturity stands in inverse relation to the number of topics discussed (not considering the monomaniac's conversational jail).

Temperamental maturity is reached when one is in a good temper on half of the occasions where one would have reason to be in a bad one.

Maturity in appreciation is reached when one is as delighted at perceiving an ash-tray on one's café-table as one is enraged at perceiving none.

Mature religiosity tolerates atheism; mature atheism tolerates religion.

Maturity in tact is reached when the ability not to be tactless is superseded by the power to react to another's tactlessness so that it is transformed into something tactful.

The higher degree of general maturity is reached when one is able to view, without retreat or resignation, every day of one's life against the background of one's death.

2   What IS Maturity?

Maturity in ambition is reached when one's ability to live up to one's ideals is increased by one's willingness to live down to one's limitations.

Maturity in courage is reached when one is able to decide beforehand what one is going to be courageous about.

Maturity in persuading one's neighbour is reached when one no longer uses him for persuading oneself.

Parental maturity stands in inverse relation not only to one's children's fear of oneself, but also to one's own fear of one's children.

Paternal maturity is reached when the father ceases to be shy about mothering his child.

Educational maturity (whether the parent's or the teacher's) is reached when one's 'need to be needed'* is superseded by one's need eventually not to be needed. [* Margaret Phillips]

Maturity in industry is reached when one isn't active just because otherwise one would feel guilty.

Maturity in passivity is reached when one's inactivity is no longer due to either one's being too lazy to do something, or one's fear of spoiling something.

Maturity in aggressiveness is reached when one's hostility towards others and towards oneself is superseded by a friendly but determined struggle against the root of much hostility: one's anxiety.

Maturity in boredom is reached when one is no longer bored because one doesn't know what to do, but rather because one does, but is prevented from doing it.

Maturity in resignation is reached when instead of retreating when it is too late, and instead of giving up too early, one stops when one has to stop, and smiles when one realises one has to.

3   On Maturity . . . (second set)

Maturity of self-sacrifice is reached when the self is left intact in spite of sacrifice.

Maturity in worry is reached when one never worries about having nothing to worry about.

Social and sexual maturity is reached when one enjoys oneself by enjoying one another.

Maturity in criticism is reached when instead of wishing that others won't do what we ourselves can't do, we wish that they would do it.

Maturity of mental balance is reached when the alternate dictatorships of emotion and of reason are superseded by democratic government within the mind.

4 Maturity

Maturity in friendship is reached when a friend is more to us than an enemy against whom we can't do anything.

Maturity in humour is reached when one's feeling that one's bad luck is a bad joke is superseded by one's realisation that it is a good one.

Occupational maturity is reached when instead of whiling away one's time one is whiled away by it.

Maturity in independence is reached when one is able to be independent even of one's independence.

5 On Maturity . . . (third set)

Maturity in idealism is reached when we depersonalise not only our ideals but also our scapegoats.

Creational maturity is reached when one realises that at times one must get an idea in order to have it.

Maturity in self-realisation is reached when one prefers being left to one's fate to being left to another person's.

Ethical maturity is reached after one has learned how important for others' happiness is one's own.

Maturity in both showing off and modesty is reached when one no longer shows off one's modesty.

Maturity in discipleship can only be reached when one is to become an heir, not a legacy hunter.

Maturity in dreaming is reached when seeing things as they aren't is superseded by seeing things as they could be.

Maturity of the wish to marry is reached when this becomes more than the mere desire for freedom from freedom.

Maturity of regret is reached when regret is no longer an excuse for not removing its cause.

Maturity in decision is reached when one realises that the only thing one can do about many a thing is, it.

Maturity of suffering is reached when one no longer carries the world's misery on another person's shoulders.

Maturity in love is reached when the beloved satisfies more than one's need for self-love by proxy.

Maturity in realism can only be reached if the child's inability to postpone satisfactions is not superseded by the man's urge to postpone them indefinitely.

Maturity in originality is reached when originality is more than lack of education; maturity in education is reached when education is more than lack of originality.

NOTES

Source

These maxims appeared in five issues of *The Psychologist*: (1) July 1945, p. 5; (2) August 1947, p. 17; (3) September 1947, p. 18; (4) October 1947, p. 31; and (5) November 1947, p. 27. There is some overlapping of concerns, especially under (5) with Keller's other aphorisms (reproduced in part I above). The September 1947 issue – Vol. 15, No. 177 – described itself as 'Published on the first of each month by Frank J. Allard at Mansfield House, 1, Southampton Street, Strand, London, W. C. 2 (Temple Bar 3980)', and comprised 32 pages as well as a densely printed cover in russet and black. The issue measures 14 x 21.5 cms. and includes main articles on 'Hypnotism and Auto-Suggestion', 'Mind and your Health', 'How you can Concentrate', 'Can Psychology Harm the Young?', 'Killing the Demon Worry', 'The Devil, Sex, and the Unpardonable Sin [against the Holy Ghost]', and so forth, together with other, smaller features such as 'advice bureau', psychological self-testing, a competition, maxims, and a full advertisement for the Pelman Institute. Keller's column 'On Maturity' belonged with – and perhaps grew out of – the small items.

In *Hans Keller and the BBC*, London, Ashgate, 2003, p. 12, Alison Garnham notes that 'the Zurich journal *Die Weltwoche* published Keller's own translation of the 1945 set under the title 'Reife' on 27 December, 1946, but turned down the next set.'

The Archive includes two further hand-written aphorisms on maturity dating from later in Keller's life:

> People consider themselves and each other mature when they can't think of anything new: watch them when they start using the word 'experience'. For the mature discoverer or inventor, experience is a private help, not a public virtue. It can certainly be a public hindrance.

> We call old people childish when, against hopeful expectation, they turn out not to be as infantile as we are. If, between the two infancies, they are guaranteed a few moments of rest, usually after retirement age, our hope turns into defensive fear and we call them senile.

*

Keller's papers from the early to mid-1940s include a single paragraph showing typically how the aphorism could be expanded into a larger statement – a maxim of a kind – about psychology and ethics:

Psychology and Ethics: a Note

The more one penetrates into what one is destined to know about the working of the human mind, the more one realises the downright fearful difficulties that confront one if one desires to make reasonable ethical suggestions. As psychologist one may be content if one has been able to throw some light on a bunch of processes, or one aspect of the psyche; as ethicist one is overpowered by the realisation that whatever one does *not* know may prove a more decisive blow to one's ethical suggestions, a blow which might prove them as noxious as one thought they would be helpful.

Psychology and Gender

Keller's concerns with sexuality (shown in Part I) and the intra-group dynamics of prostitution (shown earlier in Part II), is now crossed with a psychological enquiry into the similarities and differences between the genders, and their respective suitability for psychological research. Once again, Keller declares his indebtedness to J. C. Flugel and Margaret Phillips. As the notes show, this enquiry stood behind an instance of his music programming at the BBC in the 1970s and his remarks on the social organization of a London club. In 1975 (p. 87), Keller describes 'Male Psychology' as his 'first [formal] essay in the English language'.

Male Psychology

I Statement of Problem. Desirability of Male Psychology by Females   II Female Suitability for Proposed Task   III Female Unsuitability for Proposed Task   IV Prospects   V Summary

I Statement of Problem. Desirability of Male Psychology by Females

A quaint feeling that our title may arouse is symptomatic of the state of affairs to which the following will direct our attention.[1] The mass of psychological literature on the human female has no counterpart regarding the study of the male. Owing to the structure of our society the male is regarded as the norm, and the female, to express it exaggeratedly, as a deviation from the norm. Deviations tend to be treated specifically, especially in our time, when predilection for the study of digressions from alleged norms is making itself felt. (The psychoanalytic discovery of the female child's infantile masculinity has of course reinforced the conception of the masculinity-norm.)[2]

However, whilst women are well-nigh relegated to the department of abnormal psychology, the question arises whether a correspondingly queer being, namely, man, does not merit a similar study, or maybe even a similar relegation – so that something be done toward the attainment of that desirable state in which there would be no norm (and therefore nothing abnormal) at all.

It would, of course, be ridiculous to suggest that man has not been subjected to psychological study. But it has almost always been a study of the norm and, mostly, a study by the norm.[3] In so far as the norm is taken for granted, or is taking itself for granted, its differences from the non-norm do not attract special attention, this being rather drawn towards characteristics of the non-norm. Man is regarded as Man rather than as different from Woman.

When we deal with differentiations of a fairly impersonal nature, it is a matter of more or less indifference whether we regard phenomenon A as norm and phenomenon B as abnormal, or vice versa. From the purely rational point of view we ought, in both instances, to arrive at the same objective results. But the investigation of psychological and, above all, of sex differences is influenced by powerful motives detrimental to the rational approach. If, therefore, we are debarred from occupying an impartial standpoint when viewing the differences between the sexes, it is advisable not to stick to one single challengeable point of view, but to consider the question from different angles, either of them subjective, but each subjective in a different direction.

There is an approach to the study of sex differences which, for reasons now apparent, has been almost completely neglected: *The study of male psychology by females psychologists who investigate not the points in which they differ from men, but those in which men seem different from themselves.* Perhaps some surprises await us if 'Man' (*Mensch, anthropos*) is in this way not considered to be a man, but a woman.

The new step we thus propose should have a much-needed regenerating influence on our attitude towards this problem of sex differences. There has been of late a tendency amongst psychologists, as soon as they hear sex differences mentioned, to sit back and let Margaret Mead continue to concern herself with Samoa and New Guinea.[4] One does not like to deal with a subject that has proved so precarious, one that appears to be a phantom in that ideas of 'male' and 'female', while seeming to be clearly present at one moment, vanish into the air as soon as they are about to be grasped and used for psychological purposes.

II Female Suitability for Proposed Task

We know of a considerable number of female psychologists who, through their studies in child psychology, have either become famous, or have made momentous contributions to our psychological knowledge, or else have even proved to merit both these descriptions. We need not know much psychology in order to realize that there are many women who are interested in children. Equally, we need not acquire psychological knowledge in order to become alive to the fact that many women are interested in men.[5] Thus interest in our task will be sufficiently present, one may hope, despite the lack of past and present female authorities on male psychology.

More specifically, we have to ask ourselves now whether females on the whole markedly possess qualities favouring our placing them in the suggested situation (or whether they markedly lack qualities unfavourable in this connection), and whether this situation female-studying-male entails features conducive to success of the proposed studies.[6]

(1) The female's capacity for identification and empathy is marked. Apart from the fact that a fair degree of these powers is a necessary condition for 'guessing what's going on' in the individuals to be studied, the tendency towards identification possesses a characteristic of particular advantage in our connection: it tends to direct the identifying individual's attention to the resemblances rather than to the differences between herself and the observed subject. Since we begin to discover that sex differences have so far suffered more of an over-accentuation than of an under-estimation, an approach to the study of the male which would spontaneously pay attention to sex similarities should represent a counterpoise against preconscious attitudes of the opposite kind.

(2) The male is to a greater extent liable to sexual over-estimation[7] and to sexual under-estimation[8] of the love-object (and thus of members of the love-object's sex) than the female. With regard to this point then, the female is better equipped for the study of the male than the male is for the study of the female.

(3) It is generally conceded that a higher degree of Narcissism can be found in women than in men[9] (though it is still a matter of uncertainty whether this fact is wholly reducible to social influences prevalent in our culture or whether innate factors also play a part in it).[10] Superficial reflection would lead us to conclude from this that the over-estimation

of the self implied in Narcissism will have detrimental effects on female capacity in the sphere of male psychology, in that this over-estimation, by way of displacement and introjection, will easily come to cover the whole female sex. On close inspection, however, it appears that this view can be called into question. In the female a great amount of Narcissistic energy (ego-libido) remains dischargeable throughout life on primitive levels, i.e. the sphere of bodily decoration and clothes. This fact, for which the claims of our society are largely responsible,[11] induces us to infer that a woman will find little opportunity or necessity to displace and sublimate her ego-libido on to higher (mental) levels.

Consequently, concerning the qualities that are not immediately connected with the spheres of body and clothes, the male is more likely to over-estimate his sex than the woman hers.[12]

Now the women we have in view for our job are intellectual women and, apart from their frequent feminist attitude, it may be suggested that their highly developed mental organization often makes possible a considerable displacement of Narcissism on to the mental sphere. But in face of this it must not be forgotten that, given a highly developed psychic apparatus with the manifold outward-directed interests that this implies, the development of much of the ego-libido does not merely result in displacement. It also involves the transformation of ego-libido into (sublimated) object-libido. Remembering again that (intellectual) women are not so much subject to Narcissistic displacement as are (intellectual) men, it seems that, on the whole, women will be assisted in their new task by the line of development of their Narcissism.

(4) Connected with their capacity for empathy is the fact that women have, in the majority of cases, less difficulty in adopting in the realm of psychology the truly scientific attitude, i.e. one that is not *a priori* influenced by strong moral motives, especially motives towards negative evaluation. The female approach to questions of the human mind could be described as one of general – though sometimes perhaps not sufficiently detached – friendliness. The relative weakness of the female super-ego involves its relatively stronger dependence on (variable) external influences. Females are more liable to suggestive influences than men, a fact explainable by their strong capacity for projecting their super-ego on to other persons.[13] The passive moral attitude, its instability and adaptability which often follow from this fact are conducive to the suggested 'female approach', and thus to a relatively undistorted understanding of other people.

(5) An individual's views of others are generally less subjected to distortion than are his views of himself. In consequence of the extension of self-feeling to members of one's own sex, the latter is viewed more subjectively than the other sex. Thus woman's study of man will not be subjected to many of the disturbances which interfere with her study of her own sex.

III Female Unsuitability for Proposed Task

We turn to such aspects of our proposition as go to show that not *all* is well with it.

(1) The greater incidence of neurosis in females[14] represents a potential obstacle in the way of an impersonal investigation of the male, especially since this implies, in many of those females who do not actually develop definite psycho-neurotic symptoms, the presence of particularly strong complexes.

(2) Assuming the thirst for knowledge to be derived from infantile voyeurism, and noting that it is the female thirst for knowledge to which we here appeal, the question is whether we are asking too much of a number of females when we want to direct their scientific interest to the very sphere (i.e. the male, the 'penis-sphere') which was the centre of their infantile curiosity as well as of their sexual activity (clitoris), but which sphere they have learnt (at least partly) to avoid (both in consequence of direct external pressure (modesty barriers) and by dint of endo-psychic forces (castration-complex) (cf. III (1)). Indeed, if it could be demonstrated that one of the reasons why females have not so far concerned themselves thoroughly with the study of the male is in the last resort to be sought in the phenomena of penis-envy and the castration complex, our previous statement on female interest in the male would need some qualification in this direction.

(3) The argument adduced sub II (5) works, of course, both ways. The favourable way in which an individual regards his/her own sex is accompanied by a hostile attitude towards the other sex. If we bear in mind, however, that (i) powerful forces of attraction towards the other sex have to be counted on as well; (ii) therefore the friendliness towards the self (own sex) is on the whole stronger than the hostility towards the other; (iii) the fate of female Narcissism (*vide* II (3)) does not involve the same degree of friendliness-towards-mental-self in the female as it does in the male; we realize that the factor of hostility against man, individual conditions being fairly favourable, is not of grave significance.

(4) The ease with which the female super-ego is projected on to other persons (*vide* II (4)) involves a comparatively strong dependence on authority; hence the danger of female dependence on existing scientific views. Strong dependence on authority, especially where it is not fully conscious, may also spoil in some cases the rosy picture we have submitted of the amoralistic attitude of females. However, with regard to this latter point, we need not be too pessimistic, because we can often observe how an individual, though tending to make herself morally dependent on another person, is eventually prevented from establishing this dependence through her empathic talents: we frequently encounter a situation where a woman not only understands and at times follows the preacher, but also (in many cases to a far greater extent) understands and follows the man whom the preacher condemns.

IV Prospects

Glancing back on our considerations we find it hardly possible to present a mathematical account of the chances that our proposition would seem to promise. Nor do we want to force upon the reader conclusions which he will better form himself after his inspection of our arguments. Thus the present writer will merely, privately as it were, state his own view on our prospect.

Given fairly favourable individual circumstances, a female studying the male will work on a more auspicious psychological basis than either a female studying the female, or a male studying the female, or a male studying the male. (Perhaps we should add: taking no account of geniuses.)

Or to put the matter conservatively, the woman studying man will not, endo-psychically, encounter more hindrances than any other student of a specific psychological realm within the scope of sex differences.

Now to the question of who should do what in accordance with our proposal. Every female psychologist, as far as she has a minimum of time and interest at her disposal, should approach the subject of 'male psychology' armed with those methods which in her opinion are the best, at the same time taking just a little less knowledge for granted than she would like to.

V Summary

Owing to the structure of our society there is a specific psychology of woman, but none of man, the latter's mind being treated as the norm. The one-sided picture of the psychology of the sexes thus produced might undergo advantageous modification through studies of the male by female psychologists. The latter are psychologically equipped for this task through (1) their capacity for identification, (2) their incapacity for sexual over- and under-estimation, (3) their weak *mental* Narcissism, (4) their capacity for an amoralistic attitude, (5) their viewing the male sex more objectively than their own.

Though they may be hampered by (1) severe complexes, especially (2) the castration complex together with repression of infantile voyeurism, (3) hostility against the other sex, (4) reliance on authority, it is suggested that the prospects of the present proposal seem auspicious.

Female psychologists are asked to approach the recommended work with an open mind.

NOTES

Source

British Journal of Medical Psychology, 20, 1946, pp. 384-88. Reprinted in *World Psychology*, 2/7, July 1947. Keller claimed that it was 'the first paper published in [the] journal that had not been written by a medical man' (*1975*, p. 88). It appears to have been completed two years earlier, in 1944: a correspondence in the Archive with Dr. Karl Jena of Duke University Press about possible publication ran from 22 October, 1944 to 3 May, 1945. At the time of the reprinting, Keller commented to V. T. Searle-Jordan, editor of *World Psychology*, that the original draft had been 'thrice as long'. In a letter to a Mrs. Hummerlivert of 10 April, 1947, Keller said that at the time of writing he had not taken sufficiently into account 'female self-contempt' (the theme of the prostitutes' fieldwork described earlier).

The Archive includes another (slight) essay from the early 1940s on gender, 'Women Who Wear Trousers'. This reflects the work of J. C. Flugel on *The Psychology of Clothes* (London, Hogarth Press, 1930). Keller concludes:

> I do not think, however, that those men and women who find feminine trousers disagreeable are wholly moved by the latter's masculine significance. There is another aspect to the matter, i.e. the fact that this bifurcated costume tends to accentuate the existence of the female leg more thoroughly, and more extensively, than a skirt does. In this respect, the 'shocking' aspects of women's legs would have been transferred to the slacks. Thus, while these cover the legs more thoroughly than many a skirt, they 'uncover' them at the same time. In this sense, then, trousers, re-cover women's legs in a double sense of the term.

1   I am indebted to Margaret Phillips and Dr. J. C. Flugel for suggestions.
2   Part of the Freudian influence and part of its criticism rest on ignorance of the fact that psychoanalysis uses the term 'masculine' and 'feminine' mostly in the psychological, as distinct from the biological and sociological, sense, i.e. synonymously with 'active' and 'passive'.
3   Following a suggestion of J. C. Flugel we should perhaps remind the reader that one has, of course, to make allowance for the fact of the much lesser output of psychological papers and theses by women.
4   [Ed:] Margaret Mead (1901-78) was an American anthropologist and social psychologist who specialized in primitive cultures.
5   Female novelists have proved their interest in and understanding of the male, anticipating the knowledge that waits to be expounded in a scientific form in the same way as male novelists have forestalled the findings of various contemporary psychological schools.

6   We must of course be prepared to revise the replies we give to our question as soon as our prospective male psychology furnishes reasons therefore. (The suggestion that the present enquiry begs the question can be countered by the reminder that we cannot but work with that knowledge which investigations [so far] have yielded, investigations that started from the silent assumption of the masculinity norm.)

7   Sigmund Freud, 'Drei Abhandlung zur Sexualtheorie' ['Three Essays on the Theory of Sexuality'], *Gesammelte Werke*, 5, London, Imago, 1942, [pp. 29-145,] p. 122 [hereafter Freud, 1942; English translation by James Strachey, Standard Edition, 7, pp. 123-245]; Sigmund Freud, 'Beiträge zur Psychologie des Liebenslebens ['Investigations into the Psychology of the Love Life'], *Gesammelte Werke*, 8, London, Imago, 1943, pp. 81 and 86.

8   Freud, 1943, pp. 83 and 86.

9   Sigmund Freud, 'On Narcissism: An Introduction', trans. by C. M. Baines, *Collected Papers*, 4, London, Hogarth Press, p. 44; J. C. Flugel, *The Psychology of Clothes*, London, Hogarth Press, 1940, pp. 101, 116, 145, 208.

10   Flugel, 1940, p. 116.

11   Flugel, 1940, p. 101.

12   We note in passing that this links up with [note] 2 above.

13   Ernest Jones, 'The Nature of Auto-suggestion', *International Journal of Psychology*, 4, 1923, p. 293; Flugel, 1940, p. 152.

14   Freud, 1942, p. 123; Ernest Jones, *Freud's Psychology, Papers on Psychoanalysis*, London, Baillière, Tindall and Cox, 1918, pp. 31 ff. [hereafter, Jones, 1918]. As regards the obsessional syndromes the incidence is of course higher in the male; Jones, 1918, 'Hate and Anal Eroticism in the Obsessional Neurosis', p. 544.

Keller drew heavily on this article for an essay written during his time at the BBC (1959-79) when the Women's Lib movement had come to the fore: 'Hans Keller writes about 30 September on Radio 3, which will be a day by and about women', *Listener*, 90/2322, 27 September, 1973, pp. 428-29. He writes:

Despite its absurdities, however, despite the worst intellectual excesses of unisex, Women's Lib's suspicions are of enormous scientific and ethical strength. The clue to the thinking mind's original sin lies in the sinister ambiguity of the concept, and indeed the act, of discrimination. No sooner do we praise a discriminating mind than we have to curse it, because it seems incapable of discriminating *between* without discriminating *against* – until the horrible thought arises that the 'against' really comes first, however subterraneously, the 'between' being its rationalisation . . . A great deal is made of what women can't do, or could if the social context were fairer to them, but what needs as much consideration is what they can do, in the most unfavourable social circumstances: in the arts whose material is human beings, such as the novel, there have been female geniuses where the environmental conditions for the emergence of genius hardly obtained. In music, on the other hand, which does not primarily concern itself with specific human beings, the emancipation of feminine talent seems to depend more exclusively on the sex's own social emancipation. *Women on 3* will be a little too early to be able to feature downright composing geniuses. With performers it is a different matter: it is the performer, rather than the composer, who needs the capacity for identification.

That Keller consistently refused to equate differentiation *between* with discrimination *against* is shown by the following essay, which comes from sometime later in life. The typescript is in the Archive: it appears to have been published by the quality Sunday newspaper for which it was intended, though what the paper was and when it appeared is still unknown. According to Milein Cosman, it met with some resistance from Keller's circle. The reference to a ski club signals Keller's direct involvement in the sport.

Human's Lib

THIS ROOM IS RESERVED FOR MEMBERS
AND THEIR MALE GUESTS ONLY.
LADIES MAY NOT BE SHOWN THIS ROOM.
BY ORDER OF THE COMMITTEE

There is one thing more inimical to sheer human dignity, and hence to humanity's *raison d'être*, than this printed notice adorning the Smoking Room at the liberal Reform Club, and that is the reactions to it which my wife [Milein Cosman] and I have been collecting amongst people who call themselves civilized, who are called highly educated and are, in fact, highly intelligent, part of the cream of our society – so intelligent that they no longer see simple truths: they create subtle complications around them if and when they need to. Complexes produce complications. Our society's history of unresolved homosexuality, of its elitist 'homosociality' (J. C. Flugel), and of the other sex's unresolved reactions, is as complex-ridden as, say, the German history of the unresolved need for paternalization, for leadership, and of the other side's reactions against it. The collective antics of our Women's Liberation parallel those of the German anti-culture – so much more violent than our own.

Since the cream of our society, especially the reformed cream, tends to muse over the present newspaper of a Sunday morning, I have to spell out the simple truth at dictation speed. 'Ladies may not be shown this room' is logically and morally equivalent to 'these benches are for whites only', or 'Jews are not admitted to this ski club' – to mention but two examples of collective degradation with which I have been in personal contact in societies calling themselves civilized. Now, the most frequent answer I have encountered to my questions about the Reform Club's notice is that men are entitled to a refuge. As entitled, I admit, as whites are to a refuge from blacks, or Gentiles from Jews – or, for that matter, Jews from Gentiles. The only room from which ladies can conceivably be barred without any implied devaluation is the gentlemen's lavatory – though the Continent's frequent co-educational lavatories have not, to my knowledge, resulted in any heterosexual Sodom and Gonorrhoea.

And what I regard as a downright truism has met with an astonishing chorus of thoughtfully raised eyebrows – my submission that the dignity of the individual (pardon my pleonasm) stands or falls with the evaluation and devaluation of the individual, and of the individual only: devaluations of groups must needs involve the degradation of individuals. "So you would not collectively devalue delinquents?" one profoundly reformed mind asked me, in an attempt to pose a clarifying extreme example.

For one thing I wouldn't: Carlo Gesualdo, Prince of Venosa ([c.] 1560-1613), had his wife assassinated, together with her lover. Without tolerating murder, I suggest that a collective devaluation of delinquents, as distinct from a complex assessment of what any individual delinquent has done and hasn't (with or without the help of his delinquency), would rather miss the point about Gesualdo.

For another thing, women, blacks and racial Jews were created by an act of God, whereas delinquents were created by an act of man: all they have in common is what we regard as misdeeds – something bad. Thus my friend's rhetorical question boomerangs: is his implication that the ladies who may not be shown this room are ladies because they have something undesirable in common? Or, if it isn't, what's the remaining point of his question?

Some of the most distinguished members of the Reform Club were questioned by my wife in my absence; she told them that I intended to write about this example of not-so-mini-apartheid. "I hope he will have second thoughts," was one reply. Another: "Isn't his reaction a little twisted and exaggerated, his plan a bit ill-conceived, ungracious?" But the most usual response we got from the members was the story about the 140-year-old Smoking Room, which is the original library – the implication being that the Club's segregation is, at worst, a lovable archaism. In fact, the nearest the cream moved towards agreeing with me was to be *amused* by this retention of what is, of course, obsolete – so why fuss?

Our society's time-honoured sense of humour can be a noxious defence – especially when we laugh at something serious without being able to make a good joke about it. Laughter does not prove humour; the successful demonstration of laughability does.

I rang a charming woman who moves a great deal in Reform Club circles. "Oh well, I just find it amusing; I've seen so much of this." "That's no answer. I asked you what you thought of it." Deep telephonic silence – then: "Come to think of it, it's a bit degrading." This remains the one reply I cherish. Please, gentle reformer, come to think of it.

III

Music and Psychology,
1946-52 (and after)

The Psychology of Opera

1 Three Psychoanalytic Notes *on* Peter Grimes

A performance at Sadler's Wells of Benjamin Britten's Peter Grimes *in early 1946 turned out for Keller to be an epiphany of major proportions, even though according to friends he claimed to have gone to it 'by mistake'. (The exact repertory of Sadler's Wells at this time is still a matter or research, though it is known that productions concurrent with* Grimes *included* La bohème, Madame Butterfly *and* Sir John in Love.*) Thereafter Keller proclaimed Britten as 'the greatest of all living composers whose music I understand', openly challenged those who resisted him, and increasingly wrote about music rather than psychology.*

At first, with the 'Three Psychoanalytic Notes on *Peter Grimes', Keller simply continued with the kind of work he had been doing with Margaret Phillips on the family as a model for small-group investigation (see Part II, above). For his* Notes *he was largely dependent on Montagu Slater's separately published libretto (London, Boosey and Hawkes, 1945), an annotated copy of which survives among his papers, and less on the text printed in Erwin Stein's vocal score (London, Boosey and Hawkes, 1945). However, in his discussion of 'Grimes and His Father' (Note III), he refers to a still earlier version of the Slater libretto. Here the text corresponds to the one set by Britten in the extant sketch of the opera and alluded to in Slater's essay 'The Story of the Opera' from* Benjamin Britten's Peter Grimes, *Sadler's Wells Opera Books, 3, London, John Lane (The Bodley Head), 1945, of which Keller owned a copy. (For a facsimile of the sketch see:* The Making of 'Peter Grimes', *I, Woodbridge (Suffolk), The Boydell Press, 1996.)*

For present-day convenience, the references in the Notes *below are given in the form found in Stein's vocal score; where there are discrepancies between this and the published Montagu Slater libretto, Slater's version has been added in small type below the extract, in the form [MS:]. In the third* Note, *it has been thought necessary at one point to include* both *versions of Slater* as well as *the version found in the Stein vocal score.*

I Grimes's Character

[This section comprises eleven pages of typescript of which the first seven are missing. These are likely to have included a general introduction to Benjamin Britten's opera (in 'Three Acts and a Prologue derived from the poem by George Crabbe' to a libretto by Montagu Slater based on a draft by Peter Pears and Britten himself). This introduction might not perhaps have been dissimilar to the opening (reprinted in the notes below) of Keller's later essay, '*Peter Grimes*: The Story; the Music not Excluded'; it would have had to include a description of 'anal character'; and it may have considered Peter's character in relation both to his parent-substitutes and the Borough, a 'small fishing town on the East Coast, towards 1830'. At this point in Keller's development it may or may not have included – as later essays of his almost certainly would have done – a philosophical, or aesthetic, reflection on what it means to use notions drawn from psychology (Life) in the analyis of opera (Art).

In classifying Peter Grimes (the man) as 'obsessional', and as an 'anal type', Keller drew on the psychoanalytic papers of Ernest Jones[1] and reinforced his findings by reference to J. C. Flugel, Edward Glover, and others. However a common source was Sigmund Freud's seminal essay on 'Character and Anal Eroticism' (1908).[2] According to this, the type is one in whom the characteristics of the 'anal' stage of early development persist into adult life. (Other schools of thought – the Kleinian, for example – maintain that all stages of development remain with adults as recoverable 'positions'.) Of the three early stages – the oral, the anal, and the genital (or phallic) – the anal occurs between the ages of two and four. It derives its name from the dichotomy between expulsion and retention of faeces on the one hand, and the symbolic value attributed to them on the other. In adult life, the type is recognized by a proclivity towards orderliness, parsimony, and obstinacy. Freud writes:

> 'Orderly' covers the notion of bodily cleanliness, as well as of conscientiousness in carrying out small duties and trustworthiness. Its opposite would be 'untidy' and 'neglectful'. Parsimony may appear in the exaggerated form of avarice; and obstinacy can go over into defiance, to which rage and revengefulness are easily joined. The latter two qualities – parsimony and obstinacy – are linked with each other more closely than they are with the first – with orderliness. They are, also, the more constant element of the whole complex. Yet it seems to me incontestable that all three in some way belong together.[3]

Jottings found in the archival papers show that Keller was aware of Karl Abraham's rider that, the anal type also exhibits a dichotomous sadism that seeks to destroy an object (person) but also to retain it in its control.[4] It follows that faeces may be gifts (money) which the type likewise wishes both to give and withhold.[5]

In the course of the *Notes*, Keller describes the orderliness of Peter's hut and his exaggerated avarice (Act II, Scene 2). But he is likely to have dwelt on Grimes's obstinacy during the lost opening pages, partly because at the beginning section of the third *Note* he refers back to remarks on the conflict between the individual and the community, and partly because Peter's 'chronic attitude of defiance', his 'angry outbursts' and 'sullen fractiousness', so prominent in the 'psychological exposition' of the first Act, were evidently described in some detail there.[6] As Keller put it elsewhere, 'Peter Grimes is the living conflict. His pride, ambition, and urge for independence fight with his need for love; his self-love battles with his self-hate.'

As we have observed, Peter's obstinacy is directed in two ways, to his parent-substitutes and to the Borough, which is both a closed 'community' of men and women and an 'association' of working fishermen. In the second and third of the *Notes* Ellen and Balstrode are described as 'Mother' and 'Father' to Peter, who perceives 'good' and 'bad' aspects in both. Indeed, the relationship 'mother', 'father' and 'son' is classically (and oedipally) triangular. At the end of Act I, Scene 1, when Peter has defiantly rejected the advice of Balstrode to shelter from the storm, crying 'take your advice – and put it where your money is', it is in thoughts of Ellen that he seeks refuge:

> What harbour shelters peace?
> Away from tidal waves, away from storm
> What harbour can embrace
> Terrors and tragedies?

However, it is consistent with Keller's joint investigations with Margaret Phillips that 'mother' and 'father' can also be traced through the drama in a more ramified way (see *From Community to Association* in Part II above). For example the Law and the Church (through their representatives) assume the super-ego functions of 'father', whereas (elemental) Nature in its beautiful and violent manifestations (as Keller notes) is 'mother' – when, that is, it is not a mirror of the violence (storm) within Peter, a violence between himself and his projected father (super-ego). Mrs. Sedley, on the other hand, is clearly a 'bad mother' to Peter – indeed, she is the agent of his downfall – whereas the prostitute figures, Auntie and the nieces, in company with Ellen, display a surprising 'good mother' aspect in the middle of Act II, as Keller explains in the second of the *Notes*.

Peter's obstinacy towards the Borough emerges from the outset, in the first part of the Prologue. In the court-room hearing into the death of the fisherman's apprentice, Grimes stands apart from Swallow's terse *con forza* through a leisurely sostenuto; he shows open antagonism towards 'interferers'; and he prolongs the proceedings by declaring through the hub-bub his determination to bring his accusers to trial and 'thrust into their mouths, the truth itself!' When, in the pub-scene (Act I, Scene 2) Grimes joins the round 'Old Joe has gone fishing', a round started by Balstrode to deflect a violent exchange between Grimes and Boles (the Methodist minister), Peter can neither sing the tune nor adopt the rhythm of the group: Keller might have seen this as a psychological 'development' of the Prologue. At the end of the scene the Borough reacts to the news that Peter will take his new apprentice 'home' to his hut with the cry, 'Do you call that home?' Home, of course, is the source of our integrated image of mother, father and child, and, in the words of D. W. Winnicott, the place we start from. It is the last place the Borough associates with Grimes. Indeed, the question brings into the open an attitude hitherto concealed, namely that the devil incarnate was in their midst. Keller continues:]

*

[Now we know from Freud that the devil is certainly nothing less than] a personification of repressed unconscious instinctual life. Thus when in [this scene] the chorus sings at the appearance of Peter –

> CHORUS   Talk of the devil and there he is
> And a devil he <u>is</u>, and a devil he <u>is</u>

– they are projecting their own repressed anal sadism onto him, and it is on account of this projection that Peter's manifest sadism is far stronger in the Borough's opinion than it is in reality.[7]

[Another aspect of Peter's character emerges in the next Act.] Though some members of the anal type are capable of 'exquisite tenderness, especially with children,' 'a curious accompaniment of this tenderness is a very pronounced tendency to domineer the loved (and possessed) object . . .'[8] Thus Peter, in Act II, Scene 1 [he summons the apprentice who has been sitting in the sun with Ellen]:

> PETER   Come boy!
> ELLEN   Peter, what for?

PETER   I've seen a shoal, I need his help.
ELLEN   But if there were, then all the boats
              Would fast be launching.
PETER   I can see the shoals to which the rest are blind.
ELLEN   This is Sunday, his day of rest . . .
PETER   This is whatever day I say it is! Come boy! [Come boy!]

[MS: I can find the shoals]

And now note Peter's culminant [response. When Ellen reminds him of his 'bargain' that the boy should have 'his weekly rest', both of them having fished 'night and day without a break', he answers rudely:

PETER   He works for me, leave him alone, he's mine!]

From the above, as well as from Ellen's words following now –

ELLEN   [Hush,] Peter.
              This unrelenting work,
              This grey, unresting industry . . .

[MS: Peter, your unrelenting work]

One can gather that 'on occasion [he] will get through absolutely enormous masses of work,'[9] that his is a 'dogged persistence, and concentration, with a passion for thoroughness and completeness.'[10] At the same time, in the exclamation about the shoals, there is apparent 'the conviction that no one else can do the thing in question as well as [he] himself, and that no one else can be relied upon to do it properly.'[11]

Fish being the centre of Grimes's activities, it might be pointed out in passing that hoarding and collecting generally, as also in particular food hoarding, has anal roots. (When he intends to sell his treasures, his purpose is, of course, to exchange one copro-symbol for another, still stronger one. Further, the interest in things that are underground and in some way concealed is likewise anal.)[12]

Ellen would, of course, as Balstrode has pointed out, take Peter without his 'booty' [Act I, Scene 1], but apart from his other anal intentions regarding these copro-symbols, the latter are for him the *sine qua non* of wooing. As 'presents' for Ellen, they dominate his love life.[13]

The exposition of Peter Grimes's character ends in the first part of Act II, Scene 1. What follows, with a single exception, is 'development' and 'recapitulation' of 'anal material' previously stated. Thus we need not concern ourselves with these later parts in the present section, but it may be useful to point out that much of what has been touched upon in the earlier part of the opera (and at the same time in the above argument) receives ever-deepening support as the work unfolds itself.

However, something must be said about the above-mentioned exception, i.e. the introduction of some new characterological material at a later point.

When contemplating an abstract-musical work, one or the other reader may have encountered some seemingly surprising new matter appearing at a stage of a movement where according to its form he wouldn't have expected anything new cropping up. But on second thoughts he may have realized that this apparently new matter, though not previously stated, was really an inevitable logical consequence of earlier material, [and] was not really new therefore, in that it was implied in the old.[14]

Peter's 'new' character trait appears in his absence at the end of Act II, after his second apprentice has met his fate. The Rector and Swallow, on entering Grimes's hut, are greatly surprised about its condition:

RECTOR   Yet his hut is reasonably kept,
                Here's order, here's skill.

(Swallow draws the moral:)

SWALLOW   The whole affair gives Boro' talk
                Its – shall I say – quietus?
                Here we come pell-mell, expecting
                To find out – we know not what.
                But – all we find is a neat and empty hut.
                Gentlemen, take this to your wives:
                Less interference in our private lives.

Now the listener may be less surprised about the neatness and order in Peter's hut than the Rector and Swallow are (amongst other things because he knows Grimes better than they); yet, if we cast a correct suspicion upon him, orderliness is not exactly an attribute of Peter's that he would have expected as a matter of course. If, however, he has received some elementary psychoanalytic information, he knows that orderliness is a very essential anal feature.[15] Thus, a seemingly new little piece of characterization resolves into an implication of what has previously been brought forth.

II Grimes and His Mother

It may be quite a great fortune that in the origin of *Peter Grimes* was involved an intense feeling of nostalgia on the part of the composer.[1] For in this way he may have helped in drawing upon deep unconscious resources of phantasy, resources which all of us harbour, but which the less gifted among us can only use for more modest purposes.

Whether there is something in this view or not, it seems to me that wherever, in the course of the opera, the music is at its deepest, it is linked with 'home' or with what has an intimate psychological connection with 'home'.

With this we leave Benjamin Britten and turn again to Peter Grimes.[2] In the foregoing section some allusion has been made to Grimes's personality (an obsessional one) being – in [Edward] Glover's words – 'profoundly divided against itself'.[3] This fact is mirrored by his ambivalence towards external objects, as also by 'constantly recurring and swift alternations of feeling', and particularly by 'alternating states of attraction and repulsion' [towards] Ellen.[4] Each of these points is of course unmistakably brought out in the opera.

In his relation to Ellen he is repeating his attitude to his mother.[5] The positive (love) part of his ambivalence towards the latter is connected with feelings and ideas which are treated in the opera with the insight of tremendous intensity; the present section is mainly devoted to a short survey of these feelings and ideas as they manifest themselves in the work.

There is no doubt that Ellen is a mother figure. In fact, she says so herself [in Act II, Scene 1]:

ELLEN   They [the men] are children when they weep,
                We are mothers when they strive

> Schooling our own hearts to keep
> The bitter treasure of their love.

[MS: Men are children when they strive/We are mothers when they weep/Schooling our hearts to keep/The bitter treasure of their love.]

'We', in the present connection, are Ellen and three prostitute figures, i.e. Auntie and the Two Nieces who sing together after the men have left for Grimes's hut. This singing together, in consent with one another, occurs most naturally: a magnificent piece of work in view of the radically contrary significance of 'mother' and 'prostitute' in the conscious mind on the one hand, and the intimate connection between these ideas in the unconscious on the other hand.[6]

Ellen's mother-significance is not only obviously, but also subtly indicated, e.g. by her being a schoolmistress.[7] In what was apparently a previous version of the libretto, Ellen's first words to Peter (in the impressive, at first polytonic, senza misura recitative) were "Peter, come home!".[8] For this was substituted '. . . come away!' (perhaps because the latter is, superficially, more logical). However, Ellen's 'homely' significance to Peter goes right through the opera (its exposition finishing, incidentally, in the same scene where the characterological exposition ends).

Ellen, as 'mother' and 'home', emerges as the meeting place of Peter's deep phantasies that are concerned with *birth, pre-natal life, rebirth, and death*.[9] As psychoanalytic research has shown, these phantasies are closely interrelated.

In the recitative referred to above there are already hints as to Ellen's role both as place of rest and as originator of a new life on Peter's part. After Balstrode has left [Peter] in the storm (Act I, Scene 1), the extract quoted in section I ('what harbour shelters peace?') is sung, its continuation being:[10]

PETER   With her there'll be no quarrels,
         With her the mood will stay,
         Her breast is harbour too
         Where night is turned to day.

[MS: This time the mood will stay]

It could, of course, be said that this refers to an early post-natal state and is not anything of an intra-uterine phantasy. If only, however, because of the intimate associations of this passionate statement with death and rebirth, I, for one, do not doubt that ideas of life in the womb are here involved.[11] Thus seen, the above statement expresses, *inter alia*, Peter's desire to return to the womb, a desire, that is to say, 'to escape from the troubles, labours, anxieties, and excitements of the world' ('away from tidal waves, away from storms [. . .] terrors and tragedies') 'to a place where there is rest and peace' ('What harbour shelters peace?').[12] Further along the lines of this interpretation, the passage about the breast where night is turned to day can be taken as symbolising rebirth. The association of rebirth with a previous return to, and a brief sojourn in, the mother's womb has frequently been observed.[13]

Turning to the music of this passage, we note that it re-uses, in major, material of Peter's narrating, to Balstrode [earlier in Act I, Scene 1], the circumstances in which his first apprentice died:

PETER   We strained into the wind
         Heavily laden.
         We plunged into the waves'

> Shuddering challenge.
> Then the sea rose to a storm
> Over the gunwales,
> And the boy's silent reproach
> Turned to illness.
> Then home among fishing nets,
> Alone, alone, alone
> With a childish death.

[MS: Then the child's silent reproach]

In this passage, in the plunging into the sea, one senses something of both return to the womb and (re)birth. For the sea is a mother symbol,[14] and plunging into it does not only mean plunging into it, but also, by dint of the unconscious process of inversion, emerging from it (with apologies to the conscious layers of the mind).[15] And emerging from it means birth.[16]

Further, the 'childish death' may as such have rebirth significance, for in order to be reborn one must first become a child and 'die' (return to the womb).[17] Peter seems to identify himself strongly with the child; doubts about this are dispersed in view of his later attitudes to the Second Apprentice when the latter, too, is dead (see below).

Thus the present instance appears to be one in which operate identifications of life before birth with life after death, and of the process of birth with that of death,[18] though it is true that more obvious support for this assumption only appears later in the opera.

In the 'shuddering' and stormy aspects of the sea which do not only appear in the above-quoted passage but also in what is more purely Peter's effusion of phantasy, can perhaps be detected the negative part of the ambivalence towards the mother. This negative part would also furnish motive-power for Peter's desire for rebirth which, among other things, 'would naturally seem to give expression to the tendency [. . .] to emancipate himself from the [. . .] mother.'[19] Manifestations of this tendency, obvious in his behaviour towards Ellen, are in accordance with his character as depicted above [in section I].

Musical material of the two excerpts last discussed is reused at Grimes's entry into the pub (Act I, Scene 2), after the storm-chord has announced him, and before he starts on his arioso phantasy.[20] This monologue, in which the mother figures as the earth, develops into an overwhelming phantasy of rebirth:[21]

PETER   But if the horoscope's bewildering,
           Like a flashing turmoil of a shoal of herring[,]
           Who, who, who, who, who,
               can turn skies back and begin again?

[MS: Like flashing turmoil]

In Peter's hut monologue (Act II, Scene 2) the earth once more appears as mother-symbol, viz. in an anxiety reaction (caused by Peter's hostility to, and fear of, the father – see [section] III below) to an intra-uterine phantasy:

PETER   But dreaming builds what dreaming can disown.
           Dead fingers stretch themselves to tear it down.
           I hear those voices that will not be drowned
           Calling, there is no stone
           In earth's thickness to make a home,

That you can build with and remain alone.

[MS: But thinking builds what thinking can disown./Dead fingers are stretched out to tear it down./I hear those voices that will not be drowned/Calling, there is no peace, there is no stone/In the earth's thickness to make you a home,/That you can build with and remain alone.]

Rather than discuss the interlude preceding this scene anew from my – as it might seem, prejudiced – point of view, I would like to refer the reader to Edward Sackville-West's analysis of it, every point of which supports contentions in the present [study].[22] This analysis also contains a reference to Grimes's identification with his apprentice. It does not psychologically matter very much whether or not one distinguishes between his identification with the First and that with the Second Apprentice, since he identifies these two with one another in their turn, their relation to him being parallel.

In his hallucination in the present scene, Peter again offers a sign of his identification with the dead apprentice (cf. his 'confession' to Balstrode cited above):

(addressing the dead boy)

PETER   You'll soon be home!
             In harbour still and deep.

(According to [the] earlier version [of Montagu Slater, Peter says] 'We'll soon be home! [In harbour calm and deep.]')

Peter seems to allude here to his own approaching and his hoped-for return to the womb. Like other predictions, this partly accurate premonition springs from deep desire. The wish is not only father to the thought, but also, under certain circumstances, to reality.

During the interlude before the last scene of the work, 'a thick fog creeps in from the sea and swathes the town', producing a 'fuliginous blackness which matches that of [Grimes's] own soul.'[23] In other words, there is an intense deathly and uterine atmosphere around and in Peter; it is not only night, but the 'fog from the sea' [that] makes the situation still darker.[24] 'Grimes, weary in body and half-demented, makes his way back to the harbour and his boat – the only refuge he has left from the torment of his guilt.'[25] To vary Edith Sitwell, he is 'heavy with Death, as a woman is heavy with child',[26] being heavy with two 'childish deaths' [as he confesses to Balstrode in Act I, Scene 1] and wanting the woman to be heavy, not only with children, but with himself: he 'with the other young who were born from darkness' [is] 'returning to darkness'. (The boat is of course often closely associated with return to the womb, death and birth.)[27] In this fascinating interlude which precedes the final scene, the material first used in Peter's telling Balstrode of his first apprentice's death is used twice, it being interrupted the first time by a fragment of the music connected with the rebirth-phantasy in the hut (see above, Act II, Scene 2) and preceded and followed by other reminiscences.[28]

The constant dominant seventh on D [which is introduced as the goal of the interlude and pervades Scene 2] [sounds] like an indication of Peter's unalterable fate;[29] I have not the courage to link it more specifically with the mother, there being not sufficient evidence for this. (Add to this that I am of course already deeply prejudiced in favour of my interpretation, and that my whole emotional approach to music is not such as to make extra-musical associations particularly easy for me.) But the following two points about this dominant seventh merit at least passing interest:

1   Edward Sackville-West likens it first to 'a watery moon', and then to 'a force of
     Nature'. He thus brings forth three ideas standing for, or associated with, mother: the
     moon, water, nature.[30]

2   When the chord is taken from the muted horns by the chorus, only the females sing it.

In any case, this chord is a reminder of what should perhaps be clear enough without it, i.e.
that this interlude is not merely retrospective and referring to the present, but also prospective
– as are more extensive reminiscences of Grimes's in the scene that now follows.

This last recitative of Grimes's could almost pass without comment, so obviously does it
illustrate our interpretations:

PETER   Steady! There you are! Nearly home!
                   What is home? Calm as deep water.
                   Where's my home? Deep in calm water.
                   Water will drink my sorrows dry,
                   And the tide will turn . . .
                          . . .
                   The first one died, just died.
                   The other slipped, and died . . .
                   [And the third will . . .][31]

[The MS published libretto does <u>not</u> include the final line, although Britten's sketch, using an earlier MS
version, does.]

Now follows an open identification of Peter's with the boys, in relation to these intra-
uterine, death, and rebirth phantasies:

                   Water will drink his sorrows . . .
                                 my sorrows dry,
                   And the tide will turn.

Later, rebirth comes to the fore, indeed, receives in some respects unprecedented stress:

[*(Peter answers the chorus's calls for 'Peter Grimes')*

                   Here you are! Here I am!
                   Hurry, hurry, hurry, hurry, hurry!
                   Now is gossip put on trial
                   Bring the branding iron and knife
                   For what's done now is done for life . . .
                   "Turn the skies back and begin again."

[MS: bring the branding iron, the Knife]]

[Next there is] an ambivalent phantasy on, or rather to, Ellen [culminating in a distorted
recollection of his words, 'God have mercy upon me', his parting shot after striking Ellen in
Act II, Scene 1. Now the cry redirects the plea from humans to God ('to hell with all your

mercy!'); we note that in the earlier version, Grimes at this point cries 'to hell with all your money!', thereby retreating from his, and the Borough's, anal concerns:

> Ellen! Ellen! Give me your hand, your hand.
> There now my hope is held by you . . .
> If you leave me alone, if you . . .
> Take away your hand!
> The argument's finished, friendship lost,
> gossip is shouting, ev'rything's said . . .
> To hell with all your mercy!
> To hell with your revenge!
> And God have mercy upon you!]

[MS: There now – my hope is held by you,/ If you take it away . . ./Take away your hand . . ./The argument's finished/Friendship is lost/Gossip is shouting/Everything's said/ To hell with all your money/to hell with your revenge./And God have mercy upon you.]

[This] is followed by his last words before he roars back [his name] at the 'shouters':

> Do you hear them all shouting my name?
> D'you hear them? D'you hear them?
> Old Davy Jones shall answer:
> Come home! Come home! Come home! Come home!
>   Come home!

[MS: will answer]

As [Peter's] end draws near, his two principal mother-substitutes, Ellen and the sea, draw nearer together. Ellen and Balstrode come in while he is still singing 'Peter Grimes! Peter Grimes!' [repeatedly] in reply to the chorus; after he has calmed [down, Ellen] addresses him:

ELLEN   Peter,
         We've come to take you home.
         O come home out of this dreadful night!

Peter does not notice her though he needs her urgently: what he needs of her now is but the mother imago, and that he has inside himself. Thus he starts on his last words before he dies, his last reminiscence, the music (the only vocal dolcissimo in the opera) reverting to previous occasions where his phantasies were touched:

PETER   What harbour shelters peace,
         Away from tidal waves,
         Away from storms!
         What harbour can embrace
         Terrors and tragedies.
         Her breast is harbour too
         Where night is turned to day.

[MS: can embrace/This day[']s fair promises.]

This passage does not include the words –

> With her there'll be no quarrels,
> With her the mood will stay.

[MS: This time the mood will stay]

– which occur in the original version ([i.e. from] Act I, end of Scene 1), perhaps because these apply to Ellen as partner in life rather than to Ellen as womb, or as [an] element in the mother image relating to a very early phase of Peter's life (breast).

The idea of 'harbour' is perhaps in need of some comment. 'Harbour' involves 'away from tidal waves', away from the sea. But did not Peter just say that his home was 'deep in the calm water', that 'water would drink his sorrows dry,' does he not sail out before he actually dies?

Most probably the process of inversion, so often met with in phantasies of birth, death, and womb-life, is here at work, in the same way as when the island, instead of the water surrounding it, is used as womb symbol.[32] The stormy aspects of the sea, contrasted with the harbour's peacefulness, together with the association harbour-breast, facilitates this inversion.

After Peter has finished, Balstrode tells him to sail out and sink the boat. This time Peter does notice what is said to him: both the voice of his conscience and his instinctual urges welcome this last push in a direction in which they themselves were pointing. (This does not mean, of course, that he would have found himself in the same endo-psychic situation under different social circumstances.)

[The following] stage direction, *Balstrode leads Peter down to his boat, and helps him push it out*, [recalls the practice whereby]

> in many places the dead have been [. . .] deposited (like King Arthur) in boats and pushed out to sea. In this [. . .] practice we may probably trace the influence of an identification of the process of death with that of birth – the conception that at death we pass away by the same road that we traversed when we entered life at birth [. . .] A similar identification is chiefly responsible for the belief that the dead pass across a lake or river on the way to their new home (cf. Lethe, Styx, and Acheron in classical mythology or [the river across which Christian passes to the Celestial City in *Pilgrim's Progess*]).[33]

'Night is turned to day' as Peter makes his end meet him, (*dawn slowly begins*), a profound death in more than one sense of the hackneyed word.

The opera finishes with the chorus directly quoting Crabbe. This last phase of the work is not just a brilliant cold contrast to what happened before. Crabbe's words deal with

> CHORUS   [. . .] houses sleeping by the waterside
> [Waking] to the measured ripple of the tide.

[MS: Wake]

[or] with a

> [. . .] hollow sound that from the passing bell
> To some departed spirits bids farewell.

[MS: spirit]

The closing verse being –

> In ceaseless motion comes and goes the tide,
> Flowing it fills the channel broad and wide,
> Than back to sea with strong majestic sweep
> It rolls in ebb yet terrible and deep.[34]

[MS: vast and wide]

[Peter Pears recalls:] 'It was [Crabbe's picture of 'the whole life of a Suffolk fishing port'] with the sea behind it all which suggested to the composer an opera.'[35]

Thank heaven for the suggestion.

III *Grimes and His Father*

Pears's last-quoted sentence continues thus: 'which suggested to the composer an opera based on the conflict between society and the individual – a conflict implict in many of Crabbe's stories.' [It is] a conflict implicit in Grimes's character ([as described] above [in section I] [and at the end of the Preface]) and his Oedipus complex, part of which was of course involved in what was said [in] section II. J. C. Flugel writes:

> There can be little doubt that much of the general resistance to, and intolerance of, authority [. . .] derives its motive power from a persistence in the unconscious of parent hatreds of this [displaced] kind [. . .] the still existing desire to resist the authority of the parents [finds] outlet in a displaced form in infringements of the laws, conventions, or regulations imposed by the authority of society.[1]

And now compare:

> [Grimes] is very much of an ordinary weak person who, being at odds with the society in which he finds himself, tries to overcome it and, in doing so, offends against the conventional code, is classed by society as a criminal, and destroyed as such.[2]

Pears rightly suggests that if Grimes had lived in a city, he might have become a revolutionary.

The anti-parental tendencies which so powerfully contribute to a hostile attitude to conventional society are of course to a large extent made up of anti-paternal impulses,[3] firstly because, in childhood, rebellious impulses are more strongly excited in regard to the authority of the father than in regard to what is felt to be the less stringent and more immediately loving rule of the mother;[4] and secondly, in the case of the male child, because what is called the 'simple' or 'positive' Oedipus complex (which is normally stronger than the 'negative' Oedipus complex)[5] involves a tender attitude towards the mother and a jealous-hostile one towards the father.

As may be gathered from [section II] above, Grimes's Oedipus complex is very strong (unresolved), its positive part being abundantly manifest in the expression of his overcharged love drives towards objects representing the mother. Parallel to this marked mother-love runs his equally pronounced father-hatred. This does not merely show in his attitude towards society, but also, as will be presently seen, in a more direct way, i.e. towards more individual father substitutes.

One of the worst possible fathers within this dramatic context would of course have been Ellen's husband; but he is wisely dead, there being enough Oedipus problems without him. But, to be a little fanciful, Ellen is not Peter's only 'widowed' parent. We can also speak of Balstrode, an obvious father figure, as a 'widower', or, more exactly, as being divorced from Peter's 'mother', i.e. the sea: for Captain Balstrode is a retired merchant skipper.

Continuing a trifle more soberly, Balstrode's captainship is among the subtle indications of his position in loco parentis[6] in the same way as Ellen's profession indicates her parental significance ([see section] II above), and the fact that he is a *retired* captain, thus no longer being in a position of exercising authority, (a position that is liable to draw upon the individual occupying it a good deal of displaced parent-hatred,)[7] may well make him a little less of the stern father, a little more grandpa-ish in Peter's eyes, so suspicious of established conventional authority. Indeed, Balstrode makes quite generally the impression of being a retired father to Peter, retired, that is to say, from much of the father's bent towards ruling and dominating the son (substitute). In that way he establishes himself as a fairly 'good' father to Peter, as distinct from, and compared with, say, the 'Borough'.

In the last scene of the opera, however, Balstrode for once assumes full power, not to say omnipotence, by telling Peter to kill himself. But being a 'good' father, he releases his well-meaning murderous impulses towards the son at a time when the son manifests an unfair amount of self-murderous impulses, anyway. This last scene at the same time establishes Balstrode's fatherly role rather openly, for who else, apart from a father, will successfully give the advice, 'Now be a good boy and drown yourself'? True, this advice is, as we have said in section II, the last push in a predetermined direction, but coming from another person it would have been a counter-push.

Turning from such omnipotence as we may grant to Balstrode to his paternal omniscience, we find him endowed with a dose of it that is usually only reserved for the storyteller (and receiver). Thus he prophesies (in Act I, Scene 1):

BALSTRODE   Then the old tragedy
             Is in store [:]
             New start with new 'prentice
             Just as before!

Ellen is not so pessimistic, not only because less omniscience is attributed to her as a mother than is to the father, but also because, owing to the Oedipus complex, the father rather than the mother is interested in the son's tragedy.

A second instance of paternal omniscience is furnished when, in Act II, Scene 2, after the apprentice has fallen down the cliff and the Rector, Swallow, [and others] have fruitlessly examined the hut,

> *they all leave – except Balstrode who hesitates, looks round the hut, sees the boy's [Sunday] clothes lying around, examines them, [then goes to the path door to shut it. Balstrode goes up through the cliff door, looks out, and hurriedly climbs down the way Peter and the Boy went.]*[8]

> [MS: *THEY ALL GO OUT – all save Balstrode who has come in late who goes to the cliff side door, looks down, then closes it carefully.*]

Balstrode's paternal protection of Peter against what corresponds to the extra-familial hostile world in childhood is well brought out in [the later version of] Act I, Scene 1:

PETER (*off*)   Hi! Give us a hand!

(*Everyone stops working. G. P. [General Pause]*)

PETER   Haul the boat!

(*Nobody helps him.*)

BOLES   Haul it yourself, Grimes!

(*G. P.*)

PETER   Hi! Somebody bring the rope!

(*Peter appears, and takes a rope from the capstan to his boat, still out of sight. Balstrode and Keene move to the capstan and start pushing it round.*)

BALSTRODE   I'll give a hand, the tide is near the turn.

[MS: BOLES (*shouts back*) Haul it yourself, Grimes!   PETER (*off*) Somebody bring the rope.
*Nobody does. Presently he appears and takes the capstan rope himself and pulls it after him (*off*) to the boat. Then he returns. The FISHERMEN and WOMEN turn their backs on him and slouch away awkwardly.*]

Or, in Peter's absence, in Act II, Scene 1:

BOLES   While you worshipped idols there,
                  The Devil had his Sabbath here!
MRS. SEDLEY   . Maltreating that poor boy again!
BALSTRODE   Grimes is weatherwise and skilled
                  In the practice of his trade.
                  Let him be. Let us forget
                  What slander can invent!

And [similarly] during what follows.

But a more direct reminder of Balstrode's ('good') paternality emerges during the very scene when he also excites Peter's father-regarding hostility. This is in Act I, Scene 1, a scene which now for the third time appears to contain the end of a psychological exposition ([as described in sections] I and II above), this time that of Peter's relation to the father (substitutes).

This dialogue between Peter and Balstrode opens with the latter's offering a piece of fatherly advice:

BALSTRODE   Grimes, since you're a lonely soul,
                  Born to blocks, and spars and ropes
                  Why not try the wider sea,
                  With merchantman, or privateer?

[MS: Grimes, since you're a lonely soul/Born to block and spars and rope/Why not try the wider sea/With merchantman or privateer?]

which remains duly unappreciated by Peter. Not that this advice, to dive into Balstrode's unconscious, need be all love; we may detect a wish on his part to have Peter out of the way. After all, Balstrode's last and somewhat more radical advice (at the end of the opera), one against which Ellen protests, can be interpreted in the same way, in which case it is not without fundamental significance that this advice is pronounced after Balstrode has come in with Ellen, and before he 'takes [her] by the arm, and leads her away.' [MS: He takes ELLEN who is sobbing quietly, calms her and leads her carefully down the main street home.] The feelings of three persons are needed to make an oedipal situation.

However, throughout the upper layers of Balstrode's mind there is much friendliness towards Peter who, as the above mentioned dialogue between him and Balstrode continues, is soon confronted with a welcome piece of 'good' paternality.

> BALSTRODE   Your boy was workhouse starved;
> Maybe you're not to blame he died.

The psychotherapeutic function of this abstention from condemnation on Balstrode's part becomes immediately apparent, for Peter, reacting to these words of Balstrode's with some measure of positive transference, loses his reticence (more exactly: anal retention) for a while and discharges his confessional recollective fantasy on the First Apprentice's death ([as described in section] II above).

This is followed, after Balstrode has offered some further reassurance ['This storm is useful; you can speak your mind and never mind the Borough comment'ry' – MS: never fear], by a renewed outpouring of phantasy, predictive now (see [section I, note 12]).

But as soon as Balstrode assumes a more active paternal role and utters his omniscient, pessimistic opinion on what will happen if Peter will not listen to his advice ['then the old tragedy is in store. New start with new 'prentice just as before'], Peter manifests his hostility against what has so far been the 'good' father:[9] 'the wind has now risen to a gale height and the two men shout angrily against it.' As we have said [in section I], the storm outside Peter represents in part the storm inside Peter; and the storm inside Peter is in part a storm between him and his father (super-ego) whose external representative is again the stormy Balstrode. This last part of the dialogue clearly shows that Peter cannot tolerate a father-figure for long, not even one that he deems, at times, 'good'.

After Balstrode has left Peter, the latter again starts on a predictive phantasy, whose oedipal significance is not far to seek [cf. the introduction to section I, and section II:

> PETER   With her there'll be no quarrels
> With her the mood will stay
> A harbour evermore
> Where night is turned to day

[MS: This time the mood will stay,/Her breast is harbour too/Where night is turned to day.]]

Being thus in possession of a rough picture of some of the consequences of Peter's unusually active Oedipus complex, we are perhaps entitled to turn to two other individual father substitutes beside Balstrode, individuals whose fatherly significance is not at all apparent on first sight, but towards whom Peter manifests his oedipal ambivalence rather strikingly. These two father figures are his two apprentices.

Now since this may seem a psychoanalytic somersault too much even for the reader who has readily listened to our consideration so far, one or two words are needed to explain why one is justified in regarding a son (substitute) as a father (substitute).

To be sure, the somersault is there, but it happens spontaneously in the mind and we cannot blame the father of psychoanalysis for discovering it. The desire to be one's father's father, or one's mother's mother, is not one that altogether depends on psychoanalysis for being brought to light: one can detect it by means of ordinary observation.[10] In what is called the 'reversal of generations phantasy',[11] the child entertains the belief that as he grows bigger his parents grow smaller until eventually the reversed relation between him and his parents is established.

This phantasy serves

> as a means whereby an individual may identify his children with his parents and then direct upon the former the hostile emotions aroused in connection with the latter.[12]

The individual's oedipal wishes rouse fear of punishment proceeding from his father, and this very Oedipus complex makes the individual fear that his child may deal with him as he wants (wanted) to deal with his father ('fear of retaliation'). These 'two trends of feeling find their expression in the belief that the child is none other than the father whose revenge is feared [. . .] the child is his own resurrected grandfather.'[13]

Before we pass on to consider Peter's relation to his apprentices in the light of this knowledge, we may note in passing that the identification of the child with his grandfather (one of 'very frequent occurrence and considerable significance')[14] may easily contribute to the attractiveness, for Peter, of what we assume to be Balstrode's grandfatherly aspects ([as described] above), and also that this identification involves the idea of rebirth (of the grandfather in the grandchild), an idea which, as we have seen ([in section] II above) receives both extensive and intensive treatment throughout the opera.[15]

The best means of immediately showing now that when we associate, in Peter's mind, his apprentices (children substitutes) with his father we are not forcing our ideas upon the drama, is to inspect a passage which occurs in a former version of the libretto [prior, even, to Slater's published version] [but] has been omitted from the opera.[16] It is a passage from Peter's hut-monologue (Act II, Scene 2; see [section] II above), contained in what we anticipatorily called Peter's anxiety reaction in regard to the father. The latter is here identified with the first apprentice and is clearly threatening Peter's Oedipus wishes:

PETER   But thinking builds what thinking can disown.
    Dead fingers are stretched out to tear it down.
    I hear my father and the one that drowned
    Calling, there is no peace, there is no stone,
    In the earth's thickness to make you a home,
    That you can build with and remain alone.

(He stops. The boy watches him in fascinated horror: and Peter turns on him suddenly.)

    Sometimes I see two devils in this hut;
    They're here now by the cramp in my heart –
    My father and the boy I had
    As 'prentice until you arrived.[17]
    They sit there and their faces shine like flesh.
    Their mouths are open but I close my ears.

[MS published version: (*Line 3*) I hear those voices that will not be drowned. (*Line 7*) Sometimes I see a face here in this hut. It's there now, I can see it, it is there/His eyes are on me as they were that evil day. [The last two lines are omitted.]]
[Erwin Stein vocal score: (*Line 3*) I hear those voices that will not be drowned. (*Line 7*) Sometimes I see that boy here in this hut. He's there now – I can see him – he is there! His eyes are on me as they were that evil day.]

If a psychoanalytic observer had only known the final [i.e. published] version [of Montagu Slater's libretto] in which 'I hear those voices that will not be drowned' is substituted for 'I hear my father and the one who drowned' and in which the other reference to the father is omitted, he ought yet to have little difficulty, in view of the whole drama, in identifying the 'voices' as coming from the dead boy and the father at once. But he would have been reproached with giving free reign to his own phantasies.

Against what we have so far said, this whole passage explains itself, except for one indirect reference to the identification between apprentice and father, i.e. the two devils. Jones, in his penetrating investigation into the significance of the Devil,[18] comes to the conclusion that the latter may personify both the Father and the Son,[19] and that the 'prime aspect of the Devil' is 'the Son who defies the Father', the 'Arch-rebel'.[20] This well accords with what is probable in the case of Peter's devils. For they are not merely father and grandson to Peter, but also, in two ways, father and son:

1   As previously noted, Peter strongly identifies himself with the apprentice(s). Thereby they become himself (the Arch-rebel) his father's son(s).

2   He also identifies himself with (plays, as it were, at being) his father, manifesting in his attitude towards his apprentices the attitude of his own father (as he unconsciously imagines it) towards himself. This is a natural consequence of his Oedipus complex, involving as this does the desire to usurp the father's position. Through this identification his sons become again his father's sons.

To be sure, the reader cannot be blamed if he feels somewhat Groddecky during such considerations,[21] but we are none the worse off for such feelings. The translation of such mental processes as we are now examining into our language makes them appear more complicated than they really are, but if we are ready to take them into account we are always eventually rewarded by greater insight.

Thus Peter's behaviour towards his apprentices becomes clear to us, now that we know them to be his sons, his father, and his father's sons (himself).[22] We need not waste time on going into the love part of his attitude towards them, for there is too much in this respect that must now be self-evident. But it may be worthwhile to go into one or two implications of the hate-aspect of his emotions towards the boys.

Peter Pears (who indeed throws the boy quite a bit about the stage) points to the fact that 'Grimes was undoubtedly a harsh master',[23] and Edward Sackville-West accuses him of manslaughter.[24] To quote Reik (not, of course, on *Peter Grimes*):

We see [. . .] why he kills the child; he carries out once more the impulse of hate towards the deceased father, he kills once more his own father in the child.[25]

In being harsh to the boy(s), [Grimes] at once imitates and fights the father, and on top of it he fights himself in the boys. When he has no more boys to fight himself in, he fights (kills) himself more directly.

But we must at once qualify Peter's 'killing'. He is not, of course, a murderer;[26] as a matter of fact he is not altogether a self-murderer. Indeed the causation of the three deaths that are involved in the drama is something of a complicated matter.

Let us consider in what respects there are parallel elements in them:

1   They all happen as between Father and Son; Grimes and the apprentices on the one hand, Balstrode and Grimes on the other.
2   The manifest father figure is always involved in the son's death, without actually being guilty of it.
3   In view of the identification between an individual's father and son it can also be said that there are not just three sons' [deaths], but also three fathers', the sons being the guiltless killers.

The most satisfactory solution as to the causation of the two deaths that happen in the opera would seem to be [this].[27] The boy's death – his slipping down the cliff – is a large-scale parapraxis – i.e. an unconscious suicide, coinciding with the realization of over-determined (fatherly and sonly) unconscious death-wishes of Peter's. The boy's 'nemesis' ([to use the term] of Rosenzweig and Flugel)[28] implied in this hypothetical suicide can be accounted for by the circumstances in which he grew up, as well as by the treatment he receives from Peter's hands, and this nemesism finds expression in the boy's perpetual silence.

[Moreover,] Peter's death is a conscious suicide assisted by an unconscious 'murder' on Balstrode's part. Peter's nemesism (strongly moralized), which furnishes one of the identificatory links between him and the boy, is also related to his ill-treatment of the latter, for he is 'substituting punishment of others' (especially others-regarded-as-self) 'for unconscious self-punishment.'[29] Eventually, self-punishment gains the upper hand. Balstrode's suicide order meets Peter's need for punishment when this has developed to a high pitch. Thus, when earlier in the opera [Act I, Scene 1] Peter angrily shouts at Balstrode, 'Are you my conscience?', he but expresses his knowledge that Balstrode is, after all, the man on to whom his super-ego is liable to be projected. Expressed aphoristically, Peter, after having been twice involved in the father's death, finally welcomes the father's order to die in his turn.

It remains to draw attention to the fact that Benjamin Britten has once more proved his admirably productive empathy regarding such phenomena as need for punishment, nemesism, rebirth- and death-phantasies in his deeply conceived, and, accordingly, deeply moving, settings of *The Holy Sonnets of John Donne*.[30]

NOTES

Source

Incomplete typescript, with the first seven pages missing as indicated, dating from February/May 1946. It was published as a 52-page monograph, edited by Christopher Wintle, through the Institute of Advanced Musical Studies, King's College London, in association with the Britten-Pears Library, Aldeburgh, Suffolk, in 1995 (ISBN 1-897747-02-0). At the time thanks were extended (and are hereby renewed) to Donald Mitchell and Paul Banks (Britten-Pears Library), Barbara Diana, Madeleine Ladell, and Wendy Pank (King's College London), and Paula Lavis (British Psychoanalytical Society). The volume included the essay, printed in part II above, 'The Need for Pets', which also addresses the idea of 'reversal' raised in the third of the *Notes*. (Also included were the essays 'Self-knowledge' and 'Religion: the Psychoanalytic Standpoint' reproduced in Part II above.) The texts have been newly edited for this volume, and take into account recent research into the *Peter Grimes* libretto from the Britten-Pears Library, Aldeburgh.

Keller's typescript for the *Notes* included the following Postscript:

Open Letter to the Authors of Peter Grimes

(among whom I include Peter Pears who, besides having been associated with the work before its first bar was written, is a reproductive genius of exceptional calibre, with a distinct accent on 'productive'.)

Dear Authors,

A man comes up to you and says: "You've wasted your time on *Peter Grimes*. The text is nonsense, and the music is just a lot of noise." What will you reply? Perhaps something of this sort: "Sorry we've wasted your time, but do consider that we haven't wasted ours, nor that of a number of other people's."

Now it may be that your ideas about psychoanalysis are similar to that man's ideas about *Peter Grimes*. Concerning my present little effort, I'm perhaps particularly anxious about the reception you'll give to the first section, that on Peter's character. Freud wrote in 1910 (in a letter to F. S. Krauss) that medical men and psychologists got into a terrific rage when presented with the conception of an anal character. Since then many doctors and psychologists have grown more tolerant towards this and other elements in the psychoanalytic body of knowledge, but there are still quite a number of people who view the more 'shocking' aspect of psychoanalytic results with indignation. Maybe you are among the latter, maybe my first section, or even the whole article, is a far more thorough piece of insanity to you than Grimes's phantasies are to the above-mentioned critic. Well, in that case, I'm sorry I've wasted your time . . .

But please let me say on this occasion that I don't think you'll find a great many people who are more lastingly grateful to you for your work than I am.

> Yours, in any case, faithfully,
> H. K.

As has been noted, Keller was intensely involved with the performance of the opera in the first half of 1946 when it was revived by The Sadler's Wells Opera Company between February and June. (Keller does not appear to have attended any of the first performances between June and July 1945.) This is shown by another letter of his, to 'The Editor, *Time and Tide*', dated 16 February:

Peter Pears's Peter Grimes
[*Letter to the Editor*, Time and Tide]

I am suggesting in another place that Pears is among the greatest living reproductive artists, and I will add here that his Grimes is unsurpassable.

The invalidity of your critic's objections to Pears's rendering becomes probable (if such circuitous considerations are really needed) when one realizes that Britten himself must have been considerably stimulated by the wealth of creative powers inherent in Pears's original musical personality.

Your critic mentions that the opera is *durchkomponiert*. One is bound to add that, regarding artistic continuity, it is *durchgesungen* by Pears. An unbroken line of development runs throughout his interpretation, inevitably leading to the dolcissimo "What harbour shelters peace . . ." et seq. which is offered in a way that a listener not knowing the work will understand that here are Grimes's last words.

Against this the question whether Pears 'sounded tired' is of somewhat minor importance.

The 'place' Keller refers to in the opening line appears to have been the *National Entertainments Monthly*. For on 4 May, 1946, following an exchange of letters, Keller wrote to Pears:

Letter to Peter Pears

Thank you so much for the letter. I'm very glad that you don't mind critics more than is emotionally inevitable.

The reason why I am writing again is that I'm unhappy about the enclosed review (*National Entertainments Monthly*, a new magazine), as it is printed. Not only did this idiot of a sub-editor (who is making a habit of distorting and vulgarising my remarks) cut my detailed praise of your musical personality and your vocal capacities, but the sentence about your not being 'quite so vital on the first occasion' is all wrong. What I spoke of was the performance that was broadcast: this, I suggested, was not perhaps marked by the same vitality on your part as preceding and succeeding performances. I shall, of course, insist on a correction, and in order realistically to counterbalance the undue prominence thus given to a point of criticism of negligible importance, I shall add my conviction that you are among the most significant performers of our time, either in this country or elsewhere. (Today's performance, by the way – of which, unfortunately, I could only hear the first act and half of the second, whereafter I had to leave – was, to my mind, unsurpassed by you, and, to my imagination, unsurpassable by anyone else.)

For the rest, I can only hope that you won't be too annoyed.

Here's another point: I'm working now on a psychoanalytic study of *Peter Grimes* (psychological research is one of my occupations; my second paper is just going to press in the *British Journal of Medical Psychology*). This article, tho' more extensive than yours in the *Radio Times*, can be regarded as a complement, on the psychological level, to what you expounded on the more sociological one. Do you think that Britten is at all interested in, or at any rate not opposed to, the application to art of the psychoanalytic body of knowledge? Naturally I would only like to show him my paper when it is finished, if I knew that I wouldn't just waste his time.

Incidentally, why doesn't Sackville-West (*Peter Grimes* [Sadler's] Wells Opera Book) mention the version of his Example 5 that occurs in the storm interlude? Apart from the fact that each recurrence of this should, I think, be mentioned, its position and form in this interlude seems to be of outstanding psychological importance, since Peter's ambivalence is here inevitably impressed on the listener.

Kindly let me have the press cutting back, but please do not bother to reply if, as is probable, you have no time.

[H. K.]

The paper for the *British Journal of Medical Psychology* would appear to be 'Male Psychology', reprinted elsewhere in this volume, though it was in fact his first *published* 'paper'. The other 'paper' was probably his joint presentation with Margaret Phillips to the British Psychological Society, 'The Psychological Significance of Some Sociological Conceptions of the Group' (1945) (printed in part II above).

As indicated at the head of the essay, part of the theoretical background to the *Three Psychoanalytic Notes on 'Peter Grimes'* is set out in Keller's 'Individual Psychology and Group Psychology', included in part II of this volume. Keller wrote a long and moving tribute to Pears in 'People X: Peter Pears', *Opera* 2/6, May 1951, pp. 287-92. See also 'Not Famous Enough' later in this part.

NOTES

The following notes are Keller's unless enclosed by square brackets

[The missing opening pages may have included material used in the introduction to Keller's scene-by-scene account of *Peter Grimes*, 'The Story; the Music not Excluded', from Donald Mitchell and Hans Keller, *Benjamin Britten. A Commentary on his Works from a Group of Specialists*, London, Rockliff, 1952, pp. 111-31:

> Derived from George Crabbe's poem, *The Borough*, the scenario of *Peter Grimes* was sketched by Benjamin Britten and Peter Pears; Montagu Slater undertook the libretto. 'In writing *Peter Grimes*,' says the composer, 'I wanted to express my awareness of the perpetual struggle of men and women whose livelihood depends on the sea.' This, together with the light thrown by the story on the early nineteenth-century practice of buying apprentices from the workhouse, pertains to the sociological aspect of the work. Psychologically, however, the significance of the story transcends its time and place. Peter Pears once wrote: 'There are plenty of Grimeses around still, I think.'
>
> Peter Grimes is the living conflict. His pride, ambition, and urge for independence fight with his need for love; his self-love battles against his self-hate. Others too, he can (sometimes) love as intensely as he can despise them, but he cannot show, let alone prove his tenderness as easily as his wrath – except through the music, which, alas, the people on the stage don't hear. Thus he is destined to seem worse than he is, and not to be as good as he feels. *Peter Grimes* is the story of the man who couldn't fit in.
>
> I should go further than Pears and say that in each of us there is something of a Grimes, though most of us have outgrown or at least outwitted him sufficiently not to recognize him too consciously. But we do identify him, and ourselves consciously with him, unconsciously, which is one reason for the universal appeal of this work.
>
> Another reason is the composer's ability to satisfy both the 'connoisseurs' and the 'less learned' – I put these words in inverted commas because Mozart used them with reference to his first three Vienna piano Concertos. It is in fact the outer perfection of Britten's music that prevents some listeners from realizing its depths.

In the Archive there is also an untitled carbon copy of an 'analytical note' on *Peter Grimes* for the HMV recording company dating from 1948.]

I *Grimes's Character*

1 [Ernest Jones, *Papers on Psychoanalysis*, second edition, London, Baillière, Tindall and Cox, 1918.]

2 [Sigmund Freud, 'Charakter und Analerotik' (1908), *Gesammelte Werke*, 7, London, Imago, 1941, pp. 203-09; trans. by James Strachey as 'Character and Anal Eroticism', *Standard Edition*, 9, London, Hogarth Press, 1959, pp. 162-75. The introduction to this essay by Angela Richards in the *Pelican Freud Library*, 7, London, Pelican, 1977, pp. 205-15, lists other related writings by the author and observes that 'there are not many accounts by Freud of the nature of "character" and the mechanism of its formation' (p. 207). The same point may be found in Jones, *op. cit.*, chapter 40, 'Anal-erotic Character Traits', pp. 664-88.]

3 [Freud, *Pelican Freud*, 7, p. 209.]

4 [Karl Abraham, 'A Short Study of the Development of the Libido, Viewed in the Light of Mental Disorders', *Selected Papers*, London, Hogarth Press, 1927, pp. 422-23.]

5 [cf. Freud, *Pelican Freud*, 7, p.214. Observing further that the 'gold which the devil gives to his paramours turns into excrement after his departure,' Freud goes on to suggest that 'the contrast between the most precious substance known to men and their most worthless, which they reject as waste matter ('refuse'), has led to this specific identification of gold with faeces.' The observation is pertinent to Keller's discussion: see note 12 below.]

6 [Jones writes, *op. cit.*, p. 670: 'The person objects equally to being made to do what he doesn't want to, and to being prevented from doing what he does want to. In other words, there is an inordinate, and often extreme, sensitiveness to interference. Such people take advice badly, resent any pressure being out on them, stand on their rights and on their dignity, rebel against any authority, and insist on going their own way; they are never to be driven and can only be led.']

7 This projecting extends into the audience. Thus a good deal of talk has been going on about Peter being a 'sadist', and in addition there was even some writing about his 'demonic character', until at last Peter

Pears (*Radio Times*, 8 March, 1946) has come out with the news that 'he is not a sadist nor a demonic character, and the music quite clearly shows that.' In view of the fact that even competent listeners have shut their eyes to what 'the music clearly shows', a quite important sidelight is here thrown on how musical understanding can be prevented by such mechanisms as projection. [In *The Making of Peter Grimes, II, Notes and Commentaries*, Woodbridge, Boydell Press, 1996, p. 58, Philip Brett reports that Britten told *Time* magazine (16 February, 1948), 'The more vicious the society, the more vicious the individual' and that Peter Grimes was 'a subject very close to my heart – the struggle of the individual against the masses.']

8   Jones, *op. cit.*, p. 682.

9   Jones, *op. cit.*, p. 668.

10 Jones, *op. cit.*, p. 688.

11 Jones, *op. cit.*, p. 668.

12 [Jones, *op. cit.*, p. 681. In the typescript, this and the following paragraph were deleted.]

13 [Jones, *op. cit.*, p. 684. An interesting paradox arises here. On the one hand, there is Grimes's accusation that the Borough gossips 'listen to money, only to money' (Act I, Scene 1); and on the other there is his determination to 'fish the sea dry' and 'sell the good catches', so 'that wealthy merchant Grimes will set up household and shop' and 'you will see it all!'. In other words, Grimes denies in himself the anal cupidity, projects it onto the gossips, castigates it, and readmits it into himself by determining to beat them at their own game, thereby asserting his omnipotence. To do this, he has to exercise the single-handed manic productivity which, as Keller observes, is also intrinsic to the anal character.]

14 [In the typescript a new but unfinished paragraph followed this, beginning 'It is similar . . .']

15 Jones, *op. cit.*, pp. 665 and 682.

II   *Grimes and His Mother*]

1   [Benjamin Britten, 'Introduction', *Benjamin Britten: Peter Grimes*, Sadler's Wells Opera Books, 3, London, John Lane (The Bodley Head), 1945, pp. 7-8; reprinted in: *Peter Grimes*, ed. by Philip Brett, Cambridge Opera Handbooks, Cambridge, Cambridge University Press, 1983, pp. 148-49; and *The Making of 'Peter Grimes'*, II, ed. by Paul Banks, Woodbridge (Suffolk), 1996, pp. 1-3. Britten's opening paragraph reads: 'During the summer of 1941, while working in California, I came across a copy of *The Listener* [29 May, 1941] containing an article about George Crabbe by E. M. Forster. I did not know any of the poems of Crabbe at the time, but reading about him gave me such a feeling of nostalgia for Suffolk, where I had always lived, that I searched for a copy of his works, and made a beginning with *The Borough*. Mr. Forster's excellent account of this "entirely English poet" evoked a longing for the realities of that grim and exciting seacoast around Aldeburgh.']

2   One often encounters the view that Britten is more brilliant and witty than deep. This view seems to be based on the assumption that if music immediately appeals there must be something wrong with it, an assumption which in its turn seems to spring from the Polycrates complex ([described by] J. C. Flugel) in *Men, Morals and Society*, London, Duckworth, 1945, p. 151, owing to which we worry about having nothing to worry about. [In 'Musical Self-contempt in Britain' (see later in this part) Keller relates Flugel's 'Polycrates Complex' to Freud's essay of 1921, 'Group Psychology and the Analysis of the Ego', *Standard Edition*, 18, London, Hogarth Press, 1955, p. 67. This lecture drew upon Keller's 'Resistances to Britten's Music: Their Psychology', *Music Survey*, 2/4, 1950, pp. 227-36, reprinted in, Hans Keller, *Essays on Music*, ed. by Christopher Wintle, Cambridge, Cambridge University Press, pp. 10-17.]

3   Glover, 'Psychoneuroses', *Psychoanalysis*, London, John Bale, 1939, p. 79.

4   Glover, *op. cit.*, p. 79.

5   Glover, *op. cit.*, p. 79.

6   cf. Sigmund Freud, 'Beiträge zur Psychologie des Liebeslebens' (1910), *Gesammelte Werke*, 8, London, Imago, 1943, p. 72; [trans. by James Strachey as, 'A Special Type of Choice of Object Made by Men' (*Contributions to the Psychology of Love*, 1, *Standard Edition*, 11, pp. 163-75; *Pelican Freud Library*, 7, London, Pelican, 1977, pp. 227-42;] J. C. Flugel, *The Psychoanlaytic Study of the Family*, sixth edn., London, Hogarth Press, 1939, pp. 110ff.. [This observation may have been stimulated by Keller's fieldwork with prostitutes reported in Part II of this book under 'Prostitutes Wear Marriage-rings'.]

7   Flugel, 1939, pp. 119-20 and 234.

8   Montagu Slater, 'The Story of the Opera', *Benjamin Britten's Peter Grimes*, Sadler's Wells Opera Books, 3, London, John Lane (The Bodley Head), 1945, pp. 15-26. [The volume, which was 'ready for the first

performance [on] June 7th' [1945] included 'Essays by Benjamin Britten, E. M. Forster, Montagu Slater and Edward Sackville-West[.] Illustrated with stage and costume designs by Kenneth Green[.] Price 2/6d.]

9   Flugel, 1939, p. 66. [Flugel cites Sigmund Freud, *The Interpretation of Dreams* (1900) and Otto Rank, *Die Lohengrinssage* (1911). Keller knew the Freud essay as *Die Traumbedeutung, Gesammelte Werke* II/III (Reprint of the 8th edition), London, Imago, 1942; see also English trans. by James Strachey, London, Allen and Unwin, 1954.]

10 [The third and fourth lines of the text in Stein's vocal score read: 'A harbour evermore, Where night is turned to day.']

11 [This is amplified later in this *Note*.]

12 Flugel, 1939, p. 67.

13 Flugel, 1939, p. 71.

14 Flugel, 1939, p. 69.

15 [Flugel, 1939, pp. 66-78, cites Freud, *The Interpretation of Dreams*; similarly Jones, 'A Forgotten Dream', *Papers on Psychoanalysis*, pp. 231-41 (especially p. 232), cites Otto Rank, *Der Mythus von der Geburt des Helden* (1909) (*Myth of the Birth of the Hero*).]

16 Jones, *op.cit.*, p. 232; Flugel, 1939, p. 70.

17 Flugel, 1939, p. 70.

18 Flugel, 1939, pp. 68-9.

19 Flugel, 1939, p. 70.

20 [In 'The Musical and Dramatic Structure', *Benjamin Britten's Peter Grimes*, pp. 27-55,] Edward Sackville-West says of this that it 'creates the one moment of absolute calm and stillness in the entire scene' [p.36]. Inasmuch as dead stillness is produced by holding one's breath being taken away, I agree.

21 Jones, *op. cit.*, p. 233; Flugel, 1939, p. 69.

22 Sackville-West, *op. cit.*, pp. 43-5.

23 Sackville-West, *op. cit.*, pp. 43-5.

24 For the importance of darkness in womb symbols, cf. Jones, *op. cit.*, p. 232. See also Ernest Jones, 'The Symbolic Significance of Salt', *Essays in Applied Psychoanalysis*, London, International Psychoanalytic Press, 1923, p. 144; and Flugel, 1939, p. 66.

25 Sackville-West, *op. cit.*, pp. 43-5.

26 Edith Sitwell, 'Eurydice', *Horizon*, 12/68, 1945.

27 Flugel, 1939, pp. 69-70 and 80.

28 [The paragraph continues with an incomplete sentence, 'When that material . . .']

29 [Keller: 'The constant dominant seventh on D makes the impression of something like an indication of Peter's unalterable fate.']

30 The 'idea of water' is, of course, 'closely associated with that of birth': cf. J. C. Flugel, 1939, pp. 69-70. [Flugel also cites] Rank, *Die Lohengrinssage*, p. 46, and Freud, *The Interpretation of Dreams*, p. 243 (the reader may be reminded of a birth-dream of one of Freud's patients: 'she plunges into the dark water, at the place where it reflects the pale moon.'). [For a discussion of] Nature [as] mother substitute, cf. Flugel, 'The Psychology of Birth Control', *Men and Their Motives*, London, Kegan Paul, 1934, p.13. ['The concept of the monotheistic Christian God or of his more modern counterpart, Nature, is deeply imbued with this influence [of 'omnipotence of thought'] (the former representing – at least predominantly – a father-substitute, the latter a mother-substitute).]

31 [In the Stein vocal score, and in the earliest version of the Slater libretto (see Britten's facsimile), Grimes continues, 'And the third will . . .' He breaks off remembering verdicts at inquests past ("Accidental circumstances") and imagining, perhaps, what a verdict might be in the future. The trinity brings to mind Freud's famous essay on the 'rule of three', 'The Theme of the Three Caskets' (1913), *Standard Edition*, 12, London, Hogarth Press, 1958, pp. 223-47 (especially p. 243), whereby, as in Shakespeare's *The Merchant of Venice*, the third in a series effects a reversal of a pattern (in *Götterdämmerung*, for example, the Third Norn represents Atropos, 'the ineluctable – Death'). In this series, the two apprentices have already died, so the reversal lies in the nature of the third victim: this time, the death will be his, not an apprentice's. Keller's identification between Grimes and the boys is thus complete.]

32 Ernest Jones, 'The Island of Ireland' (1922) [in *Psycho-Myth, Psycho-History*, 2, New York, Hillstone (in two volumes, including the original American edition of *Essays in Applied Psychoanalysis*, International Psychoanalytic Press, 1923).]

33 [Flugel, 1939, p. 69. Chapter 8, pp. 66-78, is devoted entirely to 'Ideas of Birth and Pre-natal Life'.]

34 The passage is discussed more fully in, Montagu Slater, 'The Story of the Opera', *Benjamin Britten's Peter Grimes*, 1945, p. 26.]

35 Peter Pears, 'Neither a Hero nor a Villain' (1946), *Peter Grimes*, ed. by Philip Brett, 1983, pp. 150-52.

III *Grimes and His Father*

1   Flugel, 1939, p. 119.

2   Pears, 1946, pp. 150-52.

3   Flugel, 1939, p. 120n. ['Thus, as Mr.Burt has suggested to me, the influence of displaced father-hatred is probably in large measure responsible for the fact that strikes and other crude forms of rebellion against authority in industry occur principally among the working classes, where the tyranny of the father is often of a primitive and repressive type.'] and p. 28.

4   cf. (for example) Oskar Pfister, 'Neutestamentliche Seelsorge und psychoanalytische Therapie', *Imago*, 20/4, 1934, p. 431, esp. thesis 4', or Ernst Kris's review of Lucile Dooley, 'A Note on Humour', *Imago*, 20/4, 1934, p. 493.

5   Freud, 'Das Ich und das Es' (1923), *Gesammelte Werke*, 13, London, Imago, 1940, pp. 237-89 (esp. p. 261); trans. by Joan Riviere as 'The Ego and the Id', *Standard Edition*, 19, London, Hogarth Press, 1961, pp. 3-66 (especially p. 22).

6   Flugel, 1939, p. 119.

7   Flugel, 1939, p. 119.

8   [Keller's paragraph comes to a halt after attempting to reconstruct the end of Act II as a paraphrase of Slater's published libretto. The sentence begins '[. . .] examines them, and then he goes to the cliff side door, shutting it after he has looked down.']

9   [Here, and for the rest of the paragraph, Keller refers to the missing 7 pages of the first *Note*.]

10   As I write, I find a nice little instance of this that [has just been] published. A little girl had painted a cat and showed it to Daddy, saying that it was the baby cat; tomorrow she would paint the mother. Her father said that strictly speaking it should have been the other way round, as the mother came before the baby. 'No,' this little cat is her mummy's mummy.' (M. Ruben, 'A Contribution to the Education of a Parent', in *The Psychoanalytic Study of a Child*, 1, London, 1945, p. 255.)

11   Ernest Jones, 'The Significance of the Grandfather', *Papers on Psychoanalysis*, p. 652; Flugel, 1939, p. 161. [Jones interestingly relates the 'reversal' fantasy to patterns of life and death, the child growing, the parent shrinking until he or she is ready for death and rebirth. This too may throw an oblique light on the end of *Grimes*, and Peter's willingness to acquiesce in his own demise.]

12   Flugel, 1939, p. 161.

13   Theodor Reik, *Ritual: Psychoanalytic Studies*, London, Hogarth Press, 1931, p. 77.

14   Flugel, 1939, p. 86.

15   Flugel, 1939, p. 86.

16   cf. Montagu Slater, 'The Story of the Opera', p. 24. [In his copy of Slater's essay Keller has underlined 'I hear my father and the one that drowned' and added in the margin, 'Balstrode's revenge'.]

17   Is it too phantastic to point to the possibility that Peter phantasizes himself pregnant with, and giving birth to, his father together with the dead apprentice? Anyway, such a phantasy would fit perfectly into the whole psychological context.

18   Ernest Jones, 'The Devils', *On the Nightmare*, London, Hogarth Press, 1931, pp. 154-89. [Jones also cites Freud's comments on the Devil, a passage Keller draws upon at the opening of the extant part of the first *Note*.]

19   Jones, 1931, p. 166.

20   Jones, 1931, p. 180.

21   Georg Groddeck, *Das Buch vom Es. Psychoanalytische Briefe an eine Freundin* [Internationaler Psychoanalytischer Verlag, 1925)].

22   [In the typescript this paragraph is in fact deleted. Keller's identification of Grimes's father with the apprentices is not so far-fetched in view of the fact that there was an early intention to bring father and boys into the final scene of the opera, and even to introduce Grimes's father into the Prologue: see *The Making of 'Peter Grimes'*, 2, pp. 60ff. Philip Brett writes: 'Peter Pears [originally] wrote a number outline of the entire opera in which the Prologue consists of a death-bed scene for the older Grimes, attended by Ellen and disturbed by Peter, who enters drunk. In the 1975 BBC interview Pears remembers the father solemnly cursed the young man Grimes.' Although all reference to the father was removed from the final work, Keller's penetrating analysis shows that, psychologically, he is still there and has to be acknowledged.]

23   Pears, 1946, p. 152.

24   Sackville-West, *op. cit.*, p. 44.

25   Reik, op. cit., p. 78.

26   Pears, 1946, p. 150.

27 Keller gathered the following argument into two numbered points, the first starting 'The boy's death' and the second 'Peter's death'. The numbers have been dropped here in favour of continuous prose.]
28 [*Nemesism:* a propensity to acquiesce in acts of retribution against the self.]
29 Edward Glover, *The Psychology of Flogging*, second edition, London, 1937, p. 14.
30 *The Holy Sonnets of John Donne*, song cycle for tenor and piano, Op. 35, was first performed by Britten and Pears at the Wigmore Hall on 22 November, 1945.

*

A short typescript from this period held in the Archive refers to the same sources as the psychoanalytic study of *Peter Grimes* but relates them to observational material drawn from life rather than art. There is no information about the circumstances described:

A Sixteen-months-old Boy and His Mother Substitutes

1 "Mamma" – Water

Though this infant has been under my fairly continuous observation, I unfortunately missed the first occasion on which he spontaneously used "mamma" for water, nor is it possible exactly to determine what this occasion was. At any rate his sitting, together with his nine-year-old sister, in the bathtub was one of the first occasions on which, at the above age, he pronounced the expression, which subsequently was transferred to things connected with water, i.e. taps, basins, lavatories. His mother's name was, of course, "mummy".

We need not linger over the obvious interpretation of the choice of synonym for a warm fluid. The more dubious question arises whether intra-uterine memories are here involved.[1]

The problems of how we acquire ideas of birth and prenatal life, and how these ideas become invested with the significance laid bare by psychoanalytic investigations, have so far remained thoroughly unsolved. The most precise description of the chaotic state of our knowledge in these respects has been given by J. C. Flugel,[2] who also offers directives for future investigation. The first of these runs:

> To what extent (if at all) do children display – in dreams, phantasies or otherwise – knowledge as to the circumstances of their birth and pre-natal life which they could not possibly have obtained except from memory of their own past experience?

The boy's grandmother commented on the bathtub incident: "He thinks of being inside his mother's tummy." Since the grandmother could not have had any psychoanalytic knowledge as to the possible uterine meaning of the situation, I asked her why she should think so. "Because it's just as nice and warm in the bathing water." Her attitude, though not being news of interest to the psychoanalyst, may indicate to the extra-analytical observer that one needn't be bothered by depth psychology in order to attach possible uterine significance to the boy's utterance.

The question to the psychoanalyst is, was the situation womb-like only to us (the more grown-ups), or also to the boy? If it was womb-like to the boy too, it can safely be said that he 'could not possibly have obtained his knowledge from memory of his own past experience.' Here the matter rests. But a meagre piece of possible evidence is better than nothing – and nothing is exactly what we have had so far.

2 A Collective Expression for Three Mother Figures

The boy's linguistic attitude, formed at an earlier date, to his two sisters (aged 9 and 11) and to his grandmother, all of whom were living with him, merits recording.

The grandmother, a woman whose sexual organisation gave rise to a pronouncedly physical (largely oral) love relationship towards the boy, was wont to accompany her caresses with the onomatopoetic interjection "iẏea". The boy quickly availed himself of this primitive vowel formation and applied it, as constant collective name, to the three female wards to whom, apart from his mother, he manifested his strongest love.

1   For the significance of water, cf. (a) Sigmund Freud, *Die Traumbedeutung* (*The Interpretation of Dreams*), p. 404ff. (b) Otto Rank, *Die Lohengrinssage*, pp. 26ff. and 46ff. (c) Ernest Jones, 'A Forgotten Dream', *Papers on Psychoanalysis*, p. 232; and 'Dreams and Psychoneurotic Symptoms', *op. cit.*, p. 266 (d) Ernest Jones, *The Island of Ireland*, p. 408 (e) J. C. Flugel, *The Psychoanalytic Study of the Family*, pp. 69ff. [full publication details as above].
2   Flugel, op. cit, p. 76, *n.*

2 First Opera Performances in England
[Gundry, Britten (The Rape of Lucretia) and Wolf-Ferrari, 1946]

This spring and summer has brought three novelties to steadily increasing British opera audiences. In spring, we had *The Partisans*, a new work by Inglis Gundry [b. 1905] a comparatively little-known member of the younger generation of English composers.

The title of the opera indicates its subject (the libretto is the composer's). The place of action cannot be reported: in order to give it universal significance, the actual country of its setting is nameless. But one feels oneself somewhere in the Balkans.

Presented by the Workers Music Association in London, the work had a very warm reception. There can indeed be no doubt that in it both lyrical and dramatic capacities specifically suited for operatic work found skilful expression.

Whether it will survive, and whether it will ever reach other countries, among others those whose folk tunes it sensitively and organically uses (Greece and Yugoslavia), is a question dependent on other factors beside its value.

It is in any case important for music lovers abroad to realize that British opera is at the beginning of a vigorous renascence. In this Benjamin Britten, 33-year-old composer of *Peter Grimes* (which opera, completed in 1945 for the Koussevitsky Music Foundation in America, has already met with exceptional success in this country, on the Continent, and, recently, at the Berkshire Music Festival in the United States) is playing a most conspicuous part. His second opera, *The Rape of Lucretia*, which is now going through its first London performances, will shortly be performed on the Continent. It is being presented by the Glyndebourne Company, with which it will go on Continental tour; Britten also wants the original exponents of his work (whose engagement has been carried out in close collaboration with him) to present it when it goes to America.

Though this new and novel operatic creation is being greatly appreciated, the reaction here is not perhaps quite so enthusiastic as it was in the case of *Peter Grimes*. Possibly it will, more thoroughly, carry foreign audiences away. British audiences, newly and gladly conscious of the growing force of home-grown opera, inevitably approach a new British work in a national rather than in an international spirit; *Peter Grimes*, through and through English under its indubitable supra-national significance (it was composed out of home-sickness), has thus had a more intense appeal among a considerable section of opera-lovers than *Lucretia*, with its foreign scene of action.

However, the tragedy (by the young poet Ronald Duncan, after André Obey's *Le Viol de Lucrèce*, further based on Livy, Shakespeare, Nathaniel Lee, Thomas Heywood and F. Ponsard) is not only distanced in space (Rome), but also in time (500 B. C.), and the feeling of its 'dating' may affect some foreign listeners in the same way as it seems to be troubling a number of home listeners. Expressed vulgarly, this feeling amounts to "One doesn't rape nowadays, does one – not on the level of Prince Tarquinius, anyway?" who, as profligate son of the Etruscan tyrant, Tarquinius Sextus, and as "a man at the mercy of his own virility", rapes Lucretia, wife of the Roman General. The latter's forgiveness towards her increases her remorse and shame, so that she stabs herself.

Now I do not think that such feelings of this tragic climax being 'not sufficiently topical' are justified. I even believe that with those whose musical understanding is penetrating enough to grasp the whole meaning of the superbly unfolded composition this point ought not to arise at all.

But if it does, it has to be remembered that, while our sex- and other war-weapons have grown less crude, they have in many respects become more cruel, so that psychologically and ethically the tragedy is in fact more topical today than in its own historical time.

This viewpoint gains force when we consider that the rape problem is enclosed by the wider, concentric problem of (Etruscan) tyranny – again a theme that has not yet become antiquated.

Also, there is the Christian significance of the drama: the story is framed by two impersonal figures, the male and female chorus who, on the stage throughout, comment on the events (outside which they stand in time and thought) from the Christian standpoint:

> While we as two observers stand between
> This present audience and that scene,
> We'll view these human passions and these years
> With eyes which once have wept with Christ's own tears.

A recent reviewer has stated that *Lucretia* is 'utterly unlike *Peter Grimes*,' and even one of the most discerning critics in this country, Ernest Newman, suggests that 'there can be no actual comparison between two operas so different both in subject and in form.' The present writer cannot agree. As regards the libretto, there are, beneath the obvious differences, several important psychological and sociological parallels between the two stories, of which I will suggest only one, i.e. the above-mentioned tyranny-motive. In either opera this theme, a principal one, has two levels: Grimes suffers under society's tyranny, his apprentices suffer under his own. In *Lucretia*, Junius (a dubious character who challenges Tarquinius to prove Lucretia chaste in order to "make political capital out of tragedy"), as Roman General and opponent of the rulers, suffers under Etruscan tyranny; at the same time, he is a prospective tyrant himself.

The music of the two works, too, bears unmistakable affinities that will be discovered by anyone who has acquainted himself with *Grimes*, even at a first hearing of *Lucretia*. Among other things, a common characteristic between the two compositions is the well-contrived economy of thematic material, and the variety of emotional expression achieved, not in spite of this, but *thereby*.

Altogether, the music to *Lucretia* is winsomely, rather than wilfully, original, indeed original enough not to be ashamed of showing its developmental forerunners, of which there are – as there should be – several: modern, classical, and pre-classical. In matters of form the opera is rooted in the classical style.

The treatment of the orchestra is not only first rate, but also radically first-hand: eleven solo instruments (string quartet plus double bass, wind quintet, harp) and percussion, make up the whole orchestral apparatus – a new and entirely successful experiment, if one may thus call an approach that has been made with astounding assurance.

In the two alternative casts participating in Eric Crozier's impeccable production we find singers of most impressive calibre (they include, incidentally, the Danish tenor Askel Schiotz and the Czech bass-baritone Otakar Kraus). Artists like Peter Pears (a young English tenor, the exponent of the title role in *Peter Grimes* and of much else in Britten's music and already well-known abroad) and Kathleen Ferrier (contralto) belong to the best Britain, or indeed any other country, can offer. Pears (who in certain respects reminds one of the Munich tenor Julius Patzak) has in my opinion only one or two equals in the entire field of musical interpretation. The legend that Britain does not produce good solo voices is showing signs of senility.

Another first performance in England – this time not of a new, nor of a British opera – may also interest overseas readers. As a matter of fact some of them may be surprised to hear that [Ermanno] Wolf-Ferrari's *I quattro rusteghi* [1906] (*Die vier Grobiane*, or, as it has here been christened, *School for Fathers*) has had to wait until now for its (excellent) first production in England by the Sadler's Wells Company (which, it will be remembered, toured the Continent not long ago). However, there have been more serious omissions elsewhere. For instance, *Fidelio* only recently had its first performance at Pittsburgh, while the other works performed there this season, i.e. *Carmen*, *La traviata*, and *La bohème* had, I gather, had previous productions. Besides, I find that British musical life is open to an unusual extent to receive foreign works, far more so than, say, even pre-Hitlerite Austria.

It is true that the nationalist tendency upon which I touched above, while having its favourable aspects as far as British opera, and British music generally, is concerned, counteracts the friendliness prevalent (if exaggerated) in this country towards outside contributions. Thus Inglis Gundry, the composer of the first-mentioned opera, *The Partisans*, has more than once indicated his feelings "of being a musical partisan in this country, occupied so long musically by the Germans and Italians." This is perhaps putting it rather excessively: even Gundry will concede that Mozart's or Beethoven's or Verdi's 'stay' in this country has been more beneficial musically than Hitler's or Mussolini's stay in one of the occupied countries has been politically, or rather generally.

Amusingly enough, no sooner had Gundry thus pronounced, than *School for Fathers* – by a German Italian – reinforced the occupation. But the libretto of Wolf-Ferrari's opera has been Londonised, the scene having been very successfully transferred to this city from eighteenth-century Venice.

Of the three productions here reported, *The Rape of Lucretia* is by far the most important. I suggest that the development of this young genius, Benjamin Britten, be carefully heeded. This, by the way, will not be difficult: for once, the right man is being given a great deal of publicity. Yet, or rather for that very reason, he needs support. He is so successful, so lucky, that people who are not very secure in their artistic judgment tend to be increasingly suspicious of him. Notwithstanding his having turned down offers from Hollywood, these people seem to find that – to use an apt term recently coined by J. C. Flugel – he hurts their 'Polycrates complex'. The term, I trust, explains itself.

Source

Keller wrote this (typescript) survey of recent opera performances in London, including an early performance of *The Rape of Lucretia*, for syndication by 'Southern News Services' (Bexhill-on-Sea) and for consideration by the Editor of *British Features* on 'September 5th, '46'. The latter could find no outlet for it, and it is uncertain whether it was ever published.

3 *Off and On* The Little Sweep

All writing on music should be either useless or incomprehensible

(a) Who said this?
(b) What does it mean?[1]

I *Off*

Imagine writing an opera for dogs. It is, you will agree upon reflection, a fearful task. Yet it is nothing compared with the problems of writing a children's opera. For one thing, dogs are on the whole more musical than children, chiefly because they don't have unmusical piano teachers. I was supposed to be a very musical child; in fact I lived in music. I was also supposed to have an extremely keen ear. But what was I compared with my Alsation Rolf? As long as I am a musician I shall not forget him. Both he and I could recognize our car by its hoot. But he recognized it when it was so far off that I could hear nothing at all. What is more, when he heard a hoot which had the same timbre, which was played with the same sort of feeling and which had the same pitch as ours, except for a vibration or two, he would not move his tail. You may say, of course, that even the most perfect ear and the most perfect pitch are nothing in themselves; Beethoven got along without the former, and Wagner and Schoenberg without the latter. But you don't let me finish. There is a counter-melody in the slow movement of the E flat Dvořák string quartet which, bless it, is impossible. I feared as much as a child, but you know how children are, they want to be told they're right. So when the movement was played on the wireless, I gave Rolf my earphones and asked him for his opinion. No sooner had he heard the above-analysed counter-melody than his tail vanished between his legs and he started to howl pitifully. It is true that he also cried when I introduced him to my pet pieces, the first tenor aria from the Matthew Passion, the slow movement from Beethoven's Seventh, and various string quartets, but that was because he was so terribly moved.

Now it's no use saying what has all this to do with *The Little Sweep* because it has, or dogs have anyway. For even upon the most anti-canine hypothesis, it must be conceded that dogs have this advantage over children: *they have no musical history*. As soon as children show musicality, they show it in a certain way, and it's the more or less strictly diatonic way, for they carry our long and by now somewhat decrepit musical history on their little shoulders. What exactly this moving phrase means I do not know, but it certainly doesn't mean that diatonicism is 'natural', for in that case its incipience would be found in dogs. In a previous article in this journal [*Tempo*] I have tried to show that for anti-romantic reasons the raising of the norm of dissonance has proceeded more quickly than would have been necessary from a strictly musical point of view. Now that's just too bad for the child: (a) from his first (sucking) rhythm and his first 'notes' he has to rush through ages of musical development anyhow; (b) he has to cope with that recent bit of express development towards 'this modern stuff', a task which is all the more difficult since (c) his adult environment, his parents and parent figures, haven't altogether coped with it either.

Youth may be revolutionary, but the child is necessarily conservative, for you can't make a stand before you've got something to stand on. A dog probably prefers a twelve-tone opera to a diatonic pastiche, because maybe the twelve-tone opera has more archaic and instinctual energy to it; but a recent Gallup Poll (copyright reserved) showed that the number of eight-year-olds who walk about whistling twelve-tone tunes is smaller than the number of eight-year-olds who walk about not whistling twelve-tone tunes. (You may object that we don't whistle twelve-tone tunes either, but that's because we are childish.)

Here then is the first difficulty for the modern composer of a children's opera: if he wants to write vital music, he has to translate his contemporary idiom to the child without losing it in the process.

The second difficulty is psychological. When you talk to a dog you talk to a dog – it is a straightforward proposition: either you like dogs or you don't. In the face of children, however, the either-or becomes, with most of us male adults, a complex both. We are so far removed from the dog's mind that we do not recognize ourselves in it with undue frequency; whereas children are just far enough from, and near to, the adult to make him feel uncomfortable. The adult who talks to the child has to grow into what he has [taken] considerable trouble to grow out of.

Among the adults, however, who thus feel guilty about being children, the artists take their guilt least seriously: the barrier between their conscious (adult) and unconscious (infantile) minds has holes, through which childhood keeps breaking through.

[There is] no great artist who cannot be childlike, who does not like to *play*. Both the child and the artist keep common reality at a distance, though the artist uses thought-processes which demonstrably derive from child's play for the expression of ultimate realities which are hidden to the common adult. Are they also hidden to the artistic child of the artist's own time? When he successfully creates for the child, does he renounce art?

II Towards

Of all the contemporary composers, Britten is, I suggest, pre-eminently fitted to sing to the child. The barrier between him and childhood seems to consist of holes. Joseph Szigeti says that "the degree of the artist's *Einfühlungsvermögen*" [capacity for empathy][2] always seems to him "the hallmark of an artist's worth, the yardstick of his stature." With Britten the degree is extreme: his empathy embraces his own past, his own childhood. Add his extraordinary artistic maturity, and the result is, in *The Little Sweep*, that unique synthesis, mature childishness, which forms such a perfect counterpart to many an eternally precocious contemporary's childish maturity.

The second of our above-described difficulties does not then, to all appearances, exist for Britten. A real children's opera, however, cannot live on empathy alone, not even if the composer is able to surmount our first-mentioned difficulty. (How he does this we shall try to find out in Section III below.) The real children's opera must be by as well as for children. Indeed, without an intra-musical feeling for the strictly musical possibilities of the child's voice – the only instrument which the child, and only the child, can master – the greatest sympathy for, and identification with, the child would be about as useful as the sex instinct and sex appeal of a frigid woman. The comparison is not intended as piquancy, but as a simile on creativity.

Britten has in fact proved his musical feeling for the child's voice's character and timbre, a feeling that is part of his extremely subtle sensitivity to sound, from the time onwards when he outgrew his own youth. At nineteen he wrote his Three Two-part Songs for boy's voices, at twenty-one his twelve songs *Friday Afternoons* for children's voices and piano. Nineteen-forty-two's *Ceremony of Carols* for children's voice and harp proved a masterpiece of (inter alia) novel texture, while in *Albert Herring* (1947) children's voices were for the first time admitted into adult vocal society, where they have stayed ever since: in the hitherto ridiculously under-estimated St. Nicolas Cantata (one of the few occasions where genius, instead of sending a more or less competent deputy, visits our age instead), in the great *Spring Symphony*, and in the children's opera itself.

The whistling Boys' Choir in the *Spring Symphony* is a drastic example of a combined example of Britten's love for children and his musical interest in fresh sounds (in more than one sense of the adjective); some adult whistling we remember from *Albert Herring*. That his creative sympathies with the young transcend his interest in the noises they make is shown, prior to *Let's Make an Opera*, not alone by the – vocally, though nowise orchestrally – silent boy in *Peter Grimes*, but above all by the *Young Person's Guide to the Orchestra*, his first work with a 'C' certificate (adults to be accompanied by [a] child under 16).

III On and Off

His second is *The Little Sweep* wherein the big sweep Bob is a completely black little Grimes. The success of Eric Crozier's translation [for] the child of Britten's characteristic social and dramatic impulses is indeed obvious; nor, for that matter, can the librettist's problems be compared with the composer's problem of translating his contemporary idiom. We therefore say thank you very much and goodbye to Crozier and proceed to Britten. It is not easy to proceed to genius. Up there, in Section I, I have neatly outlined what ought to be Britten's first and foremost difficulty, or something. Now when I look at the music, I can't find any difficulty at all. Is it my fault? No, it's his perfection. I know of course that with him everything will sound like child's play, but I didn't quite expect that child's play would.

It wouldn't with every facile genius. But Britten has two special gifts to help him along. They clearly show in his harmonic style. First, there is his [capacity] to interpret diatonic harmony in the light of modern (his own) tonal and harmonic thinking. One who is perfectly able to translate the past into the present will have little difficulty in translating the present a bit further back into the past. Second, there is what I would call Britten's *naturalization of modality*. That is to say, he might address a newly invented modal theme as the Under Secretary of State, Home Office, addresses the newly-naturalized Britisher:–

> You have acquired to all intents and purposes the status of a natural-born modern subject . . . You are consequently entitled to all . . . rights, powers and privileges, and are subject to all obligations, duties and liabilities to which a natural-born 20th-century subject is entitled or subject.

Successful modality can serve as a strong bridge between the diatonicism of the past (child) and the anti-diatonicism of the present: the pre-diatonic is a natural mediator between the diatonic and the post-diatonic. And Britten's gift deserves all the more admiration since British music of the recent past, and (if I may say so) of the present past, is crowded with undesirable modal aliens.

A few months ago Schoenberg wrote:

> Only two of the remaining four modes [i.e. apart from the Ionian and Aeolian] ever played a role in the imagination of the composers, Dorian and to a less degree Phrygian. Except for a small number of examples, Lydian and Mixolydian failed to have real life.[3]

Like every genius (in fact like Schoenberg himself) Britten proves right theory wrong. For his Lydian and Mixolydian inventions are actually full of life: the reader will no doubt remember 'The Birth of Nicolas' (Lydian) and the motto hymn 'Whilst we as two observers stand'

(Mixolydian) from *Lucretia*. At the same time the truth of Schoenberg's theory shows even in Britten: the children's opera's third and probably best audience song (Ex. 1), which is undistinguishable from a natural-born modern – or should we say, timeless – tune, is dominated throughout by its Phrygian G minor. Not often does such a thing happen in contemporary music, where the modes are fond of hiding their artificiality by just dropping in for a moment or two.

Example 1 Benjamin Britten, The Little Sweep, *XIV, The Night Song (Audience Song III), bars 1-11*

I have noticed some members of the children's opera audiences being rather puzzled by the key-signature of the 'Night Song', since this is neither in C minor nor in E flat. If they will transpose the Phrygian scale (white keys from E) to G they will see where the third flat comes in: thus the song proceeds without accidentals. In its unspoilt spontaneity and significant simplicity, it only differs from a good folk-song in that it's better: the happiest possible meeting place of Britten's and children's feeling for folk-songs.

Example 2 Benjamin Britten, The Little Sweep, *I, The Sweeps' Song (Audience Song I), bars 1-4*

Speaking of the audience songs, there is rhythm. It is true that the relation of modern rhythms to homely (dance) rhythms is rather less world-shaking than the relation of modern melodies and their harmonies to the homely triad and its melodies.[4] This is why rhythm has not been included in Section I above,[5] notwithstanding the fact that dogs and twentieth-century composers are less bound to dance-rhythms than bears and twentieth-century children. (Exercise 1: analyse the rhythmic structure of 'Teddy Bear's Picnic'.) Now similarly as modality can form a bridge to post-diatonicism, 5/4 time, with its age-honoured folk-dance and folk-song associations (cf. for instance the various versions of 'Down by the Riverside'), offers a friendly way out of classical dance structures. And if the first two bars of the audience's overture, 'The Sweep's Song' (Ex. 2), are not quite safe in that they may seduce the audience-singer to swerve from the wrong path into duple time, the attention they need makes the audience as conscious as possible of the song's quintuple time.

But all this is really metre, and I was going to talk about rhythm – the cross-rhythms, that is to say, of the 'Sammy's Bath' interlude (Ex. 3a). Maybe, however, they're metre too. I mean this. People, including critics, have been wondering how the layman and the laychild could sing these awe-inspiring displacements of the bar-accent prima vista. The explanation is simple. Each of the ¾-melody's syncopations implies 3/2 (as can be seen from the re-written version, Ex. 3b), so that the straightforward polymetric design of the polyrhythms assures the singer that it is something easy and regular which causes the thrilling irregularities. Again a bridge here from old to new: polymeter leading the way from monometer to polyrhythm.

Example 3(a) Benjamin Britten, The Little Sweep, *IX, Sammy's Bath (Audience Song II), bars 5-14*

Example 3(b) Rewritten version of Example 3(a)

Now while the audience may at first feel uncomfortable because they can't have 60 Toscanini rehearsals for their songs, they are put at ease not only by Britten's considerate music, but also by their own reassuring number. Poor young Sammy, on the other hand, though he can have plenty of rehearsals, has to rely upon himself alone for his "'Morning 'Morning!" syncopations (Ex. 4) in the second of the two children's ensembles, "'Morning, Sammy! Lovely weather."

I mention this refrain because I had an opportunity to observe how and why a certain Sammy in a certain production of the opera made a mess of things here: it was because he relied, or was supposed to rely, on the (elsewhere) superb conductor. That is, it was all plainly the conductor's fault. In rehearsal, Sammy kept coming too soon with his second note, and the conductor kept telling him to watch the stick and wait for the second beat. Rehearsal and performance proved the method wrong. Children do not naturally feel like watching beats; they have not yet learnt to be so unmusical as to place visual movement in the foreground of their musical attention. But if they are musical they do hear and can be asked to listen. So the conductor should have told Sammy: "Wait till you've *heard* the chord inside your long note." Since the children's opera will doubtless receive many productions, I think it practical to make this point.

Example 4   Benjamin Britten, The Little Sweep, *XVI, Sam and Children, bars 3-8*

Sammy's other refrain, "Please don't send me up again", together with the first children's ensemble in which it is embedded, ties up the loose middle of my article, i.e. the query at the end of Section I. For here, in a children's ensemble of all numbers, the children's opera reaches one of its most mature moments. In fact, we here learn what and how much we meant by the phrase 'mature childishness'; we here have one of the places where child and adult alike are moved by Art with a pretty capital A. Undoubtedly the child's understanding moves on a more superficial level than the adult's. But it is just this very level that is the artistic mystery of both the children's opera in general and this ensemble in particular, and which lends the phrase of which I am so proud its real significance. There are, one would have thought, two possible surfaces, those with something inside and those with nothing inside (*Kitsch*). The first children ensemble's surface, however, while it has something inside – a distantly hidden depth that is accessible only to the adult – has another inside on the outside. It does not for its existence depend on the depth from which it has grown; it is *a surface around itself,* a surface which *includes* much of what, with other profound composers, it merely *encloses.* Almost, it would seem, against his will, Britten does not only on the slightest occasions draw upon deep sources, but also lets an essential part of his deeper personality penetrate into his very superficiality; one can imagine his being surprised at how much something means which he didn't mean to mean much. Just as his mature childishness sets itself against others' childish maturity, so his deep superficiality is opposed to other's superficial depth. Can there be an equally God-sent children's composer?

'Children's composer' means more than one likes to think. Within the limitations imposed upon him by the medium, Britten has here created what is becoming his most popular opera among adults. Not an altogether pleasant thought, this; for should not his other operas, which from the adult artistic point of view are of course immeasurably more important, receive the correspondingly greater attention? But then our annoyance may make us overlook one of the most notable aspects of *The Little Sweep*, and one entirely unnoticed.

When I say in Section I that we don't whistle twelve-tone tunes because we are childish, I mean it. Confronted with our age's, or maybe future ages' music, our age's adults become children. Schoenberg is an extreme case, wherein this state of affairs can be observed in all its tragedy. Britten is an incomparably milder case in that his surface gives glittering reflections of the past, but a case in point he remains inasmuch as the core of his music is so esoteric that you don't even notice that it is. What many of us childish adults need as introduction to Britten's music is Britten's children's music: in more than one sense the children's opera may prove the father of the man's.

GLOSSARY OF DIFFICULT WORDS

[HK:] The words marked with one or more asterisks do not actually occur in the article, but this does not seem a fair reason for excluding them from the Glossary. The number of asterisks applied to any particular word has not, as far as the present writer is aware, any special significance.

Diatonic	singable even by tenors.
Empathy	the only (and ugly) English word, a neologism, for *Einfühlung*. *Sich einfühlen* means, literally, 'to feel oneself into.'
Esoteric	what can't be turned inside out.
Modal	of the modes, i.e. pre-diatonic scales:

Dorian	*white keys from*	D
Phrygian		E
Lydian		F
Mixolydian		G
Aeolian		A
Ionian		C

*Monogamy***	humane form of polygamy (*quod vide*).
Monometre	same as *Monogamy* (*quod vide*), only with *Metre* instead of *gamy*.
*Monophagous****	monotrophic (*quod vide*).
*Monotrophic***	monophagous (*quod vide*).
Musical History	durable substitute for musical understanding.
Perfect Pitch	the ability to know that the people you're with haven't got it, so that you can safely say "E flat major" whenever you feel like it.
*Polygamy**	polygyny or polyandry.
Polymetre	same as *Polygamy* (*quod vide*), only with *metre* instead of *gamy*.
Polyrhythm	by now I dare say you've got it.
Prima vista	upon secret rehearsal.
Rolf	Alsatian musician (*b.* 1924, Vienna, *d.* 1932, Vienna).
Schoenberg	future's premature birth.
Twelve-tone	never mind, listen.

NOTES

Source

This article was intended for *Tempo* and is stamped 2 September, 1950 below Keller's initials. Although it reached proof stage, and was proof-read by the author, it mysteriously never reached print and is published here for the first time. The editor has had to provide the musical examples. The provision of a glossary – albeit a whimsical one – follows the practice of several of the psychoanalytic books in Keller's library.

The themes of maturity and reversal (the child becoming the adult's father) are dealt with elsewhere in this volume in the aphorisms *On Maturity* and the essay on *The Need for Pets* respectively. 'Reversal of generations phantasy' (Ernest Jones) is also the theme of the third of the *Three Psychoanalytic Notes on Peter Grimes*.

1   Answers to Motto Quiz: (a) Nobody (b) Nothing.
2   See 'Glossary of Difficult Words'. [This sentence caused difficulty in the proof and has been re-edited here.]
3   Arnold Schoenberg: *Harmonielehre* (1910-11) (abridged English translation), London, 1948.
4   When you read that certain classical melodies (2nd subjects) are derived from the scale, don't believe it: they're based on the triad and filled in.
5   [HK's original reads: 'in the otherwise excellent Section I.']

Extracts from *The Little Sweep* are reproduced by kind permission of Boosey and Hawkes Music Publishers Ltd. © 1950 Hawkes & Son (London) Ltd.

Keller's Writings on Benjamin Britten 1946-52: a Report

Between 1946, when he heard *Peter Grimes* at Sadler's Wells, and 1952, when he co-edited with Donald Mitchell the celebrated *Benjamin Britten: a Commentary on his Works from a Group of Specialists*, London, Rockliff, 1952, Keller devoted himself with extraordinary energy and single-mindedness to propagating the composer and his music. There are three bibliographical sources for Keller's writings on Britten in this period: (a) the bibliography to the Mitchell/Keller *Commentary* cited above, which lists 38 items, though not the 'Britten Issue' of *Music Survey*, Vol. II, No. 4, Spring, 1950 (reprinted London, Faber, 1981); (b) the bibliography included in 'Hans Keller: A Memorial Symposium', *Music Analysis*, Vol. 5, Nos. 2-3, 1986, pp. 407-40; and (c) a small group of unpublished writings held in the Hans Keller Archive in the University Library Cambridge in addition to those printed in the 'Music and Psychology' section of the present volume. This last source includes:

(i)   A straightforward introduction, 'Great British Composer' (1947), comprising eleven pages of typescript;
(ii)   An untitled adaption of (i) for young people;
(iii)   Materials relating to the [elegant and straightforward] opera-synopses booklet *Benjamin Britten: The Rape of Lucretia and Albert Herring*, London, Boosey and Hawkes, 1947;
(iv)   Materials (10 different items) relating to the essay on 'Benjamin Britten's Second [String] Quartet', *Tempo*, 3, March 1947, pp. 6-8;
(v)   Materials relating to the essay, 'A Film Analysis of the Orchestra' [on the *Young Person's Guide to the Orchestra*] for *Sight and Sound* 16/61, Spring 1971, pp. 30-31;
(vi)   6 versions of a contribution, 'A Britten Festival', to *Everybody's*, 5 June, 1948, occupying 10 pages of typescript;
(vii)   4 items, including a carbon of the original version, on 'Britten and Mozart' [1946/48 reprinted below], along with various items of correspondence with Geoffrey Sharp, Eric Blom and *Horizon*.
(viii) 'Peter Grimes', an 'HMV Analytical Note' running to 21 pages of typescript, with 2 separate versions of p. 21, along with various items of correspondence with EMI.
(ix)   A 5-page carbon copy of 'Benjamin Britten's *Albert Herring*', published in *Music Review*, 9/4, November 1948, p. 309-10.

The Psychology of Film Music

From the mid 1940s to the end of the 1950s Keller wrote copiously on film music, and represented Britain at the first international film music conference held in Florence in May 1950. The writing is predominantly technical and aesthetic, and deserves separate study. However, the following reviews show how Keller's 'overriding' interest in psychology informed this sphere of activity too.

1   *The Psychology of Film Music [on Arthur Benjamin and Georges Auric]*

Introduction

The psychology of music is the most difficult branch of applied psychology, but the psychology of what we might call applied (as distinct from absolute or pure) music offers a comparatively easy approach to the musico-psychologist. The reason, therefore, is clear. Whereas in pure music we encounter processes which, at any rate on the surface, bear little relation to such mental phenomena as have already been elucidated by psychological analysis, the processes that make up applied music, though in themselves as mysterious psychologically as those of pure music, are at least definitely related to extra-musical mental processes that have already been successfully subjected to scientific research.

But although 'the elements of art are not limited to the world of art,' though 'they reach into life and whatever extraneous knowledge we gain . . . may quicken our feelings for the work itself and even enter legitimately into those feelings,'[1] it would be disastrous for the musico-psychologist to assume, however silently, that as soon as he has explained the relation between applied music and the ideas to which it is applied, he may proceed to explain away music as such merely in terms of its extra-musical relations. This fallacy has often been committed by the psychologically-minded as well as by those who think that they are musically-minded. On the other hand, it will not, of course, do to brush aside the study of applied music's avowed association with extra-musical ideas just because such endeavour is not likely to furnish a master-key to the psychology of music. The history of science has not yet revealed a single master-key, but has, on the contrary, shown that quite a number of alleged master-keys turn out, upon examination to unlock not even a single door.

Of all branches of applied music, film music is the youngest. It has, indeed, been born into, and also out of, a psychological age, and for that reason alone it ought to be of particular interest to the psychologist, once he has noted its existence, which, so far, he has not.[2] Film music, far more than many another art form, has a well-definable psychological function: while art in general aims primarily at representing the beautiful (which sometime may be the ugly, not because the artist does not believe in beauty, but because he believes in the beauty of ugliness), film music aims to an unusual extent, indeed, often primarily, at suggesting psychological truth – thus an essential part of the psychological functions, or of the psychotechnics, of film music.

The development of the psychological, as distinct from the aesthetic aspect of music, has been going on for a long time; it indeed reached peaks before the advent of film music. Mozart was a unique figure in this as in many other respects, in that he succeeded in uniting, to the highest degree, an unsurpassed artistico-psychological insight with an unsurpassable aesthetic sense. He would not, however, have seen any point in beauty-less music; for him, indeed, music that was not primarily beautiful ceased to be music. At a later stage in the development of psychological music, however, the scales shifted: 'Music', said Mussorgsky, 'is a means of communication between men, and not an end in itself – the pursuit of beauty alone, in the literal acceptation of the word, is a childish stupidity, a rudimentary form of an art,' and Cecil Gray declares Mussorgsky 'the greatest musical psychologist of all time,'[3] a pronouncement which, to be sure, is disputable. It would not be wrong to see in a considerable section of film music the most stressedly and most conspicuously psychological music of all time. In the following two examples, some of film music's psychotechnics can without difficulty be analysed:

I.   *Master of Bankdam* (1947) adapted from the novel *The Crowthers of Bankdam* by Thomas Armstrong, produced by Walter Forde and Edward Dryhurst, and directed by Walter Forde. The music is by Arthur Benjamin, who wrote incidental scores, inter alia, for the films *The Scarlet Pimpernel* (1935), *Wings of the Morning* (1937), and *An Ideal Husband* (1947).

This is the story of Bankdam, a Yorkshire mill. Around 1860 it prospers under its old master, but later goes through several crises under his sons Zebediah and Joshua, who tend in opposite directions. Joshua dies in a mill collapse; eventually Zebediah, himself fatally ill, entrusts Bankdam not to his own son, but to Joshua's son, Simeon, who, as Zebediah realizes in the last reel, will make Bankdam prosper again.

Now the musical score centres on, and develops a theme song ('The Fire of Your Love'), which is sung, in A major, near the beginning of the film, i.e. where Joshua courts his future wife, Annie. Expressing a woman's love, the song amounts to a projection into the external world of Annie's love for Joshua. And like every theme song or Leitmotiv, 'The Fire of your Love' remains associated throughout the score with the idea that it originally suggests or underlines. Thus, for instance, it is worked out in the orchestral background to the film while Annie, after Joshua's death, is haunted by memories of her marriage. Thereby, it is true, the theme song does not make a specific, psychological contribution to the film: it does not furnish much psychological news that is not furnished by the film itself. Yet, by its constant association with Annie's love for Joshua, the song prepares for its communicating, at the end of the picture, a psychological truth which is not suggested by the visual alone. For at the end, where the dramatic situation compels the spectator to identify himself with Annie and to look at events from her point of view, we get the theme song – now, be it noted, in E major – as orchestral background to young Simeon's accession to the mastership of Bankdam. The psychological implication is obvious, at any rate to the psychologist: ' . . . the parent whose sexual emotions and tendencies have but little opportunity for discharge will be apt to lavish a greater amount of affection on his children than one who is leading a more active sexual life. Thus it is that widowers, widows, and those who are unhappily married frequently display a more than normal degree of attachment to their children, the latter receiving, in addition to the love that would ordinarily fall to their share, *the displaced affection which would otherwise find its outlet in the love of wife and husband.*'[4] The final appearance of the theme song, then imparts this piece of exact psychological information: Annie has eventually overcome her grief by displacing her cathexis of the (internal) object-imago of her husband on to an actual (external) object, i.e. her son. The fact that this final version of the theme song is in E major, i.e. the dominant of the key in which it is originally sung (*vide* above), adds a subtle finishing touch to the music's psychological significance. For the dominant, which appears of course after the tonic in the harmonic series, is the tonic's offspring, its 'child'. The reader is asked not to be misled by the expression 'dominant' for the fifth degree of the diatonic scale, for, in point of fact, as he may know from his musical experience, the tonic dominates the dominant, and not vice versa.[5]

II.   *La belle at la bête* (1946; first shown in this country [UK] in 1947), written and directed by Jean Cocteau. The music is by Georges Auric, a member of the famous group of 'Les Six' (Auric, Durey, Honegger, Milhaud, Poulenc, and Tailleferre). He contributed to incidental music, inter alia to *Alibi* (1938), *Dead of Night* (1945), *Caesar and Cleopatra* (1944-45), *Hue and Cry* (1946), *La symphonie pastorelle* (1946) and *It Always Rains on Sunday* (1947) which contains the best music [of his] I know, though not the most psychological.

This is the well-known fairytale of the Beauty and the Beast. The two complementary psychological processes on which the story centres are, (a) decomposition,[6] and (b) (re-) condensation.[7] In simpler words, the action is psychologically based on, and aesthetically unified by, the idea of three different individuals (the Beauty's suitors: The Beast, Avenant, and Ardent) who, from the point of view of depth psychology, are but three, partly conflicting aspects of a single personality (the Beauty's father substitute). Indeed, at the end of the tale, Avenant and the Beast die and dissolve into Prince Ardent, who thus resumes his identity that he had temporarily lost through a spell.

Auric and his friend Cocteau have handled the integration of music and visual with formal mastery, by which I here mean the employment of the simplest unifying, and at the same time contrasting, formal means for the purpose of suggesting the visual's deepest emotional and spiritual content. The simplest structural device in the present case was *to link every musical entry with either Avenant, or the Beast, or Ardent*, to have no music on the soundtrack that was not associated with one of these three individuals. Thereby a double psycho-technical gain is achieved: (a) music being the servant of the orectic[8] (emotional) rather than the cognitive aspect of the film, the exclusive distribution of the musical entries to the three suitors enhances the sensitive spectator-listener's awareness of the fact that the tale's deepest affective centre lies in these three figures; (b) the linking of the music with nothing but one or the other of the suitors points to the fundamental oneness of these three versions of the Father.

The unifying function of the music also applies aesthetically, for the simple reason that the artistic unity of the tale is based on the condensation with which it ends: it is this final event which, retrospectively, shows up the unidirectional current that flows through the film. The broad, unifying frame given by the music offers, of course, at the same time, ample opportunity for psychological-musical contrasts which correspond to the conflict that lies at the root of the present, as of any other, case of a mythologically 'decomposed' personality.

Now it might be suggested that Auric's plan of musical distribution is a rather obvious affair, which does not merit so much comment. Faultless psychologico-artistic method, however, is always obvious once one has noticed it, and the elemental, when recognized, is merely considered elementary. Yet I am not aware that anybody who has seen the film – the most perspicacious critics included – has shown a sign of his being intellectually alive to the organization of musical entries (though I am sure that emotionally the integration of film and music has achieved its effect). In art, as in science, the simplest thing is to scorn simplicity, the most difficult thing is to attain it.

NOTES

Source

World Psychology, 1948, pp. 23-6. (This was the journal discussed by Keller and Rickman (see Part II above).) The author is described as 'Hans Keller, L. R. A. M.'

Keller returned to *The Master of Bankdam* and its music in 'Arthur Benjamin and the Problem of Popularity', *Tempo*, 15, Spring 1950, pp. 4-15, and to 'Georges Auric at Film Music's Best' in his column 'Film Music and Beyond', *Music Review*, 15/4, November 1954, pp. 311-13 (reproduced below). In another review, 'Britain versus France', *Music Review*, November 1952, pp. 310-12, Keller writes:

> For the British musician, it is, for the rest, interesting to hear from Auric that when working on *La belle et la bête*, he had written continuous music for several concluding scenes, but that Jean Cocteau, the director, "had the excellent idea to have the music interrupted by intervals of complete silence. Thus Cocteau has made me realize the significance of silence, and I am very grateful to him." But we in Britain – and this shows the extent to which Auric's confrontation of the two film lands is still relevant – still think *La belle et la bête* severely overstuffed with (admittedly often excellent) music.

1   Lionel Trilling, 'Freud and Literature', *Horizon*, XVI/92.
2   Hans Keller, *The Need for Competent Film Music Criticism*, London, British Film Institute, 1947.
3   Cecil Gray, *History of Music*, London, 1928.
4   J. C. Flugel, *The Psychoanalytic Study of the Family* [6th edition], London, International Psychoanalytic Library, Hogarth Press, 1939.
5   Arnold Schoenberg, *Harmonielehre*, Leipzig/Vienna, 1911 (translated as *Theory of Harmony*, by Roy E. Carter, London, Faber, 1978).
6   Ernest Jones, *On the Nightmare*, London, International Psychoanalytic Library, 1931.
7   Sigmund Freud, *Die Traumdeutung* [*The Interpretation of Dreams*], *Gesammelte Werke*, 11/111, London, 1942.
8   J. C. Flugel, *Man, Morals and Society*, London, Duckworth, 1945.

2 *Georges Auric at Film Music's Best*

A Continental revival of *La p . . . respectueuse*, a 2- or 3-year-old film after Sartre's play of the same title, gave me a chance to hear an important Auric score which so far as I am aware, has never reached this country, whereas an English translation of Sartre's original drama (*The Respectable Prostitute*) has. As might be expected, the film waters down Sartre's incisive criticism of American Negrophobia. There are passages in the original dialogue which establish its author as perhaps the first virtuoso in the field of applied philosophy – an achievement which may very well prove decisive, for while pure virtuosity has died out in the realm of music in order for music to survive, philosophy can only survive as a social force if it brings forth virtuosos of the truly and honestly dazzling variety: the esoteric riddles of both the psychic and the time-space universe are being taken care of nowadays by other departments of the enquiring mind. Unfortunately, however, more than the inevitable measure of the original play's significance goes by the board in the film, whose makers have all too conscientiously tried to make at least parts of an unfilmic structure filmogenic. As a result, the entire exposition of the drama has received a kind of treatment that is exactly the opposite of artistic method as such: instead of compression, we get empty extensions that are designed to make room for filmable detail. Nevertheless, enough substance of both ethical feeling and psychologically philosophical thought has remained to stimulate Georges Auric towards one of the weightiest and, at the same time, one of the most economical film scores he has yet supplied in his somewhat over-productive career as a film composer. By way of incidental nourishment, his piece has provided us with a four-course meal for thought.

1   The Film Composer and His Film

The operative word is the possessive pronoun, the critical point the artist's possessiveness. Anyone who has had an opportunity of observing a visual artist (especially a portraitist) at work must have been struck by the fact that his mind depends for its inspiration, to a variable extent, on the psychic love- or hate-relationship which he is able to establish with his object or subject. A posteriori, this is perhaps most obvious in the case of a sexual (Toulouse-Lautrec) or religious love object on the one hand, or a political hate object (caricature) on the other; for the progeny of the latter relationship, Ernst Kris's happy characterization, 'the dissolution of unity in the interests of aggression,' springs to mind [see 'The Psychology of Caricature', *International Journal of Psychoanalysis*, XVII, 1936]. Turning to our own art, we find that the song writer, the composer of cantatas, oratorios, operas and so forth, is usually able freely to choose his love object as one human being can choose another in our society, whereas the writer of incidental music for the stage, or not so incidental music for the cinema, is often at the mercy of a complex marriage market, of matchmakers and arranged marriages. The composer of stage music can at least continue his own life up to a satisfactory point, writing his own kind of music without bothering too much about marital adjustment, but the film musician is inevitably drawn into a close relationship with the film, whether the bond be artistic or not. Anyone talking to a 'pure' musician writing for the film will be struck by the composer's intense reactions to the particular picture for which he is providing the music, and which tends to be either 'excellent' or 'rotten'. Composers are usually of the opinion that 'only good films' will produce good music in the musician's mind; it would no doubt be more accurate to say – "only films with which the composer is capable of forming a positive (love) relation", whatever their more objective value. Hate relations are of no avail in the film-musical set-up – if we disregard Malcolm Arnold's exceptional and remarkable *Captain's Paradise* [see *Music Review*, 14/3, August 1953, p. 222], which seems to show a distinctly ambivalent attitude on the part of the composer: sheltering behind the attitude of irony which the film requires him to employ, he gets his own back on 'the art of film' by laughing – unofficially, but all the more effectively and musically – at the entire film world, thus furnishing an eminently artistic example of 'the dissolution of (sham) unity in the interests of aggression'. Auric's own *La fête à Henriette*, which indulges in the selfsame destructive process, does so officially, because the film itself adopts a self-ironical, anti-filmic attitude, offering the composer an opportunity to identify himself with it.

Identification (or, in stricter psychoanalytical parlance, 'introjection') and unidentifying love ('object-cathexis', according to the psychoanalyst's vocabulary) would indeed seem to be the two positive attitudes towards a film which, separately or in combination, determine the nature of a composer's 'possessiveness' and the quality of his work, the question of whether one or the other attitude or both manifest themselves depending on the character not only of the film, but also, probably more so, of the composer himself. With Auric's better scores (*It Always Rains on Sunday*, *La belle et la bête* – to mention only two of the best-remembered), it usually appears to be a case of predominant identification, but most of his recent efforts, such as *The Titfield Thunderbolt*, the famous *Moulin Rouge* which is still being whistled all over the European continent and isles, *The Wages of Fear*, or his music for the adaptation of G. K. Chesterton's *Father Brown* stories, would seem to be the result more of matchmaking than of one or the other kind of love-making. The score for *La p . . . respectueuse*, on the other hand, strikes me as a case of identification par excellence, which is why I have permitted myself a few introductory remarks on the film itself: essentially, it is a tendentious drama, whence it offered the composer an opportunity for a twofold identification, affecting not only his conscious and unconscious self ('ego'), but also his unconscious and conscious conscience ('superego' and 'ego-ideal'). In Auric's opinion, it is no doubt an 'excellent' film. Perhaps, then, the motion picture is the only artistic or semi-artistic medium where 'committed art' easily results in good music, simply because all good film music springs from a full-blooded commitment in the first place.

2 *The Undeveloping Film Composer*

A clear conclusion emerges from our psychological analysis: as long as the film composer's 'marriages' must needs consist of what, from the standpoint of his own artistic 'love life', is a more or less accidental succession of good and (chiefly) bad matches, he can hardly develop as a film composer, even though his film work may reflect his development as a composer. In all other fields of applied music (except for incidental stage music, and including such forms as the scenic oratorio), the composer has a chance to develop along the special path chosen: Mozart developed not only as a composer, but also as an opera composer; in fact, his operatic development had diverse repercussive effects upon his development as a composer. And just as the development of opera depends to no small extent on the development of opera composers, the curious circumstance that there has not, to date, been any genuine film-musical history is due to the fact that the film composer is not allowed to develop. *La p . . . respectueuse* is chronologically surrounded by Aurician film music of comparatively feeble interest and does not prove the result of individual film-musical development, though Auric's development as a composer may possibly have something to do with the quality of this music. In a moderately ideal society, film-musical development could have a continuous refreshing influence on musical evolution; as things stand, however, the undeveloping film composer exerts a pernicious influence on the less resistant parts of both his own and other composers' creative minds. Arnold Schoenberg, who was given to radical solutions, uncompromising and unsullied, in this field as in any other, wrote his *Music for a Film Scene* (*Musik zu einer Lichtspielszene*, Op. 34) for an imaginary love-object, as it were: the film itself had not been supplied. But the laws of supply and demand have a wider application than is dreamt of in the political economist's philosophy, and if every good film composer wrote an imaginary film score every year, thus 'demanding' the appropriate kind of film, one or the other adventurous film-maker would sooner or later oblige. Man creates his love-objects in his own images' image.

3 *Film-musical Innovation*

A corollary to our conclusion is that film-musical innovations of lasting musico-dramatic or musical significance will be few and far between, as if the art suffered from an unprecedented and highly confusing complaint, namely, embryonic senility. All the more reason, then, for the music critic to notice novel features when they do turn up. Having contributed, in succeeding as well as previous films, a multitude of epigonic ideas and devices, Auric turns one of the most constant Hollywood hair-raisers upside down in *La p . . . respectueuse*, and thus introduces a highly logical device into film music. We all know those well-feared climaxes of frequent occurrence where the heroine, love-sick and re-creatively inspired, commences a not altogether unknown Chopin Nocturne upon her private pianoforte, and is anon joined by what appears to be the yearning harmony of the spheres in the form of a highly stringy orchestral accompaniment, compared with which Chopin's own attempts at concerto texture and structure are of Mozartian finesse. With a simple, almost genius-like stroke of the practised film-musician's pen, Auric inverts this procedure: a straight piece of jazz is heard as background music, continues over the change of filmic sequence, and emerges as realistic dance music in the subsequent scene. Instead of a hopeless contradiction and confusion of dramatic levels, then, we get a pre-realistic anticipation of reality: idea develops into fact, background into foreground, one musico-dramatic level into another, so that we can see the present (the sequence accompanied by background jazz) in the light of the future (the dance), the causes in the light of their effects.

Significantly enough, this tendency to turn conventional stratagems into meaningful devices, and epigonism, pastiche and quotation into characteristic commentary, is apparent throughout the score. Instead of embarrassing parodies, variational treatment, etc., of the *Kleine Nachtmusik* (*The Titfield Thunderbolt*), of an Offenbach excerpt (*Moulin Rouge*) or a Viennese-operetta phrase (*Father Brown*), instead of downright imitation music (ibid.), we hear, for instance, a sharply significant injection of boogie-woogie bass ostinato in C into a piece of a quite different nature, which would show up, if showing up were needed, the sterility of Rolf Liebermann's boogie-woogie in the first act of his new opera, *Penelope*: a bad boogie-woogie, he might have realized, does not make a good parody or caricature. His is indeed one of the most drastic examples of the results of film music's fatal influence, whereas Auric demonstrates the sort of influence film music could exert in an artistic climate.

4 Film-musical Instrumentation

Auric's stringless band (chiefly woodwind and percussion) might earn the applause of cultural opposites, such as Stravinsky on the one hand and the communists on the other. According to the latter (Hanns Eisler) school of film-musical thought, the anti-sentimental scoring would, I suppose, be praised because it corresponds to the realistic nature of the cinematic tradition. I would arrive at the same conclusion by a diametrically divergent route: the naturalism (read: pseudo-realism) of the cinema makes it, potentially and often actually, the most sentimental and unrealistic creative medium in existence (a kiss doesn't become more realistic through being shown in labial detail), whence it is the composer's task to retrieve the artistic situation, fusing, for instance, an anti-sentimental texture and a structure charged with emotion, i.e. with psychic realism.

Source

This review appeared in Keller's column 'Film Music and Beyond', *Music Review*, 15/4, November 1954, pp. 311-13. For a report on Keller's writings on film music held in the Cambridge University Library Archive, see pp. 259-60 below.

Creative Character: Its Psychology

The attempt to analyse the intra- and extra-musical creative character of individual artists and to relate the analyses to a background of established typologies preoccupied Keller throughout his life. By comparison with his nineteenth-century critical forefathers – pre-eminently Kant and Schiller – he was able to draw on mainly Freudian psychological concepts (he typically avoided reference to Carl Jung's work in the field). However, in a personal communication to the Editor just before his death, Keller claimed that nothing he had achieved in this area had really satisfied him.

Of the following two essays, the first, on Britten (1946), was matched by a long study of Keller's from much later in his life, 'Operatic Music and Britten', included in The Operas of Benjamin Britten *(ed. by David Herbert, London, Hamish Hamilton, 1979, pp. xiii-xxxi): this drew on Schiller's famous distinction between 'naïve' and 'sentimental' artists. The second, on Mozart (1947), may be more interesting for its approach than for the force of its argument (pace Keller, in Heinrich Schenker's terms, a diatonic or chromatic* Anstieg *is common enough property). Together, the essays defined Keller's two-pronged approach to characterological study, the one extra-historical and typological ('Britten and Mozart'), the other historical ('Mozart and Boccherini'). This approach in turn reflected dualisms that had dominated European critical thought since the mid-to-late eighteenth century, of which Hegel's 'noumena and phenomena', Schopenhauer's 'will and representation', and Freud's 'unconscious and conscious' are but three instances.*

1   Britten and Mozart

A Challenge in the Form of Variations on an Unfamiliar Theme

Written in 1946, this essay was first published in Music and Letters, *Vol. 29, No. 1, January 1948, after it had been rejected by four other publications that were (apparently) uneasy at the boldness of Keller's comparisons. It was reprinted 'with one or two stylistic changes' in: Donald Mitchell and Hans Keller,* Benjamin Britten, A Commentary on his Works from a Group of Specialists, *London, Rockliff, 1952, pp. 319-34, where it became the first part of a two-stage investigation into Britten's 'Musical Character'. It is the later printing that is followed here, though the notes have been modified. The two-stage investigation of 1952 followed the divisions 'extra-historical' ('Britten and Mozart') and 'historical' ('The Crisis of Beauty and Melody'): the extra-historical comparisons were fuelled by a reading of Alfred Einstein's* Mozart. His Character. His Work *(London, Cassell, 1946), whereas the historical part (which is not reprinted here) examines 'The General Cultural Situation' prevalent at the time. This latter unfolded the proposition that, 'more sexual than aggressive energies are needed for the creation of beauty; more aggressive than sexual energies are needed for the discovery of truth.' This theme was to preoccupy him in the years following 1952 and deserves a separate study.*

Remarkable similarities between Benjamin Britten and Mozart obtrude themselves on the suitably prejudiced observer, prejudiced, among other things, in favour of the view that presence of similarities does not imply absence of differences. People are wont to harp on the relation of Britten to Purcell (and to other composers, such as Mahler, whom they know Britten to admire). With Purcell, however, Britten has obviously established what in psychoanalysis one would call a superego identification – Purcell, that is to say, is Britten's father, and there is a limit to one's interest in the continuous pointing out of evident family resemblances.

Yet there is a way in which both comparisons between Purcell and Britten, and between Mozart and Britten, are equally beneficial: they counteract the current over-emphasis on the historical aspect of music, to which, in the case of the comparison with Mozart, is to be added action against the over-emphasis on the ethnological and geographical aspects.

To be sure, the exaggerated importance attached to historical factors has itself to be considered historically, as a sign of our times: the significance of the temporal environment for human activities, mental or otherwise, has once again been discovered, and to discover means to overestimate.

In music, moreover, historical explanations are particularly welcome, for the factors that go to make the individual musical character are a rather mysterious affair, and it is one of the tragedies of the mind that it prefers mysterious explanations to waiting for the facts to become a little less mysterious.

One of those who overdo the historical aspect of Britten's own work is Britten. 'It is largely a matter of when one was born. If I had been born in 1813 instead of 1913 I should have been a romantic, primarily concerned to express my personality in music . . .'[1] I don't think he would. True, he would have been more of a romantic, but in the sense in which he uses the word not primarily one. Taking into account everything depth psychology teaches us about character formation in early childhood, it is fairly safe to assume that, other things being as nearly equal as they can be, a Benjamin Britten born in 1813 would not tend (again in his own words) towards the 'point at which the composer would be the only man capable of understanding his own music.'[2] This is not to say that nature is necessarily more important for a man's artistic character than nurture, but rather that there are, not only in nature but also in nurture, character-building elements whose dependence on historical circumstances – given a large cultural frame like 'western civilization' – is negligible. In early childhood (between minus-nine months and six years) contemporary aesthetic trends are not usually of great importance even to a precocious individual such as Britten. To quote two instances cited by him, Picasso and Stravinsky did not just come because history told them to, but because they liked being told. History is of course clever afterwards: had Picasso and Stravinsky not worked against individualistic art, she would not have betrayed that she had told them to, but would have told us that they behaved according to her previous precepts.

One does not, then, understand Britten as soon as one knows that he belongs to the twentieth century and why, and that he is an Englishman and why.[3] Trying to neutralize the over-stress on historical and also on geographical interpretations (important as these admittedly are), this section will, but for a small exception, disregard them altogether.

Often when another writer's view of either composer approximates to my own, I shall give his instead of or in addition to mine, in order to exclude as far as possible the objection that I am begging the question. And wherever convenient, I shall, of course, also let the composers speak for themselves.

The most obvious common characteristic of Britten and Mozart is their youthful maturity, which concept has in either case a double meaning: proficiency early attained and maturity retaining a youthful aspect. Busoni on Mozart: 'he is young like a youth and wise like an aged man – never out of date and never modern . . .' But just because of their immense *talent*, their extreme receptivity and adjustability, their *genius* emerges and matures almost belatedly: their development contrasts sharply with Schubert's and particularly Mendelssohn's, where genius, and mature genius at that, breaks forth at an improbably early stage.

Both composers manifest their maturity in artistic behaviour that is largely classical. To me they seem to be masters in the solution of a paradox inherent in all classical art: the paradox of restrained, yet explicit emotion.

Both have an impeccable sense of form. With Britten this particular asset is even acknowledged by his sternest critics, while Mozart's sense of form can only be called, with Busoni, 'extra-human'.

Both are liable to be severely misunderstood (yes, *are*, for even in Mozart's case this is not yet a thing of the past), not only by their critics, but also by a great number of the great number of their followers. For their music is approachable on various levels, each seemingly giving a complete picture in itself, so that the superficial listener, moving on the most superficial level, may yet be strongly impressed and may think he knows all about what he hears. In this connection Mozart's attitude towards the 'popular' should be noted. Writing about the first three Vienna piano Concertos he says (letter of 28th December, 1782):

> These concertos are a happy medium between what is too easy and too difficult; they are very brilliant, pleasing to the ear, and natural, without being vapid. There are passages here and there from which connoisseurs alone can derive satisfaction; but these passages are written in such a way that the less learned cannot fail to be pleased, though without knowing why . . .

Are we not here reminded of Britten's popularity, as well as of the fact that he is at times reproached with 'making concessions'? In any case, Mozart and Britten are the only two composers I know who strongly and widely attract people who do not understand them.

Both composers are clever, supreme craftsmen, hence both are accused of trying to be clever and of lacking in the deeper emotions:

> It is a pity that in his truly artistic and beautiful compositions [he] should carry his effort after originality too far, to the detriment of the sentiment and heart of his works. His new [compositions] . . . are much too highly spiced to be palatable for any length of time.

One of Britten's more 'favourable' critics? No, one of the most favourable among the then contemporary critics of Mozart's six quartets dedicated to Haydn. 'It is perhaps the one work . . . in which he achieved real sublimity.' But this, surely, is one of Britten's 'favourable' critics, talking, I don't know, of *Grimes* (referring to 'Now the Great Bear and Pleiades'), or of the *Donne Sonnets* (referring to the sixth), or of *Lucretia* (referring to the English horn and strings passage at Lucretia's last entry) . . . No, it is a critic of Mozart again, this time one of our own age, a very favourable one; nor is he just a scribe. It is in fact one who is often above criticism – Professor Dent on *The Magic Flute* (1940). 'The "splendid isolation" of Mozartian music from the standpoint of biographical interpretation caused this music to be explained, in a period of romantic affiliation, as *academic in form, cold, empty, frivolous, superficial.*'[4] Precisely the same descriptions are not seldom given of Britten's music today, though we are not living in a period of romantic affiliation. And if it is to be objected that Britten, as distinct from Mozart, actually *is* cold and empty and superficial, we who find warmth and a rich and deep content in his music have at least this to be said in our favour: while one does not usually find things that are not there, one often does not find things that are. I would suggest that both composers sublimate not only their depths, but also their heights, i.e. they even sublimate their sublimity. (Richard Strauss, incidentally, calls Mozart 'the sublimest of all composers.')

In the music of neither Mozart nor Britten is there a sign of inhibitions (as distinct from restraint). In this respect their exact contrary is Brahms.[5] It is this freedom from inhibitions that makes a certain type of neurotic listener belittle their works: we cannot easily bear it if others do not suffer from what we deny suffering from ourselves. Hand in hand with the absence of intra-musical inhibitions goes a delight in accepting, and working within, given limitations. With Mozart this point is self-evident. As for Britten, we need not believe him too much when he gives a variety of practical reasons for the scoring of *Lucretia*, *Herring*, and *The Beggar's Opera*; for it is clear that these reasons offer him a welcome excuse for trying what he can do within the limitations of the chamber opera.

Ease, facility, effortless skill – these points are obvious in the case of either composer. Among their admirers both Mozart and Britten are known to be able to 'manage anything'. I hope there will never be any opportunity of proving that Britten can even manage things that bore him stiff; in Mozart's case such proof is furnished by the F minor *Fantasy* for what is called a barrel-organ (*Orgelwalze*) or clock (*Uhr*), 'a kind of composition which I detest', as he writes to his wife. But the general fact that both composers can write on commission as if they did not write on commission is of course established. The essence of such music for a special occasion does not with them betray external compulsion. Here the history of the Mozart *Requiem* is symbolic: an outer impulse is changed into an inner one.

The continued success of such impulse changing does not depend merely upon versatility, but also on deep-reaching agility. Britten is perhaps the most agile composer of our time. Busoni on Mozart: 'He is universal through his agility.' Universality itself has many aspects with Mozart and Britten. Two of these are particularly significant, both aesthetically and psychologically:

1 A German writer on music, Carl Gollmick (1796-1866), divides composers into two classes (he would!), i.e. 'melodists' and 'contrapuntists', and proceeds to show that Mozart satisfies the requirements of both these classes. If one wants to use this objectionable division – as a stenographic makeshift – for showing that it cannot be used in Mozart's case, and why not, one can also apply it, in almost the same way, to Britten.

2 Both composers have a sense at once of humour and of tragedy which they manifest quite clearly and which yet tends to go unrecognised by many of us because we do not easily permit ourselves to indulge, in our turn, in this double sense, and because we often find it difficult to bear contrary standpoints in the same man or work, or expressed at the same time. Yet, as the psychoanalyst Otto Rank has clearly recognized apropos of *Don Giovanni*, music is uniquely suited 'to express, at the same time, different tendencies'.[6]

This [last] point merits a little further attention, for which purpose I must, alas, once more differ from Professor Dent. Replying to the time-honoured question whether *Don Giovanni* is a serious or a comic opera, he says: 'The simplest plan is to take the opera as its author and composer intended – as an amusing comedy, with a touch of social satire and a great deal of fantastic impossibility.' One is all for taking the opera as all this, but Dent wants it to be taken as this alone. The libretto may stand such a one-sided interpretation, but the music does not. The question whether *Don Giovanni* is a serious or a comic opera does not indeed exist: it is both.[7] Similarly, *Così fan tutte* is not just 'an elaborate artificial comedy' (Dent). The great E major aria, for instance, or Act II's A major duet, suggests otherwise.

With Britten, the whole story started all over again. A prominent and otherwise perspicacious critic remarked, in view of *Lucretia* (which, upon thorough study, I deem a great work), that the composer's bent was not for 'tragic or human feeling', but solely for 'artificial comedy'. Meanwhile, Britten's first comic opera, *Herring*, had itself shown that he was able, in the words of Charles Stuart, to take 'excursions into a rarer world, with the earthiness of comic opera left behind and below.' We must recognize that there are two sides to Britten.[8] In fact I personally think that whenever there is only one side to an artist it is a wrong one.

Both composers create in the same way. Britten: "Usually I have the music complete in my head before putting pen to paper."[9] In this respect their exact contrary is Beethoven (like Brahms, a composer whom Britten does not fully understand). They also create, if I may say so, in the same way:

> When not flying or sailing to foreign opera houses and concert halls . . . Britten is perpetually rushing off to catch trains for voice-and-piano recitals with Peter Pears in remote provincial towns. The business of musical creation goes on serenely among the bustle and baggage. Looking unseeingly through train windows . . . Britten composes as fluently as if he were sitting in a soundproof cell, with quires of manuscript paper before him and a grand piano at his elbow.[10]

> And travel does not interrupt Mozart's creative activity; it rather stimulates it. When long journeys are out of the question, as for example, during the last ten years in Vienna, he is constantly changing his residence . . . from the town into the suburbs, and from the suburbs back again into town.[11]

Britten's parallel manoeuvres between London and Snape and, later, between Aldeburgh and London, are, of course, well known.[12]

Scoring: strictly speaking, this problem does not appear to be one with Mozart and Britten (except where they are concerned with other composers' works: *Messiah*, *Matinées musicales*). 'With Mozart,' Arthur Hutchings aptly observes,[13] 'such problems [of balance, tone-colour, variety, etc.] do not seem to exist. He may have been lucky; the band may have been at just the right stage of development to make instrumental thinking but one element in musical thinking as a whole . . .'[14] (Dear old History again, though it is true that Hutchings later rejects her claims.) Compare this with what one of the most discerning critics of Britten, Desmond Shawe-Taylor, says about this composer's 'musical thinking as a whole':

> One difference between Britten and most of his contemporaries is that, in the process of composition, his imaginative 'inner ear' is listening, all the time and at full stretch, to what he is doing; fascinating as his music looks on paper – for he is a master of figuration and every kind of musical device [as Mozart is – H. K.] – I feel tolerably sure that his ideas never occur to him as anything but sheer sensuous sound, and that it is to this fact that they owe the force and freshness with which they strike the listener's ear.

Thus, for instance, Mozart's and Britten's compositions for orchestra are not orchestrated, but orchestral.

Both composers seem to derive much from melodic inspiration. More materially, they are liable to be inspired by the human voice (as also by language, including foreign language), and indeed influenced by individual voices (as well as by instruments and instrumentalists). As regards Mozart, 'opera was always composed for a special occasion and for particular singers; the choice of singers influenced the vocal style and other characteristics as well.'[15] The same is true of Britten's operas to varying degrees; even Grimes was 'considerably influenced' by the

Sadler's Wells Opera Company. It would seem to me that when Britten writes for tenor or soprano he is in advance of himself in a similar way as Mozart when writing a piano concerto (in which he let himself be inspired not only by his piano playing but also, in various ways though indirectly, by vocal ideas). At the same time Britten the pianist has for me some striking similarities to what I picture to be Mozart the pianist; but as I have not heard Mozart I shall not enlarge on this point.

In any case Mozart's piano concertos and Britten's tenor compositions are instances of their common love for virtuosity, which, together with their common love of the dramatic, is also part of their intense common love for opera. Both, moreover, carry their symphonic thinking into opera, and their operatic thinking into extra-operatic music.

As for the extra-musical aspects of their operas, the psychological and sociological theme of rebellion plays an important part. Even *The Magic Flute*, it must be remembered, 'was a work of rebellion;'[16] *Grimes* and *Lucretia*, as well as *Herring* and *Budd*, centre on the motive of opposition to (society's) tyranny and *The Beggar's Opera* combines the spirit of social with that of artistic opposition.

Operatic technique (Mozart to his father, 13th October, 1781):

> Why, an opera is sure of success when the plot is well worked out, the words written solely for the music and not shoved in here and there to suit some miserable rhyme . . . I mean, words or even entire verses which ruin the composer's whole idea. Verses are indeed the most indispensable element for music – but rhymes – solely for the sake of rhyming – the most detrimental. These high and mighty people who set to work in this pedantic fashion will always come to grief, both they and their music. The best thing of all is when a good composer, who understands the stage and is talented enough to make sound suggestions, meets an able poet, that true phoenix; in that case no fears need be entertained as to the applause, even of the ignorant.

Britten:

> This 'working together' of the poet and the composer seems to be one of the secrets of writing a good opera. In the general discussion on the shape of the work – the plot, the division into recitatives, arias, ensembles and so on – the musician will have many ideas that may stimulate and influence the poet. Similarly, when the libretto is written and the composer is working on the music, possible alterations may be suggested by the flow of the music, and the libretto altered accordingly . . . The composer and poet should at all stages be working in the closest contact, from the most preliminary stages right up to the first night.[17]

Joseph Gregor has pointed out that, in spite of what there was before him, Mozart may in some respects be regarded as a founder (a 'second founder') of opera.[18] The same can already be said today, as far as the modern British – perhaps not only British – field goes, of Britten.

We cannot leave the subject of opera without quoting a criticism of *Don Giovanni*, or rather a review of *Don Giovanni*, whose resemblance with various criticisms of allegedly too favourable reactions to Britten's operas is, it will be admitted, almost uncannily striking. Einstein rightly reminds us that

> No biography should fail to reproduce . . . – as evidence of contemporary presumption, especially characteristic of Berlin – the dictum of an anonymous writer who was moved by an enthusiastic description of *Don Giovanni* by Bernhard Anselm Weber in the *Musikalisches Wochenblatt* of 1792 to the following reprimand: 'His report of Mozart's

Don Juan is highly exaggerated and one-sided. No one will misjudge Mozart, the man of great talents and the expert, prolific and pleasing composer. Yet I do not know any well-grounded connoisseur of art who considers him a correct, not to say finished, artist; still less will the critic of sound judgment consider him, in respect to poetry, a proper and fine composer.'[19]

When they are not accused of striving after originality, Mozart and Britten are accused of lacking originality, of eclecticism. In Mozart's case such an accusation will necessarily be indirect, because unfortunately it isn't done. (If it were, the lack of understanding in many a half-hearted 'admirer' would more easily be seen.) One way of thus indirectly attacking Mozart is to discover too much of him in Christian Bach, and to end up by playing Christian Bach instead of Mozart.[20]

With regard to Britten's 'eclecticism', the accusations are of course direct and numerous. Instead of allowing ourselves to be detained by them, let us look at the whole question from the other, understanding side. To begin with, Mozart again. Here is an eminent musicologist on his 'eclecticism'; we shall easily see how this applies to Britten:

> . . . [Mozart] united the musical treasures of all nations of his time. This could easily have led to a mixture without character, but . . . Mozart did not imitate anyone or anything; the external appearance of music was but a means of expression to him, never technique . . . It is not enough . . . to say that content and form balance each other in Mozart's music, for this unity is style, and while the style is constant the variety of its manifestations is as great as the number of his works. Mozart never created really new forms, but by regarding the existing styles not as unities but as phenomena which contribute towards a general style, he created a universal all-inclusive style . . .[21]
>
> We must not forget that Mozart was the child of an era customarily called the 'golden age' of musical art. Such a golden age . . . offers to the genius the richest treasures of the various artistic forms . . . he simply takes the gifts of his epoch, intact, and, as self-evident matter, utilizes them at his will . . . Mozart shuffled [the conventions of the eighteenth century] like a pack of cards and the result was a strikingly original and individual world.[22]

This is all true, I suggest, except for the over-stress on history: Britten is doing a similar shuffling without being the child of a golden age.

Let us now hear Britten's own words on his 'eclecticism'. After implying that he passes from manner to manner 'as a bee passes from flower to flower,' he declares: 'I do not see why I should lock myself inside a purely personal idiom. I write in the manner best suited to the words, theme or dramatic situation which I happen to be handling.'[23] We here remember that Einstein speaks of Mozart's 'astonishing capacity for imitation, assimilation and elaboration of whatever suited him,'[24] of his being 'the greatest master of style, or rather of all musical styles.'[25] Indeed Mozart himself wrote to his father (7th February, 1778): 'As you know, I can more or less adopt or imitate any kind and any style of composition.' Einstein suggests that this capacity counts for Mozart's super-nationality, and I would add that it also accounts for Britten's, whose success among the foreign musicians in this country and abroad is remarkable.[26] It may be interesting to note in this connection that Britten's solution of the modern sonata problem in his C major quartet has perhaps been most strongly appreciated by two ex-Austrian musicians: Erwin Stein and the present writer.[27] According to the music critic of *The Times*, sonata form 'is for all its universal validity an essentially Austrian way of thinking in music.'[28]

Britten's afore-mentioned remarks on his 'eclecticism' include a reminder that has already been partly quoted at the beginning of this [essay]: 'The romantics became so intensely personal that it looked as though we were going to reach a point at which the composer would be the only man capable of understanding his own music.'[29] And Mozart writes to his father (28th December, 1782):

> The golden mean of truth in all things is no longer either known or appreciated. In order to win applause one must write stuff that is so inane that a cabby could sing it, or so unintelligible that it pleases precisely because no sensible man can understand it.

Again, could not the following, too, have been written, *mutatis mutandis*, by Britten? –

> This is what I think [of a Concerto for two flutes by Friedrich Hartmann Graf, 1727-95]. It is not at all pleasing to the ear, not a bit natural. He often plunges into a new key far too brusquely and it is all quite devoid of charm. When it was over, I praised him very highly, for he really deserves it. The poor fellow must have taken a great deal of trouble over it and he must have studied hard enough. At last a clavichord, one of Stein's, was brought out of the inner room, an excellent instrument, but covered with dust and dirt. Herr Graf, who is director here, stood there transfixed, like someone who has always imagined that his wanderings from key to key are quite unusual and now finds that one can be even more unusual and yet not offend the ear.[30]

Reflecting upon Mozart's temperament, Einstein says:

> He yielded to an influence quite ingenuously, quite in the feminine fashion. He strove least of all for originality; because he was entirely certain of the Mozartian, personal stamp of his product. *Facile inventis addere* cannot apply to him; this adage applies indeed only to science or technique. What he derived from others was for him a fertilization, which eased the course of the spiritual and musical pregnancy and birth.[31]

And Desmond Shawe-Taylor, after mentioning, inter alia, Verdi's and Handel's influence upon *Herring*, remarks that 'in spite of such links, the whole score remains immensely characteristic of its composer'.[32] The whole problem of Mozart's and Britten's originality and eclecticism can, I think, be summed up in Einstein's words: 'Mozart belongs, like Bach, to the rare species of the conservative revolutionaries, or the revolutionary conservatives.'[33]

In a paragraph on the youthful aspects of Mozart, Lang thinks that in the composer lives all the eighteenth century's

> youthful delicacy and feminine grace, . . . its brightness and naturalness, . . . its flexibility, its loving care for the little and the fine, its fondness for variation and for the characteristic . . . But this lovable youthfulness ripens into maturity, and playful freedom and moodiness are harnessed by schooling and discipline, ingenuous feelings are formed by classic measure, ideas are deepened to symbols of universal significance.[34]

Note how very exactly the spiritual tendencies here enumerated apply to Britten, although – neo-classicism apart – one does not find the affinities between our time and the eighteenth century very striking.

One may at the same time concede that the form in which Britten's fondness for variation quite often manifests itself, i.e. the ostinato, is in part historically determined.[35]

In and beyond the art of variation, the fundamental musical principle of repetition is treated in a similar way by the two composers. Both mechanical reiteration and narcissistic re-citation are absent; thematic relationships, though frequent and really simple, often go unrecognised by the superficial listener because in the process of transformation or transplantation of themes or fragments far-reaching changes of emotional significance are secured, though of course at the same time an underlying emotional identity is preserved.

The strong drive of either composer towards economy (as distinct from poverty) of thematic material is just as obvious as the fact that economy, in either case, also radiates in other directions, e.g. the instrumental.

In an article entitled 'Back to Mozart?' Felix von Weingartner once remarked:

> . . . thus I want to give the following answer to the question put in the title: To create, with our modern means of expression, *in Mozart's spirit* – this would perhaps be the right thing . . . but . . . can there be any question 'back'? I think it must much more truly be said: *'Forward* to Mozart!'[36]

Can it be chance that Weingartner was, as far as I know, the first to call Britten (after hearing the oboe Quartet in 1934) a genius?

Before I try to round off my thesis I should like to quote some more of Busoni's aphorisms on Mozart. Their relevance will, I trust, be appreciated at this stage without further comment. 'He doesn't risk anything foolhardy.' 'He is capable of saying very much, but never says too much.' 'He carries all characters within himself, but only as an exhibitor and portraitist.' 'Together with the puzzle he gives you the solution.' 'He can always draw water from any glass because he has emptied none.' 'His smile is not that of a diplomat or actor, but that of a pure nature – yet that of a man of a world.' 'He is spirited without any nervousness – idealist without becoming immaterial, realist without ugliness.' 'It is the architectural that is most closely related to his art.'

'In respect to universality,' writes Einstein, 'Mozart may be compared only with other great masters; and in our comparisons we shall limit ourselves to the eighteenth and nineteenth centuries.'[37] He would not, I believe, have thus limited himself if he had known Britten's music.

> Nearest [to Mozart], perhaps, is Handel, the master of the cantata, the opera, the oratorio, the concerto grosso, the sonata – but we are stopped short already. Did not all this flow from one unified, mighty source, Italian vocalism, the *bel canto* of the monumental aria?[38]

On the basis of present suggestions, I submit, we cannot be stopped short in this or any other way when we compare Britten with Mozart. Britten, that is to say, is not only immeasurably nearer to Mozart than Handel because his (Britten's) universality does not spring from one unified source, but also because, beneath, above and beyond the sphere of universality, Britten and Mozart have far more in common than Handel and Mozart. 'And was Bach universal? To be sure, he left no corner uncultivated in the fields of instrumental and vocal music . . . Actually, however, all this, too, grows from one root – instrumental music . . .' And so it goes on. Gluck, Einstein's next object of comparison, need not, it will be admitted, detain us. 'Both Haydn and Beethoven are cramped by the word, they speak most freely in the instrumental fields.'[39] And even putting the question of universality apart again, can it be suggested that Haydn-Mozart comparisons or Beethoven-Mozart comparisons are comparable with a comparison between Britten and Mozart?

And this would bring us to Schubert, the composer of the 'Unfinished' and the D minor Quartet, and of hundreds of perfect songs, the only one who could be compared to Mozart, if it were not that, although he wrote operas too, the dramatic, the scenic, the feeling for the stage, were denied to him.[40]

I submit that Britten stands far nearer to Mozart than does Schubert, once more not only in respect of universality (cf. particularly 'the dramatic, the scenic, the feeling for the stage'), but also – as I hope the present [essay] tends to show – in almost every other respect. In fact, to me personally it seems that the only deep-rooted musico-characterological difference between Britten and Mozart is that the one is often strongly inspired by nature, while the other is an indoor composer.

Passing, for obvious reasons, over the rest of Einstein's list of composers to be compared, or rather not to be compared, with Mozart, we arrive at this admirable summing-up of Mozart's universality:

> When one considers the somnambulistic surefootedness and grace with which Mozart masters the vocal and the instrumental, mass and opera, quartet and concerto, one's admiration grows immeasurably at the phenomenon of his uniqueness as a universal musician.[41]

This is not the time, and I am not the man, to decide about the relative greatness of Mozart and Britten; to assess how far with Britten, too, 'the world-spirit wishes to show that here is pure sound, conforming to a weightless cosmos, triumphant over all chaotic earthliness, spirit of the world-spirit';[42] but as one who is soaked in the music of both Mozart and Britten I may be allowed to claim that for the first time Mozart, the universal musician who masters everything with a somnambulistic surefootedness and grace, has found a companion. And personally, I regard Britten as the greatest of all living composers whose music I understand.[43]

NOTES

Source

'Britten and Mozart' was written in 1946, in the same year as the *Peter Grimes* study, and first published in 1948 [*Music and Letters*, Vol. XXIX, No. 1, January 1948]; according to Keller it 'aroused comment on the continent as well as in this country.' Alison Garnham records that it was rejected by four periodicals, *Music Review, Musical Times, Polemic* and *Horizon* (*Hans Keller and the BBC*, London, Ashgate, 2003, p. 17). It was reprinted as the first part of the two-part investigation of 'The Musical Character' in: *Benjamin Britten, a Commentary on his Works from a Group of Specialists*, edited by Donald Mitchell and Hans Keller, London, Rockliff, 1952, pp. 319-34 (part I). The later printing is followed here. About this Keller remarks: 'Apart from one or two stylistic changes, the paper is here submitted in its original form, i.e. neither brought up to date (except for such obvious additions as the inclusion of *Budd* in an observation which concerns itself with *Grimes*, *Lucretia*, and *Herring*) nor down to the criticisms it has encountered . . .'

1   Anon., 'Profile – Benjamin Britten', *Observer*, 27 October, 1946.
2   Ibid.
3   It may at the same time be worth mentioning that 'from his childhood days on, [Mozart] was especially fond of England and the English' (Einstein, op. cit., p. 88).
4   Einstein, op. cit, p. 109 [italics HK's].
5   *Addendum*, 1952: At [the time I wrote this, 1947] I had, of course, no idea of Britten's actual attitude towards Brahms (nor indeed of his ideas about Mozart) as shown in [the Earl of Harewood's contribution on Britten 'The Man' to the Keller/Mitchell *Commentary*: 'his extreme dissatisfaction with Brahms's music (which he once admired) is supported by his thorough acquaintance of it'], but I think

my comparison explains his dislike. That he 'once admired' Brahms must be due to the fact that then his musical character had not yet gained definite form. His eventual aversion to Brahms's genius, while significant for the elucidation of his own, has given rise to an evaluation which, needless to add, is quite incompetent.]

6   [Ed:] Otto Rank was the editor of *Imago*, the Freudian journal of the arts. Keller knew the journal well, as is revealed in *1975 (1984 minus 9)*, p. 94, and as is clear from several scraps of paper in the Archive which refer to it. HK does not give the source of Rank's remark.

7   The two schools of interpretation, the 'tragic' and the 'comic' both equally one-sided, *can* be roughly located along historical and geographical co-ordinates. As far as the latter magnitude goes, the tragic school is predominantly German, the comic predominantly English.

8   On the basis of psychological reflections such as I have sketched above *sub* [point] 2, I ventured the prediction in June 1947 that 'the serious musical aspect of [*Herring*] will tend to be underestimated, or even neglected' ('Glyndebourne Preface', *Sound*, June 1947). Many reviewers proved me right. Among the exceptions there was Desmond Shawe-Taylor who, writing of the Threnody in the last act, pointed out that 'it is such moments as these which make it a superficial judgment to write the work off as a farce or a charade' ('Glyndebourne', *New Statesman and Nation*, 28 June 1947).

9   Anon. 'Profile – Benjamin Britten', *Observer*, 27 October, 1946.

10   Ibid.

11   Einstein, op. cit., p. 4ff..

12   See also, Peter Pears, *Benjamin Britten, a Commentary*, 'The Vocal Music', pp. 59-73.

13   'A Note on the "Additional Accompaniments"', *Music Review*, VII, 3, p. 161.

14   Hutchings's sentence ends thus: ' . . . as it is to a composer writing a chamber work.' The relevance of this phrase, however, escapes me; surely it needs qualifying. Brahms, for instance, certainly conceived music in an abstract manner even where he was concerned with chamber music, much of which clearly exhibits his surmounting instrumental problems.

15   Einstein, op. cit., p. 109.

16   Einstein, op. cit., p. 465.

17   Preface, *The Rape of Lucretia* (libretto by Ronald Duncan), London, Boosey and Hawkes, 1946.

18   *Kulturgeschichte der Oper*, Zürich, 1941.

19   Einstein, op. cit., p. 134.

20   *Pace* Christian Bach's mastery and all that Mozart owes to it.

21   P. H. Lang, *Music in Western Civilization*, 1942, p. 636.

22   Ibid., p. 137.

23   *Observer*, 27 October, 1946.

24   Einstein, op. cit., p. 110.

25   Ibid., p.129.

26   Ibid., p. 103.

27   Erwin Stein, 'Analysis of String Quartet No. 2', *Hawkes Pocket Scores*, Boosey and Hawkes, London, 1946; Hans Keller, 'Benjamin Britten's Second Quartet', *Tempo*, 3 (Old Series, 18), March 1947, pp. 6-8.

28   'English Chamber Music', *The Times*, 17 January, 1947.

29   *Observer*, 27 October, 1946.

30   Mozart to his father, 14 October, 1777.

31   Einstein, op. cit., p. 122.

32   'Britten's Comic Opera', *Listener*, 12 June, 1947.

33   Op. cit., p. 162. This is perhaps a trifle vague if one does not know Mozart so well that one doesn't need the suggestion. For those, that is to say, who refuse to divine Einstein's meaning, every genius may belong to one or other of what they might well consider two distinct 'rare species'. Perhaps it would be clearer to say that with geniuses like Beethoven and Schoenberg, the newly discovered acts in a masculine way upon the traditional which assumes a feminine role; whereas with Mozart and Britten, new inventions adopt a more passive, feminine attitude, letting the past and the already-discovered present play the active and masculine part. Thus considered, Mozart and Britten might be called 'revolutionary conservatives', Schoenberg and Beethoven 'conservative revolutionaries'.

34   Lang, op. cit., p. 624.

35   Britten's synthesis of Central-European thematicism and English monothematicism cum Stravinskyan ostinato extends, of course, over his polythematic structures too.

36   His italics. [Source unknown.]

37   Einstein, op. cit., p. 103.

38   Ibid.

39   Einstein, op. cit., p. 104.

40   Ibid.

41 Einstein, op. cit., p. 105.
42 Einstein, op. cit., p. 471. [This is the concluding sentence of the book.]
43 [Ed:] The second part of the study of the 'Creative Character' from the Mitchell-Keller *Commentary* of
     1952 examines 'The Crisis of Beauty and Truth' in three parts, 'From Beauty to Truth', 'The Melodic
     Crisis', and 'Britten: Synthesis and Solutions'. As its concerns belong properly to the 1950s it is excluded
     here. Its closing paragraphs, however, return to the question of Britten's musical character, following
     observations on how in the music 'the [interval of the] second has become beautiful and tender', 'the
     ugly' having been 'beautified' and 'the strident mollified', with the 'new sound symbolizing a new
     personality.' Keller continues:

What is this new personality? It does not show Bartók's straightforward sadism. It does not
show Stravinsky's equally uncomplicated sado-masochism. It does not manifest much interest in
the re-sexualization of music, such as has been achieved by Schoenberg, whose ear, it must
incidentally be remarked, would never have tolerated (for instance) the kind of exposed,
consecutive minor seconds which the more naïve and barbaric Bartók could allow himself.

Britten is a pacifist. It is an established fact [see Edward Glover, *War, Sadism and Pacifism*,
London, George Allen, 1947] that strong and heavily repressed sadism underlies pacifistic
attitudes. About the vital aggressive element in Britten's music (as distinct from his extra-musical
character) there cannot indeed be the faintest doubt, and those whose ears are not sensitive
enough to recognize the sadistic component at least in his treatment of the percussion, will still
be able to confirm our observation upon an inspection of his libretti, [the] children's opera
included. So far, so unenlightening: almost all our age's important minds tend to be unusually
aggressive in one way or another. What distinguishes Britten's musical personality is the violent
repressive counter-force against his sadism: by dint of character, musical history and
environment, he has become a *musical pacifist* too. This, I think, is the solution to the manifold
solutions he has effected upon our war-worn and war-weary musical scene, to the paradox of the
ruthless, yet beauty-conscious search for the truth.

In 'real' life, pacifism (as distinct from scientific research into, and consequent peaceful
organization of, aggression) is an illusion. In art, and especially in our art, pacifism is realism
par excellence, producing as it can the quickest possible communicability of new discoveries.
The only guarantee, to be sure, that pacification will not degenerate into compromise is genius.

2   Mozart and Boccherini

A Supplementary Note to Alfred Einstein's
Mozart: His Character – His Work

I

Alfred Einstein is one of those scholars who do not only always know what they are talking
about, but also often know what they are not talking about: their omissions do not spring from
ignorance, but from selection. Yet not even Einstein can know everything; in his outstanding
book on Mozart there is no mention of the intimate relation between the last movement from
one string quintet in C [major] of Boccherini and movements from at least three of Mozart's
major works. It could of course be argued that this is exactly a case of purposive omission, that
Einstein knew, but did not bother to tell. Indeed the Boccherini finale (unlike the rest of the
quintet) is relatively well known, and while Einstein says 'I cannot boast that I know all of
Boccherini's 113 quintets,'[1] it seems improbable that he does not know a movement that is
comparatively often played (though not in public). But if he knows the movement, and if he
has noticed its relation to the Mozart movements,[2] one cannot easily see why he chooses not
to discuss it. In fact, in view of the following array of circumstances, his omission becomes a
mystery: –

(a) he examines, in considerable detail, Mozart's imitations of other composers, his 'springboards' and 'plagiarisms';[3]

(b) he reminds us that Mozart owes much to Boccherini;[4]

(c) he discusses more than once Boccherini's influence on Mozart,[5]

(d) heeding particularly Boccherini's string quintets;[6]

(e) he writes, at some length, about each of the Mozart works which, as I shall try to show, are connected with the above-mentioned finale from the Boccherini Quintet, these works being the piano Concerto in E flat, K. 449, the piano Sonata in C minor, K. 457, the piano Sonata in D, K. 576, and probably also the piano and violin Sonata in D, K. 306;[7]

(f) lastly, and above all, the present instances of Mozart's using another composer's material seem to be more important than some of the examples Einstein quotes or mentions, among other things because Mozart wrote the above-mentioned E flat Concerto, and the two piano sonatas in C minor and D, in the last decade of his life when, according to Einstein, 'he relied in general upon his own ideas as springboards.'[8]

II

From one's experience of the swimming pool it would seem that, the higher the springboard, the deeper the dive. But Mozart jumps from a springboard (built by another composer) that does not reach imposing heights, and yet he reaches the bottom. Moreover, he can keep his eyes wide open in the water, never losing sight of the springboard. Nowhere is this more apparent than in the last movement of his last piano Sonata (in D, K. 576, 1789) (Ex. 1):

Example 1   W. A. Mozart, Piano Sonata in D major, K. 576, last movement, bars 1-16)

Of the four last Mozart movements I am quoting in the present article, the above is most strongly related to Boccherini (Ex. 2):

Example 2   Luigi Boccherini, String Quintet in C major, finale

With Boccherini (Ex. 3) this appears as an inversion of:

Example 3   Luigi Boccherini, String Quintet in C major, finale

The triplets and semiquavers after the promising sequence in Ex. 2 are, if I may say so, rather weak, i.e. simply a convenient way back – over-conventional in itself and at the same time forcible in its context – to the full close. I doubt whether Mozart would have allowed Thomas Attwood to do such a thing. We may perhaps assume that Boccherini's theme stuck, consciously or preconsciously,[9] in Mozart's minds, not only because of the possibilities inherent in the sequence, but also because what follows this sequence is impossible. If so, there might be a link between Boccherini's triplets (Ex. 2) and Mozart's (Ex. 1). The piano-forte dualism in either instance could be taken to reinforce this assumption, though Einstein, when discussing the relation between the Sonata for two pianos K. 448 and a piano concerto by Christian Bach, says that 'the very fact that [Mozart] avoided the dualism in Bach's announcement of the theme,' (in this case reverse dualism, i.e. forte-piano) 'is evidence of their relation'![10] In the present case Mozart did not avoid the dualism, but he modified it considerably – if he thought of it at all. Anyhow, the relation between his and Boccherini's movement is more intimate than is clear from the above quotations; unfortunately I cannot quote the entire movements (Ex. 4):

Example 4   W. A. Mozart, Piano Sonata in C minor, K. 457, first movement

In the first movement of the C minor piano Sonata K. 457 (1784) we find the Boccherini sequence in E flat major (exposition) and in C minor (recapitulation): the two keys in which it appears in Boccherini's finale. The arguable triplets also recur here, preceded by a sequence that is both based on Ex. 4 and directly related back to the Boccherini. Further, the inserted sequence (*a-b*) in Ex. 4 harks back to the Boccherini movement too.

We meet another E flat example in the last movement of the E flat piano Concerto K. 449 (the work with which Mozart started his *Verzeichnis aller meiner Werke* in 1784), a concerto 'of quite a peculiar kin', as he himself described it (Ex. 5):[11]

Example 5   W. A. Mozart, Piano Concerto in Eb major, K. 449, last movement

Note the fourth crotchet in the second and fourth bar respectively. Unlike Boccherini in his fourth quaver (Ex. 2, second and fourth bar respectively), Mozart invests his fourth beat with up-beat significance.

Example 6   W. A. Mozart, Sonata for Piano and Violin in D major, K. 306, finale, first Allegro, bars 13-18

As regards the finale of the piano and violin Sonata, K. 306 (once again in D major, Ex. 6), the reader may doubt whether we are justified in including it in our list, but if he will have a look at the coda of the finale of K. 449 (Ex. 7) –

Example 7   W. A. Mozart, Piano Sonata in Eb major, K. 449, finale

– which is of course based upon Ex. 5, his doubts will diminish. For if Ex. 6 is near-identical with Ex. 7, and Ex. 7 is based upon Ex. 5, and Ex. 5 is based on Ex. 2, then Ex. 6 is probably based on Ex. 2. Moreover, K. 306 (Ex. 6) is related to Boccherini in another way. As Einstein points out, the finale of this piano and violin sonata in D, K. 306, 'is related to the violin concertos of 1775'[12] and the model for one of these, i.e. for K. 218 in D (!), was a violin concerto in D (!) by Boccherini.[13]

III

In a recent essay, Prof. P. H. Lang reminded us that –

> Modern historiography, supported by anthropology and psychology – not to mention plain common sense – no longer believes that body and soul, the life of an artist and his creations, are two totally different entities that can be conveniently separated.[14]

With this in mind we might reflect upon the genesis of K. 576's last movement (Ex. 1), the movement, that is to say, in which Mozart makes the most intensive and extensive use of Boccherini's material, and the only movement in which he uses the Boccherini sequence as actual 'springboard', as incipit and as the basis of the principal subject.

Before formulating a hypothesis, we must assemble the circumstantial evidence:

1   Einstein thinks that an inducement for Mozart's returning to the category of the quintet in his last Vienna years was the death of Frederick the Great and the accession to the throne in Berlin of a violoncello-playing dilettante. On 21st January 1786, Boccherini had received the title of Prussian Court Composer, and Mozart habitually took careful note of lucrative appointments of that sort. We have evidence that in the following year Boccherini visited Berlin and Breslau, and perhaps also Vienna . . . This external inducement is perhaps the most plausible explanation.[15]

2   In the spring of 1789, Mozart had been in North Germany, and had apparently expected to discover greater generosity in the Royal Family of Prussia than in Vienna. He had in mind six quartets for the King and six clavier sonatas for the King's eldest daughter . . .[16]

3   The first of these quartets (in D!) was written in June, and the first (and last) sonata for Princess Friederike, i.e. our present D major sonata, was written immediately afterwards, in July.[17] The two works have not only a common external purpose (the Prussian Court), a common time of birth, and a common key, but also [common harmony and common figuration]. (Exx. 8a, from the last movement of K. 575, and 8b, from the last movement of K. 576).

Boccherini Violin Concerto in D

*Boccherini Quintet in C
(theme in E♭ and C minor)*

K.218, Violin Concerto in D

K.306, Piano-Violin Sonata in D

K.449, Piano Sonata in E♭

K.457, Piano Sonata in C minor (E♭)

Boccherini Court Composer to
  └Friedrich Wilhelm II
    └Princess Friedericke

K.575, Quartet in D

K.576, Piano Sonata in D

K.593, Quintet in D

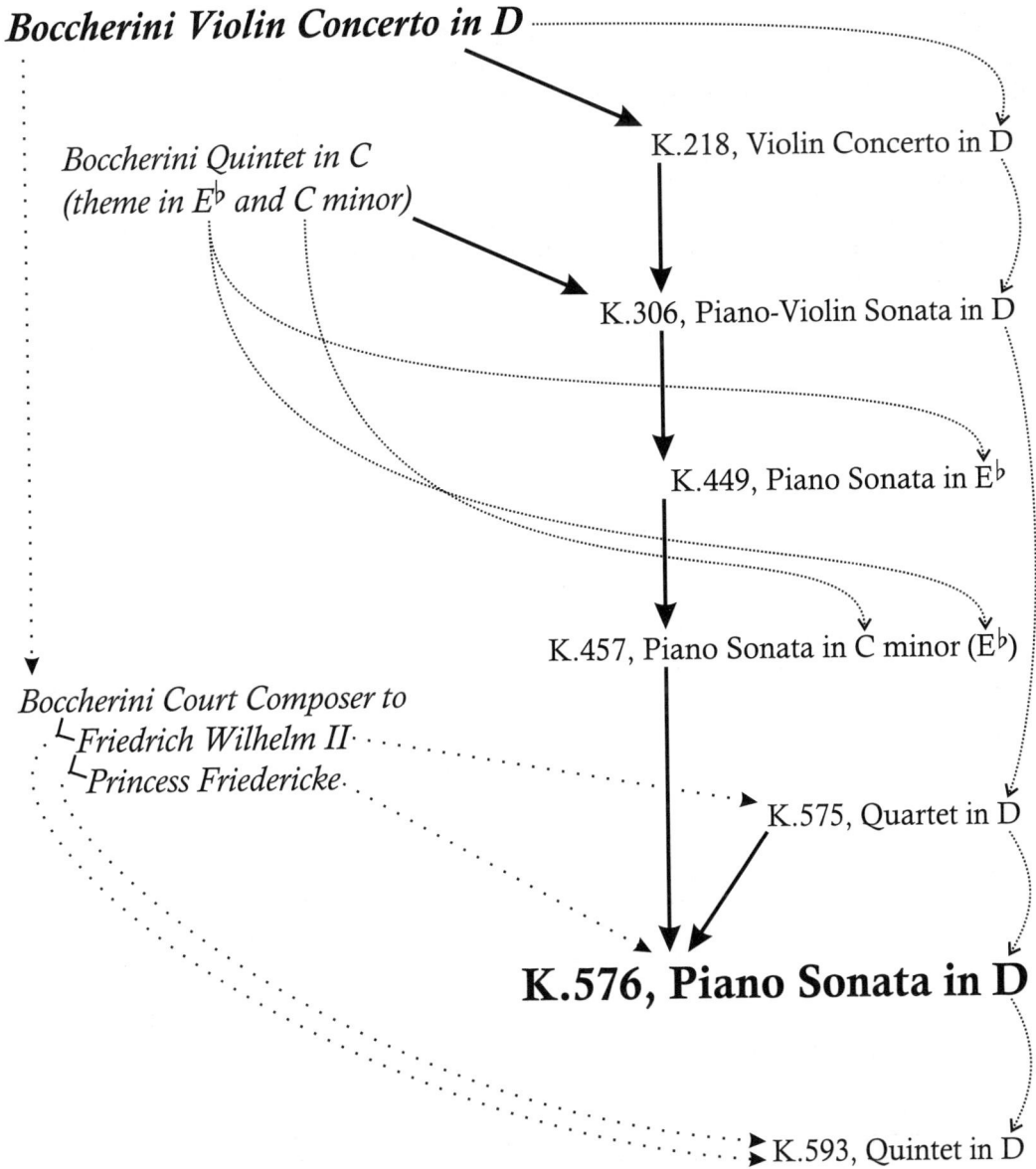

The pedigree of the last movement of Mozart's Piano Sonata in D major, K. 576

4   The Larghetto in the D major (!) Quintet, K. 593, 'juxtaposes the cello (*Mozart has not completely forgotten the King of Prussia*) and the higher instruments . . .'[18]

On [the previous] page is part of the pedigree of K. 576's last movement. So as not to be too confusing, I have not included the Quintet K. 515 (1787) in this graph; but it should be noted that this work, with its prominent cello part in the first movement (Friedrich, Wilhelm II, Boccherini!),[19] is in C major, i.e. the key of our present Boccherini quintet.

I hope the genealogical table shows clearly how the use of the Boccherini material in Mozart's last D major Sonata is – as the psychoanalyst says – 'over-determined'. I suggest that Mozart had to some extent identified himself with Boccherini via (e.g.) K. 218, K. 306, K. 449 and K. 457; later he established a more extra-musical (and more hostile)[20] identification with his lucky colleague when the latter had what Mozart wanted to have: a lucrative job. It is as if Mozart said in the last movement of K. 576: "I'll show them that I can be better than Boccherini," 'them' being Friedr. Wilhelm II, Boccherini, Mozart's own standards of perfection, and for the rest no one in particular. His previous love for the Boccherini sequence, and on the other hand his probable disgust at what Boccherini did with it, furnished him with strictly musical reasons for 'showing them' how it ought to be done. Everyone who knows something about Mozart's character will agree that his I'll-show-them attitude, while amiable, was marked. Though surely less marked than justified.

Example 8(a)   W. A. Mozart, String Quartet in D major, K. 575, last movement

Example 8(b)   W. A. Mozart, Piano Sonata in D major, K. 576, last movement

IV

As for the question of 'plagiarism', this does not, for the musician, arise:

> Mozart's 'plagiarizing' shows even more clearly than do most such examples the unreality of the concept of plagiarism.[21]

In short, Mozart was immeasurably more original in 'stealing' Boccherini's theme than Boccherini was by inventing it. Already in the piano and violin Sonata, K. 306 (cf. Ex. 6), Mozart introduces a highly original, yet astoundingly simple surprise modulation into his version of the sequences (Ex. 9) –

Example 9   W. A. Mozart, Sonata for Piano and Violin, K. 576, finale, second Allegro, bars 13-18

– a modulation whose beauty, stringent logic, and 'pull', are irresistible ("Not bad," Mozart would have said, I suppose). And Mozart's treatment of Boccherini's material in the three piano works of his last period belongs to the very greatest that music literature can offer, while the Boccherini Quintet belongs to the historian's shelf and the cellist's pastime.

But we need not waste too many words about the originality of Mozart's eclecticism; 'it is bad enough that one needs words at all.'[22]

NOTES

Source

Music Review, Vol. 8, No. 4, November 1947, pp. 241-47. The footnotes are Keller's, with references filled out:

1   Alfred Einstein, *Mozart: His Character – His Work*, London, Cassell, 1946, p. 189.
2   A relation that has not been noticed, to my knowledge, by any Mozartian, whether writer or practising musician.
3   [Einstein (*passim*):] Chapters vii, pp. 108ff., and viii, pp. 135 ff..
4   pp. 85 and 279. Incidentally, there is an index omission under 'Boccherini' where p. 279 is not given and another one under 'K. 366', where p. 255 is not given.
5   pp. 136 and 327.
6   pp. 188, 189, and 190.
7   pp. 301, 247, 250, and 255 respectively.
8   p. 137.

9   'Preconscious: mental process of which one is not aware at a given moment, but which it is possible, more or less readily, to recall to consciousness.' Ernest Jones, *Papers on Psychoanalysis*, 2nd ed., London, 1913, p. 215.

10 Einstein, p. 136.

11 I have never seen this concerto and am therefore relying for Examples 5 and 7 on acoustic memory.

12 p. 255.

13 pp. 136, 280, and 327.

14 *The Musical Quarterly*, New York, XXXII/iii, July 1946.

15 pp. 189 ff..

16 p. 250.

17 W. A. Mozart, *Verzeichnis alle meine Werke* (facsimile, ed. O. E. Deutsch, Vienna, 1938), p. 22. Mozart does not give the day of the month.

18 p. 192. Italics mine.

19 p. 190.

20 Psychoanalytic research has shown that identifications are always 'ambivalent' to a certain degree, i.e. composed of both love and hate. The hate part of the attitude is usually and largely unconscious.

21 p. 137.

22 W. A. Mozart, letter to his father, Mannheim, [22] February, 1778. Emily Anderson, *Letters of Mozart and his Family*, Vol. II, London, 1938, p. 721. [Mozart himself is not referring to music, but defending his 'good name'.]

In his first radio broadcast for the BBC, on 5 February, 1956, Keller addressed the issue of 'Mozart and Haydn: the Musical Personality' by comparing movements from the string quartets K. 481 and 589 on the one hand with movements from Op. 33, No. 2 and Op. 76, No. 2 on the other. He remarked:

> Mozart's personality emerges [distinctly] when we compare the variation theme of the finale from the second quartet he dedicated to Haydn (the D minor one) [K. 421] with the variation theme of the Haydn finale that inspired the Mozart movement [Op. 33, No. 5]. Haydn keeps the dance character of the siciliana rhythm, even though in the middle he allows himself a searching turn to the relative minor. Mozart, writing in the minor mode, uses the dance rhythm, not as a basis for his mood, but rather as a contrasting background against which he throws his dark foreground into relief . . . The profoundest humorists have always hidden a tragedy behind – far behind – their fun. With them, the tragedy lies in the past, so that there is no acute emotional contrast. Mozart, however, stands so far above his tragedies that he can afford to have them present, and to have his humour behind them, not in front of them – as in the case of Leporello's chatter behind the tragedy exposed by the Statue and Don Giovanni. With the sole exception of Franz Kafka, there is no other artistic personality that is capable of developing deep tragedy against the background of both warm and ironical humour.

Keller's typescript for this talk is held in the Cambridge University Library Archive. See Alison Garnham, *Hans Keller and the BBC*, London, Ashgate, 2003, p. 27, for a discussion of the circumstances of the broadcast.

Although Keller widened his enquiry into 'Creative Character' in later years, he never lost touch with his work of the 1940s and early '50s as expressed above and in the lecture of 1950 to the British Psychological Society, 'Musical Self-contempt in Britain' (reprinted below). As late as 1981, for instance, he contributed an essay on '[Alan] Bush's Creative Character' to *Time Remembered*, a symposium on the composer's work published in Kidderminster by Bravura Publications (pp. 11-13), in which he wrote:

> All composers who have something new to say – a minority at the time of writing, admittedly – are exceptional, distinct from any other composers who have something to say. Each of them is demonstrably unique, but some are uniquer than others, and our present subject is, demonstrably again, among the tiny band of the uniquest.
>
> The demonstration, then: for one thing, however exceptional any given English composer may be, he is likely to share one profound creative character trait with other substantial English composers, and that's *not* an idiom which can be diagnosed as English. No, even those English composers who, idiomatically, can at times behave in a Central European manner still tend to betray their Englishness through the nature of their inspiration, its sonoric nature: it can easily be shown that, ultimately, they are vocally inspired. Amongst the very few exceptions are Alan Rawsthorne, Robert Simpson and Alan Bush. It isn't merely a question of sound: as soon as a composer is instrumentally inspired, he instinctively renounces those extra-musical needs which the music of the composer who is vocally inspired inevitably carries – through its association with words.

Keller continued with a celebration of Bush's 'incomparable', 'utterly un-English' and 'unfailingly concrete' *Dialectic* for string quartet (1929), a work by a 'thematic composer *par excellence*', 'worlds removed from even the most fashionable, most elitist, most unprecedented (but not so called) sound effects of our time', which expresses 'a truth whose discovery is only artistically possible' but 'cannot be expressed in extra-artistic [i.e. Marxist] terms.'

*

On 3 April, 1945 Keller made the following (hand-written) note on a staged version of Agatha Christie's *Appointment with Death*:

Towards the Psychology of Agatha Christie's Genius

The author's castration complex has no doubt developed in the direction of identification with the male (father). The inhuman, sadistic, masterful mother in this piece is indirectly killed (through being angrily told that her days are counted on account of her physical state), her evil nature exposed (through the detection of her suicide through which the mother wanted to throw suspicions on her children), [and] her children vindicated by the female heroine, *a masculine girl (woman doctor)* who is the prospective daughter-in-law of the bad woman. "Not I, mother is the one whose guilt has to be detected, not she, I am the one who detects" is clearly felt behind the drama. The heroine is first under suspicion like everybody else (childhood-situation) until she discovers the mother's deeds and motives (wish-reversal).

In another work, *The Seven Dials*, Christie also identifies her (better) self with the masculine woman, again the heroine and (less successful) detective. The detective hero is a father (police inspector); her own father [is] conspicuous by his tolerance (just as in the present piece the evil mother is conspicuous by her intolerance). The guilty [party] is in the former case a 'brother' (member of her clique), perhaps one with regard to whom penis-envy is furiously at work as distinct from 'father' on whom the positive side of transference is lavished?

In yet another work, the *Death of Lord Edgware*, the female female, a highly narcissistic unscrupulous criminal, is the guilty [party], a father (a former French police detective, Poirot?) the detecting hero.

The Psychology of Performers

Keller's investigation into the psychology of performers was also an enquiry into society, work ethic and the conditions in which players played. Although the notice of Kyla Greenbaum's concert at the Wigmore Hall on 24 April, 1949 is remembered as the most forthright and combative of Keller's many reviews, nevertheless, like all great writing, it celebrates even more than it attacks. It also affords a glimpse of Keller's later activities as piano- and chamber-music coach (or 'anti-coach' as he preferred it).

Celebration, too, is the keynote of another piece reproduced below, in which Keller champions five performers who were 'Not Famous Enough'.

Kyla Greenbaum and the Psychology of the Modern Artist

The crisis of modern life and art, whether it manifests itself in the atom bomb or in Kyla Greenbaum, arises from man's lack of realistic responsibility, and from his inability to catch up with the techniques he creates. I say realistic responsibility, for while we molest each other, ourselves, and others' as well as our own artistic creations and interpretations with the enthusiastic support of what, subjectively, seems a conscience of the first water, our moral satisfactions depend on the degree of trouble we have taken to achieve something rather than on the objective value of the achievement. The story is not new, but it has never been more true, for with the disappearance of fairly universal ideals (e.g. religious ones, no matter whether these are right or wrong) and the inevitable suspicion which the contemporary showroom of the most modern moral models arouses, we are apt to work as hard and as brilliantly as possible in order to attain the only aim left to our bewildered psyche, namely, to hide our aimlessness behind the illusory aim to which we desperately promote every possible sort of means. Now the value of hard work is in any case liable to be over-estimated even by the healthiest of idlers. We satisfy, that is, our primitive punitive and self-punitive tendencies by making others and ourselves work. Add to this that many sources of (self-)punitive satisfaction, such as physical pain, are not nowadays what they used to be, and we readily understand why the moralization of labour is spreading epidemically. Today, in point of fact, the only difference between work and play is that we work harder at playing than at working, in order to divest play of its immorality.

Small wonder, then, that in this age of infantile man trying to create an adult society, and to make up for his intra-psychic integration by solemnly building up a world on integrated pain, the product of mental activities which is ontogenetically most closely related to love and play, namely art, shows likewise a terrifically intense moralization of heavy labour. Hence our all too exclusive concern with craftsmanship, hence our modern moral picture of the artist as, above all, a hard worker, a picture whose obsessionally enthusiastic emphasis on the uninspirational aspect of art makes it neo- rather than classical. Needless to add, the modern work-compulsion readily plays into the hands of the reaction against the Romantic Artist who writes out his stuff under the shadow of Inspiration. From the triumphant relish with which Mozart's '. . . è vero il frutto di una lunga, e laboriosa fatica' [' . . . this is truly the fruit of a long and laborious toil'] is quoted nowadays one would infer that everything he wrote with less effort must fall below the standard of the 'Haydn' quartets. The less effort, moreover, an artist has to make, the more highly will he himself regard whatever efforts he does make, and the more will he tend to overestimate, as Britten apparently does or did, the contribution of hard and regular work to his art. The very fact that work plays such an important role in art makes it easily possible to magnify its importance, for it is only the exaggeration of something unimportant that will readily show up.

With the ever-growing interest in work, technique, workmanship, practice, the art of improvisation is speedily dying out, Boris Ord of Cambridge apart, and except on the jazz level. A serious loss, this, not only for creativity, but also for interpretation, for without the power of spontaneous creation, spontaneous recreation has a more difficult life, and without the power of spontaneous recreation no performance can be alive. But then the old *Zeitgeist* looks after the public, too, so that nobody notices the difference. Indeed, the unimaginative faith in mechanical reproduction is reaching pathological proportions, whether it manifests itself in worship for the gramophone record or for Toscanini, both of whom always play the same thing in exactly the same manner. I am fully aware that Toscanini's readings are the greatest of their kind; it is their kind I am worried about, signifying as it does the decline of *Phantasie*.[1] Instead of an imaginative intellect being able to tackle a figured bass, an empty though highly diligent intelligence busies itself with figured fingerings – not, to be sure, the player's own, but those of an 'editor'. Thus a piece of music has to pass through two heads, such as they are, until it arrives at the listener. More and more the importance of the musician's own individuality, of his natural musicianship and taste is pushed into the background, for since personality and originality and talent are not to be arrived at by hard work (however hard some people try), our guilt-laden consciences ask for severer satisfactions.

It is true that most of the orchestral music one hears nowadays is under-rehearsed, but then irresponsible music-making must predominate in an age in which there are immeasurably more music-makers than musicians – a state of affairs which could not have come about without the great general advances in instrumental technique, which in their turn would not have been possible without the disproportionate, in fact, neurotic attention we have been devoting to drill. Nine-tenths of the non-orchestral music one hears played by responsible and capable musicians is indeed over-practised and over-rehearsed, such as the Beethoven-cycle of Menuhin and Kentner at last year's Edinburgh Festival. It is my considered opinion that healthy and natural musicians of these two artists' technical accomplishment and experience should not have needed more than two rehearsals for each sonata, an opinion that has not been formed and considered in the armchair. Menuhin's interpretations, in which you can always detect the influence of a parent figure, a (not necessarily actual) teacher, also illustrate splendidly the modern artist's unquenchable thirst for the supposedly healing, actually chilling waters that spring from the fountains of other people's inspirations.[2] Our age's combined need for ideals, for relief of guilt, for exercise, invests the figure of the educator with ever more towering significance. Not only is the first, and as such idiotic, question an unknown musician is asked, "Whose pupil were you?", but what in a previous era would have been an adult musical interpreter is seen and, alas, heard wandering round from teacher to teacher, "learning a lot" from everybody except the composers he is interpreting, and passing on this salad, with nothing but an overdose of pepper as his own contribution, to the listener who, having been similarly conditioned, tried to find in it the revelation he is incapable of receiving.

And what has all this to do with Kyla Greenbaum? Her playing shows more symptoms of what at the outset I have called the crisis of modern life than that of many a more renowned and less gifted musician. So gifted, indeed, is she that she could resolve the crisis more easily than many artists in whom it is less acute. It is for this very reason, namely, that her – at bottom – extraordinarily natural musicianship could doubtless catch up with her technique,

Example   W. A. Mozart, Piano Sonata in Bb major, K. 333, first movement, bars 1-24

could transform what still is often an excellent pupil's conscience into the realistic, aesthetic standards of an artist, that I have chosen her piano recital at the Wigmore Hall on 24th April this year [1949] (the only time I have heard her) for this article's point of departure and arrival. Showing the contemporary malady at, artistically, its best, her interpretations are the most irritating imaginable. She holds out a promise that she takes no steps either to break or to fulfil. The first movement of [Mozart's Piano Sonata in B flat major] K. 333, in particular, shows what a mess a potentially fine artist can make of a perfectly straightforward piece, if she works hard enough at it. Almost throughout you heard, on the one hand, the instinctively tasteful and feeling musician, and on the other hand, the conscientious practiser who had lost touch with what should be the source of all conscientious thinking-out and practice, i.e. spontaneous musicality. The result was that almost everything was just wrong. Almost everything – for the end of the movement, as distinct from the exposition's corresponding codetta, was perfectly shaped, with that natural 'taste and feeling' that used to excite Mozart's admiration. That it was at the very end of the movement that Kyla Greenbaum found herself is, I think, highly significant. The heavy task of giving an integrated rendering of the movement was virtually over, the burden of all the well-thought-out, artificial misphrasings, the victory over all the self-created difficulties belonged to the past, and there remained nothing but to let the musical mind speak for itself. To remember her interpretation of the movement in the light of what she achieved at its end was, for me, to realize the torture today's talent inflicts upon itself.

The second and third movements brought new illusory problems that, by their very nature, remained unsolved. A particularly ridiculous example of artificiality occurred in the last movement, at the end of the theme's restatement and at the later, corresponding junctures: not the kind of artificiality which manifests itself in inorganic rubato but, on the contrary, the less obtrusive kind that results in a forced adherence to strict time. Nobody but (a) a complete fool, or (b) one who has thought too much about too little, could continue the upbeat phrase after the *forte* statement of the theme in the strictest time, letting the quaver follow exactly after one quaver's time after the B flat in the bass, if not indeed sooner (See Example). Probably Miss Greenbaum's mind, instead of concerning itself with music, reacted with this sham-aesthetic phrasing against the Romantic Rubato. Reactions, however, don't make a musical performance. Her feeling intelligence could have told Miss Greenbaum that the *forte* of the theme's second statement must not be allowed to swallow up the *subito piano* of the succeeding upbeat phrase, and that, while the latter introduces something excitingly new yet growing out of the already known, the link between the 'past' and the 'future' is strengthened rather than severed by an imperceptible *Luftpause* [taking of breath] which excites our expectation for what is to follow. As it was, the listener had not time to expect anything after the end of the theme. To give an expected surprise, however, is the secret of all artistic development, creative or interpretive.

Miss Greenbaum needs, not a teacher, but a private listener, preferably not a pianist, who would encourage her to direct her conscience towards musical reality: towards her own musicianship. I should be prepared to bet that I would change her rendition of this Sonata into a first-rate interpretation, merely by listening a few times to her playing it, and by throwing in a word here and there. In the above instance, I should just say: "First (*p*) statement of theme: quasi solo. Second (*f*) statement: *quasi tutti*. Continuation: *quasi solo*." A few bars later in her performance, in the conjunct triplets, another prime fault of Miss Greenbaum's playing was manifest, i.e. the same, musically unmotivated turn to the quicker, as 'effortless' as it was unfeeling, that had already panicked the listener in the passage work of the first movement. There are triplets and triplets. Nobody (or perhaps everybody except Reginald Kell)[3] would take the first triplet in the adagio variation of [the Clarinet Quintet in A major] K. 581's finale as a strict triplet, but the point about the present triplets is that they *are* triplets, i.e. that they both relate to and contrast with the triadic *non legato* triplets at the end of the theme's second statement. The contrast is given by these conclusive, cadential *non legato* triads on the one hand, and, on the other, by the *legato* scale sequences, as they urge further afield, to the realms of the dominant. The unity underlying this contrast of structural context and function must be brought out by playing the respective triplet passages in exactly identical time. Now with a musical person, easily the chief determinant of such unmusical changes of tempo as Miss Greenbaum indulged in is over-practice. He is a very mature musician who does not run the risk, through endless practice of the same piece, of ceasing to feel through every phrase, and to feel every phrase through its context. The risk is, incidentally, all the greater in passages where technical difficulties have been brilliantly surmounted by continuous practice, for in that case the performer's satisfaction at being able to play the thing without a jolt, at its flowing like oil, may make him unaware that he plays it away. Not even Solomon is free from such dangers, though one hears that he sees them.

Miss Greenbaum's performance of Beethoven's [Piano Sonata in E major] Op. 109 offered again the sorry picture of a fight between an intense musicality and a more efficacious, unmusical musicianship. Once again Miss Greenbaum showed, not lack, but workmanlike repression of imagination, a fear of her fancy being too fanciful. She insulted what is, perhaps, music's greatest original genius (and hence, today, the least-understood classic) by not depending upon her own originality and spontaneity. If she could free herself of our time's technical and pseudo-musical obsessions, if she ceased to project her musical morality on to the outside world, on to how Mr. X. or Mr. Y. or the *Zeitgeist* 'does it', she could develop a strongly individual, independent, and intrinsically musical conscience. But if she and the other few potential musicians who inhabit our musical world will not listen to the argument of this article, we shall end in a state of affairs of which Goethe's Faust, with his usual foresight, said –

> Du hast wohl recht, ich finde nicht die Spur
> Von einem Geist, und alles ist Dressur.[4]

Faust, it will be remembered, is remarking upon the poodle, i.e. Mephistopheles. What, to be sure, is Mephistophelean about *Dressur* is that being rarely spiritless, it pretends to be spiritual.

NOTES

Source

Music Review, 10, 1949, pp. 286-90. The original occupies just four paragraphs, of which the two central ones, beginning 'Small wonder, then, . . .' and 'And what has all this to do with Kyla Greenbaum?' have been broken up here.

1   [Ed:] Keller returned to the question of Toscanini's 'time-keeping' on various occasions in his life, notably in one of 12 contributions to: Milein Cosman, *Musical Sketchbook*, Oxford, Cassirer/Faber, 1957, p. 20:

Wilhelm Furtwängler As opposed to Toscanini, the master of unchanging precision, Furtwängler was a conductor of Mahler's type: he never fixed an interpretation, always developed it. His programmes may not have varied much, but his performances of identical works showed the most striking differences. His interpretations, preferably of music that was itself of the developing kind, would even develop between the last rehearsal and the actual performance of a work. Having often watched how his rehearsals, his pre-interpretations as it were, grew into the performance in which he would trust his spontaneous intuition, I took my stop-watch along to the last rehearsal (a straight run-through on the day of the concert) and to the performance of Beethoven's Seventh at the Salzburg Festival, 1954, a few months before his death, in order to collect objective indications of this developing process. The result was surprising:

Seventh Symphony	Last Rehearsal	Performance
Allegretto	9' 49"	9' 27"
Scherzo	9' 23"	8' 10"
Finale	8' 24"	7' 04"

By friend and foe alike, Furtwängler was acknowledged to be the greatest conductor of the developmental composer *par excellence*, "the real Beethoven," as he called him, "not the academically castrated one." He was wont to describe Beethoven as the most misunderstood composer in our time, and since even one of our greatest living masters called the second subject of the Choral Symphony's Adagio "charming as a *morceau de salon*," there must be more than a kink to Furtwängler's submission. It was while he conducted this Adagio that Milein Cosman drew him, and one can see what he felt about it: "Consider the theme of the Adagio, steeped in other worldliness which properly belongs to the sphere of religion." Furtwängler was often reproached with adopting a priest-like attitude, but when sacred music is enjoyed as salon music, a priest may not be altogether out of place.

2   [Ed:] In *Musical Sketchbook*, p. 44, Keller wrote of Menuhin:

Yehudi Menuhin   Great fiddling used to be the Eastern Jew's speciality, but Yehudi Menuhin was born at New York in 1916. (Isaac Stern has meanwhile followed suit.) His equally Biblical sisters, Yaltah and Hephzibar, were born in '17 and '20 respectively. Hepzibah is herself a great musician with whom Yehudi has played ever since their famous sonata recital at the New York Town Hall in 1934. The typically Jewish family spirit has manifested itself in other ways. For one thing, Yehudi's (like Ida Händel's) father never stirred from the prodigy's side. For another, Yehudi, Yaltah, and Hephzibar all married within 50 days in 1938: if they had been triplets, there would have been a good deal of wrong theory.

Yehudi's New York debut with orchestra, at the age of 11, was one of the greatest sensations in the history of performance, but the dictionaries don't give its background: on his way to his first concerts with the New York Symphony, Fritz Busch had read in the papers about Menuhin who, upon his arrival, was suggested as soloist for one of them. The boy proposed to play the Beethoven; Busch rejoined that Jackie Coogan did not play *Hamlet*. Menuhin sen. persuaded Busch to listen before he said no. As early as the second *tutti*, Busch interrupted and said yes. "This was perfection."

A year or two later, at a private dinner after another joint triumph at Dresden, Fritz Busch spoke of the child's miraculous gifts and the responsibility they entailed – in German, which Yehudi did not understand. He only caught Busch's solemn tone, which he had not heard before. Smiling shyly at the speaker, he turned to Mrs. Goldman, the wife of the German-American banker who had given him his Stradivarius: "I knew that Mr. Busch was a very good conductor, but when I heard him speak, I thought he could also be a wonderful rabbi!"

It is an open secret amongst musicians that the man who charms every audience by his refusal to do the charming virtuoso act is often inhibiting the gifts of his childhood, for which he seems to feel over-responsible. To be or not to be the great fiddler he is, to let his personality dream freely instead of thinking dutifully and impersonally – that would seem to be the question confronting the first modest ex-prodigy on record.

It is interesting to compare this, and later remarks on Huberman (see 'Not Famous Enough' below), with another entry of Keller's from the *Musical Sketchbook* (p.12) (Keller also interpreted Elgar to the English – see 'The Psychology of Composers and Listeners' below):

Joseph Szigeti   Psychoanalysis has shown that there may be as much in a name as poets and writers have, more or less seriously, suggested throughout the ages. A musician by the name of 'Mahler', for instance, may react to his name either positively, by writing descriptive music, or negatively, by writing absolute music, or he may combine both approaches in writing universal symphonies. The Hungarian word *szigeti* means islander.

Alone among violinists of his generation – he was born in 1892 at Budapest – Szigeti has retained the old-fashioned right-arm technique, with the upper arm close to the chest when playing at the nut and on the lower strings, thus outdoing even Huberman, that arch-individualist who, though his elder by ten years, nevertheless came to adjust his right arm to modern technique. Alone among exponents of new music, he has never commissioned a new work, yet countless new concertos, rhapsodies, sonatas have been dedicated to this intimate friend of another great lonely figure – Béla Bartók. Almost alone among modern virtuosos, he puts spontaneity unconditionally above spotless technique, and his finger on the weak spots of technical strength: "we have reached the point where the string orchestra is imitating the cinema organ."

But his loneliness is for all. The *raison d'être* of his shy virtuosodom is "the irrational pleasure that communication gives: communication that transcends the barriers of language, of nationality, of race"; and what impressed him most about Kreisler's first performance of the Elgar Concerto was "that it was a *Viennese* who had transmitted the Englishness of Elgar to England and to the rest of the world." The absence of insularity and the degree of the artist's empathy has always seemed to Szigeti the yardstick of his stature.

A musician by the name of 'Szigeti' may be insular, or anti-insular, or his character may show these conflicting attitudes simultaneously. If he is a great artist and a great mind, however, conflicting elements must needs develop into complements.

3   [Ed:]   Keller discusses Reginald Kell, along with Britten, Huberman, Pears and Whyte below.
4   [Ed:]   'You may well be right, I can find no trace
                   of individuality in the spirit, and everything is down to training.'

Not Famous Enough
[on Britten, Huberman, Kell, Pears, and Whyte]

[HK:] I   Introduction: appraisal of five contemporary performers: its relation to subjectivity in music criticism.   II   The Big Five: Benjamin Britten (here as pianist), Bronislav Huberman (violin), Reginald Kell (clarinet), Peter Pears (tenor), Ian Whyte (conductor). (1) Review of common characteristics. (a) Vitality, being at the root of (i) variability of performance of the same work, (ii) organic interpretations, (iii) originality, (iv) productivity in reproduction; (b) intelligence. (2) Separate reviews. (a) Britten: Empathy. Instances cited: Purcell, Schubert, Mahler, Tippett. (b) Huberman: intensity and freedom of expression. A mixture of rhythmic structure, marriage between freedom and necessity of interpretation. Instances: (i) Lalo's Symphonie Espagnole, concertos by Tchaikovsky and Brahms, and (ii) [concertos] by Bach, Mozart, Beethoven. (c) Kell: sense of rhythmic structure, marriage between freedom and necessity of interpretation. Instances cited: clarinet quintets by Mozart and Brahms. (d) Pears: Musicianly technique. Variety of feeling, thought, timbre. Crescendo, diminuendo. Unbroken line of interpretation. Instances cited: Purcell, Rameau, Bach, Handel, Mozart, Schubert, Smetana, Fauré, Elgar, Mahler, Tippett, Britten. Two elementary qualities: unblemished intonation, moderate vibrato. (e) Whyte: superior exponent of Mozart and Mendelssohn: deep interpretations. Sensitivity to similarities between these composers.   III Conclusion: hear for yourself.[1]

I Introduction

When in the following I am trying to draw attention to what I consider quite outstanding capacities, not yet sufficiently recognized, of five contemporary performers, I realize that my observations may well smilingly be called 'subjective'. So they are (if I have to use this intriguant of a term), but not more so than many a piece of music criticism to which no such objection is taken. One must not be misled by the objective air (springing from a conscience made uneasy by the concealment of subjectivity) with which music criticism is so often expounded: a comparison between equally "objective" specimens of such reviewing shows again and again that logically they exclude each other. If, therefore, my reflections appear particularly personal, this is primarily because I am making no bones about their being as personal as they are. Though they are to some extent unusual, such unusualness is far more usual than is usually recognized.

Benjamin Britten (in the present case as pianist), Bronislaw Huberman (violin), Reginald Kell (clarinet), Peter Pears (tenor), and Ian Whyte (conductor) are, in alphabetic order, the Big Five for whom I want to make some shameless – but as is clear from their status, not altogether shameful – propaganda, in terms as little technical as possible. Each of these personalities is a personage, but the 'name' they have acquired does not generally include the notion that their interpretations arise from downright reproductive genius. It is this very notion that has prompted me to write the present article.

Let me consider first what these artists have in common (whether they like it or not). The most general and fundamental common characteristic can be indicated by a simple word: these men's interpretations are *alive*. From this common root other likenesses derive.

For instance, each of these musicians performs the same work differently on different occasions – and obviously so, once one realizes that for them each rendering is a living experience: life finds itself extremely difficult exactly to repeat itself. Here, that is to say are performers who are not just walking gramophone records. This may be one of the reasons why their fame is not greater, for the gramophone record disguised as a human being is very much in vogue nowadays, and it must be admitted that in its kind it sometimes presents itself in almost overpowering perfection. *Almost* overpowering: for in order actually to overpower an artistic happening must be highly invested with life. But then the number of listeners is considerable who don't want to hear music in order actually to be overpowered.

Again, nothing in these artists' readings is haphazard: every interpretation is an organic whole, as it is bound to be if it really lives. And every such organism is original; it is unconventional, but not in order not to be conventional: vital spontaneity is here the cause of divergence from custom.

You cannot be original without being productive. Reproduction, in the case of these performers, essentially involves production. There are those who say that the performer has nothing to do but relive the composer's experiences. Such a standpoint shows a lacking understanding of life, especially its mental manifestations. One cannot exactly relive one's own experiences, let alone those of others. And a performance suffers if at its root lies an attempt to realize an illusion. No, the reproductive musician evinces his own productivity on the basis of, and in sympathy and harmony with, the composer's. Life itself, as already indicated, produces while it reproduces.

Lastly in these general observations, I want to point to the convincing intelligence which these men possess. This is, of course, a condition for their realizing their impulses – 'realizing' in both senses of the term – and therefore for our realizing them.

And now for a more concrete word or two on each of these men of genius.

II The Big Five

In *Britten's* case, the fact that his interpretations are full of life, inconstant but always consistent, organic, original and creative, does not take us unawares, since his musical writing is, in all these respects, of outstanding calibre. More surprising to some of us, if only prima facie so, is his deep-reaching capacity to feel himself into other composers ('empathy' is the technical expression for such powers), whose musical character may be markedly different from his. But then a strong personality, in the artistic sense, will always have a highly developed sensitivity to what is going on in others' minds. Every great artist, however, self-willed and self-centred he may seem, is an intuitive psychologist and, in this sense, selfless.

Britten as pianist and accompanist, whether it be in Purcell (not to speak of pre-Purcell), Schubert, Mahler, Tippett, or, of course, Britten, is thus a unique experience: opening himself to the composer and the performer on the one hand and to his own creatively reproductive impulses on the other, he offers the perfect musical illustration of how to be actively passive.

Huberman, who to me is just as unquestionably the greatest living violinist as Casals is, to virtually all musicians and music-lovers, the greatest 'cellist, is not so widely and deeply appreciated in this country as he is (or, at any rate, was before Hitler) on the continent. In Vienna or Prague, the mentioning of Huberman used to evoke the same reactions (if not stronger ones) as 'Menuhin' does in England at the present time.

However, Huberman's recent (post-war) performances in this country have attracted and excited a far wider public than his pre-war concerts, and it is to be hoped that when he comes again in the autumn he will finally conquer our musical world. (He will, I gather, give concerts throughout Britain on that occasion in the 'International Celebrities Series'.) His, certainly, is that youthful, yet mature intensity and inner freedom of expression that should make it worth anyone's while to be captured by him. (He's in his sixties, by the way.)

For the rest, the concisest way of describing him I can think of is to call him a mixture of racy gypsy genius and classical refinement. This mixture itself always bears classical proportions that at the same time vary according to the work he interprets. Thus (to cite from his recent performances) gipsy spirit runs high in his reading of Lalo's *Symphonie Espagnole*, of the Tchaikovsky Concerto, and parts of the Brahms Concerto (the radio performance of the latter, apparently very nervous, was far weaker than the Albert Hall performance), while classical restraint (not suppression) and sublimation of passion are more conspicuous in his Bach E major, Mozart D major (the famous one), and, above all, his Beethoven Concerto. Everywhere, his singular ability of contrast (particularly as between the heroic and the lyrical) is manifest.

Reginald Kell's performances are strikingly similar to Huberman's in regard to the marked freedom with which he reads a work, and the impression of inevitable necessity that, all the same, his readings make. Such freedom has nothing to do with caprice, but develops out of incisive insight into the composition, insight that goes beyond what is printed of it. This clarinettist's unfailing sense of rhythmic structure makes it possible for him to bring about this marriage between freedom and necessity on the highest possible level. His rendering of the clarinet quintet by Brahms, in particular of the slow movement, must be noted in this connection. And as regards the clarinet's chromatic descent in the last movement's Adagio of Mozart's Clarinet Quintet, Mr. Kell is the only performer I have heard in public who has made the meaning of this passage fully (and most movingly) clear. He doesn't just play a triplet and four semi-quavers here, but expresses the melodic gravitation implied by delicately decreasing the temporal distance between the notes, without, of course, that often-heard and disastrously disintegrating accent on the first of the four semi-quavers.

Of *Peter Pears* I have already written twice elsewhere,[2] but he makes it easy for me to say something new each time I'm discussing him, if only because he is saying so very much new to me each time he's singing. By means of an exceptional – i.e. essentially musicianly – singing technique, he presents us with an astounding variety of feeling and thought, now shaded with unaffected finesse, now sharply contrasted. Lyrical portions (brought forth with that repressed vocal tear which I have only heard from one other singer, i.e. the Munich tenor Julius Patzak, who in other respects does not reach up to Pears) are given as convincingly as dramatic, heroic, pithy strokes (note the affinity with Huberman again).

Pears can play various instruments with his voice – strings, winds, and even the piano.

Capable not only of an extensively developing crescendo (in more than a physical sense), but also of a diminuendo in which musical intensity increases in proportion as loudness decreases, he always offers an unbroken line of development (and/or envelopment, as the composition demands it). *Always*: for his universality, obvious to the attentive listener even if he hears this tenor in but a single work, is unsurpassed.

Hear him in Purcell (not, again to speak of earlier composers), in Rameau, in Bach (why isn't he ever given the role of the Evangelist in the St. Matthew Passion?) and Handel, in Mozart (any chance of hearing him again in *Così fan tutte*? The A major aria and the A major duet remain unforgettable), in Schubert (the clarity of his German diction would stand out in a German company), Smetana, Fauré, (the first concert performance in London of the Shylock Suite with songs was not nearly well enough attended), Elgar (what an incomparable Gerontius! And what invalid criticism there was of this performance!), Mahler, Tippett . . . or, of course, in one of the numerous parts that Britten wrote, if I may say so, out of, and into Pears's vocal character, witness his interpreting these various channels of musical thought (unfortunately I missed him in Verdi's Requiem) and you will agree with me that he isn't an exponent of this or that, but an interpreter of music.

To end this section I would like to single out two of his more elementary qualities – elementary in his case, but, alas, rarely to be found with contemporary singers. These are, firstly, his unblemished intonation, and secondly, his moderate and at the same time vivifying vibrato.

To my mind it is as incomprehensible as it is deplorable that *Ian Whyte*, the conductor of the BBC Scottish Orchestra, is not given much wider scope. For while the orchestra is, at the present time, definitely not one of our best, the judicious radio listener can on many occasions realize that its conductor – even as he appears through this inadequate medium – is second to none of his colleagues in this country, at least as far as musical discernment goes. (No, I'm not forgetting any of the big shots.)

I would even go as far as to say that he presents Mozart and Mendelssohn with deeper understanding (there is such a thing as deeper understanding of Mendelssohn) than any of our famous or even great conductors. This double aptitude for Mozart and Mendelssohn is of fascinating interest. It is true that Mozart is in some respects the greatest of all composers, while Mendelssohn, in the words of Gerald Abraham, is 'something less than a great composer'; yet the greatness, or more exactly the depth, of both composers tends to be severely neglected, because both of them work so perfectly on the surface that people (including outstanding conductors) don't bother to look beneath the surface for deeper levels. It is Mr. Whyte's inestimable merit that he observes here, not only what moves on the surface but also what one has to bring to it.

There are other similarities between these two composers (easily overshadowed by more striking differences) that Whyte seems to grasp with exceptional sensitivity. Just to give a few clues to these resemblances: balance and proportion, lucidity, nobility, subtlety, ease; or again, to turn to something more particular, these composers' ability effortlessly and vividly to lead back from Development to Recapitulation. But here I am touching on the subject of a future article that will be parallel with the present one: I shall there try to point out *composers'* merits that are not sufficiently appreciated.[3]

III Conclusion

The [subjects of] the present article will have achieved their object if they stimulate one or the other music-lover to go and hear – or even, if I may humbly add, to rehear – for himself.

NOTES

Source

Reference to Huberman as a living player, to his post-war performances and to his impending visits to Britain in the autumn, suggest a date for this typescript of around 1946. (Huberman was born in 1882 and died on 15 June 1947.)

1 [Ed:] The introductory pages end with a disclaimer, 'the possibility of occasional linguistic imperfections is due to the writer's mother tongue not being English'. In fact, a few small changes to the text have been necessary.

2 [Ed:] It is not clear what the two previous publications on Pears would have been (not all of Keller's journalism of the time has been catalogued), though one may have been the review for the *National Entertainments Weekly* in April/May 1946 referred to in his correspondence with Pears (see 'Psychology of Opera' above). Keller later wrote about Pears in: 'Sadler's Wells: *Così fan tutte*', *Music Review*, 9/2, May 1948, pp. 110-12; 'Four Singers (de los Angeles, Christoff, Flagstad, Pears)', *Colophon*, August 1950; 'People X: Peter Pears', *Opera* 2/6, May 1951, pp. 287-292.

3 [Ed:] It is not known whether Keller ever wrote this piece. However, he did write on Mendelssohn and Mozart together in a programme note for the Wigmore Hall, 6 June, 1979, 'The Two-viola String Quintet'. This is reproduced in Keller's *The Jerusalem Diary*, London, Plumbago, 2001, pp. 209-19.

The Psychology of Composers and Listeners

Musical Self-contempt in Britain

This paper was given to the Social Psychology section of the British Psychological Society at 8 p.m. in the Physiology Theatre, University College London, Gower Street, London W.C.1 on Saturday 4 November, 1950. Keller had been ill in the weeks leading up to the event, and it appears from the correspondence that someone else read the paper on his behalf. The psychological investigation of composers and listeners is again couched within an analysis of British musical society.

This is a key text for understanding Keller's blend of psychology and music, and one that amplifies his 'Resistances to Britten: Their Psychology', Music Survey, Vol. II, No. 4, Spring 1950, pp. 227-36. It forms a natural continuity from the fieldwork Keller undertook on prostitutes' self-contempt (see Part II above).

Mr. Chairman, Ladies and Gentlemen –

As a musician and a psychological researcher who is naturally inclined to apply his psychological to his musical knowledge I am, as far as my readership is concerned, uncomfortably suspended between two stools. To put it bluntly, I cannot talk shop without someone wishing I would stop. The relation between art and psychology is not without friction: the psychologist envies the artist: the artist fears the psychologist. And musicians, especially musical musicians, are singularly uninterested in the psychology of music, not only because they resist [incursion into] the narcissistic isolation in which their art thrives, but also for the more respectable reason that music is able to express psychical realities with such unique penetration, intensity, clarity, and consistency that the question why and how it does so cannot be very fascinating to the intrinsically musical person, unless his psychological interests are exceptionally violent. After all, Ladies and Gentlemen, we must not forget that psychologists themselves are not, on the whole, unduly bothered by the psychology of psychology.

As for profoundly musical psychologists, I have not, to be candid, seen many, at any rate until five minutes ago. The great discoverer of psychoanalysis could not have been more unmusical, and most psychoanalysts have kept up the tradition, though a number of Hungarians and Frenchmen have made courageous if unappreciated attempts to apply the results of psychoanalytic research to music. However, the degree of musicality manifested in the majority of these efforts is not likely to overcome the musician's and musicologist's resistances to psychology in general and psychoanalysis in particular.

Yet, it is psychoanalysis in particular that is destined, in my considered conviction, to get the psychology of music out of its present embryonic state by shedding light on the psychology, not only of the composing process, but of the actual elements of musical structure and texture.

My task tonight, however, is more modest: it is no less concerned with the psychology of music than with the psychology of certain social attitudes towards a certain kind of music. Nevertheless, since I am here addressing not only psychologists, but also (I hope) a number of musicians, my uncomfortable position between two stools makes itself acutely felt, for the simple reason that it is impossible for me to avoid altogether the employment of the two respective technical terminologies. I shall, however, try my best to keep both psychological and particularly musical technicalities to a minimum.

*

Whence in medias res. About a year ago an English composer, whom I shall call Brown, asked me to have a look at a certain work he had recently completed, and to give him my opinion on it. After I had examined it, I did not know what to say – or rather I did, but I didn't dare say it, for fear of giving offence. For what struck me above all about this music was that no trace of any typically English style, past or present, could be detected in it; on the contrary, the work seemed to have grown out of nothing but the Austro-German tradition. At last I said: "You know, nobody can possibly guess that this has been written by an Englishman." He was not offended; on the contrary, his face lit up as if I had praised his work in the most glowing terms. Several months later, I was sharing a café table with Brown and a fellow critic. "Did I tell you," he asked my colleague with marked pride, "that Keller thinks this music quite un-English?" My colleague replied: "You *did* tell me."

Now I do not know of any other country, with the possible exception of yesterday's Hungary, where a composer would pride himself on the fact that his work was uninfluenced by his national tradition which, in fact, he would distrust and despise. Nor can Brown's attitude by any means be called unique in this country. Some time ago a British composer who is doubtless known to most of you, and whom I shall call White, asked me to write an analytical piece on his compositions. When I went through the literature on White's works, it struck me that a certain book on contemporary English music barely mentioned them. I pointed this out to White, whereupon he said, again with considerable pride: "Yes, but then I'm not an English composer!" And on several occasions he repeated this statement, to which he evidently attached great importance.

However, the cases of Brown and White are not psychologically identical. That is to say, while the music of Brown does not, to my knowledge, display any characteristics that can by any stretch of the term be called British, White's eclectic output, though cosmopolitan in its range of styles, includes at least one work that is so quintessentially English as to be quite unexportable. It would seem to follow that White's contempt of musical Englishness must carry a greater amount of in-turned aggression than Brown's.

On the other hand, when we turn our attention from the production end to the reception end of our musico-social apparatus, to the critics and listeners, the relative amount of in-turned and out-turned aggression contributing to this curious anti-British attitude becomes less easily observable; for while the creator tries his conscious or unconscious best to reveal his personality, the critic has more legitimate opportunity, and more often more illegitimate reasons, to conceal his own artistic make-up. Nevertheless, psychoanalytic research into social psychology entitles us to the a priori assumption that an Englishman's contempt of Englishness *qua* Englishness is well nigh impossible without self-contempt.

About the actual prevalence of this attitude among the listening and criticising public my experience does not leave any doubt. Particularly striking for the student of criticism have been the very hostile British reactions to the work of Benjamin Britten, whose very name seems to have had a say in the matter, as will easily be recognised by those who are familiar with the psychoanalytic investigations into the significance of names by Wilhelm Stekel, Otto Rank, Karl Abraham, Sir T. Percy Nunn, and Ingeborg Flugel. In fact, when one compares British with Continental press reactions to Benjamin Britten's work, one is surprised to note that while there is plenty of unqualified admiration for it on the Continent, British critics do not seem to find Benjamin Britten continental enough.

Fascinating in this respect were the musical-critical reactions to Britten's recent *Spring Symphony*. Even superficially the work may strike the listener as doubly English, in that it is vocal and in that it lacks the essentially Viennese sonata-developmental approach. To make things worse, it presumes up to Gustav Mahler's symphonic station, thereby reminding the guilt-laden British listener of the ideals of the Austro-German symphonic tradition, which, at the same time, he finds disregarded. Consequently British self-contempt denied the work the Austrian honorary degree 'Symphony', which title the critics considered inappropriate, in spite of this music's extended intra-musical unity and its, at bottom, classical symphonic scheme. Benjamin Britten, whose ideals are, significantly enough, Purcell and Mozart, has indeed, again and again, fallen an easy prey to British self-contempt. As my friend Wilfrid Mellers has written, 'all through his career, Benjamin Britten has been interested in the problem of effecting a rapprochement between the more provincial elements of English musical styles and the cosmopolitan techniques of Europe.'

Now the more the listener's attention is drawn to these techniques the more may he resent, if he is psychologically so inclined, their adulteration by what he feels to be wicked English styles. Thus we get the paradoxical situation that the most exclusively English composers, like [Ralph] Vaughan Williams, are likely to escape this resistance against Englishness, which in their case is taken as a matter of inevitable course and which doesn't remind you of, and tantalize you with, the methods of the good old Continentals. For those English musicians, to be sure, who have completely identified with the Austrian tradition in particular, anything and everything British is contemptible; it will not surprise you that our Mr. Brown, for instance, despises Vaughan Williams.

But how much more widely and how strongly Benjamin Britten's supra-national music stimulates the Britisher's anti-British musical tendencies was shown by a widespread rumour which preceded the first performance of the *Spring Symphony* last year, and which even found its way into what was supposed to be, and was accepted as, the most authoritative introduction to the work. As most of you will be aware, the BBC publication *The Listener* prints each week a specialist article in connection with one or more important musical broadcasts of the succeeding week or weeks. Upon the occasion of the BBC's relay of the *Spring Symphony*'s premiere at the Holland festival in Amsterdam, Scott Goddard, one of our few critics who deeply admire Benjamin Britten, came out with an article entitled 'Britten as *Instrumental* Composer.' Since the *Spring Symphony* is vocal throughout, the relevance of the article can be imagined without difficulty. It did in fact contain two sentences that were directly concerned with the work. They ran: 'The new *Spring Symphony* sounds as though it may be the kind of work that would call forth the composer's finest style of orchestral writing. It is rumoured that as well as the vocal numbers this new symphony contains a number of purely orchestral movements.'

We observe, Ladies and Gentlemen, that musical self-contempt in Britain created the wishful and completely illusory rumour among the friends of Benjamin Britten's music that the *Spring Symphony* would rehabilitate him as an instrumental composer (meaning: an un-British composer – meaning: an Austrian symphonist); we observe that this rumour was strong enough to form the unchecked, though, easily checkable basis for an official article which thus turned out to be totally beside the point; and that the article was passed by the Music Editor of *The Listener*, a highly distinguished musicologist with a strong scientific conscience. The disappointment which the unashamedly English vocal character of the Symphony brought to the minds of the rumour-mongers and their followers can now easily be imagined; even our Mr. White, who was among the first discoverers of Britten's genius and who will always remain, psychologically speaking, proud of his brilliant son, never mentions the *Spring*

Symphony, which he greatly admires, without letting you swallow this bitter pill: that it is about time now that Britten wrote extended instrumental works and proved himself master of purely instrumental styles and structures. I personally always swallow this pill with some forgivable amusement, for White himself is fundamentally a rhapsodist rather than a symphonist, whence it would appear that he projects his strongly self-contemptuous anti-English musical attitude onto Benjamin Britten – not an unusual happening as between father and son.

Far be it for me, however, to suggest that I myself am above the conflict of emotions that expresses itself in British musical self-contempt. On the contrary, Austrian by education and British by naturalisation, I am liable to manifest this artistic conflict with the superego to an acute degree. Thus, when I look back on my musico-analytical writings, I am struck by the downright obsessional insistence with which I have drawn attention to the first movement of Benjamin Britten's Second String Quartet. For it is really there that the composer may be said to have acquitted himself of the duties of an Austrian symphonist, by virtue of his frontal and, as it seems to me, successful attack on the tremendous problems of modern sonata form and style.[1]

Perhaps I have now given a sufficient outline of the attitude indicated by my title to turn to its theory without soporific effect upon the musical section of my audience. Indeed it behoves me not to hide the fact that I had the theory of self-contempt in Britain ready *before* I embarked upon systematic observations of its various manifestations. Mine was not, therefore, an unprejudiced approach. But since there isn't such a thing, one may as well try to avail oneself of the right prejudices, and call them 'working hypotheses'.

In the investigations which Margaret Phillips and I have undertaken into the psychology of small social groups, and on which each of us has delivered a preliminary paper to the Social Psychology Section of the [British Psychological Society], I encountered, in the diary of an Auxiliary Fire Brigade's group life during the war, a social-psychological attitude to which I have given the descriptive name of 'group self-contempt'.[2] This attitude seems to make its invariable appearance in any group, irrespective of its size or character, as soon as certain conditions are fulfilled. The wider groups in which I have noted the presence of group self-contempt are women, Jews, prostitutes, populations under Nazi occupation during the war, and the British musical world. You may wonder how these groups, different as they seem from each other in every conceivable respect, can be thrown under one hat, where in fact the *tertium comparationibus* lies. However, they all display the necessary degree of exclusive identification which makes the application of the term 'group' justifiable – exactly how justifiable can be gathered from the very phenomenon of group self-contempt, whose aetiology I shall now try to describe.

A group is dominated by another group in superior position: women by men, Jews by Gentiles, prostitutes by society, and so forth. The dominated group inevitably feels the dominating group to be in loco parentis. The members of the dominated group thus project part of what might loosely be called their common superego onto the dominating group. As a result, the dominated people turn part of the aggression that they would, but can't release toward the dominating group back against their own group. The introversion of frustrated aggression originally directed against a parent and substitute is of course a process that has been well channelled from infancy onwards, but in group self-contempt the course of psychic events is more complicated and, for what we might call the normally neurotic individual of our civilization, more satisfying. That is to say, group self-contempt does not present us with a straightforward inturning of aggression, but rather with an aggressive flow towards an intra-psychical object as well as towards extra-psychical objects. Inasmuch as any member of the dominated group identifies himself with it, introjects it, his group self-contempt is directed against himself; but inasmuch as he has not absorbed his group into his personality, his group self-contempt consists of extraverted aggression, namely moralized sadism taking his group, as distinct from himself, as object. From the topographical standpoint, the genuinely introverted part or aspect of group self-contempt will often manifest itself in conscious and preconscious as well as unconscious regions. But even where the conflict seems to be wholly unconscious, as for instance in the case of Mr. Brown's contempt for British music, you need not usually perform a particular feat of imagination in order to detect it, nor do you have to psychoanalyse the person in question. This is for the simple reason that many conclusive data lie in the outside world, at any rate when you are dealing with a composer.

The chief force in this conflict is, of course, the superego sadism that, in the case of intropunitive group self-contempt, is assisted by the masochism of the ego; but at the same time, we also have to reckon with a struggle within the superego, though this part of the conflict will easily be quite conscious. Mr White's superego, for instance, must harbour strong English ideals, for otherwise he could never have written a strongly English work; but from my previous description of his attitude it may already be clear to you that these ideals are nowhere near his conscious ego-ideal which, as far as music is concerned, is all cosmopolitanism. At the other extreme is my own special case: since the British part of my musical superego is comparatively young and therefore, topologically speaking, superficial, the ensuing conflict within the superego seems to be, at its deepest, preconscious, so that when as a critic I am confronted with the task of judging a typically English score, I am not seldom able to sit back and watch my Austrian and my English musical ego-ideals tearing each other to bits.

For the rest, Ladies and Gentlemen, most of you must surely have come into contact with one or other form of group self-contempt, perhaps with Jewish anti-Semitism or with female misogyny, and so you will no doubt agree that the individual adopting this attitude has really picked up an exceptionally excellent psychological bargain. For in exchange for a few ounces of reality principle – a price which even the most wretched miser is only too willing to pay – the person in question is acquiring an extremely flexible attitude which can be made to meet opposing tendencies arising out of unconscious guilt: and what more does he want? If he is in a rather intro-punitive mood today, his group self-contempt will explore the possibilities offered by the introversion of aggression; if tomorrow he should feel more extra-punitively inclined, he will lavish his aggression on his group, among whose members he will consider himself a rather fortunate exception. What is more, group self-contempt will serve him in any intermediary stage between, or compound state of, in-turned and out-turned aggression. At the same time, since group self-contempt appears to spring from the potential aggression against the dominating group, and since in any case, death instinct or no death instinct, Man's actions and attitudes are yet more aggressive than self-destructive, the extraverted components of group self-contempt will tend to gain the upper hand over the introverted components.

From the point of view of social psychology, the great flexibility of this attitude is of especial significance, for it means that a considerable variety of character types will find equal satisfaction in group self-contempt, which is no doubt the reason why it is so easy to diagnose the attitude among groups which find themselves in the situation I have described; I suggest, therefore, that unless a group is selected from some particular characterological standpoint, its group self-contempt in the British musical world, we do indeed find that there is something for everyone in this attitude. The difference in musical character between Brown and White gives some idea of the range of possible musical self-contempt; as we have seen, Brown, whose music is quite un-English, must be placed near the extreme of the predominating extraversion, whereas White's place cannot be far from the other extreme, that of predominating introversion.

Given the existence of musical self-contempt in Britain, the questions remain how and why it arose; also, it may be worth while to consider the problem of prognosis, i.e. whether, how and why this form of group self-contempt will cease.

The genesis of any form of group self-contempt can be inferred from its structure, which, in the case of British musical self-contempt, is complicated. For the dominating and the dominated group do not altogether observe the classical unities of time, space, and action. The dominated group is, or has been, the British musical world. The dominating group are, or were, the exponents of the Austro-German musical tradition. This tradition is dying. In fact, Franz Schmidt, the last great Austrian symphonist, died in 1939. The fact that a new school, Austrian in origin, and headed by the genius of Arnold Schoenberg, the discoverer of the twelve-tone technique, has emerged out of the last stages of the old Austro-German tradition, need not concern us here: for it is out of the question that these dodecaphonists are assuming the position of a dominating group in regard to British or indeed any other musical life. It is true that they have spread over the greater part of our musical civilisation and that the 76-year-old master's influence upon musical history is already considerable, but the revolution he is bringing about is up against every possible kind of violent, or irrelevant resistance, so that his followers will for a long time remain a persecuted group which, far from making other groups self-contemptuous, will probably develop group self-contempt within its own confines. For our purposes then, the Austrian symphonic school and indeed the wider Austro-German tradition is now without an important living exponent.

Now the very fact that Franz Schmidt is virtually unknown in this country – not even the Third Programme, as I may tell you from some personal experience, cares a damn about him – the very fact that Franz Schmidt does not even get a hearing over here, gives you a strong indication that the power that generates group self-contempt in Britain is a power of the past, though certainly not a past power.[3] In other words, a long-dead group dominates a living group. There is nothing to be wondered at in this state of affairs, since a good composer usually shows his full vitality only after he has died, and does not lose any of it unless and until musical history develops tendencies that run counter to his approach. The first of the galaxy of Austro-German symphonists was Haydn, and it is most probably he who is to be regarded as the first member of the dominating group. The last member commanding an overpowering influence over British musical life was undoubtedly Brahms. However, this is not to say that later exponents of the Austro-German tradition take no part at all in the structure of British group self-contempt. We have already had a glimpse of the role Mahler plays in the resistances to Benjamin Britten's *Spring Symphony*, and I may add here that Mr. Brown, whose super-ego identification with Austro-German ideals is to all appearances complete, is a passionate admirer of the German neo-romantic Hans Pfitzner, who was born in 1869 and died last year [1949], as did his diametrically opposite number, another last member in the German line, Richard Strauss.

But partly owing to the anti-romantic and neo-classical tendencies of recent musical history, all these more recent members of the dominating group have an immeasurably smaller share in the aetiology of British musical self-contempt than their forerunners; Pfitzner himself is almost as unknown in this country as Schmidt.

At this stage in our consideration, Ladies and Gentlemen, you may perhaps feel like impatiently interrupting and asking me with what scientific right I call the exponents of the Austro-German tradition a 'group'; after all, whatever sociological concept of the group we may adhere to, we all silently assume contemporaneity among its members. However, with what scientific right do we make this silent assumption?

Either the psychoanalytic concept of the group, as conceived by Freud in his 'Group Psychology and the Analysis of the Ego', and developed by others, pre-eminently by Flugel in *Men, Morals and Society* – either this concept is right or it is wrong.[4] If it is right, and if it turns out to be applicable to a piece of reality which neither Freud nor Flugel may have thought of, it does not therefore become wrong. On the contrary, it proves yet more valuable; it helps to explain more than we thought. Well, the simple fact is that the psychoanalytic concept of the group applies to the exponents of the Austro-German musical tradition. In other words, there is no doubt about their common super-ego projection upon the ideals of the tradition, principally upon the classical symphonic ideals, and more specifically upon the ideals of the organization of those extended, polythematic ternary circles which we are used to comprise under the name of 'sonata form'; and thus, quite in particular, their common superego projection upon the art of instrumental *development*, in the musico-technical sense of the term. These ideals do not exhaust all the leading ideas of the tradition, but they certainly *involve* them. Now: upon reflection you will agree, Ladies and Gentlemen, that without this common superego projection and its resulting ego identifications, the continental symphonic school could never have developed as it did.

The next question we have to consider is how this dominating group came to be the dominating group, and how the dominated group came to be the dominated group. Three interrelated factors have here to be kept in mind. First, the foreign domination of musical England prior to the rise of the classical sonata; second, the relation of English musical thinking to the thought processes required for the creation of a sonata form; and third, the state of English music itself during the 18th and 19th centuries.

The foreign influence on English musical life after Purcell is actually bound up in the popular mind with the name of Handel; but in actual fact it neither started with Handel nor did it finish with him, nor was it predominantly German – not even in Handel's own case. In fact what Eric Blom calls 'the amiable English tradition that no native musician will do if his place can possibly be given to a foreigner' seems to have started under Charles II, whose mother was French. At the same time, it would be wrong to go searching in 18th-century England, or even earlier, for some original form of musical group self-contempt, for the simple reason that English musicians did not at those times form national groups, dominated or otherwise, in any accepted sociological sense. What is undoubtedly true is that this so-called foreign domination prepared the ground for our situation of a dominated and a dominating group. But this situation could never have come about without, on the one hand, the curious disinclination of English composers to indulge in symphonic thinking, and on the other hand, what Prof. Paul Henry Lang of Columbia University has called

> . . . the arid and sentimental periods of the eighteenth and nineteenth centuries in English musical history, a decline in original composition which was at first hidden by the great variety of English musical life and which reached its obvious nadir in the earlier Victorian era, when Mendelssohn, one of the greatest and, today, one of the most underestimated masters of the symphonic-developmental thinking, dedicated his *Scottish Symphony* to the Queen.[5]

Mendelssohn's own function as member of the dominating group is of course conspicuous.

Now why did English composers not participate at all in the development of the symphony, despite the manifold stimuli they were offered for doing so? The reasons seem to be complex, one of them being the decline of English music itself, another that the English musical tradition was predominantly vocal, and in fact never attained a state of instrumental architecture from which the sonata form could spring. With considerable amazement one reads in Henry Davey's *History of English Music* the proud assertion that Richard John Samuel Stevens, who lived from 1757-1837, was the first who 'succeeded in adapting the sonata form to the glee.' Ladies and Gentlemen, I must not permit myself to enlarge upon the problems of musical form, but if you have more than the most superficial knowledge of sonata form you will realise for your yourselves that Stevens's undertaking was the most idiotic one could imagine.

Anyhow, I should like to put forward a third reason, one of greater sociological interest, why English composers remained unsymphonic, why not even Haydn and Mozart influenced them, notwithstanding the fact that early nineteenth-century London saw frequent performances of the works of these masters. It has often struck me, when observing English social life, that what one may crudely call the British character exhibits a genius for impromptu solutions of the most difficult problems, for imaginative improvisations, but has far less taste for thorough long-range organisation. Now since symphonic thinking may be said to represent musical – though not necessarily conscious – long-range organization par excellence, it is possible that their national character is in part responsible for the unwillingness of English composers to profit by the rise of the sonata tradition. However that may be, one thing is certain – that the inverse relation in strength between, on the one hand, the history of the sonata tradition and of its dissemination, and, on the other hand, the 18th- and 19th-century history of original English music determined the formation of a dominating and a dominated group in the sociological and psychoanalytic sense. Paul Henry Lang pointed out in 1941 that 'as the production as well as the appreciation of stylistic properties declined, England acquired the reputation of a "country without music" so unjustly emphasized on the Continent until recent times.' I can assure him that – totally absurd as it may now seem – this reputation is still alive among the members of the dominating group. A few months ago, for instance, while I was at the Salzburg Festival, a 19-year-old Viennese student of musicology informed me, with stressedly scientific detachment, that 'the English as a whole are curiously unmusical.' I shall in a few minutes return to the question why this reputation is still alive; for the moment, our interest centres on its early history.

'The country without music' – 'das Land ohne Musik' – this ever more widely popular expression of contempt is of German or Austro-German origin. Now, in view of what we know about the group-uniting and indeed group-forming influence of a common enemy, is it too far-fetched to assume that the Austro-German contempt of unmusical England was the first, or at any rate one of the first and strongest determinants of English musical group-formation? That it exercised its binding power long before a more positive and more obviously potent factor emerged, namely, the renascence of England's national musical styles that began in the fourth quarter of the 19th century and has developed into the present bloom of creativity? In that case the origin, or one of the origins, of English musical group formation would actually coincide with one of the origins of the English group's self-contempt.

For about the general fact that a dominating group's manifest contempt of the dominated group's self-contempt there cannot, psychoanalytically speaking, be the faintest doubt. In fact, the important question arises here whether group self-contempt can develop at all without the dominating group's superiority expressing itself *in its explicit contempt for the dominated group* – a contempt that is then incorporated in the dominated group's superegos. In the cases of female misogyny, Jewish anti-Semitism and prostitutes' anti-prostitutionalism, for instance, this element of outspoken contempt on the part of the dominating groups is certainly not lacking. But I do not think that we can give a conscientiously definite answer to this question before more detailed studies afford us sufficient insight into the various possible forms of group self-contempt to attempt something like a complete picture from the dynamic, topographic and economic points of view – a 'meta-psychological presentation', as Freud would say. Meanwhile, in our special case we can be sure that Austro-German contempt of England, strong and strongly expressed as it was, must soon have affected English musical minds, particularly when we remember the ever-increasing musical two-way traffic between England and the Continent. The English habit of studying in Germany, which started in the later 18th century and grew intense during the 19th, must indeed have stood in a circular causative relation to group self-contempt: studying in Germany must have made for group self-contempt, and group self-contempt must have made for studying in Germany. Incidentally, though this fashion naturally decreased towards the end of the 19th century, we still find, for instance, our youthful Mr. White being taken to the Continent and Germany in 1907 for the purpose of receiving advice and instruction.

But why, you may ask, this devious approach? Why not simply study critical contemporary reactions to 19th-century English music and thus find whatever direct evidence there may be of group self-contempt? The answer is that there can't be any direct evidence. That is, even the most unfavourable of these contemporary reactions would not tell us much, because English music was in such a rotten state that an Englishman's contempt of it would not necessarily indicate the presence of group self-contempt, but could simply be taken as an aesthetically realistic judgment. If you go to a medical psychologist and say: "I feel I'm utterly worthless and contemptible and don't deserve to live," he will no doubt be interested, not in your worthlessness, but in your melancholic self-depreciation. But if you go to a musical medical psychologist and say: "Can you help me: I simply cannot help feeling that 19th-century English music is utterly worthless and contemptible, and doesn't deserve to live," he will reply: "Neither can I: good morning."

We are thus in an unsatisfactory position – able to form a fairly clear picture of the psychogenesis of British musical group self-contempt without being very sure about the details of its history, though we may console ourselves that if this state of affairs happened to be reversed, our knowledge would be far more dangerously incomplete. In any case, by the time of the beginning of the national *renaissance* group self-contempt was, we may suppose, in full swing. And here we suddenly find ourselves able to contribute towards the explanation of a strange case in English musical history that, to my knowledge, has so far defied any scientific elucidation whatsoever. I mean the case of Edward Elgar. In 1947, Wilfrid Mellers wrote a paper on 'Alan Rawsthorne and the Baroque' wherein the problems of Elgar, which many do not even see, is clearly defined, though nowise explained. Mellers says: 'The great social-dramatic phase of instrumental evolution we simply bypassed, so that it is hardly surprising that when Holst and Vaughan Williams came to work towards the renaissance of our musical culture they should have returned to the great days – to Tudor polyphony and, behind that, folk-song and hence to a fundamentally vocal conception of their art. The unique case of Elgar, whose magnificently ripe symphonics [sic] are as it were THE CULMINATION OF A SYMPHONIC TRADITION THAT HAD NEVER HAPPENED, we may legitimately regard as a "sport" in our musical history.'[6]

Ladies and Gentlemen, I have the greatest respect for my colleague, whom I consider, in fact, to be one of our age's leading musicologists, but I suggest that before one 'legitimately regards' a phenomenon as a 'sport in history', one might yet more legitimately not regard it at as anything all. However, Meller's paradoxical observation that Elgar's symphonies are *the culmination of a symphonic tradition that had never happened* is a penetrating epitome of the problem. Now depth psychology leaves us in no doubt as to how to regard such manifestations of mental life as seem to be the result of something that never happened. The answer to the problem is that this something has happened, not in factual reality, but in *psychical* reality. As Freud says: 'It would not be right to underestimate this *psychical* reality in comparison with *factual* reality. Its consequences are important enough.' Well, on the assumption that group self-contempt played an active part in Elgar's musico-mental make-up – an assumption heavily supported by his own music – the psychical reality, in his own mind, of the symphonic tradition that never happened in factual reality, follows as a mere corollary. Elgar's deep-seated wish for, and unconscious fantasies of, a symphonic tradition whose factual absence we have recognised as one of the chief causes of group self-contempt, must in that case have been so powerful that he embarked upon the task of crowning, and thus proving the existence of, this non-existent British symphonic tradition: his was, if I may say so, a supremely successful flight into reality. His genius enabled him to realise what early psychoanalysis called the infantile 'omnipotence of thought' to an extreme degree that even the most imaginative critic would have been unable to foresee. The British symphonic tradition became, a posteriori, so much of a reality that we can say for certain that Wilfrid Mellers would have taken its existence for granted if he hadn't known that it wasn't there.

You will note the important difference between the roles of psychical reality in the present case and in that of a dream or a neurosis. Compulsive ceremonials, for instance, are in themselves senseless, and one can only get at the psychical reality underlying them by a retrograde reduction of the displacement of affects, of the replacement of ideas, which go to hide the psychic reality. On the other hand, the way from Elgar's two symphonies to the psychical reality underlying them is quite straight and logical; we do not find it necessary to translate anything, to resolve any displacements, because there aren't any; and there aren't any displacements because the wish for British symphonism, as distinct from, say, a death-wish is in itself nothing to worry about. The reason why Elgar's phantasies of the British symphonic tradition must nevertheless have shunned the light of consciousness was that *they were too good to be proved untrue.*

I hope that this short examination of the curious case of Elgar's symphonies will have given you some idea of the illumination we may perhaps expect from our concept of group self-contempt. Let us return to the present stage in the renaissance of English music, in the face of which our Austrian musicological student can still maintain that the English are unmusical. But can he? A hundred years ago, the Austro-German opinion of 'the country without music' was not altogether irrelevant, but today this continued expression of contempt seems to show the dominating group fighting in one of its last ditches; for last ditches are usually paved with good illusions. At the present time, British musical self-contempt takes its orders from Vienna's past and its emigrants abroad: the influence of contemporary Austrian or German music on English musical life is nil. At the same time, English musical self-respect is naturally rising, owing to the steady increase in vital original music and the gradual establishment of new compositional ideals. In fact, there seem subtle signs that British musical developments are about to exert a powerful influence on Vienna, all the more since the present extra-musical sociological situation finds Britain, as a friendly, if not always appreciated power, in loco parentis. Thus we may get, in the not too distant future, the reverse spectacle: Austrian group self-contempt with the renascent English tradition as dominating group. Meanwhile, we have to reckon with the bewildering picture of a state of flux produced by the historical overlapping between two opposite forms of group self-contempt. The weakening of Austrian dominance can already be felt, for example, in the slight weakening of British resistances against Benjamin Britten, similarly as, in another domain of group self-contempt, the weakening of male dominance has already resulted in a decrease of female misogyny.

Nevertheless, group self-contempt is undoubtedly conservative, owing to the fundamental part played in it by the primitive, unconscious super-ego, that infantile moralizing agency whose excessive severity does not, in Freud's words, 'follow a real prototype but corresponds to the strength which is used in fending off the Oedipus complex.' Similarly in childhood the super-ego does not just arise out of an incorporation of the parents' prohibitive and maybe aggressive attitudes, but rather out of a combination of these with the child's own savage, frustrated and hence in-turned aggression. [In just the same way,] in group self-contempt the dominated group's superegos, or at any rate the more relentless among them, may not rest satisfied with taking the dominant group's contempt or commands as prototype, but may be pleased to add plenty of backward-flowing sadism of their own. Thus they will tend to be over-obedient to the dominating group. It is well known that many a Jewish anti-Semite is, like the philosopher Otto Weininger, more anti-Semitic than his models; and you may remember that near the beginning of this lecture I mentioned that while Benjamin Britten's work gets unqualified praise from the Continent, English critics do not appear to find it sufficiently continental. It is unlikely that once such an over-obedience is established, once the primitive super-ego keeps a firm hold on group self-contempt, once an individual has tasted the diverse and deeply-reaching satisfactions thus offered to the Flugelian Polycrates complex – as indeed to the most varied sadistic and aggressive needs – it is unlikely that he will then, without ado, let this attitude go again. Thus we may venture the prognosis that British musical self-contempt will not cease before the renascent British tradition has established itself so securely that its ideals can act as a re-orientating magnet upon reluctant superegos, compelling them to drastic re-projections.

At the same time, we should perhaps keep another possibility in view, namely, that British musical group formation itself, as distinct from musical creativity, may again weaken or cease, owing partly to the internationalising influence of group self-contempt itself and partly to the wider development of musical history. In that case we would come to be confronted with the dialectical process of group self-contempt making for its own dissolution.

However, instead of losing ourselves in speculations about the distant future, it may be more profitable to realize that in the meantime there is no reason for despondency. For from the artistic point of view, British group self-contempt has not only an obviously harmful, but also a highly beneficial aspect. We have already seen how Elgar appears to have profited by this attitude, and upon the contemporary scene there is another, though very different, great figure, namely, Alan Rawsthorne, whose case is again highly problematic from the extra-psychological, historical point of view, and whom group self-contempt has, I think, again helped in no small measure towards attaining his present towering stature. Rawsthorne's music seems to be quite un-English, not to say anti-English. Alone among the works of the most important contemporary Britons, it is always fundamentally conceived in instrumental, as distinct from vocal terms, and Wilfrid Mellers observes in the aforementioned paper that Rawsthorne is 'the only English composer of consequence who has persistently used the kind of idiom loosely referred to as "Central European".' We note once more that on the assumption of group self-contempt playing an important part in the composer's musical mind, his exceptional position becomes easily explainable.

As I cannot, however, here go into the details of Rawsthorne's music, I may perhaps be allowed to strengthen this assumption of Rawsthorne's group self-contempt by recounting a little personal impression of a characteristically Rawsthornian attitude. As a critic I usually endeavour not to get into too close personal contact with composers whose work I am called upon to evaluate, but last May at Florence, I had the pleasure of being forced by circumstances to spend a great deal of time with Alan Rawsthorne, since we both served as delegates at the VIIth International Congress of Music.[7] In particular, I remember a walk during which I led the conversation to the subject of folk-song. Indeed, Ladies and Gentlemen, if you want to learn something from someone about his attitude towards Central European and English music, I may advise you always to start the subject of folk-song. The Austro-German and the English tradition could not be more strongly divided on this subject. German folksongs are usually bad; British folksongs are usually good. German folksongs have excited a minimal influence upon art music; English folk-songs have influenced art-music to a very considerable extent. Consequently, English musicians usually know too much about folk songs, particularly since the revival of folk music which dates from the end of the last century, while even the greatest German musicians' ignorance of folk songs, their own as well as foreign, tends to be abysmal. Richard Strauss, for instance, incorporated Luigi Denza's Neapolitan canzonet 'Funiculi, funicula' in the finale of his symphony *Aus Italien* because he thought it was a folk song!

Well, no sooner had I mentioned the subject of folk song to Rawsthorne, than he contemptuously, if perhaps not quite seriously, declared himself prepared to compose 20 first-rate folk-songs every day. (I don't remember the exact number, but it was considerable.) Now, neither the Italian sun, nor the Italian wine suffice to explain such an absurd statement on the part of a masterly composer whose extra-musical thinking is, incidentally, brilliantly articulate too. But if we are prepared to assume that Rawsthorne's mind harbours a strong measure of group self-contempt, his contempt of folk-song does not, of course, any longer surprise us. I may add here that if you mention the subject of folk song in the presence of Mr. Brown, whose musical attitude, as you will remember, is manifestly anti-British, your very life is endangered.

We must not, however, overlook the fact that Rawsthorne's group self-contempt does not work as straightforwardly as Elgar's, for Rawsthorne's music does not seem eager to link up with symphonic ideals, but rather harks back to the formal and textural conceptions of, for instance, Corelli and Bach. But this complication does not really endanger our hypothesis; we surely have to assume a displacement of affect within that region of the superego which is dominated by group self-contempt, a displacement caused by the particular nature and inclinations of Rawsthorne's genius, as well as by present trends in musical history which, owing ultimately to the harmonic crisis of our age, is inevitably growing more and more contrapuntal. However, as Mellers has pointed out, Rawsthorne's music links up with the failure of early 18th-century British music to attain to a classical stability of instrumental architecture, and it is therefore possible that the composer is actually driven by the motive of making amends for this particular defect in the British musical tradition. This would mean that group self-contempt has prompted the thoroughly different personalities of Elgar and Rawsthorne to compensate for different failures of the British tradition. And even if Rawsthorne has never had any such intention, the fact remains that he is achieving this compensation or rehabilitation of the British tradition by dint of a pre-occupation with continental methods such as can hardly be imagined without group self-contempt.

In any case, it must not be too readily assumed that Rawsthorne is, as a composer, quite so uninterested in the Austro-German tradition as his music so often suggests; in other words, the aforementioned displacement of affect within his super-ego, from the dominating group on to pre-classical continentals, is not likely to be complete. Indeed, the first movement of his recent Concerto for String Orchestra, for instance, is in fully worked-out if largely contrapuntal sonata-form and -style, and shortly we shall be hearing the first performance of his Symphony, wherein we shall perhaps find some stronger reminder that the role of the Austro-German symphonic tradition in the structure of his group self-contempt is by no means latent. Or am I perhaps now giving way to a phantasy similar to that which caused Scott Goddard's wrong prediction about Benjamin Britten's *Spring Symphony*?

And now, Ladies and Gentlemen, I have somewhat misled you throughout this paper, in that I have behaved as if the exponents of the Austro-German tradition were the only dominating group that played a part in the structures of British group self-contempt. As you will yourself have realised, things are not as simple as all that; there are other continental dominating groups which play a role in the various forms of group self-contempt among British composers, performers, critics and music-lovers. But I thought that it might be as well to concentrate, for a start, on what is, from the point of view of group psychology, the central dominating group; and that in a first outline a certain amount of over-simplification might be welcomed. So let me just add that as far as group self-contempt among performers is concerned, you may find it instructive to remind yourself of the various foreign names which British soloists have found necessary to assume; in which connection you might also consider that the various gentile names which Jews have assumed throw a good deal of light on the structure of Jewish self-contempt and its dominating groups. For the rest, Mr. Chairman, I have now been suspended for quite a time between these two stools I described to you at the beginning; in fact I have a vague suspicion that without noticing it, I may by now have fallen between them.

NOTES

Source

This talk exists in both manuscript and typescript forms in the Archive, and dates from the late summer and early autumn of 1950.

Keller wrote the paper in answer to a suggestion from J. C. Flugel (John Carl Flugel) in a formal letter of 22 June, 1950. Flugel had expressed interest and encouragement in Keller's blending of his own ideas of group self-contempt with Flugel's 'Polycrates Complex' (see 'Resistances to Britten's Music: Their Psychology', *Music Survey*, II/4, Spring 1950, pp. 227-36); Flugel also observed that a similar complex had been elaborated independently by Maryse Choisy in *L'anneau de Polycrate*. In *1975, 1984 minus 9* Keller described Flugel, who chaired this paper, as 'one of the broadest minds in the history of psychoanalysis' (p. 92). The identities of 'Mr. Brown' and 'Mr. White' are unknown.

1   [See, for example, 'Benjamin Britten's Second Quartet', *Tempo*, 3, March 1947, pp. 6-8.]
2   [See 'The Psychological Significance of Some Sociological Conceptions of the Group' (1945) under Part II, 'Psychology', above.]
3   [It was only at the end of the 1990s in the promenade concerts that the BBC moved to remedy this situation, and then only under pressure from those who had listened seriously to Keller's complaint.]
4   [J. C. Flugel, *Man, Morals and Society*, London, Duckworth, 1945; Sigmund Freud, *Group Psychology and the Analysis of the Ego* [*Crowd Psychology and the Self*] (1921), trans. by James Strachey, London, Hogarth, 1922.]
5   [P. H. Lang, *Music in Western Civilization*, New York, 1941.]
6   [Wilfrid Mellers, 'Alan Rawsthorne and the Baroque', *Studies in Contemporary Music*, London, 1947, pp. 171 ff..]
7   [For a flavour of the conference, see Keller's 'Film Music: Reply to Pizzetti', *Music Survey*, Vol. II, No. 1, 1950, pp. 42-3. Keller spoke on 'classical' [musical] quotations in film.]

Psychology and Aesthetics

At the end of his life, Keller thought that his most important contribution had been in the field of the philosophy of criticism. One striking aspect of this work was his review of aesthetics and taste from the standpoint of individual and group psychology. Two previously unpublished early exercises in this field are reproduced here. The first explicitly refers to his work with Margaret Phillips.

1 Apropos of Beauty and Reflection

Every kind of beauty is a 'reflection' in the mind of the beauty lover: on him beauty depends for its very existence. It is another question whether every kind of beauty is also a reflection in the sense that it mirrors a creator's thoughts. With works of art this is so. But with regard to nature the reply will always vary according to various metaphysical and anti-metaphysical standpoints. I have not yet seen either of these being changed by argument, and I therefore propose to leave them alone.

The difference between the receptive and creative reflection of beauty is not so clear-cut and radical as it seems at first sight. My co-researcher (in another psychological field) Margaret Phillips has shown that 'the distinction between creation and appreciation cannot be final. The attitude of appreciation itself involves creative effort.'[1]

Perhaps it would be better to substitute, for 'effort', the more general term 'activity'. There is such a thing as an effortless creation, though it probably happens more seldom than the naively idealistic onlooker thinks. Anyway, such creativeness as is involved in appreciation can be largely effortless, yet – or rather, therefore – at the same time exhaustive. Every beauty lover knows from his own experience that one can be carried down to the depths, and up to the heights, of a poem, a musical composition, a picture, without having to work for the journey. He feels that such seeming passivity can entail a great deal of creative activity – more indeed than may be possible where the creative part of appreciation constitutes an effort.

Other things being equal, the amount of effort needed for that sort of reflection that is called 'appreciation' of a work of art seems to be proportionate (not, of course, equal) to the amount of effort expended by its author. Of course it's easy for me to throw out this 'law': other things never being actually equal, you can't very well disprove it.

So to the author of beauty himself. The thoughts and feelings his work of beauty reflects may centre on what happens inside himself, without much reference to the external world, or again he may reflect in his product things and happenings of the outside world. But whether outside or inside, the material upon which he has to work has to be selected by, and then subjected to, his own creative insight and inspiration, and it is this that is the most important single element in the complex process of artistic production.

The finished work does not 'consist of' creative insight and inspiration, but is a reflection of these very personal processes in terms of that art in which the creator, together with many others, lives. More bluntly, the artist aims, to a great extent, at producing his own reflection. Now since, in order to be able to finish his work, he must, at least in anticipation, love it, one can safely say that his capability of falling in love, like Narcissus of the myth, with his own reflection, is a condition for his success as an artist.

A considerable portion of self-love ('narcissism' in psychoanalytic language), then, is absolutely necessary for good artistic authorship: it is only our distorted attitude towards problems of love and hate that makes us slow to realize that self-love need not be something 'bad', something that can only be of short-term use to the self and altogether harmful to others.

Midway between the author and his audience stands, in certain arts, another type of 'reflector', i.e. the interpreter (actor, musical performer, etc.). We have indicated that even appreciation involves creativeness: how much more must interpretation, reproduction, do so! Yet the extent to which the interpreter's 'reflection' of a work of art must be enlivened, inspired by what happens in his own heart is often underestimated; nor is it always easily attained by the interpreter himself.

That's one of the reasons why the serious beauty-lover may at times feel compelled to cut the interpreter out altogether, i.e. to stay at home and read the play or score instead of attending the performance. Yet there is no denying that thereby an important link in the chain of reflections is being lost. To which our art lover will again reply, with some justification, that he prefers a shorter chain to a longer one containing a link that is likely to break.

So far we have reflected on reflections *of* beauty. We may now turn to considering reflections *on* beauty. Sometimes the 'of' shades imperceptibly into the 'on', or the converse may happen. A piece of aesthetic writing will itself often reflect some of the beauty on which it reflects. At other times, indeed more often, 'of' and 'on' seem to confront one another as enemies – art versus science of art – though here as elsewhere one has not seldom to ask oneself whether enmity is logically necessary.

It should in any case be obvious that only he who can reflect beauty (in the sense of being able to experience it) is in a position validly to reflect on it. Though this is just another way of saying that one has to know what one is talking about, this simple truth is so little taken to heart that an overwhelming lot of nonsense is being written about beauty by people whose sense of beauty is but inadequately developed.

What's more, or – evaluatingly speaking – less, a deficient sense of beauty will quite often prompt an individual to dive, in an effort to compensate for his aesthetic shortcomings, into reflections on beauty. This is one of the many instances where intellectual activity, when (unconsciously) intended to combat what is felt to be an emotional deficiency, leads to sad results, results that, while they may seem intellectual, are certainly irrational.

When a beauty lover or artist reads a piece of such 'reflective' rubbish, he is liable to react with contempt for the scientific discipline to which the aesthetically ignorant writer may adhere. Such a reaction is unreasonable and can be a great injustice. What the artist is thinking is this: "That kind of scientific reflection on beauty is senseless," though he really ought to content himself with the statement: "That scientific reflector – the writer hasn't got any sense" (of beauty – he may be brilliant in other applications of his body of knowledge).

Again, if a certain body of knowledge has not much success in applying its findings to one or the other aspect of beauty, it is not necessarily the body of knowledge that is to blame, but maybe its representatives, or rather the lack of representatives suitable for the job.

To take a special instance, the comparatively pitiable headway that psychoanalysis has so far made in its application to music does not prove that the results of psychoanalytic research cannot be used for explaining this form of art psychologically. The lack of psychoanalytic success in this direction seems rather to be due to the fact that most of the more original and capable psychoanalysts have so far been largely or wholly unmusical, the founder of this scientific branch, Freud, being himself on top of the list of musical ignoramuses. While, however, he has not occupied himself with the psychology of music, another gifted psychoanalyst, Theodor Reik, has reflected a good deal on this topic, though, [like] Freud, he was musically incompetent. In fact, he naively confesses to what he doesn't seem to recognize as a decisive lack of qualifications for the job of a musical psychologist:

> Sometime ago I stayed as a guest in the house of a music-loving family, and there I heard a composition played by a 'cellist which, although *I am by no means musical*, made a peculiarly strong impression on me.[2]

I cannot, of course, go here into the results of his reflections. It is to be admitted that they are far better than one would expect, and usually finds them [to be], under such unfortunate circumstances. But then what is valuable about them, though mightily interesting for the psychologist, does hardly cover any ground of immediate significance from the artistic standpoint, the standpoint of musical beauty. Thus the artist lacking scientific psychological interests who reads this sort of thing will be bored to death, and his hostility or indifference towards scientific reflections on beauty will find no occasion to diminish. Yet even he must concede that given the required artistic qualifications – i.e. a sufficient sense of beauty – on the researcher's part, there remains at the very least the possibility that reflections of any kind of beauty might be extensively enriched or complemented by scientific reflections on beauty; enriched in the sense that we would more and more appreciate, not only beauty, but also our appreciation of it. Art criticism and aesthetics would here be the main usufructuaries.[3]

While one cannot easily tell whether the conflict between 'on' and 'of' is justified to any appreciable extent, one's first job is clearly to get rid of that part of the conflict that surely has no realistic foundation. The artist's opposition to science, and more particularly to psychology, has perhaps most beautifully been expressed by Oscar Wilde (though as a scientist and artist, I disagree with him from the top of my brain to the bottom of my heart):

> Psychology is in its infancy as a science. I hope, in the interest of art, it will always remain so.

At the emotional root of the artist's and beauty lover's aversion to science lies the fear that something may happen to intuition and inspiration, that these processes may be explained away. Such fears are, in part, special varieties of the general resistances to the making conscious of the unconscious, resistances each of us harbours and which in their turn are based on our being afraid of the unconscious. After all, this is one of the reasons why the unconscious is unconscious.

To turn to the scientist's contribution to the conflict between 'on' and 'of', and the wider, overlapping one between science and art generally: just as the artist's self-love is liable to centre on his inspiration, so the scientist's self-love tends to be invested in his intellect. Consequently, the scientist envies the artist the capacity of arriving at truths (if not at their expression) in a blitz sort of way, the scientist's journey towards them being a much slower affair.

The artist needn't know what he reflects as long as he reflects it. Result: resentment on the scientist's part, increased because the beautiful (artistic) reflection of truth engenders an immediately successful reflection (acceptance) of it in the mind of the perceiver. (So does, incidentally, the beautiful reflection of falsehoods. Still, if the intellect is strong enough to recognize these for what they are, their beauty does no harm, gives pleasure, and can even make us more understanding and tolerant of what, in others, we call illusions.)

Anyhow, it isn't easy for the artist to please the mediocre scientist. The latter gets angry when artistic communications are right according to his standards as well as when they are wrong. The only difference is that when the artist is right the scientist's hostility is concealed, while when the artist is wrong it isn't.

[Like] the artist, the scientist contributes to the mutual conflict with fears. Seeing how far the artist gets by predominantly emotional means, he fears that his own *intellectual* reflections may not, after all, be as much responsible for his scientific successes as he would like to think.

These fears mainly afflict, not such scientists as are appreciably rational, but those who aren't. And there are quite a lot of them about, too: nowadays one can hide one's irrationalities nowhere so easily as behind the facade of a scientific body of knowledge.

But let us not make too much of these states of tension in our effort to expose their unreason. The mature 'reflectors' of beauty and truth on the one hand, and on beauty and truth on the other hand, often show themselves capable of realizing that much of the conflict can be replaced by mutual benefit. For instance, that remarkable artist, Thomas Mann, has long ago shown an understanding and appreciation of psychoanalysis that many a scientist of today has not yet attained.

For the primitive mind, all that art and science have in common serves as occasion for outbreaks (or hidden inbreaks) of jealousy; for the grown-up mind, such common ground is the natural basis for harmony.

But 'common ground' is saying too little. It has often vaguely been suggested that in many respects artist and scientist are driving at the same thing. It can far more precisely be suggested that they often arrive at the same thing. To illustrate this suggestion, let us compare a quotation from one of the greatest musical geniuses that ever lived (in some respects perhaps the greatest musical genius) with a sentence by one of the greatest scientists. Both are offering a conclusion that has been of supreme significance for their work:

> Since death (take my words literally) is the true goal of our lives, I have made myself so well acquainted . . . with this true and best friend of mankind that the idea of it no longer holds any terror for me, but rather much that is tranquil and comforting. And I thank God that He has granted me the good fortune to obtain the opportunity (you understand my meaning) of regarding death as the key to our true happiness.
>
> [W. A. Mozart, letter to his sick father, 4 April, 1787, Vienna.]

> If we may assume . . . without exception, that all that lives dies for inner reasons, i.e. returns to the inorganic state, we can only say: "*The goal of all life is death . . .*"[4]
>
> [Sigmund Freud, *Beyond the Pleasure Principle*, 1920, section V.]

Half a minute ago, I dare say, many a reader would have thought that no two people had less in common than Mozart and Freud. However, whether or not one agrees (as I do) with their reflections, one must admit that the striking relation (or near-identity) between them may well be called beautiful.

So that's what the relation between artist and scientist can be like, at least in places. As for that other relation (not so much 'other' either) between reflections of and on beauty . . . but let's stop before we come too near the spot where we came in.

NOTES

Source

Undated typescript from the mid to late 1940s.

1   Margaret Phillips, *The Education of the Emotions*, London, Allen and Unwin, 1937, p. 192.
2   Theodor Reik, *Ritual-Psychoanalytical Studies*, London, Hogarth Press, 1931, p. 167. [HK's italics.]
3   [Ed:] 'Usufructuary': one who enjoys 'the use and advantages of another's property short of the destruction or waste of its substance.' *The New Oxford Dictionary of English*, Oxford, Oxford University Press, 1998.]
4   [Ed:] The translation of Freud is Keller's, that of Mozart possibly his too.

2   *"Bloody Little Fool": Sid's Kiss and the Problem of Taste in Opera*

[*on Benjamin Britten's* Albert Herring]

TASTE is nothing to be proud of, for it never is one's own. Or when it is one's own, it is idiosyncrasy, and that is nothing to be proud of either. Lack of taste, on the other hand, is something to be ashamed of, unless . . . and here the problem starts.

Without more than the usual epigrammatic exaggeration, it can be said that for a talent lack of taste is a danger, while for a genius taste is a danger. The great and often underestimated genius of Mendelssohn would have erupted more strongly if his had not been the most immaculate taste. Büchner, on the other hand, who in spite of his flashes of genius remains a talent, uses the word 'pischen' ad infinitum in the 4th scene of *Wozzeck* (the first of Berg's operas) without convincing us that the word is there for the scene more than the scene is there for the word. As a result, this revolutionary element of style dates and becomes childish. Because there is a limit, at any given time, to the transformability into music of vulgarity, Berg changes the word into 'husten' (cough), with the result that nobody understands what the Doctor is talking about.

The problem is insoluble: the opera house, a bulwark of taste, is the last place where you can fling vulgarisms in people's ears without any sort of preparation. In art, preparation means integration, functionalization. You can make the strongest word artistic if you have the genius to prepare it as Palestrina prepared a dissonant note. D. H. Lawrence, for instance, who remains a genius despite his infantilisms, blood and soil and the rest of them, shows himself able to prepare and use (for the first time, I believe) one of the obscenest words in the English language in a drastic demonstration of the beauty of sex.[1] This dialectic process lies at the centre of the problem of taste: an uglifying word is made to show the beauty it denies. How is this possible?

Taste means discrimination, and one cannot discriminate without discriminating against. The most primitive, and hence most widespread discrimination in which man indulges, turns against what, as an infant and child, he has learnt to regard as bad or naughty or dirty: against his (infantile) sexuality and his primitive aggression. The means by which his mental apparatus achieves the original pattern for all such spontaneous, 'instinctive' (really anti-instinctual) discrimination is *repression* in its technical sense, i.e. a wholly unconscious denial of one's own 'dirty' or 'naughty' interests. Being an unconscious process, repression does not, however, work according to laws that resemble those of reason and usually bites off more than it wants to swallow. As a result, one often 'cannot help' reacting to certain things in a certain way which, nevertheless, is felt to be the wrong way both by one's conscious conscience and one's unconscious instincts: as far as the organization of events within his own mind is concerned, man is by far the most irrational animal. He cannot help, for instance, being disgusted, even though his conscience may be disgusted at disgust – as indeed are his insights in any case, for it is against them that his disgust is directed at the deepest level.

Now, while civilization depends on successful repressions of the blatantly uncivilized, it suffers at the same time under the inevitable unrealism which discrimination-against, which every denial of the repressed, entails. This is where culture – art and science – comes in to make opposite ends meet, to reconcile civilization with uncivilized realities. In different and respective senses of the word, art and science *realize*. By realizing the repressed unconscious, culture re-establishes its truth without letting its anti-social aspect disturb social life.

While there is truth without beauty (2+2=4) and untruth without ugliness (2+2=5), there is no beauty without at least psychic truth: a beautiful woman is *true* to a strong idea. But there is no ugliness without truth either, for an ugly woman is *true* to an idea one rejects, discriminates against.

Since one tends to discriminate against everything that is new and true – the most distrustful 'news' being repressed ideas and feelings – taste always comes too late, not for civilization, but for creative culture: by the time a new truth has graduated as tasteful, it has ceased to be new.

An obscene word admits, 'realizes' a repressed wish *on disapproval*: it sneers at the truth it expresses. Hence its dynamic power, for it avails itself of the energy behind the repressed impulse as well as of the energy behind the repression. If you use it in a context that approaches the repressed both logically and stepwise, you can enlist its very ugliness in the service of beauty. The more familiar context sheds a new light on the meaning of the obscene word or, to be quite precise, it sheds an old, familiar light on the unfamiliar, admitting the bastard into the family of united, well-bred notions. Thus Lawrence.

In music one can be more tasteless, more deeply true, than in any other art without anyone noticing anything amiss. It is difficult to be musically obscene. It is true that after the premiere of *Wozzeck*, Dr. Paul Zschorlich wrote in a long article in the *Deutsche Zeitung*: 'The day cannot be far off when cohabitation will take place on the stage of the Staatsoper *corum publico*. Then only will the Schoenberg-Kleiber clique have reached the goal of its desires.[2] To find a composer for the purpose is nowadays possible without any difficulty.' But then Zschorlich had the words to help him, or at any rate to mislead him, for he promptly misunderstood them. Why? The question is important: to understand misunderstanding of art heightens one's understanding of art.

In a recent book on *Modern British Composers* (1949), Mr. Marius Flothuis has in fact found Zschorlich's 'composer for the purpose'. It is Britten: 'the orchestral accompaniment to the only really sincere moment in *Albert Herring*, that of the embrace of Nancy and Sid, is nothing less than obscene.' (Example 1) When I read and reviewed this, I was not only musically amused, but morally disgusted.

One laughs and is disgusted at the repressed. Perhaps the kissing passage avails itself, beneath its widely stretching musico-formal significance and its overt dramatic meaning, of 'tastelessness' – i.e. hitherto artistically unexpressed – primitive sex? One need not, in any case, be preoccupied with music's extramusical associations in order to feel the passage's sexual tumescence. Perhaps, however, it was my own preoccupation with the music qua music that served my repression of those feelings which, if they nourished the music, must have been stimulated in myself when I heard it? Perhaps, indeed, I did not understand the psychology, the extra- and sub-musical significance of the passage because I understood the music too well, whereas Mr. Flothuis hit on something because he didn't? Not that this kiss may be a piece of musical pornography: Lawrence is pornographic to those who mistake the psychological means for the artistic end. If we exchange Mr. Flothuis's 'obscene' for 'deeply sexual', then even his 'only really emotionally sincere moment' makes distorted sense, for we may here be presented with a moment of historically unprecedented truthfulness, with a *new realization*. And similar interpretations may apply to *Wozzeck* and Zschorlich.

The reason, then, why of all the arts, music can afford to be deepest is that its logic does not – need not – remind the musician of its sub-musical, instinctual depth. For if the 'kiss' passage had occurred in a symphonic work, not even Mr. Flothius would have raised his hands in decent horror. On the other hand, he may still have disliked it, for the same motives for which he dislikes it in its dramatic context, without, however, knowing why. Possibly he would have called it tasteless and artificial. Since 'natural' is what one is used to, one might even go so far as to say it is absolutely necessary for new depth, new naturalness, to sound artificial: nothing goes so strongly against known nature as unknown nature.

The problem of taste in opera makes the problem of taste in music acute. Words and particularly the stage divest music of its psychological anonymity; at the same time, music heightens one's sensitivity towards the word and the stage event. Beethoven, himself a ruthlessly tasteless genius, could not get over *Giovanni* or *Cosi*. *Tosca*'s torture scene is still unacceptable although the opera has become historical and its action, or worse actions, most acceptable to the modern playgoer who swallows Sartre.

For the present-day composer, moreover, the problem (however unconscious) is at its acutest, because truth is ever further advancing into the realm of beauty, beautifying itself or being uglified according to the historical status of the onlooker. Mozart could still say that

> . . . passions, whether violent or not, must never be expressed in such a way as to excite disgust, and music, even in the most terrible situations, must never offend the ear, but must please the hearer, or in other words must never cease to be *music* . . .[3]

[whereas] Schoenberg, self-confessedly Mozart's pupil, and the first to insist that music must always remain music, has written in his *Harmonielehre* (1911) that

> . . . beauty comes into being when the uncreative begin to miss it. Before that it does not exist, for the artist does not need it. For him truthfulness is enough.[4]

Likewise Picasso: 'The beautiful does not matter to me.' Partly, of course, we now call 'true' what formerly was called 'beautiful', but part of what we now call 'good' will never be called 'beautiful', not even by the uncreative when they begin to like it.

With Britten, who is as conservative and, *mutatis mutandis*, as beauty-conscious as Mozart, the advance of truth is particularly interesting in that, even in his work, it is particularly strong. Intra-musically, Erwin Stein, for instance, points out in a forthcoming symposium,[5] that the chaos of the 'Dies Irae' in the *Sinfonia da Requiem* is 'painted somewhat differently from the opening of Haydn's *Creation*,' and that disorder has never 'before been conveyed in so convincing a musical form' as in the recapitulation's disintegration. Operatically, there is, for example, the integrated disintegration of *Grimes's* 'Mad' Interlude;[6] or, quite generally, Britten's ever stronger love for the universal truths of everyday life, or ordinariness, which, incidentally, owes a great deal to *Wozzeck*. (The inartistic aspect of Büchner's tastelessness was needed to make some of Britten's artistic tastelessness possible.)

"Bloody little fool" at the end of Herring's Act I adds common language to the material for Britten's discoveries of the uncommonness of the common – commonplace, the common people, common sense, the common apparent even in such a piece of revolutionism: at this time of the day, the use of 'bloody' unites Bermondsey with Bloomsbury and only the lower middle class remains to be convinced, whose less musical members, however, tend to feel guilty in the opera house anyway.

The difference between Sid's kiss and "Bloody little fool" is that the tastelessness, the realization, is essentially musical in the former and essentially conceptual in the latter. (Psychologically speaking, 'bloody' has the significance of an obscene word – seriously weakened nowadays, but powerfully reinforced by its operatic appearance.) We shall have to expect Britten's methods of preparation and familiarization (see above: Büchner on the negative and Lawrence on the positive side) to vary accordingly. In one case it is a question of fitting 'unfamiliar' music into a 'familiar' musical context; in the other, of musically contextualizing a verbal phrase. The basic answers are, thematic anticipation and integration of the music, and rhythmic structuralization of the verbal phrase respectively.

Example 1 Benjamin Britten, Albert Herring, *Op. 39 (1947), Sid's 'long, passionate kiss' (Act II)*

The thematic anticipation and integration of the introduction to the kiss starts with Sid's love-offer to Nancy in Act I, scene ii, "Have a nice peach!" etc. (p. 121 of the vocal score),[7] which is resumed as Sid says, "Give us a kiss, Nancy!" (p. 129). The latter passage, including the voice part, is enlarged upon at Sid's renewed, and this time more successful, "Give us a kiss, Nancy" etc. (p. 266 ff.) which in its turn prepares the way for the 'obscene' passage. At the end of the opera, as Albert appeases the children with the words, "Have a nice peach?" (p. 369), his notes are the same as Sid's (on p. 121), thus, a posteriori, desexualising the 'obscene' association of unconscious ideas created in the listener. The kiss itself, moreover, is thematically prepared by Albert's drinking feat (p. 230), [a passage that] in its turn [has] been prepared by the ironic use of the love potion from *Tristan* that accompanies Sid's pouring rum into Albert's lemonade (p. 184).[8]

The formalization of "Bloody little fool" offers a vastly different picture. Though there is some immediate thematic preparation be way of Mum's tune (first exposed when she first bustles in in Act I, scene ii, p. 139 ff.), thematification definitely takes second place; in fact, the phrase is not really set to music, but occurs first in a tiny recitative passage and then, in its repetition, even *à la Sprechgesang*, or rather *Sprechgeschrei*. (Example 2) Strict musicalization would have increased the shock and decreased the fun; it would have made the phrase ridiculous instead of comic. Instead, an element of familiarization that plays a subsidiary part in the integration of the kiss passage, i.e. a posteriori contextualization, here takes first place – within a narrow space, to be sure, and, as I said, in the form of rhythmic structuralization. By means of the repetition and – most important – the general pause before the last *fff*, the phrase becomes an integral, refrainish part of a highly original rhythmic structure which rolls cadential extension and compression into one.

Thus "Bloody little fool" is 'prepared' after it has happened – a thing which is only possible in a structure of strong inner-musical logic: 'the two-or-more-dimensional space in which musical ideas are presented is a unit,' says Schoenberg in his essay on 'Composition with Twelve Tones'.[9] (An extreme example which, I think, has not yet been noticed by anyone: the working-out section of the Prague Symphony's first movement develops a figure which is first stated in the recapitulation.)

And here, with the repetition of "Bloody little fool", we encounter a problem of taste that I have not yet been able to solve for myself. Britten succeeds in applying one of the most unrealistic devices in operatic word-music formalization, i.e. repetition of (verbal) phrases, to an unprecedentedly realistic phrase – applying it with new formal meaning. The trouble, however, is, not that Mum couldn't have shouted the phrase twice, but that she could. The listener's attention is therefore diverted from the excellent musico-dramatic structure to the apparent naughtiness of a seemingly faithful (unselective) reproduction of Mum's embarrassingly vulgar behaviour. Why apparently naughty? Because naturalism harbours an element of assent. I do not say that naturalism was the intention; in fact, it is clear from the structure that it wasn't, but for me the inescapable irony of this artistic situation consists in the fact that by the very act of contextualization, of de-vulgarization, of structuralization, the passage, accidentally as it were, approaches real (because insignificant) vulgarity so closely that it takes the mind [away] from its meaning: a significant tastelessness runs the risk of being taken for an insignificant one. I personally prefer looking at the passage in score to listening to the isolated laughs after the repetition of the phrase (as distinct from the general and legitimate laughter after its first occurrence).

But then, I'm beginning to be proud of my taste.

Example 2 Benjamin Britten, Albert Herring, *Op. 39 (1947), "Bloody little fool!" (close of Act I)*

NOTES

Extracts from *Albert Herring* are reproduced by kind permission of Boosey and Hawkes Music Publishers Ltd. Text © copyright 1947 by Hawkes & Son (London) Ltd. Music © copyright 1948 by Hawkes & Son (London) Ltd. Copyright for all countries.

Source

Typescript from 1951, intended 'For OPERA (Autumn 1951) No draft.' Keller's self-examination of taste and resistances found echoes later in his life, notably in 'Whose Fault is the Speaking Voice', *Tempo* 75, 1965-66, pp. 12-17 (he bridled when he first heard Arnold Schoenberg's *Pierrot Lunaire*) and a review of Benjamin Britten's *A Midsummer Night's Dream*, *Music Review*, 22/2, May 1961, pp. 173-74 (he disliked counter-tenor). Keller also examined the dynamics of taste in 'Wolf-Ferrari', *Listener*, 7 September, 1972, pp. 314-15, and 'Benjamin Britten's *Albert Herring*' in *Music Review*, 9/4, November 1948, p. 309-10.

1   [Ed:] In 'À Propos of *Lady Chatterley's Lover*' (1929), D. H. Lawrence writes: 'This is the real point of the book. I want men and women to be able to think sex, fully, completely, honestly, and cleanly' . . . 'The mind has to catch up, in sex: indeed, in all the physical acts . . . it means being able to use the so-called obscene words, because these are a natural part of the mind's consciousness of the body. Obscenity only comes in when the mind despises and fears the body, and the body hates and resists the mind.' *'À Propos of Lady Chatterley's Lover' and Other Essays*, London, Penguin, 1961, pp. 89-90. A representative example of what Keller has in mind might be the following (the gamekeeper is talking to Lady Chatterley):

> Then with the same eyes darkened with another flame of consciousness, almost like sleep, he looked at her. "Dunna ax me nowt now," he said. "Let me be. I like thee. I luv thee when tha lies theer. A woman's a lovely thing when 'er's deep ter fuck, and cunt's good . . ." And softly he laid his hand over her mound of Venus, on the soft brown maiden hair, and himself sat still and naked on the bed, his face motionless in physical abstraction, almost like the face of Buddha.
> *[Lady Chatterley's Lover* (1928), London, 1961, p. 221]

2   [Ed:] Erich Kleiber conducted the first performance of Alban Berg's *Wozzeck* (1917-22) at the Berlin State Opera on 14 December, 1925.

3   [Ed:] W. A. Mozart, the celebrated letter to his father on Osmin's rage, 26 September, 1781, Vienna. The translation is by Emily Anderson, and was originally published in London by Macmillan and Co. in 1938.

4   [Ed:] Arnold Schoenberg, *Theory of Harmony* (*Harmonielehre*, 1911), translated by Roy E. Carter. Keller developed the theme of the 'crisis' of Beauty and Truth (and melody) in his contribution to Benjamin Britten: A Commentary on His Works from a Group of Specialists, London, Rockliff, 1952, pp. 334-51.

5   [Ed:] Erwin Stein, 'Britten's Symphonies', Orpheus in New Guises, London, Rockliff, 1953, pp. 142-43.

6   [Ed:] See: Hans Keller, 'Britten: Thematic Relations and the "Mad" Interlude's 5th Motif', Music Survey (1949-1952), eds. Donald Mitchell and Hans Keller, London, Faber Music, 1981, IV, pp. 332-34.

7   [Ed:] In the typescript Keller has written 'the accompaniment of' below 'the thematic anticipation' without making it clear whether this part of the sentence should be reconstructed or the line below that should be amended to 'with the accompaniment of Sid's offer to Nancy.' There are similar problems in four other places in this paragraph; but as the revisions are even more obscure, the original form has been left intact.

8   I had no space to mention these relations in my booklet on Lucretia and Herring (Covent Garden Operas, 1947). [This stylish little booklet is essentially an opera guide containing a scene-by-scene account of the action. Keller begins:

> If the comedy of Albert Herring is a pendant to the tragedy of Lucretia, it is also a pendant to that of Peter Grimes. This is not just because of their common setting – Suffolk – but also because the theme of opposition to tyranny plays a fundamental part in all three operas . . . but whereas Grimes suffers from being too independent, Herring suffers from being not nearly independent enough. (p. 19)]

9   [Ed:] Arnold Schoenberg, Style and Idea, New York, 1950 and London, 1951; expanded edition edited by Leonard Stein, London, Faber, 1975.

The Psychology of Genius: Two Later Essays

These essays have been included to show the development of Keller's investigation of 'creative character' in the mid 1950s. The focus is now on the concept of 'genius', a topic that preoccupied him throughout his life as it had done his twentieth- and nineteenth-century forebears. The essays also raise other important concerns: the achievement of Stravinsky and the 'mourning of the lost object'; reactions to the work of Theodor Adorno; the writing of biography; the status of history; love, aggression and their relation to psychology and art; Dementia praecox (see the Afterword *to this section for Keller's observational material); the madness of 'our age's' rationalism; and the need to defend great music.*

1 Towards the Psychology of Stravinsky's Genius

This was written to mark a number of concerts of Stravinsky's music conducted by the composer himself: the Symphony in C, Symphony of Psalms *and* Pulcinella *were broadcast at 8.00 p.m. (Home [Service]) and 9.15 p.m. (Third [Programme]) on Wednesday, December 5 [1956], and again at 8.00 p.m. on Friday, December 7 (Third). The first English performance of* Canticum Sacrum *was given at 8.15 p.m. on Tuesday, December 11 (Third).*

In his penetrating though often fallacious *Philosophie der neuen Musik*, Theodor W. Adorno plays off Schoenberg against Stravinsky whom he calls a death-mask of the past.[1] Professor Adorno usually knows what he is talking about, but his talk is not always equal to his knowledge, chiefly because it is not inspired by that respect for a great genius without which the truest observation on him lacks perspective.

The fact remains that Stravinsky's creative character in general, and his attitude to the past in particular, has proved a headache to most musicians and critics, for the simple reason that we have never encountered this kind of great composer before. All good composers start out from the past; most bad composers remain stuck in it; but Stravinsky is the first great creator who speaks through it.

Where history fails, psychology must take its place. The problem of Stravinsky's creative character is that of our time – the problem of aggression. But the problem of his aggression is, paradoxically enough, the problem of his love.

Apropos of his treatment of Pergolesi's melodies in the ballet *Pulcinella* (1919-20), Stravinsky asked: "Should my line of action be dominated by my love or by my respect for Pergolesi's music? Is it love or respect that urges us to possess a woman? Is it not by love alone that we succeed in penetrating to the very essence of a being? But then does love diminish respect? Respect alone remains barren and can never serve as a productive or creative factor. In order to create, there must be a dynamic force, and what force is more potent than love?" He felt his 'conscience to be innocent of sacrilege' and moreover considered that his attitude towards Pergolesi was 'the only possible one towards the music of earlier ages'. Less known, but equally relevant, is Stravinsky's suggestion that 'rape may be justified by the creation of a child'. Paul Valéry changed the metaphor: 'A lion consists of digested lambs'.

Psychoanalysis recognises two basic types of love, self-love apart. Genetically the more primitive is identification, which stems from the earliest, sucking stage of infancy and whose protype is oral incorporation: hence the technical term 'introjection' for the 'absorbtion of the environment into the personality' (Ernest Jones); hence, too Valéry's metaphor. The other type, 'object love', is what we commonly understand by love. In monosyllables, identification is based on the need to *be* someone, object love on the need to *have* someone. Identification is the more ambivalent of the two, not only because you destroy what you eat, but also because you want to replace the person you want to be.

Ordinary artistic development always starts with identification: while the composer's own creative ego is still weak, he identifies himself with his teachers and with older masters and proceeds to imitate them. As his originality grows, these father figures recede or are absorbed by his conscience and, if nothing drastic happens (such as the Bach crisis in Mozart's life), his creative 'love relations' with the music of other composers amount to no more than sporadic flirtations resulting in, say, variations on another composer's theme, which will be children of 'object love' rather than of identification.

Alone among geniuses, with the possible exception of Picasso, Stravinsky has actually developed his capacity for identification together with the unfolding of his intense originality. At the same time, as his commentary on *Pulcinella* indicates, his creative mind also employs a good deal of highly aggressive 'object love': he makes the aggressive best of both love worlds, though identification remains the basic 'dynamic force'. No previous composer has shown any desire to compose his way 'into the very essence of a being'.

> And all men kill the thing they love,
> By all let this be heard,
> Some do it with a bitter look,
> Some with a flattering word,
> The coward does it with a kiss,
> The brave man with a sword!

There is some special pleading here [in these words of Oscar Wilde's], but there is a truth too. Stravinsky has in fact himself employed the bitter look, the flattering word, and the sword, but he has never killed the past by kissing it, as so many of his followers and other neo-classicists have done.

The two symphonies which he will conduct twice next week are extremely healthy children of his ambivalent identification with more than one past, and if the first movement of the Symphony in C (1939-40) is a little uneasy about its synthesis of Stravinsky's characteristic, undeveloping *ostinato* technique and classical sonata development, the resultant formal friction turns out to be as valid a part of the structure as is, for instance, Beethoven's un-operatic attitude in *Fidelio*.

The *Symphony of Psalms* (1930), on the other hand, does not evince such seeming imperfections: it is a spotless and gigantic masterpiece, profoundly expressive in its very suppression of expressionism, its in-turned, self-castigating aggression. Identifications with the past span a wide field, stretching back into the archaic, and when the opening four-part fugue of the second movement (with the answer in the dominant) raises its voice through what we might call the life-mask of Bach, we realise that the term 'neo-classicism' is just not good enough.

The severe limitations that Stravinsky's identifications impose upon his intense imagination are precisely what he wants. His urge towards formal stringency and simplicity goes beyond the requirements of unity and clarity: he does not discipline his inspiration; rather he is more lavishly inspired by self-discipline than any other composer. Again, his love, this time his artistic self-love or self-respect, is unlike the usual artist's: again it is vehemently ambivalent, combined with, perhaps even outweighed by, aggression turned inward.

Symbolic of this self-restrictive, form-conscious simplicity is the fact that all three major works in next week's programme show cyclic devices on the one hand, and recognise C as their tonality on the other (though two of them do not start out from home): no doubt the first concert programme of this kind in our entire history.

After Schoenberg's death, and too late for Professor Adorno to revise his theory about the antithesis of Stravinsky's and Schoenberg's attitudes, Stravinsky embarked on his serial period which has now culminated in his first twelve-tone music – the three middle movements of the *Canticum Sacrum* (1955), whose first and fifth movements, moreover, mirror each other in self-restrictive retrograde motion. My own little hypothesis, on the other hand, here seems to receive its final confirmation. The 'identification with the lost object' (Freud, *Mourning and Melancholia*, 1916) is no news to the psychoanalyst, who will see in the previous ambivalent relation between the two musical leaders of our time an ideal foundation for Stravinsky's 'introjection' of Schoenberg's method: by way of creative mourning, Stravinsky identified with Schoenberg's serialism as soon as it had become a thing of the past. In justice to Professor Adorno, we must remind ourselves that his 'death mask of the past' now assumes a new significance, but we must continue to reject the negative evaluation implied in, or insinuated by, his formulation.

For the rest, great geniuses are few and far between, and we cannot afford to miss them when they come.

NOTES

Source: The Listener, 56/1444, 29 November, 1956, p. 897.

1   [Ed:] Keller had reviewed Theodor Adorno's *Philosophy of New Music* (in its German edition, J. C. B. Mohr (Paul Siebeck), Tübingen, 1949) in *Tempo*, 16, Summer 1950, p. 32:

Adorno's Philosophy of New Music

Unreadables attract each other on their basis for their common contempt for the common idiot. Thus Adorno and his unsuccessful pupil in matters twelve-tonal, Thomas Mann, appear to like each other more than they need to, and thus, too, I myself am prejudiced in favour of the present book. But while the truth is invariably unreadable because it is always complicated and usually beneath expectations, unreadability is not always the reader's fault, but sometimes nobody's (as in the case of Kant, whose thought processes necessitated a special language), and sometimes, as in the case of Adorno, everybody's. As far as it is the author's, it consists of (a) condensations which cannot be due to space considerations, since he often says the same thing five times over in five differently condensed groups of propositions, where a single full-length exposition would have needed far less space; (b) his highly developed art of begging all questions of evaluation; (c) his obsession for using the same word, twice in a sentence, for different concepts and leaving it entirely to God to decide how far A is the contrary of A (this is known as dialectics); (d) Anglicisms of vocabulary as well as grammar which seem to require a readership composed of German-, Austrian-, or Swiss-born naturalized British or American subjects who have retained a firm knowledge of German philosophical terminology and at the same time made English their mother tongue; (e) a snobbish and quite forgivable partiality for what, in music, he himself detests, i.e. archaic language ('denn' instead of 'als' [than], 'ward' instead of 'wurde' [was], etc.).

Yet Dr. Adorno offers innumerable penetrating and imaginative observations, interspersed with strokes of genius-like insight, on almost everything except the subject indicated by his title (for 'philosophy' read often 'psychology'). No excuse for the reader who puts the book aside because it is too tough (which it isn't) or because it could be much less tough (which it could). I personally shall read it thrice. Meanwhile I cannot refrain from taking my savage revenge upon the author's torrent of equivalent condensations by condensing them into a single sentence: the upshot of it all is that while Schoenberg is a true map of psychic life, Stravinsky is a false death mask of the past. True, this doesn't say all Dr. Adorno means, but then, does Dr. Adorno?

2   Schumann after Freud

This essay from 1956 introduced a number of radio programmes commemorating the centenary of Robert Schumann's death. The broadcasts took place at 9.30 p.m. on Sunday, 29 July (Third Programme) and at 10.15 p.m. on Tuesday, 31 July (Home Service). Schumann was also 'This Week's Composer'.

Robert Schumann died mad [on 29 July 1856] twelve weeks after Freud was born. Freud died [on 23 September 1939] three weeks after the age of insanity had begun to reach one of its climaxes [the declaration of war on 3 September]. Freud would not have been able to help Schumann to any decisive degree, but he can help our age's attitude towards Schumann.

In the current *Monthly Musical Record*, the editor suggests that 'Schumann's music can only be fully understood in terms of Schumann the man', and that 'we need a new interpretation of the facts – preferably by some biographer who knows how to use the tools of Freudian research.' Schumann seems to have suffered from a form of schizophrenia. Amongst music critics, this is still known by Emil Kraepelin's term *dementia praecox*, which Eugen Bleuler, in a monograph (1911) partly based on Freud, replaced by 'schizophrenia', while Freud's own 'paraphrenia' has made little progress. (Music critics do, of course, use the term 'schizophrenia' – chiefly for hysteria. They also use 'hysteria', chiefly for normal love and hate.)

Schizophrenia, whose relation to musical talent has been demonstrated but not yet explained, 'is an omnibus group which covers a diversity of psychotic conditions' (Edward Glover), and the magic word in itself does not greatly advance our knowledge of Schumann. A Freudian study of Schumann's psychosis will doubtless shed light not only on the sources of the defects in Schumann's music but also on some of its innovatory merits. In particular, I am thinking of an achievement which Einstein calls the 'Romantic disintegration of Classical structure', and which can easily be observed in such forms as 'Overture, Scherzo, and Finale' or, on the highest level, the Piano Concerto.

Where I beg to differ from the editor of the *Record* is in the artistic appraisal of any knowledge thus gained. Good music can be understood only in terms of what happens within it, and the fullest knowledge of Schumann the man will not increase our *musical* understanding of a single quaver rest, unless it be a bad one. The editor acutely observes that 'Schumann is now an unfashionable composer', that 'he stands for so much that the present generation values least'. A reassessment of his stature will be helped by a study, not of his madness, but of our own.

This is the maddest of all ages because ours is a case of pseudo-rational insanity. At no previous stage in our culture was irrationality so powerfully rationalised. Neurotic religions were bad enough; psychotic sciences are sometimes worse. Times change but the unconscious does not change with them, and our attitude towards mental illness itself has not changed half as much as have our words about it. True, lunatics are no longer purified by fire, but normality itself is regarded with almost religious reverence, and every 'normal' empty-head shrieks with joy when he discovers a neurotic symptom in a genius. The eternal fear of mental illness, which is a fear of the unconscious, is nowadays rationalised into an attitude of *ambivalent patronisation* that goes by the name of 'balanced' or 'objective' opinion.

Combined with our anti-romanticism, then, which in itself is our fear of our madness, it is our awareness of Schumann's eventual disintegration that has produced our stand-offish attitude towards much of his music. My suggestion may be wrong and indeed sound absurd; at the same time, it must needs sound absurd if it is right, for it describes a reaction which would not be unconscious if it were acceptable. This is where Freud helps us.

How, without him, are we to explain the curious coincidence that, of all the geniuses among the more popular composers, it is Schumann alone who, especially in knowledgeable circles, arouses just this patronising response? that much of his best music is little-known or under-known? that his shortcomings, especially in the matter of scoring, have become almost proverbial, whereas, say, Brahms's instrumental failings (in the chamber music) are merely whispered about? 'I once read in an examination paper of a sophomore who had studied only a little harmony and much music appreciation, but who had certainly not heard much "live music", that "Schumann's orchestration is gloomy and unclear". This information was derived directly and verbally from the textbook used in class.' (Schoenberg). And by way of indirect evidence, we may remind ourselves that a less popular madman, Hugo Wolf, is very similarly treated.

How many Schumannians are there who realise that 'no other Romantic, not even Chopin, is comparable to Schumann in youthfulness and originality' (Einstein)? One of them, Kathleen Dale, writes that 'it was rare for him to invent phrases of uneven bar-lengths', whereas in point of fact he was one of the greatest rhythmic and melodic innovators of all times. Here for instance, is the breath-taking inspiration from one of those works – the A major Quartet (1842) – of whose very existence even some Schumann lovers have to be reminded:

Example   Robert Schumann, String Quartet No. 3 in A major (1842), first movement, bars 8-11

(The 'repeat' notation is, of course, mine.) Superficially, there are 'even bar-lengths' indeed, but what happens within the 4-bar phrases? 1 + 3! Joan Chissell traces this theme back to Beethoven [Piano Sonata in E flat major] Op. 31, No. 3. Formally, however, a comparison with Mendelssohn's contemporaneous 'Song without Words', Op. 62, No. 1, is far more relevant: we there find almost the same rhythmic structure, likewise introduced by a quasi-vocal call before the quaver rest that opens the consequent. The difference lies in the character of the consequent itself. Mendelssohn, true to his purpose, continues the 'song'; whereas Schumann contrasts his vocal antecedent with an instrumental consequent, thus sharpening the asymmetry within his symmetry. Absolute music's conquest and assimilation of poetic and dramatic means of expression is a typically romantic exploit to which Schumann contributed more than any other composer.

Dika Newlin has sensitively drawn attention to the '"operatic" tonal conception' that lies at the root of progressive tonality (i.e. a tonal structure that does not centre on one key),[1] but what seems to have remained unobserved is that Schumann was the first who succeeded in thus 'disintegrating' pure music: in another hardly known work, which we might call the 'schizophrenic' A minor Quartet, the first movement stands in F major. I would submit that Schumann is the father of Mahler's progressive tonalities, and one of the grandparents of Schoenberg's dis- and re-integration of tonality.

The editor of the *Monthly Musical Record*, one of Schumann's leading advocates, thinks he was 'not a great man'. Our attitude towards Schumann will have become sane when we have out-Schumanned the Schumannians.

NOTES

Source

The Listener, 56/1426, 26 July, 1956, p. 141.

1   [Ed:] Keller reviewed Dika Newlin's *Bruckner-Mahler-Schoenberg* in *Tempo*, 9, Autumn 1948, pp. 210-14.

Biography's Truths

Keller again raised the issue of Freudian attitudes to a musician's – Mahler's – mental disturbances in the course of the following review of Ronald W. Clark's Freud: The Man and the Cause, *London, Weidenfeld and Nicholson, 652 pp. (0 297 77661 4). The typescript (a carbon copy) dates from the early 1980s and has the appearance of a contribution to a periodical or journal. However, the piece is not listed in the* Music Analysis *bibliography, and if and where it appeared is unknown.*

The biographies I trust without disquieting reservations can be counted on the fingers of a gravely crippled hand: the first volume of Cosima Wagner's *Diaries* is one of them, the second the other. Year in, year out, she sat down every night and wrote down what Richard said and did. The result is sensationally truthful, characteristically Wagnerian. On the other hand, consider what you think of A's view of B. As distinct from the usual biographer, A knew B well; so, for that matter, did you. And it is because you did that you can clearly see how A misunderstood, even invented him. As for my personal experience and evidence, through no fault of my own, I keep being interviewed. It's been going on for decades – yet I only remember a single interviewer, a blind reporter from *The New Yorker*, who actually said I said what I said. And at the time of writing, I am correcting a distinguished interviewer's transmutation of a transcript of an interview that was recorded on tape: he even got that wrong.

How does it all happen? As a professional biographer, Ronald W. Clark, a distinguished writer with numerous previous convictions (among them richly praised biographical assaults on Bertrand Russell, Einstein, and the Huxleys), has at least one answer to every question, including, of course, this one:

> Thirty years after Freud had developed his theory of the unconscious, Werner Heisenberg, the world-famous German physicist, was showing that in the physical world, at the subatomic level, the mere act of observing inevitably affected what was being observed.

How much more on the mental level, our biographer concludes, sensibly enough. So Freud's psychology, or what, in another place, Clark is pleased to call his neurotic make-up (he probably means the make-up of his neurosis), inevitably affected psychoanalysis. Fair enough – but why doesn't Clark subject his own act of observing Freud to equivalent reflections?

Has any biography of anyone you knew ever left you satisfied, unperturbed at its having been written? Nor is this my complete case against biographies. After all, we live in an age of psychobiographies, about which Clark is comprehensively and commendably cautious, however lenient he may be towards his own psychobiographical inclinations. He thus merely repeats an inconsistent attitude towards psychobiography and psychohistory which Freud himself had evinced in the first place; in fact, in a letter to Lytton Strachey which Clark has, happily, unearthed, the father of these disciplines turns into their step-father and, by the way, into my brother:

. . . we cannot divine men's motives and the essence of their minds and so cannot interpret their actions. Our psychological analysis does not suffice even with those who are near us in space and time, unless we can make them the object of years of the closest investigation, and even then it breaks down before the incompleteness of our knowledge and the clumsiness of our synthesis. So that with regard to the people of past times we are in the same position as with dreams to which we have been given no associations – and only a layman could expect us to interpret such dreams as those.

Unless the interpreter is Freud, of course.

What completes my case, however, are not psycho-biographical dreams (which, at least latently, underlie all biography that does not confine itself to a curriculum vitae), but even the truest biography's sheer irrelevance. The brutal truth is that the greater the mind, the smaller the interest in his life – for the simple reason that the greater the mind, the more of his life lies in his work: it's there that he is unlike the rest of humanity and its psychology. But then, we write and read biographies in order to bring him down to earth, to make his life show, misleadingly, that he is like the rest of the species. So he is, of course, outside his work, I mean his pleasure. His life, therefore, is supremely uninteresting – obvious. A small composer's deafness, to be sure, would be a riveting story, a heart-rending tragedy; whereas Beethoven's produced an isolation, acoustic as well as social, which enabled him to create unprecedented, unsurpassed, unparalleled art. The excitement, the truth lies in the late quartets and nowhere else – not in the countless, interminable musicological reflections on what his deafness meant in his so-called life – inevitable misrepresentations anyway: A at least knew B, remember?

A great mind's biography then, tends to be even less true to life than obscenity to love, but so long as there's no law against it – or at least against its defamations which, were its victim alive, would be actionable – we must be grateful not alone to Cosima Wagner but also, yes, to Ronald Clark: his firm conscience does test his knowledge and his sheer news. He has, in fact, got hold of quite a bit of new or novel documentary evidence – novel in that it's new to you or me, though it may have been available to the specialist researcher. For the afore-quoted, fascinating letter, for instance, we'd have had to go as far as Michael Holroyd's *Lytton Strachey* Vol. II (London and New York, 1968), and who would have shown us the way?

Ernest Jones's Freud biography could, of course, have been included in my single-handed list: *mutatis mutandis*, he was indeed another Cosima Wagner, in that his *Sigmund Freud: Life and Work* [1953-57] is, psychoanalytically, as mistakeless as Cosima's *Diaries* are musically. One can hardly suppress a smile, therefore, when Clark's blurb proudly presents 'the first full-scale biography of the founder of psycho-analysis [hyphenated here, though not within] to be written for nearly a quarter of a century', as if stop-press Freud biographies were due at regular intervals. If, Cosima's apart, any biography can claim to be at least intermittently definitive, it is Jones's.

Nor does Clark improve on it, but he does complement it and, occasionally, offer new thought – not to speak of some new and impressive photos, unknown even to the most visual Freudians I could lay my hands on. At the same time, he naturally cannot rid himself of what is both the biographer's and the historian's original sin: however deep and wide, his knowledge will always be inadequate, because his terms of reference force him to write about more than he can possibly know and understand. Clark's ignorance is, in fact, as striking as his knowledge; what is worse, it is two-dimensional, in that there are gaping holes in both his psychoanalytic and his cultural outfit.

I personally doubt that you can, faultlessly, write about psychoanalysis at all without having experienced it first-hand; to me it makes as much sense as writing about music without having been inside it. But it isn't only inside knowledge that is lacking; since he had decided to write about 'the Cause' too, the outsider would have had to inform himself more fully about the latest advances in our knowledge of psychoanalysis as a religion. The outstanding observer and thinker in this field is Thomas Szasz – amongst psychiatrists the most independent psychoanalytic (or psychoanalytically experienced) mind since Freud himself. Clark is dimly aware of his existence and importance, but does not seem to know more than his near-journalistic, highly exaggerated, and proportionately weak book on *Karl Kraus and the Soul-Doctors* (London, 1977), as well as an earlyish paper on 'Freud as a leader'. The result is that he ignores almost the entire Szaszian case and anti-cause – Szasz's close, critical analysis of psychoanalytic ideology (as distinct from psychoanalytic practice and the causeless facts of both psychoanalytic theory and the psychoanalytic body of knowledge). Paradoxically, though, perhaps helped by his ignorance, Clark is more objective, fairer to Freud's genius, than Szasz proves upon occasion – but his fairness could have gained in substance if it had been based on knowledge of what has happened to 'the Cause' behind the biographer's back.

In matters cultural, Clark's diverse ignorances (which deserve the introduction of my neologistic plural, so diverse are they) turn out to be equally embarrassing, equally central. Take Freud's historic encounter with Mahler – a half-explored event in all conscience, into which our biographer could well get his teeth, after doing something about their cavities, the worst of which is his unawareness of almost the entire literature on the subject. Thus he talks about Egon Gartenberg (*Mahler: The Man and the Music*, London and New York, 1978) as 'his [i.e. Mahler's] biographer', as if there were no other comparable eminence – oblivious, that is, to the detailed work done on Freud's analytic blitz on Mahler by Donald Mitchell, in the two published volumes of what is going to be a 4-volume work on the man and his music. I myself have a burning question here which neither Jones, not Mitchell, nor indeed Clark has answered.

It concerns what – as Clark rightly reports – Freud considered Mahler's 'Holy Mary complex', i.e. his mother fixation (*Mutterbindung*), which made him identify his wife with his mother. At the same time, however, Mahler suffered from a lifelong tic in one of his legs – which, as Mitchell points out, can be taken as a sure sign of his own identification with his lame mother. Well then, here is an opportunity for some responsible psychobiography – on the nature of these conflicting identifications: on the one hand, Mahler's wife was his mother, while on the other, he was! Freud must have been violently struck by the composer's conflict: is there no record of his having remarked upon it, however privately? If anybody, Clark might know – or know where to look for a possible answer.

Most surprising, perhaps, is Clark's gravely defective knowledge of, and about, Vienna as the birthplace of much of our century's culture. As a matter of fact, he doesn't even seem to have informed himself about the place as a place: 'Freud's summer house at Grinzig, outside Vienna' was well inside Vienna: Grinzing is part of the nineteenth metropolitan district (where I was born); outside Vienna it was in Beethoven's time. And in his discussion of Freud's hatred of Vienna, Clark moves dangerously close to cultural illiteracy:

> . . . genius that he was, Freud could . . . claim that Vienna was a city in which, after fifty years' residence, he had never met a new idea; yet this, within his own experience, had been the city of Mach, Schlick, Carnap and Wittgenstein, as well as of Frank Kafka and Gustav Mahler . . .

A baffling list, especially since it is not meant to be incomplete. Kafka was neither born nor bred in Vienna, nor did he live there; whereas such creators of the twentieth century as Schoenberg, Berg, Webern, Klimt, Kokoschka, Schiele, and Herzl (whom Clark notices elsewhere in the book) remain unlisted, not to speak of such minor major figures as Schnitzler, Hofmannsthal, and Werfel. In Clark's defence, you might think that he left out the great composers because Freud was utterly unmusical – but he didn't: there's Mahler.

Inevitably, his unfamiliarity with Vienna's cultural and civilisational history blurs his picture of Freud's role in Viennese society – or, psychobiographically speaking, of Freud's motives and reasons for doing things or not doing them. In order to appreciate the exceptional morality of Freud's refusal to abandon, for opportunist reasons, a religion he didn't believe in, one has to know that the stand he thus took was equally exceptional, downright unique: I know of no other case. That is to say, in agnostic or atheistic Jewish circles it was absolute form to abandon Judaism if the social or professional need arose. But while Clark remarks that 'more and more Jews took the road of baptism, the "admission ticket to European civilisation" as Heine called it,' he doesn't realise that by the time Freud was confronted with the opportunity for opportunism, everybody else availed himself of it; he merely singles out one or two examples – without, incidentally, including Mahler, whose baptism he mentions close on 200 pages later, unaware of the fact that Mahler had thus secured himself the directorship of the Vienna Court Opera. In due course and much against his character, Schoenberg followed suit – in his early twenties. So it wasn't just that 'Freud trod the harder road'; within his social context, he was a downright saint, and a passionately anti-religious one into the bargain.

But don't let me go on: I'm getting into the biographical swing myself.

The Psychology of Music and Its Effects:
Two Fragments

1 Manifestations of the Primary Process in Musical Composition

The papers in the Archive show that, through fragments of quotation and aborted essays, Keller tried to develop a psychological approach to both meta- and intra-musical questions in the 1940s without ever achieving a satisfactory first base (this came a decade later and is the subject of the third section of Essays on Music, *CUP, 1994). From an undisclosed source he learnt what is evident from the Hoffer experiment outlined in (2) below, namely 'that one may attach a considerable degree of importance to the voice and to music generally as a method of sexual appeal' and that 'the musical belief in the moralizing influence of music has survived into modern times mainly in a somewhat more scientific form as a belief in its therapeutic effects in disordered nervous and mental conditions.' From Ernest Jones's* Essays in Applied Psychoanalysis *he also learnt how 'That [an] infantile interest [in] the sound accompanying the passage of the flatus may be transferred in later life to the subject of* music *was first pointed out by Ferenczi [in 1911, Zentralb. für Psa. I, p. 395].' He took notes from the handful of essays on music published in the Freudian journal* Imago *edited by Otto Rank (he was impressed by an essay of Mosonyi's (see below)); and he drew on* Musical Forms *(1878) by Ernst Pauer for definitions of 'Transposition of the Accent' ('for the sake of special effect a deviation often takes place from the established order of the accent by transposing it. The accent is transferred from the thesis to the nearest arsis.') and 'Syncopation' (the obsessive concern of the* 'Manifestations' *project): both definitions are also used below.*

However, it was with the fragment entitled 'Manifestations of the Primary Process in Musical Composition' that he began to lay out his argument, taking as a starting point the 'definitions of terms' and processes described in Freud's Interpretation of Dreams *(1899).*

In view of the unusual ideational contents with which we have to deal in a psychological analysis of musical composition it is necessary to define very carefully those psychological terms which we know from the study of other spheres of psychical activity and which we intend to apply to musical phenomena. The three terms denoting essential characteristics of the primary process that are of the greatest importance to us in the present connection are (1) displacement, (2) condensation, (3) representation through the opposite.

This leads straight on to another untitled typescript, this time of 21 pages, which is his most substantial document on musical form from this time. Keller turns at once to the development section of classical sonata form, and although his remarks are both incomplete, sketchy, and not entirely coherent, they still establish the thought processes that would crystallise in, for example, his essay on 'The Chamber Music' from The Mozart Companion *(London, Faber) of 1956. This extract reproduces pages 1-6 of the typescript covering sections 1-4 of the list drawn up in 'The Primary Process in the Development' (see below): thereafter Keller abandons the orderly presentation and pursues his preliminary thoughts on syncopation obsessively, to the detriment of the whole (this section is not included).*

Selection of Observational Material

We shall focus our attention mainly, though not exclusively, on the development section of the classical sonata form and on this form generally. The reasons why this seems to be a convenient choice are the following:

1   Of all musical styles, the classical style is best known to educated laymen who have an interest in serious music.
2   The classical development section is a unique meeting-place of the diverse elements of style. A psychological discussion of this part of a movement in sonata form will at the same time represent an examination of formal elements and compositional devices which, when isolated, can be regarded as essential components of the manners of artistic expression at various periods.
3   The relation of the development section to the exposition and to the recapitulation is from the psychoanalytical standpoint an especially fascinating field of investigation. A similar relation can be shown to exist between different sections of movements in other styles, but again it is the development section of the sonata form where various manifestations of this relation are displayed in an unmistakeable way.

The Primary Process in the Development

The various means by which the ideas used in the exposition are represented in a new light in the development are the following:

1   Transposition and change of mode
2   Alteration of harmony
3   Ornamentation
4   Altered accent or time [tempo]
5   Fragmental representation
6   Imitation, sequential repetition
7   Employment of double counterpoint, canon, fugue

There is much overlapping between these groups of devices. In all of them two principles are at work: (1) repetition, (2) modification. It is the latter aspect, that of modification or even transformation, with which we are primarily concerned when observing manifestations of the primary process and of the mechanisms of distortion; the element of repetition will be discussed in a later section.

1   Transposition and Change of Mode

In *transposing a subject* from the main key or from the nearest related key to another key, the composer is at the same time transposing the affective value with which he invested the original idea to the idea which he is modifying through change of key. The new key has now become full of interest although originally it had been – from the standpoint of listening to, or creating the exposition – without significance. The different ideational components of the primary idea are melodically centred [on] the tonic of the main or the related key; the corresponding elements of the secondary idea avail themselves of a very different centre: the tonic of the new key (cf. Freud, *Interpretation of Dreams*). The whole process of transposition is bound up with the 'transference of affect from one idea to another' (Ernest Jones). Thus there are striking similarities between this displacement and that originally known to us from the study of dream-formation; but there are also striking differences which should give us a clue as to the function of this displacement. Before the discussion of this question, however, we have to attempt to acquire a fairly comprehensive knowledge about the musical manifestations of the mechanisms participating in dream formation.

The *change of mode* does not only, through the secondary idea again replacing, and being the representative of, the primary conception, involve a (partial) displacement of the affect on to the former, but it also entails so drastic an alteration of the quality of the affect that the affect accompanying the representative of the original idea appears to be the opposite of that attached to the latter. Thus the change of mode yields an obvious example of a musical inversion of affect (cf. Jones, op. cit., p. 248), again [offering a] parallel to the inversion of affect in dream formation. Further, as in dream-inversion, the inverted affect (i.e. that accompanying the context as it appears in the exposition) is dynamically and chronologically the more important one.

2 Alteration of Harmony

Here, as in *3 Ornamentation*, we have again one idea replacing another one with which it is associated through common elements.

4 Alteration of Accent or Time [Tempo]

Until now we [have] inspected only such modifications of musical ideas as are based upon alterations of pitch [and then] of course only from the surface level of observation. When inspecting alterations of accent and time, we are confronted to a large extent with the rhythmical aspect of musical ideas. The simplest way of changing the accents of a motive is what is conveniently known in music theory as 'displacement of accent' (the German term 'Akzentverschiebung' also corresponds to the Freudian term). Indeed we meet here with one of those not too frequent cases where one and the same word is not used for widely different things. For the musical accent, in representing an 'inhibited discharge' (Mosonyi), is certainly a 'psychic accent' (Freud), and being displaced from one ideational element (the thesis of the original idea) to the other (the arsis of the replacing idea) it is a very clear example of the appearance in music of the mechanism of displacement.

We know that [what] the working mode of the primary process achieves is not acceptable to our intellect, which rejects it as incompatible with the established laws of reasoning, as abnormal (Freud); similarly, the displacement of accent in music represents a 'deviation from the established order of the accent' (Pauer). To be sure, we accept the rhythmic illogicality with pleasure and even sanction it through special terms just as we accept all the other deviations from original musical statements that we have enumerated. In the present instance, our readiness is, according to Pauer, based on the 'special effect' that is presented to us through this device. We shall analyse the nature of this special effect in a later section.

A very frequent element of musical form wherein the displacement of accent is employed is *syncopation*. The above definition would make us believe that accent-displacement and syncope are identical, which, however, is not the case. In syncopation we find another process besides displacement at work, i.e. the fusion of two originally separated elements (a thesis and an arsis) into one single element. Harmonically this implies the appearance of a preparatory dissonance (a suspension) or else an anticipation.

Both suspension and anticipation are, in consequence of the mentioned fusion, characterized by what German musical terminology calls 'harmoniefremde Töne', i.e. through notes which appear together in a harmony to which they are foreign. Translated into psychological language this means that two musical ideas are <u>condensed</u> into one idea, [and that] their three mental aspects, the rhythmic, the melodic and the harmonic, are all undergoing condensation: the first in that two beats are, for all practical purposes, compressed into one, the second because two notes with a certain interval (a unison) have become a single note, and the third in that the differentiating characteristic between the two different harmonies is neglected through an element of one chord becoming an element of another to which it is foreign. The 'composition' thus achieved (in the psychoanalytic sense described by Jones) exhibits elements of similarity between the original ideas: the melodic and the rhythmic (and metric) condensation makes use of the two separate notes having the same pitch, the rhythmic (metric) condensation itself is frequently facilitated through the original separate elements having the same, or almost the same, time-value.

Keller here turns to a 'practical example' of a (hypothetical?) 'development of a sonata' derived from 'Stoehr' in which he compares two passages, the original idea from the exposition, and its syncopated reworking in the development. The examples are not included in the typescript and hence the intricate argument pursued over several pages of typescript (pp. 7-11) cannot be followed; but he does challenge the application of psychoanalytic theory to music by adding to the idea of 'condensation' its 'opposite': this he describes as 'diffusion' ('Zerstreung'), and marks it out for later explication. After further philosophising about the musical examples (to page 14), Keller describes a childhood confusion of the terms 'suspension' and 'anticipation'. After this, the text begins to dissolve with an incoherent sporting comparison, and breaks off with sketchy definitions of categories (6) Imitation, Sequential repetition ('it is obvious that these devices rest upon the mechanism of displacement in a similar way . . . as described under (1) and (2) above') and '(7) Imitation in contrary motion. (Inversion.)'. For this last he announces a comparison of the first phrase of the principal subject of Haydn's String Quartet Op. 76, No. 2 (first movement) with 'the first 6 bars of the development section.'

He appears to have missed out a category, (5) Fragmental Representation.

NOTES

Source

Neither of the incomplete overlapping typescripts 'Manifestations of the Primary Process in Musical Composition' (3 pp.), nor an incomplete essay in German comprising ten pages of manuscript with the same title, nor 'Selection of Observational Material' (22 pp.), is dated, though the appearance of the materials suggests a time in the early to mid 1940s. Also related to this is an undated draft of an essay, 'Dream-work and Development in Sonata Form' (8 pp.). A longer manuscript of 33 pages held in the Archive, 'A. Analytischer Abschnitt' (n.d.), may have been intended to relate to the above material. Other undated fragments include: 'Akzentverschiebung' (four pages of text) and the related ' . . . während meiner vorliegende Notierung sei korrekt . . . ' (eleven pages); 'Die abnormen Vorgänge in der Musik' (two pages); 'Ansätze zur psychoanalytischen Musikbetrachtung' (three pages); and 'Studies in the Psychoanalysis of Music' (two pages). A purely musical entry from 1951 on 'Panchromaticism' for *Groves Dictionary of Music and Musicians,* fifth edition, edited by Eric Blom, was discarded on grounds of complexity, as is revealed by an exchange of letters in the Archive accompanying the entry.

2 Notes on a Case of Dementia Praecox
(Bleuler's Schizophrenia)
and Attempts at a Musico-psychological Treatment

At the beginning of 1945 Keller was sent a patient for treatment by Willi Hoffer, 'a psychoanalyst of the old guard' (1975 (1984 minus 9), London, Dobson, pp. 86-7). The course of treatment was brief and unsuccessful (the patient had a mental breakdown). Nevertheless, Keller had time to make notes of the first meeting on 18 January. These notes are reproduced here lightly edited:

I undertook the case at the instigation of Willi Hoffer. The latter informed me that the patient, a 20-year-old refugee boy of wealthy parents, was largely occupied with musical ideas; he wanted to learn the piano and compose. My first telephone talk with the patient revealed his extremely slow speech (already mentioned by Hoffer) and slight difficulties in spelling the name of the street where he lived. The first session [took place] at the patient's house: Hoffer informed me that it was safest meeting there as sometimes the patient did not find [his way] home.

Speech Tempo seems to vary. I have the uncertain impression that inhibitions increase when the patient wants to object to something, also generally when the subject [of conversation] induces affective reaction. Speech [itself] seems to be usually announced by varying facial or bodily movements. On the other hand these also take place without a following speech. [The patient] speaks good educated English, [with] excellent pronunciation.

Intellect With regard to speech content, he makes a strikingly normal impression.

Memory [He probably] has extensive amnesias. He speaks of several months of piano-study, undertaken some years ago, but does not seem to remember more about the time. He says that he has difficulties in reading and writing, musical or otherwise. He plays a not-too-easy piece fairly correctly with the notes in front of him, but [without ever] looking at them: "Can't read and play at the same time." He can hardly read [music] at all, and changes the subject when asked to give the name of a piano key (C) or a note. When hearing a triad several times (C-E-G), and asked to reproduce it "or something similar", he first plays G-B-D, then G-E-C, and, when asked, states correctly which was the exact repetition (all this not without difficulty). When hearing a dominant 7th, again downwards, G-F-D-B several times, he is unable to repeat it, plays 4 notes in downward thirds. He mentions something about "different fingerings", but does not explain what he means. He agrees to practice this "ear training" for purposes of composing.

Musical Phantasies He seems to play chords at random, with certain repetitions, mostly of what seem to be meant as dominant 7ths. For the rest, he plays mainly dissonances, and calls his productions "jungles of sounds". He regrets that he is unable adequately to express his feelings musically.

Course of Treatment as Indicated by Hoffer Encouraging. [There is] praise for his compositional talent etc. [He] promised to do a twofold course, theory and free composition. He wants to play quickly in order to be able to play his own compositions quickly (and talks about increasing the subtlety and strength of his fingers). He is keen on as many lessons as possible.

Some Further Motor Reactions [He places his] hand over [his] eyes (apparently [out of] embarrassment) [and runs it] through his hair (slight states of trance?). He blows tobacco ash about the table, and smokes whenever he is offered a cigarette. Sometimes he stares prolongedly into my eyes, especially whenever offered a light.

NOTES

[Ed:]   As far as the musico-psychological treatment of patients was concerned, Keller might have remembered a startling observation of Melanie Klein's he once jotted down from the *International Journal of Psychology* (VII, p. 59):

> In Felix, who was 13 years old and up till then had shown no musical talent, a marked love of music gradually developed during analysis . . . it proved that sounds, some of which he had heard proceeding from his parents' bed and the rest of which he had phantasized, had formed the basis of a very strong and very early inhibited interest in music, an interest which was liberated again during analysis. This determination of the interest in and gift for music I found present (side by side with anal determination) in other cases as well, and I believe it to be typical.

Aphorisms on Music

The first set of aphorisms, Food for Music-love and -thought, *was written in about 1941 and appears never to have been published; the typescript matches that of the aphorisms reproduced in Part I above. The second set,* Short and Bitter, *was published in* Music Survey, *Vol. II, No. 2, Autumn 1949, p. 71.*

1 Food for Music-love and -thought

Whether or not music be the food for love, love is the food for music.

So often the platform turns playing into placarding.

To composers, performers, and listeners: there is only one convincing way out of a phrase, and that's the way into the next.

In one way or another, you can express everything in music – except music criticism.

Comprehending listening means re-composing.

Behind the veil of music man's deepest feelings dare emerge.

You know a good lullaby by the fact that it keeps you awake.

The superficial listener is happy that music whiles away his time. The penetrating listener is unhappy that time whiles away his music.

Musical composition is the only art in which the conflict between illusion and reality becomes, not just unimportant, but meaningless.

In Beethoven and Brahms a performer can show his competence, in Bach and Mozart his incompetence.

A musical man who cannot be moved to tears by music seems to belong to a remarkable type of creature found among both sexes, i.e. a woman trying to be a man.

Ultimately, every important instrumentalist comes to realize that the instrument is of no ultimate importance.

The perfect musician understands both the language of music and the music of language.

Reaction to late Beethoven: "It couldn't be done better." And to mature Mozart: "It couldn't have been done otherwise."

A piece can be played better than it is.

Some listeners cannot enjoy the music they like. In a recess of their mind there resides a thought highly charged with feelings of inferiority and guilt: "Whatever fascinates me can't be much good." They must be elaborately bored in order to be able unreservedly to praise. (‡With acknowledgment to *National Entertainments Monthly*.)

Every great composer is succeeded, not only by his heirs, but also by his legacy hunters.

2   Short and Bitter

Nothing is further from the truth of music than its partial understanding.

While the beautiful is always right, the ugly is not always wrong. Which makes many deem the ugly beautiful.

Every composer must start by imitating others. None should end up by imitating himself.

Genius remains genius. When a talent is born into the storm created by genius, it rarely remains a talent: the billows either bear it high or drown it.

The great have done more and been less than the small think.

Good music cannot prosper without the support of those who pretend to like it.

The God of Art is an angry god, for he makes the talentless industrious.

Intellectual music is emotional music we do not understand.

A conscience without originality is pitiable; originality without a conscience is a pity.

The modern need for simplification, unlike the classical need for simplicity, is the result of a decrease of leisure among the intelligent and the increased literacy among idiots.

There isn't such a thing as a courageous artist. When you have something to say you need no courage to say it.

What seems morbid [in] music frees the feelings our morbidity makes us fear.

The bad artist is created by his times. The mediocre creates for his time. The better artist creates for posterity. The great creates posterity.

A truism is a truth stated without having been re-discovered.

The need of the hour is mental birth control.

The mature artist's ability to live up to his ideals is increased by his willingness to live down to his limitations.

'The appreciation of music' makes as much sense to me as 'the appreciation of God'.

Later Aphorisms on Music

The Archive includes a number of later aphorisms on music (and life) in addition to those published in the 'Memorial Symposium', Music Analysis, *Vol. 5, 2-3, 1986. pp. 368-70. The following is a selection:*

Art as a precursor of scientific thought is second-rate. Art as a successor to scientific thought is trash. Art that remains a precursor of scientific thought which never catches up with it – that's art.

The arts' jealousy of music is incurable: it has the precision of conceptual thought without its retarding disadvantage, its cause: incarceration by static definition.

One of the most pleasant ways of passing what feels like an hour with nothing is to listen to Stravinsky's complete *Pulcinella* – a spiritual source of that powerful advanced school of compositional thoughtlessness which replaces art by playing games. In fact, if some advanced composers knew their sources, they'd do something else instead – or perhaps, again, nothing.

The word 'brilliant' ought not to be used to describe achievements and achievers: what it fairly describes is that violin sound of D major as opposed to that of A flat major. But as for you and what you do, you either can or you can't. 'Brilliant' was invented by those who can't but think they can a bit; inevitably they soon found plenty of sympathizers: we all can, though we aren't brilliant, but maybe we're all the deeper for that. Have you ever heard a man whom they call brilliant describe anything or anybody as brilliant?

When it is not plain stupidity, which is surprisingly rare, all inarticulateness is self-love – a withdrawal in view of the fact that one can't say everything. So what? Saying nothing is worse – unless you have nothing to say; in which case, say so.

The world's problems would be solved if we knew what to do about the talentless, or if they knew what to do about themselves. Their degradation is a misuse of the degraders' talents, their self-denigration a function of the civilized world's success-hunting – public, social, or endo-psychic. Yet a harmless total failure towers above a harmful success – and how many harmless successes are there?

The Psychology of Everyday Musical Life

Keller was not just a keen and articulate psychological observer but also an astute adviser. He was as ready to instruct performers (before and after the event), composers (including Benjamin Britten on handling string-quartet form and texture), critics (in the error of their ways), film-makers and educationalists, as he was anybody else with whom he came into contact, footballers not excluded. In an autobiographical radio interview later in his life, he deemed it a mark of his 'personality' that he felt compelled to involve himself passionately in whatever caught his interest, and in particular he campaigned for the abolition of capital punishment in the UK. The following three essays offer early examples of his advice to opera management, parents, and broadcasters.

1   Announce Opera Casts!

Imagine this concert notice:

> Triple Concerto for piano, violin, 'cello, and orchestra in C (Beethoven). The soloists will be *either* Mr. Jones, Mr. Smith, and Mr. Brown, *or* Mr. James, Mr.Black, and Mr. Green, *or* Mr. Jones, Mr. Black, and Mr. Brown, *or* Mr. James, Mr. Smith, and Mr. Green (etc., etc.).

One would doubtless take exception to such neglectful treatment of one's potential expectations. Yet, with many a forthcoming opera performance, one knows just as little (indeed often less) about who are to be the singers, and opera audiences have so far voiced no protest.

It seems that there are two distinct factors that may determine an indifferent attitude towards the question of which interpreter one is going to hear. To begin with the more sophisticated mental agent, there are what could be called the 'anti-star' motives. As far as their rational, or at any rate, rationalized, aspect goes, they centre on the view that the composer's work is so much more important than the performer's that we oughtn't to bother too much about who the latter is, provided that he can be expected to be tolerably competent.

We sometimes even find a variety of this view applied, not primarily to the relation between performer and composer, but to that between the composer and his work:

> The works themselves are, or at least should be, of course, the thing that matters most . . . and not the names or personalities of the authors . . . One wonders if it would not be preferable – though not to some of the professional critics – to have musical works performed without indicating the names of their composers.
>
> (Béla Bartók, *Tempo*, 14, 1946)

Though Bartók's suggestion does not concern itself with performers' names, it implicitly concerns them all the same: if the composer's name does not sufficiently matter to merit indication, the interpreter's name certainly isn't worth mentioning [either].

Anybody can see that arguments along these lines have a strong point. Directed against conceptions of 'stars' and 'personalities', they are indeed in harmony with the general trend of mental development, which, as psychoanalytic research in particular has shown, proceeds towards the depersonalisation of values. However, fundamentally inartistic admiration of stars apart, a composer's or performer's name clearly has artistic significance. I'm not interested in Peter Pears's favourite dish, but I like to know whether I shall be able to enjoy his art in a particular performance – a legitimate musical interest, I submit.

In fact, the validity of anti-star arguments is often threatened by a non-sequitur that smoothly grows inside them: A is far more important than B, therefore B is unimportant. We generally tend towards such simplifying exaggerations, it being easier to think in terms of mutually exclusive contrasts than of mutually expediting contrasts.

But leaving on one side the question how far anti-star motives are justified in a particular case, it is clear that their influence cannot be decisive in producing opera audiences' indifference to casting. Otherwise, we would expect a similar indifference towards soloists in recitals and concerts. In point of fact, concert-goers do care more about the question of who is going to perform than opera audiences, although the latter are on the whole, not less, but more star-conscious.

How resolve this contradiction? I suggest that beside anti-star motives there is another and far more important cause of the indifference towards interpreters, viz., simply, ignorance. In this country knowledge of operatic art is more modest than any other musical knowledge (though this state of affairs is rapidly changing). If one doesn't know anything about a work one cannot possibly care a lot about different forms of its interpretation.

Now this indifference towards differentiation between singers does not exclude intense star-love, which, however, must in this case be promiscuous. "Give me a singer and he'll be my star for tonight." [It is] in some way like this the promiscuous listener feels when he buys his ticket. Nor is he an exception with what to others seems his self-contradictory attitude. We can observe this wherever love promiscuity manifests itself. Even the male addicted to prostitutes, little selectively though he behaves in his love choice, can invest his idea of his short-lived love-object with a sufficient amount of feeling to make her, for the duration of his blitz love-relation, his star.

If the contention that comparative ignorance is at the root of the unconcern about casting be correct, it would follow that the claims of knowledgeable opera audiences are sufficiently urgent to make the detailed announcement of casts a rule. This is indeed the case. In (pre-Hitlerite) Vienna, for instance, each of the chief dailies and evening papers brought, every day, the complete casts for both of the daily opera programmes (Staatsoper and Volksoper); in addition, forthcoming casts were announced. It would have been quite unimaginable for any music-lover not to be thus informed.

When I here propose that in this country, too, the musical public should not be left in the dark about forthcoming opera casts, I feel that I am only slightly in advance of the tide. The ever-decreasing ignorance of our opera audiences, that is to say, may soon result in their attitude towards opera singers running parallel to the concertgoer's attitude towards soloists.

It is true that the actor-singer is liable to pave the way to a regression to adolescent and pre-adolescent hero (star) worship to a more dangerous extent than the concert soloist. But I suggest that the disadvantage that may thus be involved in paying greater publicity attention to casts is outweighed by the advantages that the serious art lover must derive from detailed information about who will be singing on particular occasions. In any case these advantages are greater in the field of opera than elsewhere in musical life. Firstly, the opera performer offers both musical and histrionic interpretation, and the possible variety of different shades of expression, many of them equally valuable, is correspondingly wider in the field of opera than in the concert hall. The wider the variety, the more pressing is the advanced listener's need for diagnosing the different types of interpretation and for being in a position to look forward to the experience of a particular type.

Secondly, and far less subtly, deficient interpretations are at the present time still more widespread in our realm of opera than in any other of our musical spheres. Consequently, if one doesn't know the cast beforehand, the chances are pretty high that one will have to endure some rotten piece of performance.

A word, finally, on how to go about this publicity business. If it should prove difficult to announce casts in the dailies, or at least in the weekly gloomies, it could surely be arranged that information be available, as soon as the casts are settled, at the opera house in question. Leaflets would be best, but posters (customary at the Vienna State Opera) would also do the job, if the glamorous photos of singers (far be it for me to protest against their adorning foyers) could be induced to leave a spot of room.

Source

Typescript dating from 1946 or 1947, originally entitled 'Opera Casts and Audiences'. On the first page is the (at the time) familiar hand-written warning that 'the possibility of occasional linguistic imperfections is due to the writer's mother tongue not being English'.

In the period leading up to the closure (for redevelopment) of the Royal Opera House, Covent Garden – i.e. in the 1980s and 90s – casts were indeed announced as Keller proposed. However, since the reopening – in the new millennium – the practice has been abandoned.

2 Your Child and Music

The Teacher

You should really get to know your child's music teacher if possible, and see whether you like him or her. Unfortunately there are music teachers who combine great musical knowledge and ability with a considerable lack of psychological insight. Some indeed seem surprised if a child, at his first violin lesson, does not exactly behave like Heifetz.

The teacher's outlook should be as tolerant and understanding – as parental, that is – as, I am sure, yours is. For the following reason it is quite important that there be no essential differences between the teacher's and your own general attitude to the child. The latter is gradually building up in his own mind an internal 'parent', consisting largely of his idea of yourself, but also of quasi-parental figures such as teachers. Part of this 'incorporated' parent will eventually come to be his adult conscience, or, in music, his standard of artistic valuation – his musical conscience and his musical ideals.

Now if the persons whose images contribute to the development of conscience show themselves very different, conscience will not in itself be united, but [will be] divided by mental conflict mirroring the once actual discrepancies. Awkward as we know that conflict between our conscience and our less moral self is, conflict within conscience itself is of course also a danger to our happiness and efficiency. Especially in music, the reproduction of which requires a mind that knows exactly what it wants, harmonious ideals are of great importance.

Try also to see whether the teacher not only tolerates but actually follows your child's inclinations. I suppose I am telling you no news when I suggest that the successful teacher is taught by his pupil's capacities how to teach.

Practice

As I write this, a passage from a young woman's report on her work as a general hand at a garage (a report required for some group-psychological work I am doing) strikes me as having a bearing on the present subject: 'I have had many different jobs before this one . . . The thing I like best about it is that you have not [got] a boss standing over you watching what you do. We do pretty well what we like provided we get our job done.'

Garage work may be different from musical practice, adults may be different from children, but doing work without a boss watching you is not only pleasurable, but psychologically wholesome in widely different spheres of activity, and at widely different ages. Learning an instrument, as learning to live, involves the presence of a watching eye, but not its perpetual presence. Don't play too much the role of a second teacher; don't supervise and instruct your child in his practice all the time. Never mind if there is some irregularity in time, duration, or content of periods of practice. Ideally, practice should (and can) be a pure pleasure to the child. If you use your 'musts' and 'mustn'ts' sparingly, you are working towards this ideal.

Your child's conscience (which, we said, is your representative in his mind) should not only come to harmonise with itself (as we have seen before) but also be on fairly good terms with his more immediate desires. To achieve this you will find it useful not to introduce demands into his conscience to which there is not much of a response on the part of his spontaneous inclinations, nor demands that show him that there is a tremendous distance between what he is able to do and what he should be able to do.

Playing whilst Playing

You will have noticed that we use the word 'play' both for musical (and theatrical) activities and for (children's) games. Indeed, virtually all psychological schools agree (which means a good deal) that play has a number of affinities to art. Do not prevent your child from 'playing' during his practice, even if he is engaged in compository activities reminiscent of the things that you switch off when you hear them on the wireless. But tell his teacher that he should concern himself with your child's creative impulses. There is much joy in composing; besides, if one has some idea of how to produce there is more fun in reproducing. If playing an instrument generally assumes to your child the significance of 'playing', he must needs find what would be difficult and irksome to others a child's play.

Taste

The development of harmony (or otherwise) between musical conscience and inclinations is of course related to the development of taste. Some teachers treat tastes as some doctors treat medicines. They prescribe them and don't care a hoot whether the individual is going to be sick after taking them. "It's good for him, anyway."

As I indicated before, the teacher and you should take special care of your child's natural likings. These can be guided and developed, but tastes cannot profitably be imposed on the child's mind. Not only should he not be induced to 'learn' to like what he doesn't like, but, similarly, there is not the least point in making him (pretend to) abhor compositions which he really likes. Neither those who like some of what is considered 'bad' music, nor those who 'can . . . without shame let people hear them call a famous symphony a nuisance' (to vary a well-known sentence by William James) are necessarily musically incompetent. The teacher and you should take special care of your child's natural likings.

That the selection of pieces to be played should be carefully adjusted to the child's musical needs (not merely to his technical standard) should, one thinks, be obvious. However, how often does it happen?

Group Music

As soon as possible your child should be given frequent opportunity to 'play' with others, not solely with the teacher or with you, but also with musical playmates. In the first place, chamber-musical activities will enormously accelerate the child's musical development. Secondly, the social ties formed, and to be formed, in this way will prove valuable stepping-stones in the somewhat complex jumps from the family to wider social units.

If You are Unmusical

Don't neglect your child's musical inclinations (if there are any) simply because you yourself are not musical. After all, his interests may differ from yours.

Life, we know, often necessitates awkward tensions in our minds. We are not justified in depriving our children of a possibility of releasing perhaps a considerable amount of these tensions (and, incidentally, of creating pleasurable tensions) in a way which does not only bring joy to themselves, but also to others – in a way indeed highly valued by a large part of our society.

Source

(a) Manuscript of two large hand-written sheets with an introductory fragment of typescript dating from the mid 1940s; and (b) a fully evolved typescript including an amplified opening section by 'Hans Keller L.R.A.M.' The title of the section *Group Music* was altered twice, from *Chamber Music* and *Social Music*.

It was possibly Keller's earliest essay on musical education, a subject to which he frequently returned, notably in 'Education and Its Discontents', *Listener*, 81/2080, 6 February, 1969, p. 185.

3   The BBC's Victory over Schoenberg

The death of Arnold Schoenberg on 13 July, 1951 was commemorated by the BBC in a number of broadcast talks and performances. The following review of these events appeared in The Music Review, *May 1952, pp. 130-31, originally appended with a lively 'footnote by Donald Mitchell' (a footnote that reinforced Keller's views). Keller and Mitchell had themselves marked Schoenberg's death with a collection of obituaries in* Music Survey, *Vol. IV, No. 1, pp. 312-17, to which they added a commemorative issue, Vol. IV, No. 3 (June 1952). This issue included: a number of letters of Schoenberg's; the talk by Mátyás Seiber on 'Composing with Twelve Tones' mentioned below; a brief discussion by O. W. Neighbour on Schoenberg's String Trio; and a very brief review by Humphrey Searle of the broadcast of Schoenberg's Stefan George Songs Op. 15, also mentioned below. In their introduction, 'A Bedside Editorial for the BBC', the editors note that they cover much the same ground as the review below, though with a further observation: 'We shall no doubt be accused of the "sour grapes" line of argument, but the basic question is whether the grapes were in fact sour. Besides, one of us (Keller) had to spend many a working hour on gratis advice and information that he had to give in reply to backstage enquiries from actual and potential contributors to the series; no doubt Erwin Stein, the great Schoenberg expert who was not asked to contribute at all, had similar, if not worse experiences. 'That was when the grapes turned bitter.'*

The following review shows Keller's characteristic readiness to expose the lack of credentials of fellow critics and musicians (a release of almost suicidal aggression within a loose 'group', a kind of 'critical anti-criticism'), and to couch his assault in formal psychological terms. The 'scientific' enumeration of paragraphs is also typical.

Schoenberg dies. The horde, true to primordial savage precedent, falls upon the father and devours him. *Music and Letters*, orgiastically forgetful of its otherwise unceasing respectability, publishes, instead of an obituary, a symposium in which the half-grown and the senile vie with each other in murdering the dead. Marion Scott secures herself a place in the annals of posterity by compressing her reaction to Schoenberg and his death into a single sentence: 'Inevitable, no doubt; but not interesting.' Richard Capell, a man of otherwise impeccable culture and taste, has made himself responsible for printing a collection of wrong facts and infantile opinions that soon becomes ill-famed over the whole of musical Europe. Nor does the daily and weekly press wish to stand aside when all have their mouths full, and 'obituaries' are published which betray the psychological root of their death-notice rather than its cultural purpose. It remains to un-cultural, money-ridden, ruthless America, it remains to the *New York Times*, to pay homage to the adopted son, to end its obituary tribute with the words: 'We are proud to have been his contemporaries'.

But the ambivalence towards the murdered father has two opposite sides, and the fear of retaliation, more widely known as remorse, presently sets in. *Music and Letters* accepts a reasoned article, 'In Defence of Schoenberg', and the Third Programme launches an extended Schoenberg series that does not bring the composer any satisfaction or money; for, on the contrary, he had to pay for it with his death.

Sure enough, it immediately emerges that the series is a child of ambivalence rather than of unmixed love. It emerges from the choice of the editor, of the speakers, of the performers, it emerges from the general disorganization which includes the provision of disastrously short rehearsal times in at least three important instances. Nevertheless, ambivalence has two opposite sides, and though the negative side gains the upper hand, the series comes to include events for which the artistic listener has to be unqualifiedly grateful. In fact, the listener too is forced into a position of ambivalence.

(1) The *General Editor* is Michael Tippett, who approaches his task unprejudiced by any digested knowledge. It is at once apparent that the Third has chosen the 'objective approach' – a wonderful rationalization of ambivalence that conveniently forgets that, applied to an as-yet esoteric composer, objectivity must needs mean ignorance. The result is, according to the informed listener's temperament, tragic or comic in the extreme. Tippett tries his pathetic best (his second talk is already less windy than his first), he learns as quickly and as much as he can, but it is humanly impossible for him to emerge, in the short time at his disposal, as anything else than a good pupil at his best, and a bad pupil at his second-best. His *status*, however, is that of a teacher, to which his preaching tone gives the finishing touch. More than half of his facts are wrong, and less than half of his thoughts are baked. He dabbles here, he dabbles there, he leaves a muddle everywhere. At any one point he tries himself as a brilliant second-rate journalist of the effective variety, at others he tries his hand at philosophy, mysticism, astrology, numerology, comparative psychology and sociology, all the time fitting his facts to his fancies, which isn't difficult since the former are few and the latter inconstant. At the same time his actual insight into Schoenberg's music runs continuously near the zero level, so that practically every remark on the music itself contains a hair-raising technical or emotional blunder. And when he comes to compare Schoenberg with Freud – a parallel

which, alas, he may have from me: I should have gone into it or else not mentioned it at all – he shows that his knowledge of Freud and psychoanalysis equals his understanding of Schoenberg and twelve-tone music. Nevertheless, an impressive parallel emerges, for the two misconceptions will parallel each other as neatly as their unrecognised facts if they arise in the same brain that misunderstands similar data in a similar manner. I have the greatest respect for Tippett the composer and Tippett the thinker, but none for his accepting this job: it is as if I were to accept the general editorship of a Sibelius or Delius series.

(2) *Of the other speakers*, three are outstanding: Seiber on Schoenberg's technique, [Edward] Clark on the Berlin, and [Rudolf] Kolisch on the American years: islands of facts in a sea of unoriginal and irrelevant phantasies. [Egon] Wellesz is another of those wonderfully ambivalent, 'objective' selections: the only Schoenberg pupil who turned away from Schoenberg. He makes an honest job of his talk and tries indeed to be objective, but that is not enough, for his waning interest in Schoenberg renders him incompetent, in fact ignorant, as far as the composer's later works and theoretical concepts are concerned. It is sad to get from the first and enthusiastic Schoenberg biographer such doubly wrong information as that 'from now on' (i.e. after *Pierrot Lunaire*) Schoenberg used as the basis for every (*sic*) composition a theme (*sic*) consisting of all the notes of the chromatic scale, or that Schoenberg rejected 'atonal' in favour of 'atonical', which was true enough at the time, but meanwhile the composer, in his as yet unpublished book on *Structural Functions of Harmony*, had (without Wellesz's knowledge) developed the concept of 'pantonality' instead. Besides, Wellesz mistranslates a crucial passage in Schoenberg's manifesto-like programme note for the 'George' songs, putting 'craftsmanship' for 'Sicherheit'. The motley array of speakers includes Alan Pryce-Jones who isn't even a musician and fortunately knows absolutely nothing about Schoenberg so that he is compelled to confine himself to irrelevant remarks on 'The Background of Old Vienna' (Schoenberg should have listened to that one!), and Alfred Polgar, whom to interview the BBC apparently pays Tippett a journey to Switzerland, the yield being of course nil, for Polgar (a first-class essayist, literary and dramatic critic and with Freud the best German stylist since Schopenhauer) knows as much about Schoenberg as any old Viennese intellectual.

(3) In the *selection of performers* too, an ambivalent attitude, or/and an abysmal ignorance is apparent, in that there is a definite tendency to choose well-qualified musicians for the one job for which they aren't. The Second Quartet is given to the New London, whose highly promising young leader hasn't the first idea about this music (already the tempo of the opening finishes everything) and to Patricia Neway (somewhat better in *Erwartung*) whose approach could not be wronger. The best possible, because practical, criticism of her performance is unintentionally given by Wellesz when he plays the opening of the fourth movement on a record of an excellent performance: suddenly the virginal listener understands what the music means. Perhaps the most amusing case is that of the 'George' songs which are given, at outrageously short notice, to Esther Salamon and Paul Hamburger. Musical musicians, and unprejudicedly adventurous ones too, in all conscience, but the trouble is that Schoenberg did not write the work for mezzo (a fact which the BBC, with its thorough objectivity, does not find out), so that Miss Salamon has to transpose some of the songs and thereby eliminate the harmonic structure from the performance. Literally opposite Broadcasting House sits Erwin Stein, Schoenberg's oldest pupil, the first exponent of the twelve-tone method, and the first coach of the 'George' songs.

The series has not finished at the time of writing, but the BBC's score over Schoenberg is so high that victory is certain.

Musical Criticism (including Film Music Criticism) and Other Writings: a Report

1 General Music Criticism

There are three categories of musical-cum-critical writings held in the Archive. The first includes about 45 typescripts, carbons or manuscripts of items that were taken on to publication and are listed in the 'Memorial Symposium' bibliography in *Music Analysis*, 5/2-3, 1986, pp. 407-40. These pieces were written for the journals Keller contributed to at the time: *Colophon*, *Hallé*, *Music Review*, *Music Survey*, *Opera* and *Tempo*. There is no need to list them again here. The second involves materials relating to just a few published items. A 19-page typescript of an analytical note on 'Prokofiev's Symphony No. 5 in B flat' comes with multiple versions of several of its pages and a correspondence with EMI. There is a draft for a piece on 'The New London Opera Company', of which the published version in *Music Parade*, Vol. I, No. 8, July-September, 1948, p. 3 ff. is incomplete. There are also various materials, including a copy of the published version, relating to 'New Music in the Old Year', *Music Parade*, Vol. I, No. 10, January-March, 1949, p. 37. The third contains one or two unpublished pieces: a 5-page typescript describing 'Music in London: Some Future Events' from January 1946; a 2-page typescript review of the Stravinsky Mass (1948) intended for *Music Review*, August 1951; and a 3-page typescript on the 'Haydn Festival at the Conway Hall' from November, 1951. There is also an undated 2-page fragment on 'Criticism and Prognosis'.

2 Film Music Criticism, 1946-52

A preliminary list of Keller's film music criticism may be found in the 'Memorial Symposium', *Music Analysis*, Vol. 5, Nos. 2/3, 1986, pp. 437-38. The following notes are in addition to this.

Alison Garnham's catalogue for the Cambridge University Library Keller Archive includes 'Noise as Leitmotif' (1948), a typescript of 11 pages; 'The News and the Muse', an unpublished contribution to *Sight and Sound* comprising 10 pages of typescript; 'Music in the Films', an incomplete manuscript of four pages; 'Film Music: *Frieda'*, a typescript of 4 pages; and 'Listen and Look', a fragmentary page of manuscript intended as part of a 'handbook of film-musical appreciation and depreciation' for the British Film Institute. (The printed copy of his BFI monograph, *The Need for Competent Film Music Criticism*, London, October 1947, is accompanied by fragments of an earlier draft.)

In the Archive there are published typescripts, together with printed copies, for publications such as: *Sight and Sound* ('A Film Analysis of the Orchestra' [on Britten's *Young Person's Guide to the Orchestra*], 16/61, Spring 1947; 'The First Filmized Opera: Revolution or Retrogression?' [Rossini's *Barber of Seville*], 16/62, Summer 1947; 'Hollywood Music: Another View', 16/64, Winter 1947/48 [but NOT the only other article for this journal, 'Film Music: Some Objections', 15/60, Winter 1946/47]); *Tribune* ('A Note on Film Music', 13 June, 1947); *Contemporary Cinema* ('Film Music: "Time Out of Mind"', 1/8, September 1947, pp. 229-31; 'Film-musical Atmosphere', 1/9, October 1947, pp. 277-79; 'Film Music: The Edinburgh Festival', 1/10, November 1947, pp. 307-11); *Film Monthly Review* ('Film Music: Variations' , 6/6, March 1948, pp. 10-11; 'Films and the Ballet', 6/11, August 1948, pp. 4-5; 'Another Filmed Opera' [Verdi's *Rigoletto*] 6/14, December 1948, pp. 16-17); and *Music Review* ('Film Music and No Film Music', 10/1, February 1949, pp. 50-51; 'Vaughan Williams's *Scott of the Antarctic*', 10/2, May 1949, p. 138; 'Bax's *Oliver Twist*', 9/3, August 1949, pp. 198-99).

In 1947-48 Keller wrote, as a script of 26 pages, 'Film Music Notes' for the British Film Institute, some extracts of which were published anonymously in the BFI's *Monthly Film Music Bulletin*: 19 November, 1947 (*Mine Own Executioner*, Benjamin Frankel); 25 November, 1947 (*It Always Rains on Sunday*, Georges Auric and Ernest Irving/Billi Mayerl); 16 January, 1948 (*L'ange de la nuit*, Maurice Thiriet); 29 January, 1948 (*The World is Rich*, Clifton Parker); 30 January, 1948 (*Death Valley Outlaws*, Cy Feuer); 11 February, 1948 (*Night Beat*, Benjamin Frankel, and *The British - Are They Artistic?*); 11 February, 1948 (*Against the Wind*, Leslie Bridgewater); 12 February, 1948 (*Call of the Blood*, Ludovico Lunghi); 17 February, 1948 (*The Three Weird Sisters*, Hans May); 18 February, 1948 (*Blanche Fury*, Clifton Parker); 23 March, 1948 (*The Greed of William Hart*, and *Snowbound*, Cedric Thorpe Davie); 6 April, 1948 (*Blackmail*, Mort Gickman, and *Miranda*, Temple Abady); 19 May, 1948 (*Daybreak*, Benjamin Frankel, and *A Double Life*, Miklos Rosza); 20 July, 1948 (*The Red Shoes*, Brian Easdale); 3 August,

1948 (*Le silence est d'or*, Georges Van Parys); 19 August, 1948 (*The Fallen Idol*, William Alwyn); 30 August, 1948 (*Un revenant*, Arthur Honegger); 6 October, 1948 (*Sleeping Car to Trieste*, Benjamin Frankel); 11 November, 1948 (*The Small Voice*, Stanley Black, and *It's Hard to be Good*); 17 November, 1948 (*Rope*, Leo F. Forbstein).

In 1952 Keller proposed a contribution (unpublished) to his column 'Film Music and Beyond' for the February 1953 edition of *Music Review*, 'An Open Note to the Queen'. See also a letter in *Music Review*, 24 December, 1952.

3   Other Writings

Keller's writings in general are shot through with a forthright concern for moral conduct, and can take the form of stories, poems, plays, public letters, lengthy formal responses and open rebuke, in addition to the public advice as offered above. His strictures over a female Chelsea novelist, for instance, appear in a ms. 'The Rotten Novel: a Blessing', to which 'Frustration: a Blessing', about 'John, Joan, and other people in plenty' with a 'chorus behind the scenes' seems a companion piece. 'Joad and Psychoanalysis' is a combative response to 'Joad's contribution to the *Rationalist Annual*, 1946, pp. 65-75' and in the Archive is accompanied by letters to the editor of *The New English Weekly* (20 December, 1945, 11 January, 1946, and 17 January, 1946 – the last two being typed on the reverse of letters to the *Sheffield Weekly Telegraph*, 20 November, 1945, and to H. Grotte, 6 January, 1946).

Appendix

Two Stories and a Play

Two Stories and a Play

The Archive contains a number of stories and poems that are, in effect, exercises in applied psychology. Of the two stories included here, the first, 'Freedom from Freedom', dates from late 1945 or after and was apparently unpublished; the second, 'Don Juan Again', appeared in Kite, *December 1945, p. 16.*

Freedom from Freedom

He was acquitted. Charged with the murder of his wife who had vanished from their home, who had had a secret lover, secret to everybody but him, who . . . no point in repeating the whole story. He was acquitted.

He was acquitted. He repeated the words . . . the words repeated themselves over and over again.

He had proved his innocence. True, there was a flaw about it. He wasn't innocent. To be exact, he had murdered his wife.

He had done it cleverly. Need he tell you how? He was acquitted. Was he glad about it? He thought he was. Something fishy about thinking so.

The day of his acquittal should have meant an appointment with happiness. He was disappointed.

Walking home, he realized that he started thinking mad things.

Did I murder her in order not to murder him? In order to save him from her? Rubbish. Did I murder her in order not to be guilty of murdering him? Did I murder her in order to be guilty of something? But I am not guilty. "Not guilty." But I am guilty. Terribly guilty. Why haven't I murdered someone else? I could murder someone for my murdering her. Why am I feeling so guilty? Because I loved her. Because I love her. Why did I kill her then? Because I wanted to prove that I didn't love her.

Why haven't they sentenced me? Why haven't they sentenced me? I could have proved then that I loved her after all. I want to prove that I love her after all. Shall I kill myself?

Slowly he ascended the stairs to their . . . to his home. His home. His own home.

I shall enter this home, my home, for the first time as a free man. Free from her, free from fear of punishment, free!!! Don't I believe myself? Can I never be satisfied? Not even now? If I kill myself I'm free from myself. But not before. That's the trouble, not before.

"Stop repeating phrases," he said aloud, and opened the door.

He walked about the rooms. Her belongings did not touch him. She hadn't touched him for a long time, anyway. But he had touched her, ha, ha, some farewell touch. It was a trifle rude to think like that. So what.

I am free! I just have to realize it. I am free! I think I feel it now; I am free!

What was that? A scrap of paper, a phone number scribbled on it, her handwriting.

He dialled. He asked for him. They gave him another number.

He dialled again, with the immediacy of hesitation overcome.

He asked him for a meeting.

For some reason or other he didn't do it cleverly this time. Maybe that was why he gave himself up to the police.

Don Juan Again

And so, for the . . . tieth time, he kissed for the first time. True, it was innocence that he was after. But innocence never had anything to do with the woman. Innocent was everyone whom HE touched for the first time. If she had been touched before, well, he couldn't help it; or was it even better then? Not that he couldn't tell – he didn't want to tell: he could tell too much. Never was there any thrill in his mind, only in his body, or maybe also just in that portion of his mind that was attached to his body.

Part of the tragedy, he thought, as he felt an innocent though thoroughly experienced tongue, was not that he had no pleasure in morality, it was that he had none in immorality. His pleasures had nothing to do with morality, either way round. Those who hated him envied him for something he hadn't got.

Oh, that he could never kiss without thinking of the woman before and the one after.

Into his kisses, he wanted to say: "You are a whore, or let's say a bore, because there is something in your kisses that tastes of the kisses of the one before you."

In a way, there was only one Woman to him, and she always had betrayed him with him. Don Juan was his own rival.

And what about the woman after? Why, as he kissed, had he to think of her? Because the present woman was already passed? No – because the present one showed how past the future one would be.

And beneath all this, there was the yearning for the woman whom, after he'd had her, he could forget. These fools, they thought he forgot every woman; none could he forget. That was another part of the tragedy. To him, miscarried hopes were unredeemed promises. And unredeemed promises one does not forget.

Where was the woman who could envelop his mind, in whom he could forget himself, and whom he could therefore forget afterwards?

He kissed, and kissed his . . . tieth first kisses with the passion of the desperate. Sadly he looked at this passion.

The woman, quivering under his kisses, suddenly noticed that his eyes were always open.

"I am looking at me, darling, I am looking at me!" he replied to the pain in her heart. The truth did not console her, nor was there anything consoling for her in it. Besides, she didn't understand what he meant.

She wanted him and he came to her.

And whilst he whispered: "Never could I love anyone more than I love you", and whilst she thought he lied, he knew that he spoke the bitter, bitter truth.

NOTES

Source

About 'The Factory Journal' *Kite* in which 'Don Juan Again' appeared, Alison Garnham writes (in *Hans Keller and the BBC*, London, Ashgate, 2003, p. 12) that it

> . . . was a publication whose policy was 'presenting the best which the writer in industry has to offer'. According to the editorial in the issue in which Keller's story appeared (the fourth), its contributors were 'all factory workers', and it is unclear from Keller's correspondence with the magazine why they decided to depart from this policy in his case. Certainly his contributor's biography looks unusual among those of the metal turners and electricians who appeared alongside him.

Keller included the last two sentences of 'Don Juan Again' in his early aphorisms printed in Part I above.

Stories, Poems and Other Genres: A Report

Other stories, or fragments of stories of this time include: 'Escape', 'Mens Sana in What?', 'Shameless, not Shameful' (fictional letter 'to an unkown lovee'), 'A Lady Weary of Life' (fragment), 'Appointments with Boredom' (a study of 'Sunday afternoon in Kensington Gardens', with the fourth of its five typescript pages missing), 'The Impatient Patient', 'The Rival', and 'A Short Story without a Point'. One of the most substantial stories is in German and occupies 5 pages of typescript: 'Nichts erfährst du durch Erfahrung' ('Nothing do you learn from experience'). A further item entitled 'Short Stories' comprises 36 stories of 1,2, or 3 lines apiece, e.g. 'He claimed to make history whilst undoing it'; 'She spent a sleepless night because he did not wake her'; etc. There is a novel which went no further than a first page and a 2-page postscript: *Ursache und Schuld: Roman von Hans Heinrich Keller*; this comes with a fragmentary page, 'Der Engländer in uns.'

Of Keller's poems, which are again applied psychology, two examples are included below: the first is marked in the typescript 13 October, 1950; the typeface of the second suggests more or less the same date. Other poems from this time include: 'Song of the Potentially Happy', 'Truth and Tact', '!', 'Upright', 'Lies', 'Future's Pimples' and 'Antisemitism' ('When a Jew/Has a flu/That's something new', included in the play *Antiwhatism* (below)).

Keller was in fact diffident about his relation to verse. In a letter to John Greening of 3 December, 1980 kept in the Archive, he writes, 'as you know, my understanding of poetry is sub-normal'. (See Alison Garnham, *Hans Keller and the BBC*, London, Ashgate, 2003, p. 11.) Yet his experience at versifying seems to have been useful for his later work on opera texts (as with his original libretto for the posthumously performed *Der Turm*, to music by Josef Tal).

The Other Consummation

Unforgetting, with one higher and one lower brow
He approached her room.
He would never do it if he didn't do it now.
Undecided, he decided on the smaller, nearer,
                        rather than the larger, latent doom.

The door gave way to his fume.
What would she be doing now?
She lay naked on their bed.
But instead
He kicked up the first decided row.

A Short History of the World

There was a time when every thought was new,
And every prostitute enjoyed a cup of tea;
When our self seemed more or less a You,
And our commonplace made us see.

The time is over; so is our life:
We live a debt which nobody can pay
Except for God – but He Himself is eighty-five:
For all he cares He may not live another day.

(*Note* This is very morbid.) [HK]

Other writings from the early 1940s show Keller trying more genres still. An (unsuccessful) entry for a BBC variety show beginning 'Ladies and gentle males . . .' reveals a strain of whimsy that was to pervade his life's work. There are also three entries for literary competitions, 'Six of the world's best books to be left behind when setting out for a desert island' (*Time and Tide*), 'Special Home and Overseas Competition' and notably 'What one book . . . would you particularly recommend for reading during the later years of life' (*John o' London's Weekly*).

Antiwhatism

A One-act Experiment Including Some Moral or Other

Have we the courage plainly to indicate what they mean,
Even if they mean nothing above the meaningless?

CHARACTERS (*in alphabetical order*)

Helen (Thorpe)
Herbert
Maid
Muriel, Herbert's wife
Rosenbergh
Spencer, Muriel's brother

Note According to the writer's views, directions are given sparingly in order to enable actors and producer to make essential use of their creative abilities.

Antiwhatism

London. Herbert's and Muriel's flat: living-room. Evening. Herbert and Muriel.

Herbert It's idiotic. As far as I am concerned anyone can seduce almost anyone, I don't care, and if I care I don't care whether or not it's a Jew who does the seducing.

Muriel You don't see the point, darling. It's perfectly typically Jewish, the whole thing. It isn't that Rosenbergh has no values; I suppose he's got them all right. But they only crop up where he is dealing with Jews, his own 'chosen' lot. A Gentile girl is . . . well, you know what I mean. They're all like that, these Jewish gentlemen, and then they complain about anti-Semitism!

Herbert I married you because you were stupid, darling, but I slowly realize that I myself was stupid enough not to know that stupidity can be irritating at times, at least in marriage.

Muriel Don't start an intimate quarrel with your wife, nobody is listening. Besides, our impersonal and serious quarrel is much more important.

Herbert Why something that concerns a third person should be impersonal I can't see.

Muriel Ah, but it isn't impersonal because it concerns a third person, but because it doesn't. It concerns a race.

Herbert Does it?

Muriel Now really, I can't start the whole argument all over again.

Herbert I'm sure you could, darling, I'm quite sure you could. But I'm relieved to hear that you think you can't. There's some hope that you won't.

Muriel I told you once before there was no point in joking about it.

Herbert I'm joking about you.

Muriel You're always joking about anti-Semitism.

Herbert I'm always joking when I want to cry, but see that there wouldn't be any point in crying. This, my dear, is humour, a thing which you haven't got, and, by the way, a thing the Jews have got very extensively.

Muriel Why bring it into connection with Jews? You just said you'd got it; well, you aren't a Jew.

Herbert Why bring seduction into connection with the Jews? (*Spencer enters and joins the company; Herbert continues.*) What the devil is typically Jewish about seduction? I for my part even object to bringing seduction into primary connection with men, but that may be sex prejudice. Anyway, that's beside the point. Now then, I ask you, why should Jews be born seducers?

Spencer <u>They have no guts,</u> that's what it is. Look at Rosenbergh and imagine a decent chap in his place. Why a decent chap might have raped Helen, or something; I mean, he'd have made a straightforward affair out of it, even if he'd been a criminal. But what does Rosenbergh do? He . . .

Herbert Now look here, although I quite agree that rape is indicative of a higher virtue . . .

Muriel Stop it. This is not a thing to be stupidly funny about. It's really distasteful that such a thing should happen to a girl who is a friend of ours, or at any rate is going to be one . . .

Herbert How do you know? We wouldn't know anything of her or about her if Spencer hadn't run after her and, well, failed to rape her . . .

Spencer I don't like the level this conversation is descending to. Yes, yes, I did run after her; I did want to make love to her; but, dearest brother-in-law, I did not intend to make her a baby. Yes I also admit that I'm jealous, but I don't admit that my jealousy has anything to do with me regarding Rosenbergh's doings a dirty Jewish business.

Muriel   'Jewish' will do, 'dirty' is a pleonasm or whatever you call it.

Herbert   As I was saying, we don't know much about Helen, nor, for that matter, do we know a great deal about Rosenbergh, except that he's doing nothing. So . . .

Muriel   It's quite a lot if you know of a chap that he isn't doing anything. It throws a lot of light on him. Especially when he is a Jew.

Herbert   Laziness can be a virtue as well as a vice. It depends on what the fellow would do instead of being lazy.

Spencer   I don't exactly like that line of yours. Rosenbergh could have said such a thing, or some other Jewish intellectual could. Because it sounds like Oscar Wilde. Decadent stuff, I mean.

Herbert   Anyway, Wilde wasn't a Jew, was he?

Spencer   He could have been one, that's the point.

Herbert   So could you, you're just enough of an anti-Semite for a certain type of them.

Spencer   (*ignoring Herbert's remark*) Wilde also got into trouble about that sex business, as all Jews do, or would do, if they weren't too smart to be caught. Sex, that's their sphere. Just remember Freud. And they always get away with it. Rosenbergh left London yesterday.

Muriel   Did he really? The day before yesterday I dropped him a line asking him to come here tonight. In part Herbert incited me to do that. He said he always liked to talk with objects of rumours, because such a talk regularly turned out to be either a moral duty or else a pleasure. If the rumour was exaggerated, he said, it was a moral duty to destroy it. If on the other hand the rumour included too little, it was a pleasure to destroy it and circulate a more appropriate one.

Spencer   Rumours are in any case despicable.

Herbert   Not when they are called 'information' . . . by those who forgot why they wanted them.

Muriel   Anyhow, Rosenbergh replied at once indicating that he would be pleased to come.

Spencer   Ha. He would say that. And I bet you he won't come. "He would be pleased to come." He can tell that to the Jews. He knows alright that we like Helen and he won't be keen on spending an evening with people who like her in another way than he 'likes' her, or liked her. Why, how could a Jew have the courage to come? Anyway, it isn't very probable that he'll come. To say the least, it's unlikely. Unless of course some Jewish cheek is working in him. But even then, he wouldn't dare to face decent people on that issue. (*Pause. Then Spencer gets up.*) Anyway, I'm off because I don't want to meet him.

Herbert   Never mind, old chap, please do stay. There are enemies whom we want out of the way and there are enemies whom we want right in the way in order that we [can] say that we want them out of it. I suppose the Jews want the anti-Semites out of the way, and the anti-Semites want the Jews in the way. So be a good little anti-Semite and don't rush away. After all, you don't meet a bloody Jew and a bloody rival all in one every day, do you?

Muriel   (*reproachfully, but not very forcefully*) Herbert!

Herbert   (*kissing her*) Bliss No. 2 of married life is that you're always called by your proper name when you say something improper.

Spencer   (*still standing*) What then is bliss No. 1?

Herbert   Brothers-in-law who don't run away but keep sisters' husbands company. Look here, as you said, Rosenbergh may not come, at any rate he'd be a fool if he did, well, and then I'd be quite alone with my wife. If I would be an anti-Semite I would yet say that there's one thing which is still worse than a Jew, and that is a wife and nothing but a wife. She gives you an opportunity to experience the agonies of being alone and of not being alone all at once.

(*Spencer sits down again, temporarily as it were.*)

Muriel   Darling, Spencer told you before, he didn't like the level of this conversation. You must treat anti-Semitism seriously, even if you don't agree with it.

Herbert   (*teasingly*) Must you? (*After a pause, more seriously*) Perhaps you must. Yes, maybe you must. Anyway I can't. Really, I cannot. I can't treat something as serious which seems utterly nonsensical to me. People like you two have been [trained] seriously with little success. You just go on delivering your nasty nonsense. Perhaps people like me have a function in laughing – instead of fighting – that nonsense down.

Muriel   Herbert darling, please don't talk to me like that. For a moment you sounded as if I were your enemy. This rotten business isn't worth, er, isn't worth . . .

Herbert   (*smiling again*) Well, don't tell me then to treat anti-Semitism seriously. That would involve taking you seriously . . . well you know where married life comes to if things are once going that way.

Spencer   Sometimes I think you would have made quite a good Jew. They're just as cynical as you are, only you're really a decent fellow below it; but . . .

Herbert   (*impatiently*) We've had that before. Skip it, I really can't bear it. If anti-Semitism weren't the most indecent thing you can imagine, it would still remain the most boring one.

Muriel   Sententiousness doesn't substitute arguments, darling.

Herbert   That depends. Surely my sententiousness more than substitutes your arguments?

Spencer   You're side-tracking all the time.

Herbert   When one has been led round a circle for a number of times, one naturally tries to find a way out of it.

Muriel   And always these abstract things! They're tiring.

Herbert   When I'm tired I'm tiring back.

Spencer   You certainly are.

Herbert   Tired?

Muriel   Tiring! Now who is the one who is circling?

Herbert   The trouble is we, or some of us, aren't clever enough to talk about one and the same subject all the time. If you stick to one subject you either . . .

(*A bell*)

Spencer   Rosenbergh!

Muriel   Keep quiet.

Maid   (*enters*) Miss Thorpe!

Herbert   (*to Spencer*) Helen! So you were wrong. Or right, if we consider your first prognosis.

(*Meanwhile Helen has entered and the maid left the room. Helen is an unusually attractive girl.*)

Helen   Good evening . . .

Herbert   How are you, Miss Thorpe? So glad you dropped in.

Spencer   Hello Helen, how are you?

Helen   Hello, Spencer, how are you? (*To Muriel*) I must apologize for . . .

Muriel   Do sit down. Well, and how are you, my dear?

Helen   Oh, I'm fine, thank you? How are you?

Muriel   I'm so glad you've come . . .

Spencer   I hope you're keeping fine, Helen?

Helen   Oh yes, I'm very well, thank you.

Herbert   (*prestissimo*) And how am I? I don't know, thank you. I'll tell you next week because I can only tell in retrospect, thank you. And thus I take the liberty to close this subject, thank you.

(*Laughter*)

Spencer   We were just talking about anti-Semitism.

(*Herbert releases an unsuccessfully suppressed sigh.*)

Helen   Oh really? That's very funny, because this morning I saw a nice little poem about anti-Semitism in the *Thinker's Magazine*, quite simple and obvious, maybe too obvious, but it was really logical. Mummy said it was cheap and you ought to treat such a problem seriously, but I didn't think it was so bad . . . did any of you see it by chance?

(*General indications of "No"*)

Spencer   I must have a look at it. It's good to be simple and obvious about the Jews.

Helen   I know it by heart, I think.

Spencer   Come, out with it.

Helen   –

> When a Jew
> Has a flu
> That's something new.
>
> Seeing him lie in bed
> They presently see red,
> And write to the *Evening Gazette*:
>
> 'Sir, what I say is true:
> Immediate action is due
> Against the Jewish flu!'
> (Or else the fluish Jew.)

(*Spencer is taken aback, wants to say something, but is anticipated by Herbert.*)

Herbert   Very nice, as far as spirit and that sort of thing goes. I don't like the setting, though, makes you feel the whole thing is a bagatelle.

Spencer   Curious that you should say so. This poem could have been by you.

Herbert   As a matter of fact, it is.

(*General surprise, especially on the part of Muriel*)

Herbert   Some time ago when, er, when the subject, er, we talked about before started circling amongst us, I received an express inspiration, er well, well and so on.

Spencer   Helen, that <u>you</u> should like the spirit behind this poem, er, er, at the present time, is something that is thoroughly beyond me.

Helen   Why I don't understand what you mean.

Herbert   Never mind what Spencer means, it's even less important than what he says.

Helen   (*to Spencer*) What do you mean by "at the present time"? You're shy about it, so has it something to do with my being pregnant?

(*Spencer is shocked.*)

Herbert   You mustn't talk to him like that, Miss Thorpe, he has a collection of things in mind which for some mysterious reason he regards as dirty. Amongst them are sex and J . . .

Helen   (*breaks in innocently*) Oh well, to be honest, formerly people didn't talk about sex because they were ashamed of it. Nowadays they talk about it for the same reason. So much, then, for my straightforwardness.

(*A bell*)

Herbert   (*to Helen*) That might be Mr. Rosenbergh. Did you know that he might be coming here tonight?

Helen   No. I haven't seen him for some time.

(*The maid has entered*)

Maid   Mr. Rosenbergh.

(*They await Mr. Rosenbergh's entry and the maid's exit in silence.*)

Herbert   (*to Rosenbergh*) So glad to see you, double.

(*During this dialogue with Herbert, Rosenbergh transmits his silent greetings to all the others.*)

Rosenbergh   At the present moment, I'm single.

Herbert   Why, are you going to marry somebody?

Rosenbergh   Good heavens, no! I de-married someone not long ago. What did you mean by double, anyway?

Herbert   Spencer (*points at Spencer*) thinks that if I weren't I, I could be you.

Rosenbergh   So you could, I should think. In fact I wouldn't be at all surprised if you exhibited undreamed-of capacities as soon as you weren't you.

Spencer   (*to Rosenbergh, offensively*) We were talking about anti-Semitism when this theme, er, of doubles, er, came to our minds.

Rosenbergh   Were you really? I don't see the connection, but that may be all to the good because people too often tend to see connections where there are none.

Herbert   (*to Spenser, interpetatively*) He means that this may also apply to anti-Semitism.

Rosenbergh   Pleased to hear that I meant that. It's always nice to learn how clever one is. In fact one way of becoming intelligent is to surround oneself with intelligent listeners.

Muriel   Mr. Rosenbergh, we would like to have a number of things straight out tonight. In view of this fact (if I may be honest) I first thought it unfortunate that Miss Thorpe was here, but I gather she's a very straightforward girl, so perhaps it will be just as well for her to be present.

Helen   You are alluding to my past relation with Mr. Rosenbergh and to my future child. Though I have no secrets in that direction may I ask you what business that is of yours? Mind you, I'm not offended and I don't want to offend you, I'm just interested in *your* interest in, well, what really is my own business.

Rosenbergh   But Helen, have you ever seen people who are interested in their own business? That's why nobody knows anything about his own business. He – with 'he' I mean any somebody who's a nobody – wants to learn about human nature, about other human natures, to be sure; in other words, he wants somebody whom he can abuse.

Herbert   You're quite right, but I plead to be excepted from this charge. Or rather, I'd like to qualify it as far as it refers to me. I do want people whom I can abuse, but they must be abusing people.

Rosenbergh   Charge withdrawn, as far as you are concerned.

Spencer   Mr. Rosenbergh, I think we are the people who are going to do a bit of charging tonight, and you are the one to be charged.

Rosenbergh   I can assure you that I do not doubt that you think that.

Helen   Now really, all this preposterous.

Herbert   The only thing to do is to smile. It is a very great art to be able to start smiling and afterwards to find something to smile about. In fact it is, if I be allowed to make a colourless and therefore serious interjection, the art of life which I have now been describing in minute detail.

Rosenbergh   The art of life consists in dying without having even noticed that one has lived. The art of anything consists in having done the anything without having too much noticed that one has done it.

Spencer   All this is quite incorrect.

Rosenbergh   It never was intended to be correct and therefore has little chance to be *quite* incorrect.

Spenser   It is quite impossible to argue in this way.

Rosenbergh   Thank heaven that you realise this. It's always impossible to argue; the only thing one can attempt is to make people realise now and then that there's no point in their trying to start arguing.

Helen   One can argue with oneself.

Herbert   Yes, but one can never convince oneself, unless one tries to convince oneself of something which is the opinion of someone with whom one is in love.

Rosenbergh   That sentence definitely was too long; for the rest it was alright.

Muriel   What I intended to say was . . .

Spencer   Perhaps it would be better if I told Mr. Rosenbergh what we intended to say to him, and what we intended him to explain to us.

Herbert   It certainly would not be better.

Rosenbergh   It doesn't make any difference.

Spencer   It does, because I'm going to come straight to the point, whilst Muriel wouldn't do so. Mr. Rosenbergh, I told you before, we intend to charge you . . .

Muriel   Now don't let's talk about it in this way. We feel that Miss Thorpe – may I say Helen – hasn't been treated very nicely by you, Mr. Rosenbergh, and we just want to know, I mean we naturally want to ascertain, whether this is really true, and if so, whether we can help her a little, and whether we can bring Mr. Rosenbergh to . . . well, to be frank, we want to show him how . . . how not at all nice his attitude is, er, has been.

Rosenbergh   Why people always state their first reasons last.

Herbert   That's not true, not always, not even mostly. In most cases they don't state their first reasons at all.

Helen   In most cases they don't know them.

Rosenbergh   In many cases they knew them and cowardly forgot them

Muriel   Anyway, that's neither here nor there.

Rosenbergh   On the contrary, it's almost everywhere. Let's take an imaginary instance which by utter chance would seem to happen to occur to me, a man sleeps with a woman, she gets a child, he doesn't marry her. Why doesn't he marry her? Think of the coward's reasons! But think of them only, don't tell me them, or else I'll go sick. And the worst thing is, he has forgotten his first reasons. He has reached the most abject stage of hypocrisy, namely that where he does no longer know that he is a hypocrite.

Herbert   Oh yes, I quite agree, the worst hypocrite is the honest one.

Rosenbergh   Precisely. Now take one of those few who have some courage left in them, as for instance, to take a slightly less imaginary example, myself.

Herbert   Nobody is so imaginary as oneself is. For it is primarily oneself whom one habitually imagines to be different from oneself.

Rosenbergh   I grant that. What I was going to say was that my simple, and truly first reasons why I do not marry Helen are, one, that I don't like her and two, well, let's remain brave and let it be one reason only.

Spencer   (*to Helen*) And what have you to say to this, Helen?

Helen   As I don't like him either I can't be cross with him, or with fate, or something, can I? Nor does it matter whether he likes me or not, because naturally I wouldn't marry him even he would like to.

Muriel   May I know then how the whole thing started?

Rosenbergh   No. But you may know that I liked her, and that she liked me.

Spencer   (*to Helen*) Is that true, Helen?

Helen   Yes

Herbert   The whole thing is a subject for a bad play of . . ty years ago.

Rosenbergh   And for a good play of today. The more intellectually commonplace a subject becomes, the better the play must be if it wants to be a play. Besides, the subject is only *intellectually* commonplace, as I said. Emotionally it remains a hit, as the majority of ladies and gentlemen present could testify – if they were amongst the courageous I talked about a minute ago.

Muriel   (*to Rosenbergh*) Please do not be insulting. We don't insult you, though we could.

Herbert   (*to Muriel*) I humbly doubt whether you could, darling.

Rosenbergh   That's what I was going to say, had it not been for a reminder just received not to be insulting. Anyhow, the reason why I was invited here tonight was that very hope for the emotional hit . . . but since it's a commonplace intellectually, I may be permitted to start yawning. (*He does not yawn.*)

Spencer   You are clever, Mr. Rosenbergh, but you do not know, er, that there are wider implications involved in our interest in your doings, implications, if I may say so, er, of a sociological, er or rather anthropological nature.

Rosenbergh   (*to Herbert*) What does he mean? Is he out of his mind?

Spencer   (*to Rosenbergh*) You'd better appreciate that I do not express myself more directly. (*Silence. Gradually a thoughtful smile manifests itself on Rosenbergh's face.*)

Rosenbergh   Something begins to dawn on me. (*To Helen*) Does it by any chance dawn inside you, too?

Helen   It does. And something else is dawning too, quite vehemently.

Rosenbergh   Something else? Ah, perhaps I see what you mean.

Spencer   I do not quite see what Helen or Mr. Rosenbergh should mean by "something else", though I quite see what is at last dawning upon Mr. Rosenbergh's mind. But you, Helen, didn't you know from the beginning . . .

Helen   Listen, Spencer . . .

Rosenbergh   Don't! For the love of my not loving you, *please* Helen shut up! You know I never asked you for a favour before.

Helen   Oh yes you did, you asked me some time ago why I ever cared for you. (*To Herbert*) That, he said, was the only thing about me he couldn't understand.

Rosenbergh   Yes, just as the only thing I can understand about myself is why I care for myself.

Helen   (*further to Herbert*) That *was* asking for a big favour, wasn't it? To tell a man for whom you don't care why you cared for him.

Herbert   I can understand that, for an honest girl like you it must mean doing a favour if you decide to do some lying.

Helen   Why lying?

Herbert   One never cared for someone for whom one doesn't care.

Rosenbergh   Look at him, he's starting to moralize. May I remind him that one never cares for people for whom one cared?

Herbert   Oh, spare me that stuff. Modern Don Juans ought to think of something less tedious.

Rosenbergh   They would like to, but they can't. They experience it all the time. That's just why – as you say – it's boring. If the truth weren't so boring there would be more interest in it.

Helen   (*to Spencer*) You might remember that tonight when you lie in bed. It's . . .

Rosenbergh   (*to Helen*) Stop it.

Muriel   We seem to be drifting from what we wanted to discuss.

Rosenbergh   Quite. We wanted to discuss the subject 'man seduces girl', and there also seems to be a small but essential number of intentions to discuss, or to allude to – Jews or anti-

Semitism. We shall begin with the first mentioned subject. Mr Rosenbergh, why did you seduce that girl? Because . . .

Muriel   I don't think the level on which you start this is quite . . .

Rosenbergh   (*very decidedly, to the surprise of all*) Never mind about levels. I'm going to start and to finish in my own way and if you don't like it you can turn me out of here. I have come here for the sole purpose of enjoying myself. In fact I'm going to enjoy myself more than I expected and, what's more, I'm also going to make Helen enjoy herself. Is that true, Helen, or not?

Helen   The enjoyment will be, well, a little childish, but I'd better be honest and admit, well, that there may be fun.

Muriel   I think I am completely mystified.

Herbert   I know Spencer is. But Rosenbergh, you forgot me. I'm enjoying myself immensely already.

Rosenbergh   So you should. But I wanted to add that since the poor seduced girl admits that she is going to have fun, you'd better let me have my way, for after all you wanted to do something for that girl, didn't you? Now then I resume my interrogation. Mr. Rosenbergh, tell us in your own words why you seduced Helen. Because I have no will power. The disquieting thing about will power is that people who are suffering from it succumb to it completely. They walk about willing things instead of doing them. I, on the other hand, being not affiliated by this disease, did what I didn't want to do. Not that I wanted to do anything else, in fact I'm never wanting.

Herbert   Spencer thought before you came that you were.

Muriel   I think all this is unbearable.

Rosenbergh   I'll bear it for you. Mr. Rosenbergh, why don't you marry Helen. Because . . .

Spencer   I think there is no point in continuing with this.

Herbert   (*to Rosenbergh*) I would rather have asked you, why didn't you choose a married woman instead of Helen? Being what you are that would have been the most natural course.

Muriel   Herbert!

Herbert   I wasn't saying that it was desirable, darling, that he should seduce a married woman; I merely put the question why he, being what he is, did not do it.

Rosenbergh   In the first place, the one doesn't exclude the other. One can seduce married women, and one can seduce Helen. In fact, I seduced a married woman not long ago; the flaw about it was that she was married to me. However, that wasn't what (*to Herbert*) you meant. You meant, why don't I generally have affairs with married women? The answer is, because you never get rid of them. An unmarried woman will presently fall in love with someone else, but in the case of the married woman *one is the someone else*, and the husband is the deserted, happy one. And women are intolerably constant as far as the someone-elses are concerned.

Spencer   What you say is very, very obscene, and very, very, er, typical.

Rosenbergh   What you call, sir, obscene, is what you know is true but do not dare to say so. Being *really* obscene means saying something indecent. Maybe what I say is indecent, but it's far more decent than what people use to say who think and act as I do. I put it to you that it's more decent to be honest about oneself than to be honest about others. (*Further to Spencer*) I'm quite sure you are able to say just the same things as I do, only you don't speak in the first person, but you are talking of what *others* are doing and thinking. And then you think they are obscene, not you.

Herbert   (*to Rosenbergh*) The gist of your argument may be alright, but there are one or two fallacies . . .

Rosenbergh   There are just one or two abbreviations. For we have to get on to (directs his thumb towards Spencer) this gentleman's second observation, that what I say is typical.

Helen   (*to Rosenbergh*) Hurry up, I think I've had enough of it. I'm not curious about your private views, I want this situation solved.

Rosenbergh   Alright, alright, we're just coming to it. (*To Spencer*) Now may I begin by enquiring, what is typical of what?

Spencer   (*after a pause*) If you want it frankly, your, er, behaviour towards women, and your way of talking about sex, are typically Jewish.

Rosenbergh   Indeed. In view of such unexpected frankness I shall discontinue questioning myself, for there are now more important things which await . . .

Muriel   It might be as well if we told you now that all of us, perhaps with the exception of my husband, do not on the whole think much of Jews. I say all of us, because I want to take the liberty to include Helen. At present she may not yet be quite clear about these things, in fact she recited us what appeared to be a philo-Semitic poem, and seemed to approve it, but I'm pretty sure that in view of, er, her recent experiences she will soon come to see the Jewish case in its proper perspective, the anti-Semitic perspective that is, to be quite honest. So I'm including her amongst us. I'm a little older and a little more mature than she is, and I may therefore speak for her, not as she is at present, but as she will be. (*Warmly*) She is a nice girl, Helen is, and I think we shall care for her, and also for her child, although it will be half a Jew.

Herbert   You'll care for the Gentile, and I for the Jewish part.

Muriel   Herbert please, you may laugh about what you like, but really you mustn't laugh about whatever you choose.

Spencer   (*as offensively as he can, which is quite a lot*) Mr. Rosenbergh, we don't like Jews, and therefore we don't like you.

Rosenbergh   In itself, the inference is without a flaw. If I may return the compliment in a slightly modified version, you bore me. Don't take this to heart too seriously, though; you're not the only one who does that to me. I was born to life only to be bored to death.

Herbert   I propose a new anti-Semitic slogan: 'Let's bore the Jews to death!'

Rosenbergh   As soon as people will no longer be able to promote Jewish death or misery, they'll necessarily bore the Jews to death unless they cease to be anti-Semites.

Herbert   More active anti-Semitism won't stop so quickly. Like other nasty things, it is practiced by many who condemn it.

Rosenbergh   Well, it's less often condemned than other nasty things.

Herbert   Because it condemns.

Helen   Yes, it's easier to condemn the condemned than to condemn the condemnation.

Muriel   Really, Helen, I don't think you have an objective view of the whole problem. (*To Rosenbergh*) It is interesting how you succeed in infecting her mind although she does not like you.

Rosenbergh   Infecting with what?

Spencer   With a good opinion of bad men.

Rosenbergh   (*to Spencer*) has it never occurred to you that it might just be that you infect people's minds with a bad opinion of good men?

Muriel   (*to Rosenbergh*)You would even suggest that all Jews are good? Of course you would . .

Rosenbergh   Would you kindly let me answer your question before you answer it . . .

Helen   (*to Rosenbergh, impatiently*) You said you'd come to the point. Please don't get lost somewhere else, I can't stand it much longer.

(*Pause*)

Rosenbergh   <u>Alright</u>.

(*Pause*)

Rosenbergh   (*to Spencer*) Please answer me this question . . .

Muriel   Mr. Rosenbergh, when I come to think of it, I find it shameless, well, and typical, that you haven't left this place, after all the insults you received tonight.

Rosenbergh   You can never find things shameless late enough. (*To Spencer*) You were saying a little while ago that you quite saw what was then dawning on me. Well, what did you see?

Spencer   I suppose you discovered at long last that we knew you were a Jew.

Rosenbergh   On the contrary. I discovered after a relatively short period that you did not know that I was not a Jew. I do hope that I have spoken clearly enough and that you will prove capable of taking it in.

(*Consternation*)

Muriel   Did you say . . . did you say you weren't a Jew?

Rosenbergh   Now listen again carefully. I admit it's pretty bad news: I am no Jew, and what's distinctly more – or less – in this case, I never was one.

Spencer   But . . . but . . . but how did we come to know, er, to think, that he was one?

Muriel   I . . . I don't know. Didn't Elsie say . . .

Herbert   Never mind what Elsie said. Congratulations old girl, rejoice, my dearest wife, you may care now for a fully Gentile child! And I needn't care for anybody.

Helen   (*rising, to Herbert*) Before I go I just want to go into what you said just now.

Herbert   Who, I? I'm sorry if I've hurt your feelings in any way, it was just a silly joke . . .

Helen   Oh no, you haven't hurt me in any way. But what you said just now reminded me that what your wife said about my child this evening was, well, was perhaps the only correct observation she made this evening.

(*Pause*)

Herbert   I think I see. (*To Muriel*) So it looks as if I'll have to care for half the child after all.

Muriel   What do you mean?

Herbert   You mean, what does Miss Thorpe mean? Miss Thorpe, darling, has just communicated to us the fact that her child will be half a Jew after all. It therefore looks as if Miss Thorpe is a Jewess. Do you see, darling?

Spencer   (*to Helen*) Is that true?

Helen   It is true. And with that I thank the hostess for a highly interesting, and, may I add, fairly disgusting evening. Goodbye.

(*Exit*)

Herbert   That's that, to summarize.

(*Lengthy pause.*)

Herbert   Well, we could turn the argument upside down now, couldn't we? Gentile rascal seduces Jewish girl, and the rest of it. Of course it would be equally idiotic. Apart from arguments which you can't have both ways, there are some which you can't have either way.

Spencer   (*slowly recovering from consternation*) You don't understand, Herbert. You want to generalize. The fact that one indecent man has proved not to be a Jew is no proof that all indecent men aren't Jews.

Rosenbergh   I suppose not even then, not even if there weren't any indecent Jews, would you get tired of anti-Semitising.

Herbert   It seems that anti-Semitism is the only Jewish historical and modern theme that hasn't got anything to do with the Jews.

Rosenbergh   Judging by what we witnessed tonight that would almost appear to be correct. However, Helen, or any other Jew, would probably not agree with you.

Spencer   Nor would an anti-Semite.

Herbert   True, an anti-Semite never would but a Jew would agree if he saw what I meant.

Muriel   Herbert darling, I think I'm going to bed. Kindly excuse me, gentlemen. Goodnight. (*Exit*)

Rosenbergh   Now, though I would never call myself an anti-Semite, I don't like the thought that the fact that I seduced and did not marry Helen was considered typically Jewish. I never behave typically Jewish as far as sexual matters are concerned. A typical Jew <u>hasn't got the guts</u> to do the things I'm doing. He's got a terrible lot of family-sense and therefore marries all the time. No really, regarding sex, Jews are terribly banal and virtuous.

Spencer   (*with some relief, however uncertain, to hear something in the nature of an anti-Semitic remark from Rosenbergh, to Herbert*) Well, there you are! Rosenbergh himself doesn't like the Jews. There you are.

Herbert   Am I?

Curtain

NOTES

Source

The typescript includes a few corrections and suggests a date sometime in the 1940s, possibly – and notwithstanding the command of language and genre – as early as 1942, given the shared concerns of this and the early 'Jewish' writings in German (see Part I above). There is no indication that the play was ever performed. In the manuscript Keller typically double-spaced each letter of those words intended for special emphasis. This double spacing has been replaced here by underlining.

The play focuses a host of issues and traits typical of Keller's early years: 'anti-Semitics', sexual mores, social comedy, differentiation between the genders, a thorough-going application of psychologism, and a delight in (structural) paradox and aphoristic diction (principally with the Wilde-like Rosenbergh, possibly named (ironically) after the 'pseudo-synthesizing' Nazi Alfred Rosenberg described in Keller's essay, 'On National Socialism and "Being German" ' printed in Part I above).

Antiwhatism also prepares the ground for later dramatic work: the 2-act play, Is Opera Really Necessary? (Opera, 2/7, June 1951, pp. 337-45, and 2/8, July 1951, pp. 402-09); the original libretto for Der Turm (Josef Tal, 1986); and the libretti for Hamlet (after William Shakespeare, Humphrey Searle, London, Faber, 1967) and Marching Song (after John Whiting, Benjamin Frankel, 1971-72). The experience would have fed into his translations into and out of German of some of the later dramatic works of Benjamin Britten: The Golden Vanity (1967), The Prodigal Son (1968), and Death in Venice (1975).

Keller does not refer to, and may not have known Arnold Schoenberg's remarks on anti-Semitism and in-turned Jewish aggression. These appear in the second of two speeches on the Jewish situation (1935). See: Arnold Schoenberg, *Style and Idea*, edited by Leonard Stein, London, Faber, 1980, pp. 501-04.

Index

Excluding references to Hans Keller and the topics listed in the table of contents

Abady, Temple 169
Abraham, Gerald 204
Abraham, Karl 122, 144, 207
Adler, Oskar 40-1
Adorno, Theodor 79, 232-35
Altenberg, Peter 9-10
Alwyn, William 169
Anti-Semitism 25, 266-78
Aristotle 21
Arnold, Malcolm 166
Atcherson, Renée xiii
Attwood, Thomas 185
Auric, Georges 161-69

Bach, J. C. 176, 181, 185
Bach, J. S. 5, 8, 152, 200, 202-03, 217, 233-34, 248
Bales, R. E. xvii
Bardus, Willy xvi
Barnes, James and Patience 79-82
Bartók, Béla xvi, 199, 251-52
Bax, Arnold 169
Beethoven, Ludwig van xii, 152, 174, 179, 182, 194, 197-98, 200, 202, 227, 233, 237, 239, 241, 248-49, 251
Benjamin, Arthur 161-63
Berg, Alban 225, 227, 231, 241
Black, Stanley 169
Blanco, Matte xviii
Bleuler, Eugen 236
Blom, Eric 212, 246
Boccherini, Luigi 183-90
Böcklin, Arnold 82
Bollas, Christopher xviii
Brahms, Johannes 172, 174, 181, 200, 202, 211, 236, 248
Brett, Philip 144
Bridgewater, Leslie 169
Brill, A. 73
British Psychological Society xiv
Britten, Benjamin xii-xiii, xvi, 121-60, 169, 170-82, 194, 200-03, 207-08, 211, 215-19, 227, 231, 251, 278
    Peter Grimes 121-48, 227
    Rape of Lucretia 149-51
    The Little Sweep 151-60
    Albert Herring 154, 225-31

Bruckner, Anton 10-11
Büchner, Georg 225, 229
Busch, Fritz 199
Bush, Alan 191-92
Busoni, Ferruccio 172-3, 179
Byron, Lord 5, 26

Capell, Richard 256
Capital punishment 31
Carnap, Rudolf 241
Catell, R. B. 100
Chaplin, Charles 24
Chamberlain, Neville 10-11, 80
Chesterton, G. K. 166
Chijs, A. van der xv
Chissell, Joan 237
Chopin, Fryderyk 167, 237
Choisy, Maryse 219
Christie, Agatha 192
Christoff, Boris 204
Clare, Anthony 107
Clark, Edward 257
Clark, Ronald W. 238-41
Cocteau, Jean 163
Coleridge, Samuel 4
Colombos, C. J. 103
Coogan, Jackie 199
Corelli, Arcangelo 217
Cosman, Milein xiii, 117, 198-200
Crabbe, George 121, 132-33, 144
Crozier, Eric 150

Dale, Kathleen 237
Darwin, Charles 22
Davey, Cedric Thorpe 169
Davey, Henry 212
Delius, Frederick 257
De los Angeles, Victoria 204
Dent, Edward J. 172, 174
Denza, Luigi 217
Donington, Robert xviii
Dostoyevsky, Fyodor xiv, 4, 10-11, 23
Duncan, Ronald 149
Dvořak, Antonin 152

Easdale, Brian 169
Ebner, Mayer 25-6
Eden, Anthony 10-11
Einstein, Albert 238
Einstein, Alfred 170, 176-83, 236-37

Eisler, Hanns 168
Elgar, Edward 200, 203, 214-17
Ellis, Havelock xv, 47, 50, 90-1
Elster, Alexander xvi
Engels, Friedrich 21

Fauré, Gabriel 200, 203
Fenichel, Otto xv
Ferenczi, Sándor xv, 242
Ferrier, Kathleen 151
Feuerbach, Ludwig 21
Feuer, Cy 169
Fichte, Johann 5, 7, 23
Flagstad, Kirsten 204
Flothius, Marius 226-27
Flugel, Ingeborg 207
Flugel, J. C. xvi-xviii, 41, 47, 50, 57, 61, 68, 75-6,
     85, 93-4, 99, 112, 116-18, 122, 133, 140,
     145-48, 164, 211, 219
Forbstein, Leo F. 169
Forster, E. M. 144
Frankel, Benjamin 169, 278
Frederick the Great 187-89
Freud, Anna 61
Freud, Sigmund xii, xv-xviii, 5-6, 17, 28, 41, 50,
     57, 60-3, 73, 74, 77, 79, 85, 92, 94, 101,
     104, 106, 117, 122, 124, 143-48, 164, 170,
     211, 213-14, 216, 222, 224, 234, 235-36,
     238-241, 242-45
Friedlander, Kate 68
Friederike, Princesss 187-88
Furtwängler, Wilhelm xii, 198

Gartenberg, Egon 240
'Germain' xvi
Gesualdo, Carlo 118
Gickman, Mort 169
Glover, Edward 61, 85, 101, 104, 122, 126, 145,
     147, 182, 236
Gluck, C. W. 179
Goddard, Scott 207, 218
Godwin, William 5
Goebbels, Josef 10, 24
Gollmick, Carl 173
Goehr, Alexander xiii
Göring, Hermann 16
Goethe, J. W. 3, 5, 10, 23, 26, 197
Graf, Friedrich Hermann 178
Graf, Max xvi
Gray, Cecil 162, 164
Greenbaum, Kyla 193-98
Gregor, Joseph 176
Grillparzer, Franz 26
Groddeck, Georg 147
Grottc, H. 259
Gruber, Gerold xiii
Gundry, Inglis 149, 151

Halifax, Lord 10-11
Hamburger, Paul 258

Hamsun, Knut 10
Händel, Ida 199
Handel, G. F. 178-79, 203, 212
Harbison, Robert 80
Harewood, Earl of 181
Haydn, F. J. 172, 179, 212, 227, 259
Hegel, G. W. F. 7, 10, 21, 25, 27, 170
Heine, Heinrich 9-10, 26, 241
Heisenberg, Werner 238
Hendricks, Ivan 85
Herzl, Theodor 27, 241
Heywood, Thomas 149
Himmler, Heinrich 16
Hindenburg, Field-Marshal 80
Hitler, Adolf 10-11, 16, 20, 23-4, 79-82, 101-02,
     106, 252
Hodler, Ferdinand 82
Hoffer, Willi 53-4, 83, 91, 246
Hofmannsthal, Hugo von 241
Hoffman, Josef 82
Holroyd, Michael 240
Holst, Gustav 214
Honnegger, Arthur 169
Horkheimer, Max 79
Huberman, Bronislaw 200-02
Hume, David 3, 22
Hutchings, Arthur 175
'Huxleys', the 238

Irving, Ernest 169

Jäger, Gustav 28, 50
James, William 255
Jones, Ernest 85, 99, 101, 117, 122, 139, 143-48,
     160, 164, 191, 233, 240, 242, 244-45
Jones, Kathleen 106
Jung, Carl xviii

Kafka, Franz 191, 241
Kant, Immanuel xvi, 4, 7, 9-10, 20, 21, 24, 25, 28,
     235
Kell, Reginald 197, 200-03
Kentner, Louis 194
Kleiber, Erich 226, 231
Klein, Melanie xvi, 107
Kleist, Heinrich von 23
Klimt, Gustav 82, 241
Kokoschka, Oscar
Kolisch, Rudolf 257
Kraepelin, Emil 236
Kramasoff, Ivan 20
Kraus, Karl 10, 151
Krauss, F. S. 141
Kreisler, Fritz 199
Kris, Ernst 165
Kristallnacht 81

Lachs, Robert xvi
Laing, R. D. 106
Lalo, Édouard 200, 202

Lang, Paul Henry 178, 182, 187, 212-13, 219
Lanvan, Marc 91
Lao Tse 10-11
Laughton, Charles 20
Lawrence, D. H. 5, 225-26, 229, 231
Learner, 'Mrs. G.' xiv
Lee, Nathaniel 149
Lenin, V. I. 22
Lessing, Gotthold 13, 23
Les Six 163
Liebermann, Rolf 168
Livy 149
Lunghi, Ludovico 169

Mach, Ernst 6-7, 241
Mahler, Gustav 171, 198, 200-03, 207, 211, 238, 240-41
Mann, Thomas 223, 235
Marle, 'Miss G[erturd].' 41, 47
Marx, Karl 21-2
Maturin, Sybil 41
May, Hans 169
Mayerl, Billi 169
Mead, Margaret 116
Meerlo, A. M. 91
Mellers, Wilfrid 207, 214-16
Mendelssohn, Felix xii, 172, 200, 203-04, 212, 225, 237
Menuhin, Yehudi xii, 194, 198-99
Miles, Catherine Cox 85
Mill, John Stuart 3
Minchinson, Carl 85
Mitchell, Donald xii-xiii, xvi, 143, 160, 170, 180, 182, 231, 240, 256
Moorhead, Alan 104
Moser, Kolo 82
Mosonyi 242, 244
Mozart, W. A. 14, 162, 166, 170-82, 194-97, 200, 202-04, 207, 212, 224, 227, 231, 233, 242, 248-49
Mussorgsky, Modest 162

National Socialism 13, 23-4
Neighbour, O. W. 256
Neway, Patricia 258
Newlin, Dika 237-38
Newman, Ernest 150
Nietzsche, Friedrich 6, 9-10, 23-4, 26
Nunn, Sir T. Percy 207

Obey, André 149
Offenbach, Jacques 168
Ord, Boris 194

Palestrina, G. P. da 225
Paret, Peter 79-82
Parker, Clifton 169
Parsons, Talcott xvii
Patzak, Julius 151, 203
Parys, Georges Van 169

Pauer, Ernst 242, 245
Pears, Peter 120-21, 133, 139, 141-47, 151, 174, 181, 200-04, 252
Pergolesi 232-33
Pfeifer, Sigmund xv-xvi
Pfitzner, Hans 211
Phillips, Margaret xiii, xvi-xvii, 41-82, 83, 89, 91-2, 112, 116, 121, 123, 143, 208, 220, 224
Picasso, Pablo 171, 227, 233
Plato 10-11
Polgar, Alfred 13, 258
Ponsard, F. 149
Popper, Karl 80
Prokofiev, Sergei 259
Pryce-Jones, Alan 258
Puccini, Giacomo (*Tosca*) 227
Purcell, Henry 171, 200, 202-03, 207, 212
Putnam, S. 85

Rank, Otto 145-46, 148, 181, 207, 242
Rawsthorne, Alan 214, 216-19
Reik, Theodor xvi, 57, 139, 147, 222, 224
Rickman, John xviii, 83, 91-4
Riemann, Hugo xvi
Rosenberg, Alfred 5, 23-4, 278
Rosenzweig, Saul 93, 140
Rossini, Gioacchino 169
Rosza, Miklos 169
Russell, Bertrand 238

Sackville-West, Edward 128-29, 139, 142, 145, 147
Salamon, Esther 258
Sartre, Jean-Paul 165-67, 227
Schenker, Heinrich 170
Schiele, Egon 241
Schiotz, Askel 150
Schiller, Friedrich 4, 9-10, 26
Schlick, Moritz 241
Schmidt, Franz 41, 210-11
Schnitzler, Arthur 241
Schoenberg, Arnold xiv, xvi, 152, 155, 159-60, 164, 167, 182, 210, 227, 231, 232, 235, 237, 241, 256-58, 278
Schopenhauer, Arthur 9-10, 26, 80, 170, 258
Schubert, Franz 172, 180, 200, 202-03
Schumann, Robert 235-38
Scott, Marion 256
Searle, Humphrey 256, 278
Seiber, Mátyás 256-57
Settle, Alison 33
Shakespeare, William 4, 149, 278
Shawe-Taylor, Desmond 175, 178, 181
Shaw, G. B. 10
Shelley, Percy Bysshe 3-5, 26
Sibelius, Jan 257
Sitwell, Edith 145
Slater, Montagu 121, 129, 138, 145-47
Smetana, Bedřich 26, 200, 203
Snowman, Daniel xiii, 47

Sophocles 22
Spengler, Oswald 3, 80
Spinoza 22
Sprott, W. J. H. 59
Stalin, Josef xi, 21-2
Stein, Erwin 121, 177, 181, 227, 231, 256, 258
Stekel, Wilhelm 207
Stevens, Richard 212
Stone, Norman 79-82
Storr, Anthony xvi
Strachey, Lytton 239-40
Strauss, Richard 211, 217
Stravinsky, Igor 168, 171, 182, 232-35, 250, 259
Streicher, Julius 31
Stuart, Charles 174
Szasz, Thomas xii, 105-07, 240
Szigeti, Joseph xii, 153, 199-200

Tippett, Michael xviii, 200, 202-03, 257-58
Toscanini, Arturo 157, 194, 198
Toulouse-Lautrec, Henri de 165
Trilling, Lionel 164
Trumpeldor, Josef 27

Valéry, Paul 233
Vaughan, William 79-82, 207
Vaughan Williams, Ralph 47, 169, 214
Verdi, Giuseppe 169, 178

Vogelweide, Walter von der 10
Vogler, Edith 16

Wagner, Cosima 238-40
Wagner, Richard 9-10, 14, 16, 152, 238
Weber, Bernhard Anselm 176
Webern, Anton 241
Weingartner, Felix von 179
Weininger, Otto 26, 28, 92, 216
Wellesz, Egon 257-58
Werfel, Fritz 241
Whiting, John 278
Whyte, Ian 200-04
Wilde, Oscar 5, 222, 233, 268
Wilson, Bryan 59
Winckelmann, J. J. 23
Windsor, Edward, Duke of 84, 91, 93-4
Winnicott, D. W. 123
Winterstern, A. xvi
Wittgenstein, Ludwig 241
Wolf, Hugo 237
Wolf-Ferrari, Ermanno 151, 231
Wordsworth, William 4

Zeitspiegel 14
Zionism 26, 27-31
Zola, Emil 22
Zschorlich, Paul 226-27